AF802487

Basic Theories of Intellectual Property Transaction

Ming Yang

Basic Theories of Intellectual Property Transaction

知识产权出版社
全国百佳图书出版单位

Springer

Ming Yang
Peking University Law School
Peking University
Beijing, China

ISBN 978-981-96-7038-3 ISBN 978-981-96-7039-0 (eBook)
https://doi.org/10.1007/978-981-96-7039-0

Jointly published with Intellectual Property Publishing House Co., Ltd.
The printed edition is not for sale in Mainland China. Customers from Mainland China please order the print book from Intellectual Property Publishing House Co., Ltd.

Translation from the Chinese Simplified language edition: "知识产权交易基本理论" by Ming Yang, © Intellectual Property Publishing House Co., Ltd. 2024. Published by Intellectual Property Publishing House Co., Ltd.. All Rights Reserved.

© Intellectual Property Publishing House Co., Ltd. 2025

This work is subject to copyright. All rights are solely and exclusively licensed by the Publisher, whether the whole or part of the material is concerned, specifically the rights of translation, reprinting, reuse of illustrations, recitation, broadcasting, reproduction on microfilms or in any other physical way, and transmission or information storage and retrieval, electronic adaptation, computer software, or by similar or dissimilar methodology now known or hereafter developed.
The use of general descriptive names, registered names, trademarks, service marks, etc. in this publication does not imply, even in the absence of a specific statement, that such names are exempt from the relevant protective laws and regulations and therefore free for general use.
The publishers, the authors, and the editors are safe to assume that the advice and information in this book are believed to be true and accurate at the date of publication. Neither the publishers nor the authors or the editors give a warranty, express or implied, with respect to the material contained herein or for any errors or omissions that may have been made. The publishers remain neutral with regard to jurisdictional claims in published maps and institutional affiliations.

This Springer imprint is published by the registered company Springer Nature Singapore Pte Ltd.
The registered company address is: 152 Beach Road, #21-01/04 Gateway East, Singapore 189721, Singapore

If disposing of this product, please recycle the paper.

Contents

Abbreviations

CNIPA	China National Intellectual Property Administration
CTEA	Copyright Term Extension Act
IP	Intellectual Property
PTI	Patent Transformation Indicator
R&D	Research and Development
SEP	Standard Essential Patent
TRIPS	Trade-Related Aspects of Intellectual Property Rights Agreement (TRIPS)
WIPO	World Intellectual Property Organization
WTO	World Trade Organization

Chapter 1
Introduction

Since its inception, the intellectual property system in the context of private law has a history of nearly four hundred years.[1] There has been a plethora of research both domestically and internationally on the understanding and interpretation of this system. This includes interpretations of the justification of intellectual property from perspectives such as natural law, positive law, philosophy, economics, and even public policy. It also encompasses the theoretical foundation for the design and reform of specific norms for intellectual property, as well as doctrinal and empirical research on the application of specific intellectual property regimes or rules. However, despite this extensive body of research, through years of observation of judicial practice and theoretical research in intellectual property, it seems that there is less and less consensus that can be reached in the field. This is particularly evident in China's intellectual property arena, where every concept, regime, and rule in intellectual property law seems to be fraught with uncertainty and controversy.[2] Many may dismiss these uncertainties and disputes as merely the result of the impact of technological and economic development, rather than attributing them to flaws in the research paradigms and methodologies of intellectual property law.

In the author's view, the aforementioned shortcomings cannot be ignored. While it is true that the controversies surrounding the basic concepts of intellectual property rights, specific institutional designs, and their applications are related to the flexibility of the boundaries of rights resulting from the intangible nature of the subject matters

[1] Although there are some debates, the *Statute of Monopolies* of 1624 in the United Kingdom is generally regarded as the earliest legislation on intellectual property in the private law sense. For discussions on 'whether the *Statute of Monopolies* served as the origin and foundation for modern patent law', see Sherman, B. and Bently, L. (1999). *The making of modern intellectual property law: The british experience 1706–1911*. Cambridge University Press. 206–212.

[2] During the period from 2019 to 2020, China completed the revisions of the *Trademark Law*, *Copyright Law*, and *Patent Law*. However, through the consultation process of the draft amendments, it can be observed that almost every provision has been subject to disagreements, with particularly intense debates surrounding key provisions, such as the provisions regarding content of rights in the *Copyright Law* and the provisions on employee invention in the *Patent Law*.

© Intellectual Property Publishing House Co., Ltd. 2025

M. Yang, *Basic Theories of Intellectual Property Transaction*,
https://doi.org/10.1007/978-981-96-7039-0_1

of intellectual property, this cannot surely justify our belief that 'there is no right or wrong opinions as long as the logic is consistent'. Such a notion is detrimental to legislative amendments, law applications, and academic research. If we trace the origins of the system, we can certainly find that the development of science and economy is the fundamental driving force behind the continuous evolution of intellectual property rights systems. However, if we do not delve into the level of behavioral choices to study institutional design issues, that is, to explore the impact of science and economy on human behavioral choices and how to guide human behavioral choices through institutional arrangements, the so-called institutional configuration will be superficial, often falling into the pitfall of 'merely treating the symptoms but not tracing the root causes' or the consequentialist subjectivism trap. Behavioral research aims to reveal the underlying framework of 'society (the organic unity of people and material) - economy (the sum of the static and dynamic relationships of material) - technology (the conditions for transforming material) - politics (the upper structure)' behind institutional arrangements, otherwise, we cannot answer the questions of 'why this system is needed' (that is, the clear purpose of the system) and 'how to make the institutional arrangement to make the institutional purpose compatible with a specific social structure'.

1.1 Three Reflections on the Theory and Current Practice of Intellectual Property Law

Although some textbooks on intellectual property law provide definitions or descriptions of the concept of 'intellectual property law', such as: "Intellectual property law is the sum of legal norms regulating various social relationships arising from intellectual property. It is a specialized legal system internationally recognized by peers for confirming, protecting, and exploiting copyright, industrial property rights, and other proprietary rights of intellectual achievements."[3] "Intellectual property law creates proprietary rights in various things and also prescribes rights for various marks applicable to goods and services."[4] etc. It is not difficult to see that these definitions are essentially similar, but more importantly, they do not offer much help in revealing the essence of intellectual property law as an economic mechanism (a mechanism for distributing interests), nor do they aid to understand the continuous transformation of the social structure that plays a decisive role behind the facade of institutional evolution (mainly manifested in expansion).

Intellectual property holds a significant place within the framework of private rights, indicating the necessity and specificity of entitlement over specific objects, and the significance of entitlement is to delineate the boundaries of conducts of

[3] Wu, H. D. (2021). *Zhishi chanquan fa [Intellectual property law]*. Falü Chubanshe [Law Press]. 46.

[4] Bently, L., Sherman, B., Gangjee, D., & Johnson, P. (2018). *Intellectual property law* (5th ed.). Oxford University Press. 1.

non-right holders.[5] Therefore, from a normative perspective, intellectual property law revolves around a complete chain of right, including 'conditions for granting entitlement' (the generation of rights), 'scope of the right to exclude' (the content and limitations of rights, i.e., behaviors that are prohibited or permitted to non-right holders), and 'remedies for infringement of rights' (bar on prohibited behaviors). It aims to design specific rules and form a collection of behavioral norms around this chain of rights, rather than simply understanding it as a sum of rights and obligations concerning intellectual property. Based on this understanding, the author believes that the following three aspects of China's longstanding intellectual property law doctrines and corresponding knowledge systems (whether in legislation, judiciary, or theoretical research) need to be reconsidered:

Firstly, there is a neglect of market principles. Market principles are the theoretical cornerstone underpins the design and application of intellectual property systems. The absence of these principles in the process of specific institutional design and judicial application will lead to a deviation from the basic rationale of intellectual property law in understanding core issues such as 'why granting entitlements', 'boundaries of property rights', 'why property rights should be limited' and 'private remedies'. This often results in speculative debates on philosophical levels. The issues of intellectual property that intellectual property law aims to regulate are fundamentally revolved around transactions and competition. As Peter Drahos puts it, "intellectual property and the market are closely linked."[6]Therefore, the logical thread for formulating the fundamental legal framework of intellectual property law should be 'knowledge production - intellectual property - transactions - market'. Only within a market can we address the distribution of benefits derived from transactions based on intellectual property, and through this understanding that we can grasp the notion why intellectual property law is essentially an economic mechanism. However, many scholars and practitioners in the field of intellectual property overlook the importance of market principles in intellectual property law. As a result, when debating the grounding issues of why a particular regime is needed or how a certain regime should be deployed, they are often caught up in disputes driven by ideological interpretations. Despite the continuous development and changes in the economic and technical underpinnings of intellectual property systems, relying on market principles can nonetheless help achieve alignment between societal realities and the original purpose of the system in interpreting and applying specific rules. For example, the determination

[5] There may be controversies regarding the delineation of the boundaries of behaviour in property rights—whether the boundaries are defined for the right holders or for non-right holders. Many may assume it is the former, but this is not the case as it holds no significant meaning in that case. It is only by imposing constraints on the behaviour of non-right holders that the exclusivity of property rights is truly realized, because the essence of exclusivity is the right to refuse compulsory transactions. Mark Lemley, in his article discussing the empowerment model of trade secrets, has discussed how to understand the exclusivity of property rights models. Lemley, M. (2008). 'The surprising virtues of treating trade secrets as IP rights'.*Stanford Law Review*, 61(2), 311–353. 324–326.

[6] Drahos, P. (1996). *A philosophy of intellectual property*. Dartmouth Publishing. 74–75.

of infringement on 'multi-parties implementing a method patent' in patent law,[7] and the establishment of the 'private copying compensation regime' in copyright law,[8] can both be reconsidered in light of the market principles.

Secondly, there is a lack of a behavioral perspective and approach in intellectual property law. A rough examination can even reveal the fundamental differences between the civil law system and the common law system regarding the origin of intellectual property law. Although modern intellectual property systems (mainly the copyright system and the patent system) originated in England in the context of private law, both systems have had significant influences on the birth and evolution of intellectual property system within China's private law framework. This has resulted in many inconsistencies and even distortions in both theoretical and institutional systems in China.[9] It is well known that the common law system explains the fundamental purpose of the intellectual property system through incentive mechanisms, "Innovators should have property rights based on their investment outcomes, which can motivate individuals and businesses to invest in research and development activities,"[10] and Clause 8 of Article 1(8) of the *United States Constitution* is often regarded as benchmark of the incentive theory evident at the legislative level, which gives rise to broad and profound impacts. According to this theory, the establishment of intellectual property systems is for the continuous creation of intellectual property, thereby promoting overall social welfare. Therefore, the common law system perceives the fundamental issues of intellectual property law to an exchange between 'incentive' and 'access'.[11] Although the author has different views in treating 'incentive mechanisms' as the essence of the system, but nevertheless strongly agrees with a notion of this theory: intellectual property law is an interests distribution mechanism guiding the behavioral choices of creators and users of intellectual property. Only by looking from a behavioral perspective can we deeply understand how specific rules actually function and whether they align with the original intent of the system design. Consequently, we would refrain from frequently proposing new systems (or rules) or changing existing ones. In contrast, the ground for the establishment of intellectual property law in civil law system is entirely different, as its legislative conception is unrelated to incentives but is based on natural rights theory.[12] It is

---

[7] For example, the *Shenzhen Jixiang Tengda Technology Co., Ltd. and Shenzhen Dunjun Technology Co., Ltd. Infringement of Invention Patent Rights Dispute Case* Supreme People's Court (2019) SPC Civil Judgment No. 147.

[8] Yang, M. (2021). 'Siren fuzhi de zhuzuoquan fa zhidu yingdui: Cong jixie fuzhi dao yun fuwu' ['The copyright law system's response to private copying: from mechanical reproduction to cloud services']. *Zhongguo Faxue* [*Chinese Journal of Law*], 1. 189–209.

[9] For example, regarding the institutional arrangements for the creation, utilization, and change of title of rights, the relevant provisions in China's *Patent Law* and *Copyright Law* typically reflect the logical inconsistency arising from the mixture of the two major legal systems.

[10] Holyoak, J. & Torremans, P. (1995). *Intellectual property law*. Butterworths. 13–14.

[11] Posner, R. (2005). 'Intellectual property: The law and economics approach'. *The Journal of Economic Perspectives*, 19(2), 57.

[12] We can clearly see the notion of natural rights in the French *Patent Law* of 1791.See Tang, Z. (2003). *Zhuanli fa jiaocheng* [*Textbook on patent law*]. Falü Chubanshe [Law Press]. 9.

evident that natural rights theory 'focuses on' explaining the justification of intellectual property, serving as a value declaration for institutionalizing the results of creation based on static thinkings. Its flaw is the inability to explain how the production behavior of intellectual property is motivated, what form and structure of rights the creators pursue, and how various entities choose transaction arrangements for the assignment and licensing of their rights to maximize their own utility. In fact, many disputes in judicial practice arise from applying specific systems (rules) under static thinking, thus result in a deviation from the original intent of the institutional design. Therefore, whether it is legislation (including amendments), interpretation, or law application, a behavioral perspective with dynamic thinking is crucial. This approach allows the institutional value to be concretized in the constantly changing social situation, thereby achieving optimal effectiveness in interest distribution mechanisms. Hence, behavioral studies not only reveal why people choose to engage in specific behaviors but also help people to form rational expectations about the consequences of their actions.

The third reflection pertains to the insufficient level of systematization in both the fundamental theories and specific regimes of intellectual property law. Of course, this issue is closely related to the two aspects mentioned above. From recent judicial practices and academic research, it is apparent that the awareness of problem is increasing in China's intellectual property law field, yet research on these issues is becoming micro. The consequence of not emphasizing systematic thinking is that people lack a general understanding of basic concepts, theories, and the system. As a result, the same rules are often inconsistently interpreted and applied across different cases. For example, there is a lack of clarity in the Chinese intellectual property field regarding the concept of 'trademark use', consequently, in the application of different regimes within trademark law, such as confirmation of trademark authorization, determination on trademark infringement, and the 'three withdrawals' regimes, there exist inconsistencies regarding the interpretation of 'trademark use'.[13]

Similar to Professor Sun Xianzhong's analysis of 'the shortcomings of Chinese legal studies in scientific thinking within the continental law system',[14] fragmented viewpoints have brought significant challenges to the implementation of intellectual property law. The author believes that no legal system ever exists in isolation, 'the three most important characteristics of law are its coerciveness, systematicness, and normativity'.[15] Employing systematic thinking to understand the typological nature of specific norms in different systems is essential for the qualitative analysis we often undertake. Systematization is the legal technique required to achieve 'formal rationality' and move from 'the general to the specific', as well as a scientific means to

[13] For a unified understanding on the principle of 'trademark use', see Wang, T. (2021) 'Shangbiao fa shang shangbiao shiyong gainian de tongyi ji qi zhidu wanshan' ['The unified understanding of the concept of 'trademark use' and the improvement of its system in trademark law']. *Zhongwai Faxue [Chinese and Foreign Legal Studies]*, 4, 1027–1047.

[14] Sun, X. (2022). 'Minfa tixihua kexue siwei de wenti yanjiu' ['Research on the issues of systematic scientific thinking in civil law']. *Falv Kexue [Legal Science]*, 1, 36–38.

[15] Raz, J. (2003). *Falv tixi de gainian [The concept of a legal system]* (Wu, Y trans.). Zhongguo Fazhi Chubanshe [China Legal Publishing House]. 201.

prevent arbitrary legislation, amendments, or judicial practice. Not only does codification in the civil law system reflect a consistent pursuit of systematic thinking, but the common law legal system also highly values the study and application of systematic approaches to law, particularly in the field of intellectual property law. In this regard, the author suggests that in order to perceive and apply intellectual property law accurately, we should adopt the endogenous relationship between 'institutions', 'markets' and 'behaviours' as the logical framework for systematization, and implement systematic thinkings sufficiently and comprehensively in pursuant to systematic effects.

1.2 Why Choose 'Intellectual Property Transactions' as the Research Object?

Why do we need property rights? According to Demsetz, "Property rights are an instrument of society and derive their significance from the fact that they help a man form those expectations which he can reasonably hold in his dealings with others."[16] So we say that property rights are not actually arrangements between people and things, but rather refer to the relationships between people that arise from the existence and utilization of things. People must respect the interactive relationships among them or bear the consequences (costs) of not adhering to these relationships. Whether it is the typical property right of ownership based on tangible objects, or intellectual property rights with intangible products as the subject matters, the significance of granting and confirming rights lies in meeting the needs of property transfer. The institutional arrangement of property rights establishes the boundary of behaviours between right holders and non-right holders, more precisely, the behavioural norms of non-right holders. In this vein, individuals can determine the allocation, utilization, and restructuring of resources in a specific and predictable manner, and transactions are the primary means of achieving these objectives. Transactions occur because relevant parties believe that they can optimize the utility of property combinations on these grounds. Individuals have an inherent incentive to maximize their own interests, therefore, it is not difficult to see that transactions externalize this endogenous demand into social activities.

The economic essence of property rights suggests that they are meaningful only when they are both exclusive and transferable. Transferability is indeed a very important attribute of rights because it ensures that property can be utilized by the entity that values it the most.[17] We know that in order to facilitate property transfer and ensure

[16] Demsetz, H. (1967). 'Toward a theory of property rights'. *The American Economic Review*, 57(2), 347.

[17] The transferability here refers to the circulation of property, specifically reflected through means such as licensing, transfer, and capitalization, rather than merely referring to the transfer of property rights under civil law.

transaction security, there are many complex and sophisticated mechanisms established in civil law. Based on the positioning of intellectual property rights within the civil rights system, these institutional norms can certainly be applied to intellectual property transactions. Therefore, there is no need to redundantly establish general or foundational systems regarding transactions in sector specific legislation of the intellectual property. However, due to the intangible nature of the subject matters of intellectual property, their stronger characteristics as public goods, and the possibility of erroneous intellectual property authorizations, transactions involving intellectual property are more complex compared to general property transfers in civil law. Therefore, it is necessary to establish corresponding rules in sector specific legislation for intellectual property. It can be seen that legal rules related to intellectual property transactions are divided into two categories: general civil law principles and norms applicable in the field of intellectual property, and sui generis rules designed for the characteristics of intellectual property. Based on the current state of theoretical research and judicial practice in intellectual property law in China, both the level of understanding and the effectiveness of applying these two types of rules for intellectual property transactions are not ideal. There are many instances of non-compliance of the logical framework of the civil law system, which make some straightforward issues to become contentious and difficult, at the same time, the creation of some sector specific rules lacks clear theoretical underpinning and thus appears to be arbitrary.

The research object of intellectual property transactions is not only a simple and scattered study of how different types of intellectual property transactions are conducted. In order to provide security to transactions and protect the legitimate rights and interests of transacting parties and even bona fide third parties, this book takes 'intellectual property transactions' as the logical thread and analytical grip, aiming to study the coupling relationship between 'intellectual property transactions, related regimes, and market entity behaviours'. The author will analyse the behavioural choices of the market entities in intellectual property transactions and examining the operation and effects of the basic system and sector specific rules of intellectual property law. If we categorize the specific norms of various sector specific laws of intellectual property, it is not difficult to find that the so-called institutional arrangement can be divided into three levels: the production of intellectual property (generation of rights), the utilization of intellectual property (licensing, assignment), and the remedies for intellectual property (infringement determination, remedial methods, legal responsibility), 'Intellectual property transactions' can span these three levels accordingly. Starting from the perspective of behavioural choices, by revealing how specific intellectual property transactions occur in the market, people can understand how specific institutional arrangements such as the confirmation of intellectual property authorization, rights delineation, and remedies for infringement actually function. Therefore, taking 'intellectual property transactions' as the logical thread of this book, and aligning it with the research methods of behaviourism, helps us clarify how the intellectual property system has shaped the economic environment of the market, and consequently how it influences the behavioural choices of market entities. At the same time, it also helps us reflect on the rationality of the current system, laying a solid foundation for proposing suggestions for institutional reform or advancing methodological improvements in law application.

As mentioned earlier in the above paragraphs regarding the relationship between intellectual property rights and the market, intellectual property law aims to address various issues in the implementation of intellectual property rights in relevant markets. It is well known that intellectual property owners have two main approaches to derive benefits from their intellectual assets: they can either utilize the intellectual property rights themselves or license others to exploit them. In the former case, the most important legal significance for granting property rights (confirmation of authorization) is that, unless subject to statutory limitations, right holders have the right to refuse to deal. Furthermore, their legal position of not being compelled to deal is a baseline to fully embody the principle of autonomy of wills in intellectual property transactions. In the latter case, whether transactions can be completed smoothly is significantly influenced by information costs. The institutional system constructed by intellectual property law, including entitlement (generation of rights, enforceability of rights, and boundaries of rights), rights exploitation and remedies, plays a fundamental role in reducing the information costs of transactions (enhancing the ability of both parties to understand each other – 'know thyself, know thy enemy').

Therefore, the comprehensive institutional construction of intellectual property law, though manifested in different nodes along the complete rights chain, is essentially aimed at meeting the requirements for the exploitation of intellectual property in the market. More specifically, it pertains to how parties should adhere to behavioural norms in resolving disputes when there is a market failure, as rules become necessary when autonomy fails to resolve disputes. Hence, when referring to 'intellectual property transactions' in this book, it is not merely concerning the trade-off of interests by way of contracts under traditional civil law. Instead, it is a refinement of the comprehensive issue of how intellectual property operates or how it is exploited in the market. Approaching the study from the perspective of intellectual property transactions helps us clarify the interaction between 'the operation of the system' and 'market behaviour'. This in turn allows a rethinking on the complete system of intellectual property constituted by rights generation, changes in titles of rights, rights limitations, and remedies. For instance, it prompts questions like whether the current system is rational and whether there is a need for institutional improvement. The standard for assessing the rationality of the existing systems and rules lies in whether they achieve the maximization of social utility in terms of benefit distribution. This understanding is most smoothly achieved when placed within the framework and system of intellectual property transactions.

1.3 Research Approach and Content of This Book

Overall, this book takes a market-oriented perspective and starts from the theory of behavioral choice to explore the basic theory and operational mechanisms of intellectual property transactions. Its aim is to gain a deep understanding of how specific intellectual property institutions and rules operate or are applied through the extrinsic forms of institutional operation. The book closely examines the coupling relationship between 'implementation of the institution' and 'behavioral choice', following the logical thread of intellectual property transactions, to investigate the institutional mechanisms behind specific transaction forms and conduct benefit analysis. Through this approach, it provides a profound interpretation of the economic mechanism of intellectual property system from both theoretical and practical perspectives.

In pursuit of this research objective, the book will unfold along the following logical framework: Firstly, it will delve into the initial and fundamental issues of intellectual property transactions, namely the theoretical basis for using property rights rules to protect intellectual assets. It seeks to analyze the market environment formed by the current system, starting from the principle of entitlement of intellectual property rights, attempting to reveal the institutional implications of the generation of rights, boundaries and attributes of rights. Secondly, by analyzing the question of 'how intellectual property transactions should be understood', it will comprehensively examine the compatibility between the current intellectual property system and the operation of the intellectual property market, thus expose specific manifestations of the institutional inadequacies in delivering the value realization of intellectual assets. Thirdly, considering that intellectual property transactions are essentially contractual issues, this book chooses the 'incomplete contract theory' and 'price theory' from economics as the theoretical foundation for intellectual property transactions. By analyzing the relationship between market environment and behavioral choices, it aims to clarify the endogenous logic among 'system', 'markets', and 'behavior'. Finally, based on the mutual influence between institutional operation and market behavior, the book will discuss the assignment, licensing, and capitalization operations of intellectual property respectively, as well as explore issues such as restrictions on right holders and competition exclusion in intellectual property transactions. Its goal is to reveal how the current system and rules impact specific intellectual property transactions, identify the challenges posed by the rapid development of technology and the evolving business practices to the existing laws, and ultimately provide strategies for addressing these issues.

Based on the research thread mentioned above, the content for each chapter in this book is arranged as the following:

Chapter 2: Intellectual Property Creation and Cumulative Innovation—A Behavioral Study of Property Rights. The effectiveness and boundaries of rights are the starting point and foundation to assess whether the value of intellectual property can be fully realized. Under this premise, intellectual property transactions can proceed smoothly. Research on entitlement issues can not only help the transacting parties to reduce information costs but also limit the space for rent-seeking behaviors of intellectual property right holders through the system. Although intellectual property is created spontaneously, and sometimes for non-market-oriented purpose, they can still be protected by intellectual property law. Nonetheless, non-utilitarian motives for creation do not prevent right holders from relying on intellectual property law to control the market and pursue profit maximization. Intellectual property producers who are inherently market-oriented are more concerned with decision-making based on the institutional arrangements of existing laws when making behavioral choices, and they strive to gain a competitive advantage in horizontal and even vertical competitive relationships. Intellectual property law is in fact established by virtue of the latter and is essentially an economic mechanism. Understanding why it is necessary to grant intellectual property entitlement allows us to understand why intellectual property transactions occur.

Chapter 3: A Behavioural Analysis of Intellectual Property Transactions and Insufficient Supply of Legal Systems. From its appearance, intellectual property transactions are economic behaviors pursued by the parties involved for their own utility, and of course, are also shown as a legal form. But from a deeper perspective, it can be seen that the smooth implementation of intellectual property transactions is a guarantee for the supply of knowledge products in the market, especially for ensuring the continuous supply of innovative products. It is only from the perspective of intellectual property transactions that we can thoroughly understand that intellectual property law is a mechanism that seeks to find the optimal balance between dynamic and static efficiency.[18] Whether for self-use or authorizing others to use, the efficiency of intellectual property protection is reflected not only in the ability of knowledge property producers to obtain sufficient returns on investment but also in the promotion of knowledge dissemination, thereby encouraging cumulative innovation and promoting the continuous advancement for knowledge property creation. However, the practice of the operation and development of intellectual property transactions has shown that the supply of legal institutions underpinning them is often insufficient. The first reason is the possible loopholes in the legal system itself, and the second is the inadequacy of the methodology for legal application. Therefore, it is significant to explore the connotation of intellectual property transactions from a behavioral perspective and clarify the insufficient supply of legal institutions on intellectual property so as to improve legislation and promote the development of relevant industries.

Chapter 4: Contract Theory in Intellectual Property Transactions. Simply put -- in order to achieve the exchange of benefits, specific parties negotiate and reach agreement on a combination of various conditions to bind all parties to certain behaviors or inaction — this is a contract. The conditions for transaction as the content of the contract, are reached by the parties based on the information they hold over the subject matters of the transaction. Due to the complexity of transactions, differences in the capacities of the parties (including technical capacity, capital capacity, etc.), and factors such as information asymmetry, contracts are often incomplete in many respects, which may lead to incentive or transaction cost issues. Therefore, using contract theory to analyze the negotiation of transaction conditions and how contracts will be fulfilled can help us better understand transactions based on the 'interaction between the system and behavior', especially regarding the issue of uncertainty, which are more adaptive for intangible assets like intellectual property. Observing the relevant systems and judicial decisions of intellectual property law in China

[18] Belleflamme, P. & Peitz, M. (2010). *Industrial organization: Markets and strategies*. Cambridge University Press. 508.

from the perspective of contract theory in economics can enrich the methodology for analyzing whether there are flaws in institutional construction and operation, thereby enhancing the theoretical solidness and persuasiveness of institutional improvement.

Chapter 5: Price Theory in Intellectual Property Transactions. If transactions are considered as economic mechanisms guiding efficient resource allocation, then prices are the tools that determine the realization of this efficient allocation because 'prices themselves can guide efficient economic decisions'.[19] Historically, there has been very little attention paid to price theory in China's intellectual property law academia, and the few studies that exist mainly focus on abstract discussions of the aspect of 'consideration', with little concern to the more practical issue of how prices guide decisions (behavioral choices). Moreover, some important institutions and practical hotspots in intellectual property law such as compulsory (statutory) licensing, determination of licensing fees for standard-essential patents, whether to issue injunctions against infringement, and calculation of damages for infringement, all revolve around pricing issues. Therefore, this chapter aims to examine whether there are loopholes in the current intellectual property system or whether there are unreasonable aspects in rule design by reviewing the development and system of price theory and exploring how it functions in intellectual property transactions, thereby further enhancing awareness of the interaction between the system and behaviors.

Chapter 6: Specific Types of Intellectual Property Transactions. This chapter will return to the perspective of traditional legal systems, distinguishing between different types of transaction models and providing a detailed analysis of how intellectual property transactions are conducted. It is well known that intellectual property transactions include three forms: assignment, licensing, and capital operations. Legislative rules have been designed for each type of intellectual property transaction, but they are often rough, showing not only logical confusion in emphasizing the coordination between the special attributes of intellectual property and the application of basic principles of civil law, but also failing to meet the practical needs of industrial development. In view of this, this chapter aims to explore the effectiveness and shortcomings of the current system by examining the specific types of intellectual property transactions and to propose institutional improvement schemes based on this analysis.

Chapter 7: Antitrust Issues in Intellectual Property Transactions. The objective and outcome of transactions are resource allocation, closely related to market competition. Intellectual property transactions may be related to horizontal competition and may also affect vertical competition. In either case, if intellectual property right holders have sufficient bargaining power, they may have the motives to abuse their market position, seeking to exclude or restrict competition in relevant markets through transaction arrangements. Therefore, antitrust issues shall not be ignored in the analysis of intellectual property transactions. This chapter begins by analyzing

[19] Milgrom, P. (2020). *Jiage lilun [Discovering prices]* (Han, C. trans). CITIC Publishing Group [Zhongxin Chubanshe]. 37.

potential monopolistic conducts in intellectual property transactions within the traditional analytical framework. It then reflects on the controversies arising from industrial development and antitrust practices. Finally, it discusses the breakthroughs and innovations that should be incorporated into the anti-trust regulations related to intellectual property transactions in the new economic era by deploying the new theories and methodological development in anti-trust analysis.

References

Belleflamme, P. & Peitz, M. (2010). *Industrial organization: Markets and strategies*. Cambridge University Press

Bently, L., Sherman, B., Gangjee, D., & Johnson, P. (2018). *Intellectual property law* (5th ed.). Oxford University Press

Demsetz, H. (1967). Toward a theory of property rights. *The American Economic Review, 57*(2), 347

Drahos, P. (1996). *A philosophy of intellectual property*. Dartmouth Publishing

Holyoak, J., & Torremans, P. (1995). Intellectual property law. Butterworths

Lemley, M. (2008). 'The surprising virtues of treating trade secrets as IP rights'. *Stanford Law Review, 61*(2), 311–353

Milgrom, P. (2020). *Jiage lilun [Discovering prices]* (Han, C., Trans). CITIC Publishing Group [Zhongxin Chubanshe]

Posner, R. (2005). Intellectual property: The law and economics approach. *The Journal of Economic Perspectives, 19*(2), 57

Raz, J. (2003). *Falv tixi de gainian [The concept of a legal system]* (Wu, Y., Trans.). Zhongguo Fazhi Chubanshe [China Legal Publishing House]

Sherman, B., & Bently, L. (1999). The making of modern intellectual property law: The British experience 1706–1911. Cambridge University Press

Sun, X. (2022). Minfa tixihua kexue siwei de wenti yanjiu [Research on the issues of systematic scientific thinking in civil law]. *Falv Kexue [Legal Science], 1*, 36–38.

Tang, Z. (2003). *Zhuanli fa jiaocheng [Textbook on patent law]*. Falü Chubanshe [Law Press].

Wang, T. (2021). Shangbiao fa shang shangbiao shiyong gainian de tongyi ji qi zhidu wanshan [The unified understanding of the concept of 'trademark use' and the improvement of its system in trademark law]. *Zhongwai Faxue [Chinese and Foreign Legal Studies], 4* , 1027–1047.

Wu, H.(2021). *Zhishi chanquan fa [Intellectual property law]*. Falü Chubanshe [Law Press]

Yang, M. (2021). Siren fuzhi de zhuzuoquan fa zhidu yingdui: Cong jixie fuzhi dao yun fuwu [The copyright law system's response to private copying: From mechanical reproduction to cloud services]. *Zhongguo Faxue [Chinese Journal of Law], 1*, 189–209.

Chapter 2
Intellectual Property Creation and Cumulative Innovation: A Behavioural Study of Property Rights

2.1 Creation of Intellectual Property and Claims of Property Rights

For a long time, theoretical research in the field of intellectual property law in China, as well as studies on related institutional designs and their specific applications, have generally been static. Of course, this is closely related to the private law tradition of China, and it is evident from the extensive discussions over the justifications of intellectual property that are deeply influenced by naturalism and transcendental philosophical thoughts.[1] It must be recognized that the static thinking mode has indispensable significance for the creation of the intellectual property system 'from scratch' in China that of a civil law tradition. However, being completely immersed in philosophical speculation tends to make us overlook the essence of the intellectual property law as economic mechanisms, and disregard to study from the perspective of the interaction between institutions and behavioural choices. This often leads to either result-oriented and logically uncoherent conclusions, or simply adopt international treaties or refer to case precedents in other countries when making court decisions or institutional modification proposals. Although there are often fierce debates occur between the theoretical and practical fields, in fact, it is simply due to the flaws in the research approaches. Therefore in the author's opinion, the key in the study of intellectual property law is the emphasis on methodology, rather than the pursuit of so-called discoveries and research over 'new' problems. As long as there are scientific and abundant methodological underpinnings, we can readily deal with the legal disputes arising from the rapid development of technologies and industries,

---

[1] Professor Peter Drahos has provided a detailed analysis of the philosophical theoretical foundation of the justification of intellectual property. From his analysis, it is evident that naturalist and transcendental philosophical thoughts serve as important theoretical tools in the arguments for the justification of intellectual property. Drahos, P. (1996). *A philosophy of intellectual property*. Dartmouth Publishing. 41–69,73–91.

© Intellectual Property Publishing House Co., Ltd. 2025

M. Yang, *Basic Theories of Intellectual Property Transaction*,
https://doi.org/10.1007/978-981-96-7039-0_2

and it will also be easier to achieve consensus in designing reasonable solutions in institutional reform.

The transferability of property is its fundamental attribute for value realization. To facilitate smooth transfers, especially when transaction costs are unavoidable, establishing initial entitlement of property rights is crucial.[2] In fact, the clear delineation of property rights, along with the construction and implementation of corresponding legal systems, are aimed at reducing transaction costs and facilitating smooth market transactions. As advocated by the school of transaction cost economics represented by Coase, Arrow, and Williamson, the extent of transaction freedom and the level of transaction costs are crucial factors for determining whether market operations and resource allocation can effectively carry out.[3] Especially for intangible subject matters like intellectual property, the issue of rights delineation is particularly crucial. Therefore, whether property rights can be granted and whether the boundaries of rights are clear have a significant impact on people's decisions on whether to engage in creative activities related to property. Property rights essentially address a fundamental question—what kinds of items can be privately owned. This means that property owners enjoy such a legal status: they have the right to use a specific item while have the right to prohibit anyone else from using that item.[4] Therefore, for market participants, engaging in intellectual property creation so that to acquire related intellectual property rights is a crucial component of their market strategy to participate in market competition, and serves as a vital starting point and cornerstone.

As widely recognized, the creation of intellectual property originates from two distinct levels of demand: one is the material need at the economic level, and the other is the fulfilment of self-realization at the spiritual level. The history of creative activities in human society, including literary and artistic creations as well as technological inventions, stretches back far into antiquity. However, setting compatible property right systems for intellectual property creations only became prominent after the Industrial Revolution. This indicates that creative activities driven purely by spiritual pursuit are completely motivated by internal incentives regardless of external conditions. On the other hand, creative activities driven by economic interests have a high demand for external incentives. The higher the level of industrialization and the more complex the social structure, the greater the need to achieve an optimal balance between internal motivations and external incentives. It is easily understood if we analyse the institutional history of intellectual property law. Of course, regardless of people's motivations for engaging in intellectual property creation, there is no difference in their pursuit of profit from utilizing the results of their creation. Therefore, the impact of the system of intellectual property on people's behavioural choices can be divided into two types: firstly, the choice of whether to engage in a specific

---

[2] This statement does not contradict the Coase Theorem, as it is based on the premise that transaction costs are not zero.

[3] For an introduction on the basic arguments on transaction cost economics, see Williamson, O. (2010). 'Transaction cost economics: the natural progression'. *The American Economic Review*, 100(3), 673–690. 675.

[4] Shavell, S. (2004). *Foundations of economic analysis of law*. The Belknap Press of Harvard University Press. 9.

intellectual property creation activity and the selection of which intellectual property protection to seek for the created results; secondly, how intellectual property right holders decide between utilizing their intellectual property themselves or authorizing others to exploit it. The former will be discussed in this chapter and the latter will be discussed in the next chapter. In the following discussion, the author will distinguish between different scenarios and examine how market participants can select property rights claims that align with specific intellectual property creation activities.

2.1.1 Whether to Invest in R&D?

"Numerous technologies come together to create something we call 'economy'. Economy is a manifestation of technology and evolves with the advancement of these technologies."[5] Therefore, it is not difficult to understand why R&D capabilities on technologies have become a decisive factor in modern market competition, and intellectual property rights represent a typical institutional form of these capabilities, which are currently the most important tools for gaining competitive advantages in the market. For technology-focused enterprises, choosing the right timing, direction (technological fields), and target markets for engaging in R&D activities is crucial to gaining an advantageous position in the competition. Simply put, whether a firm invests in a particular technological R&D activity depends on the results of a 'cost–benefit' analysis. In this analysis, the firm needs to examine several aspects:

Firstly, understanding the level of R&Ds in the relevant technological field, that is, grasping the existing technologies (prior art), especially when a firm is preparing to enter into a new market. Certainly, from a purely scientific research perspective, this is usually not a difficult issue, but for enterprises, understanding the level of technological advancement is essential to assess the costs for R&D. Therefore, the anticipated technological level that a firm expects to achieve through its R&D efforts (which, in a sense, also reflects the anticipated industrial level) directly influence cost analysis.

Secondly, analysing the horizontal and vertical market structures to clarify the competitive landscape within relevant markets. Clearly, analysing market structure and competitive conditions is very complex, it varies not only based on whether the R&D enterprises are incumbent firms or new entrants, but also on factors such as the homogeneity or heterogeneity of competitors, and whether future applications of technological achievements will increase product differentiation. However, what can be certain is that the more intense the competition in relevant markets, the higher the expectations of the investors of R&Ds on the net value of technological achievements.[6] This expectation leads to more cautious investment decisions.

---

[5] Arthur, B. (2018). *Jishu de benzhi* [*The nature of technology*] (Cao, D. & Wang, J. trans.) Zhejiang Renmin Chubanshe [Zhejiang People's Publishing House]. 214.

[6] If the number of competitors in the relevant market is N and the industry average cost is C, then a firm will only have the incentive to invest in technological R&D when the net value of

Thirdly, assessing potential market demand. This issue is crucial in assessing the value of technological achievements, it is highly important and also complex. Throughout human history, groundbreaking inventions such as the telephone, automobile, and airplane were initially ridiculed as useless. This illustrates that there is often a gap between scientific and technological advancements and their practical applications (result transformations), the value of technology may not always be fully recognized immediately upon the completion of an invention. Furthermore, considering the potential interactions between technologies and the final products, and the network effects that can arise through usage, assessing market demand for a particular invention is more challenging compared to traditional industrial products.[7]

2.1.2 *Patent or Trade Secret?*

Whether to engage in specific technological R&D activities is just the first step in implementing corporate market strategies, once successfully obtaining the R&D outcomes, enterprises then immediately face the question of choosing the path of which intellectual property to take. Certainly, for most of the time, enterprises make decisions regarding whether to invest in R&D and what type of rights protection to seek for anticipated outcomes simultaneously. The intellectual property protection modes related to technological R&D outcomes mainly refer to the patent system and the trade secret protection system. For developers and researchers to choose between patent rights and trade secrets, they first need to understand the differences between these two modes.[8] The author believes that the difference between the two can be summarized as the following:

Firstly, the characteristics of the patent system include public disclosure in exchange for protection. On the other hand, a crucial premise for obtaining protection under trade secret is the secrecy of the technical solution. Therefore, the protection under patent law operates under the principle of 'ex ante publication against the world, and presumption of fault on the part of the unauthorized implementor',[9]

---

the technological outcome is greater than C × N. The rationale is that if the N competitors are homogeneous, the probability of success for any one firm is 1/N. Therefore, considering opportunity costs, the net value must exceed C × N in order for competitors to decide to invest. Of course, if the competitors are not homogeneous, then competitors with higher production efficiency can assign a lower valuation to the net value of the technological outcome than C × N, because their probability of success is closer to 1 within the range of [1/N, 1].

[7] On the relationship between product interactions and network effects, see Belleflamme, P. & Peitz, M. (2010). *Industrial organization: Markets and strategies*. Cambridge University Press. 531.

[8] Of course, the analysis in this book is based on the premise that the outcome of a certain R&D activity can meet the conditions for patent application and can also be protected as a trade secret. If this premise is not met, the R&D firm would not face a choice between the two.

[9] According to the principles of tort law, the liability for damages is based on the fault principle, meaning that a condition for the tortfeasor to bear compensation liability includes the element of 'fault of the tortfeasor'. In specific cases, when applying the law, due to the public nature of patents

whereas protection under trade secret operates under the principle of 'ex post delineation of rights, where the plaintiff must provide preliminary evidence of fault on the part of the defendant'.[10]

Secondly, to acquire patent rights, inventions and creations must satisfy the criteria of novelty and inventiveness. Whereas for a technical solution to receive trade secret protection, it is not required to examine these two aspects, the only requirement is to ensure that the solution meets the criterion of secrecy (not accessible through public channels).

Thirdly, for owners of trade secrets to receive protection, they must meet the requirement of having taken reasonable confidentiality measures. In contrast, if they choose the approach of patent protection, there is no such requirement for confidentiality measures. The requirement for trade secret owners to have taken confidentiality measures is connected with the earlier requirement regarding secrecy.

Fourthly, in terms of patent protection, as long as the technology involved in the alleged infringement falls within the scope of the patent claims, the infringement can thereby be established, regardless of whether the infringer acted 'intentionally'. However, concerning the protection of trade secrets, even if the technology involved in the alleged infringement is substantially identical to the content of the trade secret, so long as the alleged infringer can prove that the technology they used was independently developed or by reverse engineering, it does not constitute an infringement of the trade secret.

Due to these differences, there is a common misconception in practice that trade secret law protects only low-level technological innovations, and that developers only seek trade secret protection when they cannot obtain a patent.[11] This is clearly a misunderstanding. In fact, when faced with the following situations, R&D enterprises tend to prefer using trade secrets to protect their technological achievements: (1) once a product is publicly sold, its technological details can be easily reverse engineered by others, but the value of the technological results is relatively low. (2) when the technology fails to meet the substantive requirements for patentability, particularly the criterion of inventiveness. (3) when the technological achievements are significantly ahead of competitors and are difficult to reverse engineer. Specifically, when choosing between a patenting strategy and a trade secret strategy, R&D enterprises typically need to consider the following factors: the cost of protection under different strategies, the strength of protection provided by each strategy, and the cost of remedy against infringement. These factors are not static and vary depending on the value of the R&D achievements, and they are not linearly related.

In the first scenario, the value of the R&D outcome is low. Simply put, the marginal benefits of this technology may quickly diminish to zero. At this point, the cost of

---

(*in rem*), once a judge determines that an infringement has occurred, the tortfeasor is presumed to have subjective fault.

[10] The so-called 'ex post delineation of rights' here refers to the situation where the scope of the trade secret being protected and the identification of the rights holder are only defined when the owner of a trade secret files an infringement lawsuit.

[11] Landes, W. & Posner, R. (2003). *The economic structure of intellectual property law*. Harvard University Press. 357.

filing a patent application is significantly higher than the cost of protecting it as a trade secret, and moreover, patents can offer stronger protection compared to trade secrets, although the costs associated with remedy against infringement are higher for patents than for trade secrets. Nevertheless, by taking all the above considerations into account, R&D enterprises shall tend to choose the trade secret mode to protect their outcomes when the value of the technological achievement is low.

In the second scenario, the value of the R&D outcomes is extremely high, for instance, its technological advantage can sustain even longer than the protection period of an invention patent. In this circumstance, the cost of acquiring rights under the trade secret mode increases significantly, as it is related to the adoption of reasonable confidentiality measures, since the more complex and valuable the technology, the higher the cost of maintaining confidential measures. On the other hand, the cost of the patent protection mode is less affected by changes in the value of the technological outcomes.[12] Regarding the strength of protection, as mentioned earlier, trade secret protection does not exclude independent development or reverse engineering, as a result, patent rights provide stronger market control for R&D enterprises than trade secrets. Thus it is generally believed that patents offer greater strength for protection. However, when the technological advantage is so significant that competitors cannot conduct independent development nor reverse engineering to achieve the technology, there is no significant difference in terms of the protection strength between the two modes.

As for the cost of remedy against infringement, because the value of the R&D outcomes is significantly high, which implies that the technology involved is extremely complex, thus the cost for delineating the right over trade secret is high. However, under the premise assumed in the above discussion that the technological advantage of the R&D is extremely significant, it can, to some extent, limit the growth of the costs in delineating the right. At the same time, we shall see that the complexity of the technology would also affect the identification of the scope of patent protection, as the judicial decisions on patent infringement follows the doctrine of equivalents, and the scope of patent protection is based on the claims. Therefore, the more complex the technology, the higher the costs of delineating the right based on the doctrine of equivalents and claim interpretations. Overall, when the technological advantage is sufficiently large, due to the value of a patent is limited by the protection period, protecting R&D outcomes through trade secrets can bring more benefits to right holders. Therefore, as long as the sum of the costs of acquiring rights and the additional costs of delineating the right in remedy is less than the increased benefits gained, adopting a trade secret protection mode becomes more desirable.

---

[12] It should be noted that under China's patent system, the simpler the technological outcome, the more likely developers are to apply for a utility model patent. On the other hand, the higher the technological level, the more developers tend to apply for an invention patent. Transitioning from a utility model patent to an invention patent changes the patent examination procedure, with the most significant impact being a longer application processing time. If opportunity costs are not considered, the actual cost of applying for a patent does not increase significantly.

In the third scenario, when the value of R&D outcomes falls between the two extreme situations mentioned above, that means the duration of which the technological advantage can sustain is not long enough, at this point, the returns generated by the technological achievements in both modes are the same. In the patent mode, the cost of acquiring rights and the cost of remedy are not affected by the value of the technological achievements. However, in the trade secret mode, the greater the value of the technological achievement, the higher both of costs mentioned above will be. Therefore, measuring with 'returns minus the two costs', it can be seen that adopting the patent mode is typically more reasonable for R&D enterprises. However, there exists a specific value point for the value of R&D outcomes, at which point there is no significant difference for developers in choosing either of the two protection modes. Furthermore, even if the premise of our discussion is that the R&D outcomes meet the substantive requirements of a patent, the quality of the patent application drafting is another factor that needs to be considered. If the quality is less desirable, it can pose additional risks of losing the overall patent rights. Therefore, when choosing a protection strategy, R&D enterprises must be able to eliminate the risk of patent rights being declared invalid when selecting the patent strategy.

2.1.3 Copyright[13] or Patent Right?

There are very significant differences between works and technical solutions, although both are creations protected under the intellectual property system as 'things' (knowledge products exist in certain forms), what 'objects' are truly protected for is different.[14] Whether scientific and technological innovation or literary and artistic creation, in order to grant entitlements over intellectual properties, all such creative 'things' require certain mediums (material form) to be made known to the outside world. As Hegel said, "In abstract law, spiritual skills and scientific knowledge, etc. are considered possessions only insofar as they are recognized as legally, and are thus subject to examination."[15] However, in certain circumstances, inventions and creative works share similar external forms. In such instances, producers of intellectual property face a choice in deciding whether using copyright or patent right

[13] When discussing the relevant concepts in common law countries, this book should ideally use the term 'copyright' as adopted by these countries. However, since China's legislation, judiciary, and the majority of academic discourse use the term '著作权' (author's rights), in order to maintain consistency in terminology, the Chinese version of this book will use the term '著作权', and the English version of this book will use the term 'copyright' instead.

[14] Both patent rights and copyright protect the expression of a creative 'thing', but they focus on different aspects of that expression: patent rights protect 'technical ideas', which refer to the functionality intended to be achieved by a technical solution; copyright, on the other hand, protects the expression itself, without extending to the underlying ideas.

[15] Hegel, G. (1961). *Fazhexue yuanli [The philosophy of right]* (Fan, Y. & Zhang, Q. trans), Shangwu Chubanshe [The Commercial Press]. §43, 52.

to protect the intellectual property 'fixed' in these forms.[16] So, what exactly do these instances refer to? We know that the subject matters of patent rights include products and methods, among which there are two types that may share similar material expressions with creative works: one is computer software, and the other is industrial designs, each of them will be discussed respectively below.

2.1.3.1 Computer Software

Computer software is a combination of 'programs + text', thus can be protected by copyright. Traditionally, software has always been protected by copyright, especially in Europe, the *Munich Convention* of 1973 excluded software from the scope of patentable subject matter.[17] However, as the digitization of traditional industrial products continues to advance, and business models arising from digital technologies increasingly dominate people's daily lives, patent protection has been increasingly applied to software, albeit in a seemingly conservative manner. Limited by the research objectives of this chapter, the author has no intention to explore the issue of patentability of computer software as there already have been sufficient research on this topic. However, significant disagreements persist without any majority consensus reached.[18] In the current era dominated by digital technology, countries around the world are gradually relaxing their scrutiny over patent applications for computer software. However, software still cannot be granted with independent patent rights. Against this background, this book aims to discuss how developers can choose the most advantageous approaches for their software as a form of intellectual property that can be protected by both copyright and patents.

Although there are controversies regarding the patentability of computer software, the main disagreement revolves around the view of 'inventions must utilize natural laws'—specifically, whether adhering to 'machinery relationship standard or physical transformation standard' as the sole criterion for patentability, rather than solely concerning the purely technical aspects—whether technical problems can be solved, whether technical means are employed, and whether technical achievements are gained—to deny the patentability of computer software and even entire business

[16] Many jurisdictions, including China, do not exclude the possibility of dual-track protection for certain objects under copyright and patent legislation. However, what the author wishes to emphasize is that, although certain objects can be simultaneously protected by both copyright and patent rights, as mentioned earlier, the subjects of protection under these two rights are actually different. Moreover, simultaneously seeking protection under both rights may not be the optimal state for R&D firms. Therefore, developers typically choose the protection model that best benefits them, based on the level of technological development, industry structure, and market demand.

[17] Belleflamme, P. & Peitz, M. (2010). *Industrial organization: Markets and strategies*. Cambridge University Press. 510. The 1973 *Munich Convention* referred to by the author of the book is the *European Patent Convention*, under which Article 52 of the *European Patent Convention* at that time explicitly stated that 'programs for computers' are not patentable.

[18] For example, in the famous case of *CLS Bank v. Alice* (2013) 717 F.3d 1269, there was a 5–5 split among all the judges. In academic discussions, the patentability of 'computer software' is also a topic of ongoing debate.

methods.[19] Given this premise, we can now discuss whether to choose copyright or patent rights to protect software:

Firstly, based on the principle of entitlement, it is understood that the essence of the copyright system is to grant authors (including de facto authors and de jure owners of copyrights) control over the dissemination of their works in the market. In the era of mechanical reproduction, the system was built surrounding 'reproduction rights + distribution rights', whereas in the digital communication era it revolves around 'wired + wireless communication'. However, regardless of its evolutionary paths, the material basis of the copyright system has always been the market of works. Consequently, to circumvent the market control of copyright holders, it is clear that substantively different expressions must be adopted in terms of procedures and texts. The principle of entitlement for patent rights is different, it confers inventors a monopoly position in specific technology markets. The technology market corresponds to technical solutions, which are composed of 'problem—solution—effect'. Therefore, patent rights are pointing at the functionalities of software. Even if a non-right holder replicates the program or text of the software, so long as they do not engage in activities such as using, producing, selling, or offering to sell under patent law, there is no infringement of the patent. However, even if a non-right holder does not directly replicate the patented program (essentially the code) or text, if it can be determined that the software used by the infringing party operates in a manner that is 'essentially identical in method, achieves essentially the same functionality, and produces essentially the same results' as the software of patent holder, patent infringement is so established.[20] In light of this, if a R&D enterprise seeks protection aimed at monopolizing a specific functionality and technical effect in a technological market, then choosing the patent rights approach is appropriate. However, if the goal is to gain control over the distribution market of software carriers (including carriers in digital formats), then the copyright approach should be chosen.

Secondly, we need to understand why for quite a long time, mainstream views (especially in Europe) advocated for protecting computer software by copyright. For this issue, it is difficult to provide a reasonable explanation if the perspective is limited to the intellectual property system itself. In fact, we can find the answer in the development process of industrial forms and patterns. For a considerable period of time, the distribution of copies (such as CDs) was a major business model in the software industry. Therefore, copyright protection has been crucial for the software industry and has been deemed sufficient for developers. However, as business methods (patterns) increasingly appear in the form of software while product functionalities are implemented through software, the software industry is no longer solely

[19] For example, in the *Bilski case*, the U.S. Supreme Court adhered to this standard, ruling that Bilski's patent application involved an abstract idea and was not patentable. See *In re Bilski* (2008) 545 F.3d 943.

[20] This means a consistency in the 'function-way-result' test, which is the basic meaning of the standard for determining patent infringement—equivalence infringement.

dependent on software distribution, the integration of digital technology with traditional industries (manufacturing) has become a key developing direction for the software industry, and correspondingly, there is a growing emphasis on the patentability of software. Especially in recent years, the proportion of software-driven industrial products (services) in the industrial structure has been continuously increasing. Smart manufacturing (the era of Industry 4.0) has risen to become a national strategy, consequently, many R&D enterprises call for applying patent protection to software for the development of new formats and models.[21] However, accompanying with the advocacy for software patent protection, opposite voices have never ceased. For instance, the European Union launched a plan in 2002 aimed at promoting software patents, but it quickly became an arena of policy conflicts.[22] It is not hard to imagine that supporters are primarily the existing giants in the software development industry, while opponents are mainly advocates of open-source software, academics, small and medium enterprises, and an important group—sellers in the software distribution market. Despite the fact that the underlying issue in the debate is essentially about distribution of interests, but a significant reason for opposing software patent protection on the surface of the debate is that considering the inherent cumulative nature of software development—its sequentiality and complementarity—software patents may indeed benefit industrial development, though their net effect tends to hinder innovation and reduce competition.[23]

From the above, it is clear that the choice between software copyright protection and software patent protection is an exceptionally complex issue, involving both technical considerations and public policy choices. Therefore, whenever a classic case emerges that changes the rules (such as the cases of *State Street Bank*, *Bilski*, *Alice* in the United States), or when a new legal document containing a new public policy orientation is proposed or enacted (for example, the draft of the *Directive on the Patentability of Computer-Implemented Inventions* was proposed by the European Commission in 2005, which was later rejected by the European Parliament), they essentially reflect an integration and consolidation of the strategic gaming within the relevant industries. Whether software patent protection will ultimately stifle or promote innovation within a certain period needs to be verified by ex post empirical analysis.[24] However, for enterprises involved in this landscape, they can only base their decisions on the existing rules and policies considering their position and strategic goals within the industry structure, so as to make behavioral choices that are conducive for utility maximization.

---

[21] Section 2.3, Chapter 8, Part 3 of the *14th Five-Year Plan for National Economic and Social Development of the People's Republic of China and the Vision for 2035* provides a basic description of 'what intelligent manufacturing is'.

[22] Belleflamme, P. & Peitz, M. (2010). *Industrial organization: Markets and strategies*. Cambridge University Press. 510.

[23] Ibid., 511.

[24] For example, James Bessen and Robert Hunt conducted an empirical study analyzing the impact of rule changes on software patents in the United States. See Bessen, J. & Hunt, R. (2007). 'An empirical look at software patents'. *Journal of Economics & Management Strategy*, 16(1), 157–189.

2.1.3.2 Appearance Design

According to Paragraph 4 of Article 2 of *Patent Law* of China: "Appearance design refers to a new design that embodies the overall or partial shape of a product, pattern, or their composition, as well as the composition of color with shape or pattern, which has a certain degree of artistic merit and is suitable for industrial application." It can be seen that appearance design includes both the shape and structure of a product while also presents as a work with a certain degree of artistic merit, and consequently gives rise to the issue of 'cross-protection' for designs.[25] If appearance design can receive both copyright and patent rights protections, then there would be an absolute overlapping protection compared to computer software where the substantive objects of protection under the two rights are actually different. The root for the overlapping protection problem of appearance design lies in the fact that this particular form of expression possesses both the characteristics of being 'a certain degree of artistic merit' and 'suitable for industrial production', the key is whether the right holder intends to produce the design by industrial methods—if yes, the act falls under the meaning of 'manufacture' as defined in the *Patent Law* (Article 11 of China's *Patent Law*)[26]; if no, the right holder is entitled to control the act of making copies within the meaning of copyright law (Article 10 of China's *Copyright Law*). On this basis, what we need to consider is that if the legislation a particular jurisdiction permits dual protection (as is the case in most countries), would the designer still face the problem of behavioural choice?[27] Would they always seek to obtain protection under both rights in all circumstance?

In order to answer the above questions, we may need to trace back to the origins of the appearance design systems to gain some insights. The appearance design protection system was originally established for the purpose of providing legal protection for industrial product designs, which is inherently inseparable from the Industrial Revolution. More specifically, it gained prominence and developed in the eighteenth

[25] The term 'cross-protection' in the book was intended to refer to overlapping protection of appearance designs through both copyright and patent rights. However, some countries such as the United Kingdom and Japan exclude the overlapping protection regime.

[26] Taking 'industrial production' as the economic basis for protecting industrial designs, some countries adopt a separate legislative model to protect industrial designs, while others include them under patent law for protection. In fact, the principles and specific rights associated with the separate protection model are essentially no different from those of patent rights.

[27] Some scholars, based on Article 2(7) of the *Berne Convention*, have argued that "prototypes of industrial products that do not constitute works (including applied art works) lack artistic value and are solely used for the production or manufacture of industrial products, and therefore should not be protected under China's *Copyright Law*." See Wang, Q. (2011). 'Moxing Zuopin Dingyi Chonggou'['Reconstruction of the definition of 'model works"]. *Huadong Zhengfa Daxue Xuebao [Journal of East China University of Political Science and Law]*, 3, 22. However, it should be noted that regardless of whether one agrees with this view, the conclusion does not prevent the *Patent Law* from providing protection for applied art works under design patents. Therefore, dual protection remains the norm, as long as the copyright law of a country does not explicitly exclude 'applied art works' from the scope of protection.

century in the United Kingdom due to the rapid growth of the textile industry.[28] To enhance the aesthetic quality of industrial products, the UK Parliament enacted the *Design Registration Act* in 1839 and introduced the design registration system, which provided: "If the applicant submits a registration application for a new and original design related to an industrial product, the design may be granted a monopoly right for a period not exceeding three years."[29] Apparently, this system adopted an independent protection model, and the protection it offered to ornamental designs is largely equivalent to the protection of appearance design patent under China's patent law (apart from the term of protection). As the concept of design protection became more ingrained, the protection of designs in the Britain later expanded from the independent monopoly model towards copyright protection. This shift extended the concept of right entitlements to a broader scope that covers functional designs and decorative designs, especially driven by the Arts and Crafts movement which emerged with the revival of traditional craftsmanship and advocated for copyright protection for both functional and decorative designs.[30] Interestingly, compared to the design of a registration system, the Arts and Crafts movement in Britain had greater influences on the United States and civil law countries, whereas United States, France, and Germany placed more emphasis on distinguishing between copyright protection and the protection of industrial designs.[31]

In addressing the protection of designs, whether a country ultimately adopts a 'parallel' or 'sequential' structure to handle the relationship between the two modes, it inevitably involves two crucial concepts—namely 'industrial production' and 'artistic merit'. Whether these two concepts can be clearly defined (which, for businesses, directly relates to the cost of rights delineation and opportunity costs) has a decisive impact on corporate decision-making. The term 'industrial production' lacks a normative definition. In the United Kingdom, where design protection originated, the standard for determining whether something falls under 'industrial application' is: "… [where] the design is applied to more than fifty articles, which do not all together constitute a single set of articles … or …where the design is applied to goods manufactured in lengths or pieces, not being hand-made goods."[32] The criterion of 'not being hand-made' and the number '50' are certainly objective standards, and although they have been in use since the established in the *The Registered Design Rules* in 1920, it is difficult to say that there is any scientific basis that

[28] Zhu, N. (2016). 'Yingguo Gongyepin Waiguan Sheji Baohu Zhidu De Bianqian Ji Pingjia'['The evolution and evaluation of the industrial design protection system in the united kingdom']. *Shanghai Zhengfa Xueyuan Xuebao* [*Journal of Shanghai University of Political Science and Law*], 3, 110–112.

[29] Bently, L., Sherman, B., Gangjee, D. & Johnson, P. (2018). *Intellectual property law* (5th ed.), Oxford University Press. 720–721.

[30] See Zhu, *supra* note 28.

[31] Therefore, the protection of industrial designs in the United States and civil law countries represents a true dual protection model. In contrast, the United Kingdom essentially arranges copyright and design registration as a linking model, with the connecting point being 'whether it is used in industrial production'.

[32] Schedule 2, Part 2, Para.12(a) & (b), *The Registered Designs Rules* (as amended in 2006) of UK.

underpinned them. Thus, these standards may be explained as merely a result of public policy choices.

Compared to 'industrial production', the judgment on 'artistic merit' is even more abstract. Despite the fact that many rulings on whether the subject matters in question reach a 'artistic merit' often do not provoke controversy in judicial practice, for instance, in cases such as *Shenzhen Qiaokai Industrial Development Company v. Shenzhen Saikede Intelligent Technology Company* involving the 'foreign currency notes detecter housing',[33] *Pivot Point Intern., v. Charlene Prods, Inc.,* involving the mannequin head 'Mara',[34] and *Hart v. Dan Chase Taxidermy Supply Co.,Inc.,* involving animal mannequins.[35] It is relatively easy to reach a consensus over the subject matters in these cases, as stated in the *Lego case* that ' the general public is sufficient to view it as a work of art'.[36] However, if we apply Hegal's definition of 'art' which is: "[t]he content of art is the idea, and the form of art is the image that appeals to the senses. Art seeks to harmonize these two aspects into a free and unified whole",[37] it becomes difficult to clearly articulate what level of artistic standard that 'the general public is sufficient to view it as a work of art' refers to.

In this regard, it is relatively easy for designers to obtain protection through patent rights or specialized rights, whereas acquiring copyright protection is more challenging. In comparison, the advantage of copyright protection is that there is no requirement for registration or examination as prerequisite, while the protection term is much longer. However, its disadvantage lies in the ambiguity of the cost in delineating rights and the risk of losing rights thereby. Considering the relevant legal provisions and judicial practice in China, it is possible for a separate patent application to be filed for appearance designs that are protected by copyright law, but if it was purely an industrial product design, it could not receive copyright protection. Therefore, the target market anticipated by the designers has a crucial impact on how they choose their protection approach: if the designer is expecting large-scale industrial production, seeking copyright protection may not be necessary. On the contrary, if the target of the designer is the art market and its derivative markets, then copyright becomes crucial. However, if the designer seeks for dual protection, they must not put their work into production and sell it in the market before the patent application is filed, as this would fail to meet the novelty requirement for patent applications. Additionally, it is noteworthy that a design of artistic merit does not necessarily mean it meets the substantive requirement of 'originality' for copyright protection, especially when the design is not so regarded as art in the eyes of the general public. Therefore, if a designer believes their 'work' falls into the realm of highly abstract, distinctive, or avant-garde art that may not be readily accepted by the

---

33 See *Guangdong Provincial Higher People's Court (2005) Yue Gao Fa Min San Zhong Zi No. 378 Civil Judgment.*

34 (2004) 372 F. 3d, 913, p932.

35 (1995) 884 F.Supp. 71, p74.

36 See *Beijing Municipal Higher People's Court (2002) Gao Min Zhong Zi No. 279 Civil Judgment.*

37 Hegel, G. (1996). *Mei Xue(Di Yi Juan)*[*Aesthetics (Vol. 1)*] (Zhu G. trans), *Shangwu Chubanshe* [*Commercial Press]*. 87.

general public, they should prioritize an application for patent protection for their designs so as to avoid the risk of being left unprotected on both fronts.

2.1.4 How to Choose a Trademark Registration Strategy?

Enterprises accumulate goodwill by the use of trademarks, which is essentially a production behaviour of intellectual property. Unlike technology R&D and the creation of literary and artistic works, trademarks are inherently related to the market, and cannot exist purely in the realm of spiritual pursuit. In modern commercial activities, trademarks have become an indispensable factor for market competition that cannot be neglected by enterprises.[38] For an enterprise, how to choose a trademark when entering the market? There are essentially two ways: one is to use an existing trademark owned by others, and the other is to register its own trademark. The former refers to the situation of acquiring a right to use by authorisation, which may take the form of standard commercial licensing (such as the trademark licensing agreement between the predecessor of *JDB Group* and *Wanglaoji*) or franchising. If a company chooses to register its own trademark, it would have various options. For instance, it can create a new mark for registration (like the well-known '*Xerox*' trademark) or utilize existing elements to register a trademark (for example, using a 'common name'[39] or applying for registration based on the secondary meaning doctrine, such as the '*Little Sheep*' trademark; alternatively, the company may use symbols that are as closely associated with the product or service as possible, with a typical example being the '*Microsoft*' trademark.).

The advantage of using another's trademark is that the licensee can easily enter into the relevant market.[40] However, the drawback is that it becomes difficult for the licensee to accumulate goodwill of their own. Additionally, depending on the types of license (ordinary license, sole license, or exclusive license), there may be potential disputes over the distribution of goodwill once the licensing term expires.[41] Of course,

[38] Unlike a business name (trade name), a company is not legally obligated to register or use a trademark; the registration and use of a trademark are not compulsory for a business. Moreover, in the past, during periods of economic underdevelopment, factors such as population density and geographical distribution influenced commercial activities, which were not yet as dense or widespread. As a result, there were fewer entities offering homogeneous or competing goods and services in the market, and therefore, the significance of trademarks was not as pronounced.

[39] The term 'common name' used in this book refers to the collective term for the marks stipulated in Article 11(1) of the *Trademark Law* (2019) of China.

[40] If a trademark is used through commercial licensing, it must be a trademark with a relatively high level of recognition (at least within a specific region). From an incentive perspective, businesses are unlikely to have any willingness to license a trademark that has no recognition (i.e., is entirely unfamiliar to the relevant public).

[41] The series of lawsuits between *Wang Laoji* and *Jia Duo Bao* can be considered a typical example of this issue, such as the infringement lawsuit arising from the advertising slogan 'The best-selling red-can herbal tea in the country renamed Jia Duo Bao.' See the Supreme People's Court (2017) Supreme Law Min Shen Zai No. 152 Judgment.

since the licensor and licensee are independent legal entities, and the licensee usually has their own trade names, decorations for product or service, and distinctive signs, etc., as a result, the licensee is still motivated to develop and accumulate its own goodwill even when using another's trademark, though the cost of doing so will be higher in order to distinguish itself from the trademark owner. However, franchising is different. Franchising is a legal form in which the licensor granting a bundle of intangible assets, including trademarks and corporate logos, to the licensee.[42] From a market competition perspective, the licensee acts as a branch of the licensor (although they remain independent legal entities), as defined in the *Illinois Franchise Disclosure Act* that a franchisee is authorized '... to engage in the distribution of goods and services ... under a marketing plan or system prescribed or suggested in substantial part by a franchisor.'[43] The licensee can enter the relevant market more easily through this method, but they may only generate revenue by exploiting business resources of the franchisor, rather than accumulating their own goodwill. In summary, if a business chooses to enter a market by using a trademark of others, then the choice between ordinary commercial licensing and franchising is based on the premise that the business has a clear market positioning. Factors for consideration include the number of competitors and the structure of the relevant market, the market power of the trademark owner in horizontal competition, the influence of the trademark owner on upstream and downstream markets, the scale of operation of the potential entrant, geographical scope, competitive objectives and so on.

On the other hand, registering a trademark of one's own entails a completely different strategy. It is generally considered natural and logical for business owners to design trademarks themselves and proceed with the registration process. However, the situation is not so simple in practice. The uncertainties associated with trademark examination is something that cannot be ignored. Even after incurring costs for trademark searches and analysis, an applicant may still fail to pass the examination and thus cannot obtain a registered trademark. Although there are subsequent remedies of the trademark review procedures that may reverse the decision, the process is yet complex and costly.[44] If a business owner is confident that the designed mark is a fanciful trademark, a successful registration is usually not difficult to complete. However, fanciful trademarks offer no advantages when it comes to building goodwill for the business—due to the lack of recognition and publicity, the trademark owner

---

[42] See Article 3 of the *Regulations on the Administration of Commercial Franchising* (effective May 1, 2007) of China for the definition of 'commercial franchising'.

[43] Sec.3 (1) (a) & (b) *Illinois Franchise Disclosure Act 1987*.

[44] The trademark dispute between Shanxi *Little Sheep* and Xi'an *Little Sheep* over the 'LITTLE SHEEP and logo' illustrates this point well. See *Shaanxi Little Sheep Industrial Co., Ltd. v. Trademark Review and Adjudication Board of the State Administration for Industry and Commerce, Trademark Administrative Dispute Appeal Case* (Beijing Municipal Higher People's Court, 2006 Gao Xing Zhong Zi No. 92 Judgment) and *Xi'an Little Sheep Barbecue Restaurant v. Trademark Review and Adjudication Board of the State Administration for Industry and Commerce, Trademark Administrative Dispute Appeal Case* (Beijing Municipal Higher People's Court, 2006 Gao Xing Zhong Zi No. 94 Judgment).

faces higher costs in promoting the trademark and accumulating goodwill.[45] The role of a trademark is to reduce search costs for consumers, searching is in essence the process of matching prices.[46] In all markets, even the homogeneous goods (or services) markets, prices are dispersed because price dispersion is a manifestation of ignorance in the market.[47] Trademarks can serve as tools to overcome this market ignorance, because no two products (or services) are completely identical based on the correspondence between product quality and sales conditions (notably, the producer himself is part of the sales conditions), trademarks can thus help to correct the information distortion that may arise from relying solely on price indicators. The degree of price dispersion is closely related to the state of market competition. The larger the market and the more intense the competition, the greater the price dispersion would be. Trademarks, as tools to overcome market ignorance, function as means (mediums) to provide information to potential consumers. However, if the trademark is a fanciful trademark, the information it can provide is very limited in the early stages of the trademark owner's business. The owner will need to bear additional promotional costs, such as advertising. This is what is meant by the aforementioned 'lack of cost advantage'.

Compared to the registration of fanciful trademarks, it is more difficult for a business to register a trademark based on the secondary meaning theory. Marks that may only be registered based on the theory of secondary meaning—'common name'—show a certain 'commons' attributes. However, many people misunderstand that such marks lack distinctiveness and therefore cannot be registered until they have been used (as trademarks). In reality, the 'commons' attribute does not imply that the mark itself lacks any distinctiveness (or source-identifying capacity); any symbol possesses a degree of recognizability in commercial activities. However, the entitlement of property rights based on the specific method for the use of different symbols (using the symbol for specific goods or services) gives rise to different outcomes: confer entitlements to marks with inherent distinctiveness brings minimal impacts on non-right holders while creates significant benefits to the trademark owner, thus leading to an overall increase in social utility even when such symbols have not been used[48]; Conversely, if it is a 'common name', conferring entitlements before or soon after it was put in use would impose considerable costs on other competitors in the market who offer identical or similar goods (services) as they must adopt alternative

[45] A more detailed analysis shows that it is not necessarily the case that the cost of cultivating the recognition of a coined trademark is always higher. Many factors are involved, with the most important being the company's existing recognition, or more specifically, its goodwill, which exerts a radiating effect on all of its business activities (including the use of a new trademark). For a well-known company, even if it registers a new coined trademark, the cost of promoting that trademark to achieve recognition among the relevant public will be lower. Therefore, the high promotional cost of a coined trademark mainly applies to new market entrants.

[46] Landes, W. & Posner, R. (1987). Trademark law: An economic perspective. *Journal of Law and Economics*, 30(2), 265–309. 269.

[47] Stigler, G. (1961). The economics of information. *Journal of Political Economy*, 69(3), 213–225. 213–214.

[48] See Landes & Posner, *supra* note 11, 287–288.

means to mark their goods (services) to avoid infringement risks.[49] At this point, we need to compare the 'increase in benefits to right holders' with the 'increase in avoidance costs to competitors' to determine which has a greater absolute value. In practice, it is not difficult to reach a conclusion on this assessment: at the initial stage of use, the 'commons' attribute of a 'common name' significantly outweighs its ability to point to a specific business, thus, even if it can be registered, the incremental benefit it brings to the rights holder are very limited. But meanwhile, competitors in the market are forced to use other symbols to describe their goods or services, which inevitably incurs substantial costs to avoid the 'common name'. In summary, if exclusive rights of trademark are granted to 'common names' from the beginning or within a short period after it is put in use, it is obviously a wrongful entitlement that diminishes the overall social welfare.

However, it does not necessarily mean that the common name cannot be used without entitlement. As the duration of use gradually increases, should the attitude toward granting right to 'common names' change? The author believes the answer is yes. Since the accumulation of usage over time would enhance the ability of 'common names' in reducing search costs for consumers, thereby generating benefits for users. Attracted by commercial value, competing businesses are motivated to join in the group of 'common names' users in the hope of profits sharing. Therefore, on the one hand, the act of use promotes an increase in the value of the 'common name', but on the other hand, with more users join in (of course, on the premise that it does not constitute unfair competition) would cause a rent dissipation of the 'common name', this is a reflection on the principle of diminishing marginal returns, i.e. the more competing businesses that engage in using the 'common name', the faster the rent dissipates, until the marginal returns equal the marginal costs, at which point the net value of the used mark becomes zero. Apparently, the point at which marginal returns equal marginal costs is the optimal time to confer an entitlement for the 'common name'. If entitlements are granted too early, the avoidance costs for non-right holders may be excessively high, leading to a net loss of overall social welfare. Conversely, if entitlements are granted too late, not only will there be issues with avoidance costs, but the net value of the mark in reducing search costs may also become negative. Moreover, although granting rights after a period of use (i.e. 'acquired distinctiveness' as referred to in Paragraph 2, Article 11 of the *Trademark Law* of China) may still be efficient, but they should be granted only on an exclusive basis rather than joint. Because if the entitlements are granted jointly to two or more users, any one of the right holders will be motivated to invest in costs in order to capture as much of the net value as possible from the trademark. If the co-owners cannot negotiate effectively regarding cost inputs and profit distribution, it may lead to a situation where the net value of the trademark becomes lower than in the case when the 'common name' is exclusively granted.[50]

---

[49] Ibid., 291–292.

[50] For a comparison of the efficiency of granting rights to 'shared names' in exclusive or shared ways, see Yang, M. & Zhang, W. (2010). 'Gongyong mingcheng zhi shang chanquan zhengduo

Using symbols that are closely associated with products or services as trademarks is indeed a strategy that can help businesses nourishing their own trademarks, while there are successful examples like '*Microsoft*', '*Caterpillar*',[51] and '*Lai Yi Tong*', yet the opportunity costs for businesses can be relatively high given the risk of violating Paragraph 1 of Article 11 of the *Trademark Law* of China if not managed properly. Meanwhile, it can be challenging for such trademarks to effectively counter competitors using similar strategies. For instance, the trademark owner of '*Lai Yi Tong*' once opposed to the '*Zhongdan Lai Yi Tong*' trademark application of the *Qingdao Beer (Yangzhou) Co., Ltd.* but failed eventually.[52] In summing up, using trademarks that can easily link the marks to products or services is a feasible strategy, but business owners must recognize that this approach poses challenges on the capacity of the examination and review agencies as well as judges in understanding and applying Paragraph 1 of Article 11 of the *Trademark Law* of the trademark properly. Therefore, different businesses need to assess various factors, including their market positioning, competitive landscape, industry characteristics, and expectations regarding goodwill, so as to make behavioral choices that suit their specific situations.

2.2 Intellectual Property Protection and the Promotion of Cumulative Innovation

Anyone can freely utilize what they have created, whether it is tangible or intangible property. This freedom of use is independent of whether there is a statutory entitlement over that property. The fundamental significance of property rights entitlement lies in the right to refuse: unauthorized use of the property by non-right holders is prohibited without the consent of the owner, that means the owner enjoys freedom from forced transactions. In economics, ownership is refered as residual control rights, which effectively summarizes this feature: people acquire ownership of assets primarily for the purpose of obtaining such residual control rights.[53] Clarifying that property owners have legal control to refuse forced transactions is particularly important for intellectual property, as the intangible nature of knowledge property often exhibits characteristics of public goods, namely non-exclusivity and non-competitiveness. Therefore, the freedom granted to rights holders to refuse forced

de jingjixue he faxue fenxi' ['An economic and legal analysis of the property rights struggle over 'shared names'']. *Qinghua Faxue [Tsinghua Law Journal]*, 4, 68–69.

[51] *Caterpillar* was later adopted by *Caterpillar Inc.* as a trademark for its crawler tractors. The image of a caterpillar is easily associated with a track due to their visual similarity. Today, *Caterpillar* has become a world-renowned brand.

[52] See Trademark Review and Adjudication Board Decision No. 02187 of 2007. It should be noted that during the 2019 central government institutional reform, the Trademark Review and Adjudication Board was integrated into the Trademark Office of the China National Intellectual Property Administration (CNIPA), and is no longer maintained as a separate entity.

[53] Grossman, S. & Hart, O. (1986). 'The costs and benefits of ownership: a theory of vertical and lateral integration'. *Journal of Political Economy*, 94(4), pp. 692, 716.

transactions effectively gives them a certain degree of market control. However, due to the public nature of knowledge property, the control conferred to rights holders should be subject to some limitations. Consequently, it is necessary to strike a balance between the free exploitation of intellectual property and the appropriate 'access' for the public when granting entitlements to intellectual property rights owners. This balance can be described on both external and internal dimensions, where the former refers to economic discussions on the length and breadth[54] of intellectual property protection, while the latter pertains to the rights limitation regimes established by intellectual property law. This chapter will explore the issues surrounding length and breadth of protection.

2.2.1 *The Impact of the Length of Intellectual Property Protection on Cumulative Innovation*

The length of intellectual property protection refers to the duration of protection as stipulated by the intellectual property legislations in various jurisdictions. Among all types of intellectual property, the protection of trademark is rather unique. Although rights holders must apply for renewal at specified intervals and may only obtain another protection period upon approval, but in theory, trademark rights can be protected permanently. Therefore, the length of protection periods and the inconsistencies of regulations in different jurisdiction concern primarily copyrights and patent rights. As we know that the duration of patent protection is largely consistent across different jurisdictions, whereas there are certain discrepancies regarding copyright protection periods. Although the *Agreement on Trade-Related Aspects of Intellectual Property Rights* (*TRIPS*) strives to establish a set of harmonized international rules, it merely sets a minimum protection period that member states must provide. This raises an interesting question: why different countries can reach a consensus on the duration of patent protection but set different provisions on the duration for copyright protection? One possible reason is that the impacts of inventions (technical solutions) vis-a-vis literary and artistic creations (works) differ on cumulative innovations. In the more industrialized realm of patents, countries may find it easier to agree on a specific length of patent protection to control its effects on cumulative innovation.

As mentioned earlier, rights holders gain a degree of market control based on intellectual property entitlements. When prior intellectual property exists, it inevitably constrains subsequent cumulative innovation activities. Later creators may either find ways to circumvent these rights or obtain authorization from the rights holders. Each

[54] The 'breadth' of intellectual property protection is not a legal concept. In legal terms, 'breadth' refers to the boundaries of intellectual property. In economics, however, 'breadth' is commonly used to describe the impact of intellectual property on horizontal competition (the substitutability between technological solutions) and the ease or difficulty of intellectual property iteration and updating.

choice entails corresponding costs, and there are significant differences between copyright and patent rights in this context—the restrictive impacts of prior copyrights are far less than those of prior patents because, despite the different degrees of reliance on 'existing technology/existing works' in scientific and technological innovation vis-a-vis literary creation, later entrants have greater freedom to offer substitute products in the market for works compared to the market for technological products. The differences will be discussed respectively below:

2.2.1.1 Copyright Protection and Cumulative Innovation

After the enactment of the first copyright law within the realm of private law in human society—the British *Statute of Anne 1710*—a historic debate took place. The topic of debate was that should copyright be a perpetual property right or a property right limited in duration? Notably, more than a century later, this question was raised again by scholars when they sought to explore the nature of authorship and copyright based on German transcendental philosophy and the personality theory of property. However, the significances of these two debates differ greatly, with the former being more directly related to the essence of the property right nature of copyright. As Mark Rose points out: "The literary-property question was a legal and commercial struggle".[55] Therefore, copyright entitlements can determine the cost of utilizing prior works in subsequent commercial activities, while the transcendental philosophical view of authorship cannot provide an analytical framework for understanding its impact on cumulative innovation.

The arguments for and against treating copyright as a perpetual property right reflect differing attitudes towards cumulative innovation. Proponents believe perpetual protection provides incentives for authors while opponents argue that it harms the development of literature. Lord Camden, a leading opponent in this regard, expressed this view in a romantically phrased statement: "Providence has taken care that there shall not be wanting the noble motives and incentives for men of genius to communicate to the world those truths and discoveries which are nothing if uncommunicated."[56] Of course, nowadays, it is a general rule and common sense in all jurisdictions that copyrights as property rights enjoy exclusive protection only within a certain period of time, the more important question is, what is the difference in the impact on cumulative innovation before and after the expiration of the protection period? In the author's opinion, the key difference is the cost of subsequent creations using the works of the 'geniuses', therefore it is not difficult to understand that the change in the length of copyright protection period will have a profound impact on the cultural and creative industry.

We know that the duration of protection for copyright is divided into general provisions and special provisions. Regarding the former, many countries set the general term of protection as 'the lifetime of the author and 50 years after the author's death',

[55] Rose, M. (1993). *Authors and owners: the invention of copyright*. Harvard University Press. 104.

[56] Ibid., 105.

while the latter applies to specific types of works (such as films, computer software, etc.). Among the major jurisdictions, the United States and Germany provide longer general copyright protection terms—'the lifetime of the author and 70 years after the author's death'. This provides an excellent sample for analysing the impact of copyright protection on cumulative innovation. In 1998, the United States enacted the *Copyright Term Extension Act* (*CTEA*), as a result, *Disney*'s copyright over the *Mickey Mouse* series—which was set to expire in 2003 and would have entered the public domain—was extended by another 20 years on the ground of this Act, *Disney* thus obtained an additional 20 years of exclusive status. Hence, the *CTEA* is also nicknamed as the '*Mickey Mouse Act*'.[57] Although before this law was passed, Nobel winners such as Akerlof, Arrow, and many renowned economists strongly opposed it and took active actions in the believe that extending the copyright term would do nothing more than maintain the market control of copyright holders, which offering no further incentives for authors. But apparently their efforts ultimately failed. Shortly after the *CTEA* was enacted, the famous case *Eldred v. Ashcroft*[58] (also known as the '*Mickey Mouse* lawsuit') was filed. The case went all the way to the U.S. Supreme Court but the plaintiffs lost eventually. Although the case was based on the fact that *CTEA* violated the right to freedom of speech stipulated in *The U.S. Constitution*, it actually reflects the impact of copyright protection on the market for works. Specifically, this impact works through prices, that is, the longer the copyright protection period, the higher the price of using the work. Economists have conducted effective empirical research proving that 'copyright raises prices'.[59] Although Germany, as similar to the United States, also adopts the '70-year standard', the justification for extending the copyright protection period is rather different: "…as the average human life expectancy increases, the close relatives of authors often outlive the 50-year term after the author's death, thus unable to benefit from the author's works."[60]

Whether from the perspective of authors of natural person or corporate authors, the outcomes of extending the copyright protection term are the same: non-rights holders will need to pay licensing fees for a longer period when using a work for subsequent creative purposes.[61] While this cost may result in an exchange for the increase in the producer surplus of the original work, what needs to be contemplated by lawmakers is the question of whether extending the protection period will

[57] Schwartz, P. & Treanor, W. (2003). 'Eldred and lochner: copyright term extension and intellectual property as constitutional property'. *The Yale Law Journal*, 112(8), 2331–2414. 2333.

[58] (2003). 537 U.S. 186.

[59] Li, X., MacGarvie, M. & Moser, P. (2018). 'Dead Poets' property—How does copyright influence price?', *RAND Journal of Economics*, 49(1), 181–205. The paper is considered the first comprehensive empirical study on how copyright protection increases prices.

[60] Schriftlicher Bericht zu BT-Drucks.IV/3401,S.12; Yu, L. (2020). 'Zhuzuoquan baohu qixian biaozhun de shenshen yu chonggou' ['A review and reconstruction of the standards for copyright protection duration']. *Faxuejia[Jurist]*, 3, 159.

[61] In fact, regardless of the standard, it is largely unrelated to the author themselves, as the beneficiaries are the author's descendants. The concept of 'providing economic care for the author's descendants' originates from the *Berne Convention*, but the Convention does not explain the legitimacy of such economic care.

reduce the market supply in the cultural and creative industries (i.e., fewer derivative works)? This is the core concern of economists like Akerlof and Arrow. Some may argue that even if the market for derivative works is significantly affected by the extended protection period, the creation of original works remains unharmed, as creators who are unwilling to pay the license fees can simply shift to producing original works. However, the boundary between derivative and original works is far from clear than expected. For example, cases such as *Qiong Yao v. Yu Zheng*[62] (on copyright infringement) and *Jin Yong v. Jiang Nan*[63] (on copyright infringement and unfair competition) illustrate this well—copyright infringement was established in the former case but not in the latter (although it constitutes unfair competition), which demonstrated that the perception over the distinction between 'derivative' and 'original' works is highly subjective, once a dispute arises, the view of the creator may not be accepted by the judges and a consensus can hardly be reached in subsequent cases even there exist precedent rulings in this regard. Therefore, when the extension of copyright protection period leads to an increase in the cost of cumulative innovation, the market supply of derivative works will decrease within a certain period. At the same time, the market for original works will not necessarily become more active, instead, people will invest more costs in preventing the risks of infringement, therefore the overall welfare of society will decrease.

The decision not to extent the duration of copyright protection in the third revision of copyright law of China in 2020 is, in the author's view, a right choice. Assessing from the impact that an extended protection period would have on the market for work—including the changes in producer surplus for both original and derivative works, as well as consumer surplus—there is no evidence that the overall social welfare will be improved.[64] However, it should be noted that the copyright protection period for special circumstances stipulated in the *Copyright Law* of China is relatively limited (only in Article 23, Paragraphs 2 and 3 of the *Copyright Law (2020)*). In other words, in most cases, the copyright protection period is subject to the 'fifty-year standard', which may result in a suboptimal balance between the copyright holder's free use and the public's access to such works in most cases, such as for photographic works, computer software, graphic works, online games, etc. Therefore, the author suggests that without altering the general terms on the duration of copyright protection, more *sui generis* provisions could be implemented that point to specific types of works or industries, as well as setting varying lengths of copyright protection respectively. By doing so, such provisions can play a more elaborated role in adjusting specific markets for creative works by optimizing the relationship between the copyright holder's control and non-rights holders' freedom of use, prevent excessive impact on the producer surplus of original creators while incentivizing cumulative innovation and increasing the supply in the derivative works market.

---

[62] See Beijing Higher People's Court (2015) Gao Min (Zhi) Zhong Zi No. 1039 Judgment.

[63] See Guangzhou Tianhe District People's Court (2016) Yue 0106 Min Chu No. 12068 Judgment.

[64] The empirical study conducted by Xing Li, Megan MacGarvie, and Petra Moser, mentioned above provides us with a valuable reference.

2.2.1.2 Patent Protection and Cumulative Innovation

As Professor Scotchmer noted: "Most innovators stand on the shoulders of giants, and never more so than in the current evolution of high technologies, where almost all technical progress builds on a foundation provided by earlier innovators."[65] This is clearly a description on a broad basis and all-encompassing, including both horizontal and vertical competition, where everyone continues to advance technological progress based on the work of predecessors. However, when analyzing the impact of the length of patent protection on cumulative innovation, it refers to the narrower concept of 'standing on the shoulders of giants', i.e. the control that earlier patent rights exert over subsequent R&D activities, in other words, new R&D involves the use of earlier patented technologies, users must pay the patent holders appropriate considerations. In real-world economic activities, the narrower form of cumulative innovations is more common, which includes quality improvement, process improvement, new applications, and cost reduction. As previously mentioned, compared to the literary and artistic fields, cumulative innovation in the technological field has a greater impact on the market, especially in sectors like telecommunications, electronics, and software. Therefore, the length of patent protection requires a more precise institutional design, or an empirical examination of the impact that existing regulations have brought on cumulative innovations.

Determining the length of patent protection is a systemic challenge faced by legislators. On one hand, patent technology requires a certain amount of social return as rewards for the inventors on their investments in R&Ds and their efforts in advancing technology progress (a manifestation of the incentive theory). This is especially true when a patented technology is indispensable, which shows its technological superiority and industry reliance on that particular technology. From a R&D perspective, inventors indeed deserve to be rewarded in that circumstances. But on the other hand, societal progress relies on continuous innovation, necessitating a continous involvement of new researchers in innovative activities. Given that patent protection shields inventors from competition, it should not come at the cost of hindering sequential innovation.[66] Therefore, the length of patent protection should aim to maximize the social returns from innovation. These social returns comprise three components: the monopolistic profits of innovators, industry profits,[67] and consumer surplus. Different schemes for patent protection duration will influence the quantitative relationships among these three components, ultimately leading to varied calculations of social returns. Thus, finding the optimal length of patent protection involves balancing dynamic gains against static losses.

---

[65] Scotchmer, S. (1991). 'Standing on the shoulders of giants: cumulative research and the patent law'. *The Journal of Economic Perspectives*, 5(1), 29–41. 29.

[66] Landes & Posner, *supra* note 11, 297.

[67] Here, the term 'industry' in 'industry profits' refers to the industries related to the use of patented technologies.

It is well-known that when the patent system was first established, the protection period was not as long as it is stipulated under current laws.[68] Today, most countries provide a 20-year protection period for invention patents, but why 20 years? Is this protection period at appropriate length? Does the impact of patent protection length on cumulative innovation vary across different sectors? To answer these questions, we must consider the industry practice of sequential competition, in other words, most market participants enter sequentially in practice, and in order to compete with incumbent firms, later entrants make behavioral decisions based on industry structure, patent distribution, existing technology levels and the homogeneity or heterogeneity of competitors. Since patent information is completely public, later entrants must conduct thorough searches and analyses of existing technologies to determine whether they can circumvent prior patents. And if choosing to license, they also need to assess the associated transaction costs and licensing fees. The concept of circumventing prior patent rights refers to the idea that invention patents can be substituted, allowing later entrants to offer substitute technologies or products without using prior patented technology. Based on the ability to circumvent patents, there are three possible routes for later entrants: first, if they cannot circumvent prior patents, they must trade with patent holders; second, even if they can circumvent prior patents, they may still choose to trade with patent holders; third, if they can circumvent prior patents, they might opt to conduct their own R&D.

In the following discussion, we will focus on invention patents and explore how the length of patent protection affects social returns from innovation in the above three scenarios respectively:

Start with the first scenario. 'Cannot circumvent a patent' may be caused by technological incapabilities and excessive costs. Therefore, for later entrants, obtaining a patent license becomes the optimal choice. Generally speaking, the higher the inventiveness of a patent at the time of application, the lower the likelihood that later entrants can circumvent it. For example, the more patent-intensive the industry is, the stronger of substitutability of patents there will be, because of sufficient and fierce competition within that industry.[69] On the contrary, in fields with high R&D and fixed costs, it is more likely that patent technologies cannot be bypassed. The length of patent protection reflects different patent structures. Assuming that certain patent technologies cannot be circumvented, a specific quantitative relationship can form between the number of market entrants (i.e., competitors) and market prices (referring to technology market prices, i.e., licensing fees). Hence, if extending the patent protection period, the monopolistic profits of patent holders will then increase, and the number of implementers entering the market through licensing will also rise. However, as the market price of the technology (licensing fee) will not decrease, leading to a reduction in average industry profits. Moreover, compared to the original

[68] The patent protection period specified in the 1623 *Statute of Monopolies* of the United Kingdom was 14 years. See Bently et.al, *supra* note 29, 395.

[69] Certainly, apart from the technological level of advancement, in practice, there are often situations where, although there is no longer a technological advantage, the patented technology is still effectively non-circumventable due to factors such as policy exclusion and market segmentation.

protection period, the extended patent protection will further reduce both industry profits and consumer surplus. Therefore, in this first scenario, an extended patent protection period benefits businesses with clear technological advantages but puts their competitors and consumers in a disadvantageous position, and the legislative choice should depend on whether public policies are aimed at encouraging investment in specific industries.

Next, let us move to the second scenario. In this scenario, while the prior patent may not be highly advanced technologically, the cost for later entrants to develop substitute technologies is still higher than the combined 'transaction costs of patent licensing + licensing fees'. In such circumstances, they are likely to choose the licensing route, especially given the risks associated with R&D failures. This situation often occurs in industries with high fixed costs but low technological intensity, where information is abundant and symmetric, leaving little room for negotiation between the patent holders and patent implementors. Because in such industries, the likelihood of later entrants choosing to conduct their own R&D is low due to fixed cost constraints, and the low transaction cost will not create obstacles for patent licensing. Imagine if the patent protection period is extended under this structure, the patent holder may benefit from collecting more licensing fees for a longer period, thereby increasing their monopolistic profits; however, since the patent can be circumvented, the extension of protection period will also motivate competitors to engage in R&Ds. During this R&D period, both industry profits and consumer surplus will decline, resulting in an overall net loss in social returns. If we move the time point of this thought experiment forward, when designing patent protection lengths for industries with high fixed costs and low technological intensity, it is advisable not to make the protection period overly long, otherwise the pace of industrial upgrading will be significantly slow.

Finally, let us examine the third scenario. We know that in order to apply for a patent, an invention needs to be fully disclosed, the spillover effect of information means that patented technology can only be partially proprietary.[70] If the prior patent is relatively easy to circumvent (with low technological advancement), and the cost for competitors in the homogenous market to develop substitute technology is lower than the combined costs of 'patent licensing transaction costs + licensing fees', then that particular patent can hardly hinder competition in the relevant market. In this case, competition in the technology market is robust, and substitute technologies are readily available. It can be further seen that the existence of prior patents has no substantial impact on the cost structure in related industries, but can merely serve to resist and combat pure technology 'pirates'. Whether the patent protection period is extended or shortened, the three components of social returns from innovation remain unaffected. Therefore, for industries in this third scenario, i.e. those with low fixed costs but that are technology-intensive, it is inefficient to alter the length of patent protection; in other words, how the patent protection length is designed is less critical, but the key consideration is whether the competitive returns for patent holders are sufficient to recover their R&D costs.

---

[70] See Landes & Posner, *supra* note 11, 299.

In summing up, the analysis shows that the length of patent protection for inventions has varying impacts on cumulative innovation across different industries, ultimately affecting industry development efficiency and the social returns from innovation. Therefore, an efficient institutional design should avoid a one-size-fits-all approach to patent protection durations. It would be advisable to learn from the legislative model of copyright law, establishing general provisions while adding *sui generis* provisions for specific circumstances (typically involving shorter patent protection periods). In this context, the provision of a 10-year protection period for utility model patents and design patents in the patent law of China is a reasonable and efficient institutional arrangement.[71] In practice, industries that frequently employ utility patents and design patents largely fall into the second and third scenarios described earlier, where shorter patent protection lengths facilitate innovation and effective competition in relevant technical fields. However, a simple distinction among invention patent, utility patent, and design patents is insufficient; a more idealized institutional design should also incorporate special provisions devote to special categories of patents, even further subdividing utility patents and design patents into more specific categories so as to better meet the needs of contemporary industrial development.

We should also recognize that the one-size-fits-all provisions regarding the protection period for invention patents in patent law have given rise to many market strategies that we are very familiar with in practice, such as cross-licensing, no-challenge clauses and grant-back clauses in patent license agreements, and reverse payment agreement for pharmaceutical patents, etc. These market arrangements, born from specific industries and implemented through contractual mechanisms, can be seen as adjustments made by the contractual parties in response to the rigid patent protection lengths under the current law. However, it is evident that some of these strategies aim to promote cumulative innovation, while others are designed to hinder it and exclude competition. Therefore, a diversified institutional arrangement for the length of patent protection are also conducive to suppressing the motivation to adopt those market strategies with negative effects.

Moreover, considering the difficulty in reforming the provisions regarding patent protection lengths, the above discussion on the relationship between patent protection lengths and cumulative innovation is also meaningful in the sense that such analysis can be used in individual cases to determine whether to grant injunctions as a remedy for patent infringement. Let us take the recent amendment to the *Patent Law of Germany* as an example. Germany completed the amendment to its *Patent Law* in August 2021, in which an important change that has attracted attention concerning the application of the proportionality principle in patent infringement injunction remedies. Article 139 of the law adds a new provision that the remedy of injunctive relief for patent infringement are ought to be considered in light of many factors,

[71] In fact, the academic debate over the patent protection models for utility models and design patents is not related to their relatively short protection periods, but primarily concerns the patent application examination process and the strength of protection.

among which, 'the economic impact of the injunction' and 'complex products'[72] are closely related to cumulative innovation. That is to say, in patent infringement cases, if the injunction will lead to the suppression of innovation input or the weakening of competition in a specific industry, then the injunction should not be issued as a remedy. Obviously, the consideration over innovation and competition here is in fact the content of an economic analysis on the lengths of patent protection.

2.2.2 *The Impact of the Breadth of Intellectual Property Protection on Cumulative Innovation*

The so-called breadth of intellectual property protection refers to the issue of the boundaries of intellectual property rights. Compared to the issue of the length of right, the breadth of right brings a relatively more straightforward impact on cumulative innovation. As mentioned earlier, it primarily involves horizontal competition and the iterative regeneration of intellectual property. Both the length and breadth of intellectual property rights serve as public policy tools to prevent the granting of excessive monopoly power to intellectual property rights, which could negatively impact cumulative innovation. However, since the term of protection is generally stipulated as fixed numbers in the legislations of different countries (with the copyright laws as a whole show some diversity),[73] 'breadth' becomes the most important tool under current legislation for regulating the relationship between intellectual property protection and the promotion of cumulative innovation.

Although intellectual property legislation explicitly proclaims the entitlement model of intellectual property rights—namely, the property rights model—the boundaries of these rights are not directly defined by law; rather, they are a matter of interpretation. This can be understood through the criteria of copyright infringement, i.e. substantial similarity, as well as the protection scope of patent rights which is based on the claims of the patent. The breadth of intellectual property falls within the realm of public policy and is inherently linked to the non-material attributes of the subject matters of rights. Therefore, the entitlement essentially involves correcting the externalities associated with intellectual property. On the other hand, knowledge shows the characteristics of public goods, meaning that the externalities cannot be entirely eliminated through entitlement, a certain degree of access to knowledge must be preserved for the public. This is referred to as the elasticity of intellectual property

[72] See *Diskussionsentwurf des Bundesministeriums Justiz und für Verbraucherschutz, Entwurf eines Zweiten Gesetzes zur Vereinfachung und Modernisierung des Patentrechts*, p. 61, from https://www.bmj.de/SharedDocs/Gesetzgebungsverfahren/Dokumente/DiskE_2_PatMoG.pdf?__blob=publicationFile&v=1, Accessed 24 July 2022.

[73] In fact, the protection period of trademark rights can be quite flexible, i.e., it can be extended through the trademark renewal system. However, firstly, trademark rights are unrelated to innovation, and secondly, the protection period of trademark rights remains fixed within each protection cycle. Therefore, this book does not address the issue of trademark protection duration. The subsequent discussion on the issue of scope also does not involve trademark rights.

rights, reflecting a dynamic delineation of the public–private boundary. It should be noted that overcoming the externalities of intellectual property is not a static result but a case-by-case judgment aimed at achieving specific value objectives in particular contexts. More specifically, it requires analysis of the behavioral choices of intellectual property holders, competing businesses, and the public (the ultimate consumers of knowledge products) to determine the breadth of intellectual property rights with the goal of utility maximization.

2.2.2.1 The Breadth of Copyright: An Expression Cost Perspective

In recent years, different methods for creation have emerged in copyright judicial practice, including concepts such as 'creative commons', 'tribute works', 'secondary creations', and 'fan works'. The reason why they have caused heated discussions is essentially a problem led by the unclear public–private boundaries. In previous discussions, people prefer to analyze the scope of copyright protection from the perspective of public interest and freedom of expression, and then reach a conclusion that the scope should be restricted to a certain extent.[74] This is certainly correct, but not so helpful in establishing a sense of the boundaries of copyright, just like the famous theoretical totem in copyright law—the 'idea-expression dichotomy'—everyone knows what it means literally, but it is too vague to convey any substantive information. Regardless of the forms of 'creation' as mentioned above, there is a consensus that later creations must have 'borrowed' something from prior works. The dispute or doubt is whether such type of 'borrowing' touches the boundaries of copyright. If yes, whether the 'borrower' should bear the liability for infringement? Putting these two questions together, they shape the breadth of copyright precisely.

If the 'idea-expression dichotomy' is seen as the origin, then the issue of copyright breadth has a long history with the earliest judicial practice that can be traced back to the case of *Sayre v. Moore* in the United States in 1785.[75] Even today, despite that the 'idea-expression dichotomy' is deeply rooted in peoples' minds and seen as an institutional cornerstone of copyright law, there seems to be no clear definitions of what constitutes 'idea' and 'expression' respectively. Moreover, the common understanding of 'ideas' often differs significantly from the interpretation of 'ideas' in judicial rulings. For instance, the judge in the leading case of *Baker v. Selden* interpreted 'idea' as creative material, which may give the impression of a reverse causality where 'the effect has led to the cause'.[76] Under such judicial interpretations, this dichotomy seems meaningless. While acknowledging this issue, the author does

---

[74] As early as 2006, the video work *A Bun Sparks a Bloodshed* sparked a heated debate in the Chinese academic community, with representative papers such as Su, L. (2006). 'Xifang de falv baohu he xianzhi——Cong <yi ge mantou yinfade xue'an> qieru' ['Legal protection and limitations of parody—A case study of *A Bun Sparks a Bloodshed*']. *Zhongguo Faxue*[*China Legal Studies*], 3, 3–16. Although there were differences in viewpoints, the direction of the argument was generally consistent.

[75] (1785) 102 Eng. Rep. 138, 139–40 n.(b); 1 East 358, 361–62.

[76] (1879) 101 U.S. 99.

not attempt to 'risk the world's condemnation' and call for the abandonment of the theory. Instead, by shifting the discourse to the public–private boundary through the lens of copyright breadth seems to be a better approach that can avoid ineffective discussions that appear on different dimensions.

In what circumstances is the breadth of copyright significant? Undoubtedly, it is when subsequent creations need to make use of prior works. If someone merely disseminate existing works, the boundaries of copyright are unlikely to attract any attention.[77] However, in the case of subsequent creation, copyright holders of prior works are likely to scrutinize the creative activities closely with wide open eyes. There has been a long history of literary and artistic creation in human society, and today, there exist an abundance of prior works available for use that are still protected by copyright. Thus, the extent to which subsequent creators can freely use these works cannot be explained simply by abstract values (such as 'for the sake of cultural heritage'). According to the classic theory of 'standing on the shoulders of giants', limiting the breadth of copyright to a certain scope is intended to prevent the loss of overall social welfare caused by monopolization of ideas.[78] In the author's view, exploring the issue from the perspective of 'idea monopolization' cannot help one to understand the basic principles of copyright protection. Throughout human history, the regulation of press publishing has existed much longer than the history of copyright protection, and the functions of these two mechanisms are entirely different, whereas the regulation of press publishing is truly a mechanism that is related to 'idea monopolization'. However, the purpose of copyright law is to address the distribution of benefits arising from the dissemination of works, which is closely linked with the market, yet the creation and dissemination of literary and artistic works do not necessarily involve market factors.

Thus, the familiar logical chain we often encounter—where the boundary of copyright lies in the division between ideas and expressions, aimed at preventing idea monopolization, which would otherwise lead to welfare loss—raises a crucial point about the vague concept of 'welfare'. What exactly does it refer to? If it merely pertains to the public access and appreciation of works of others—purely spiritual benefits independent of market factors (often termed public interest in many studies)—then 'welfare' would not be diminished due to unclear boundaries between 'ideas' and 'expressions' or because 'ideas' are granted with copyright protection. As mentioned earlier, copyright protection aims to ensure that copyright holders

---

77 As the saying goes, copyright infringement can be divided into two categories: one is piracy-type infringement, and the other is plagiarism-type infringement. In reality, both the academic and practical circles have not fully recognized how important it is to distinguish between these two types of behavior. A typical example is when the legislative body designs the 'platform liability for intellectual property infringement' system, where it uniformly regulates the platform's duty of care without making a distinction between the two types of infringement.

78 The term 'ideas' here differs in meaning from the 'idea-expression dichotomy' mentioned earlier. As the subject of the discussion on the scope of copyright, 'avoiding the monopoly of ideas' refers to the idea that even content with originality should allow non-rights holders some freedom to use it, in order to prevent the cost of supplying cultural products to society from becoming excessively high.

receive economic benefits, which stem from the market dissemination of works.[79] Once copyright holders place their works in the market, the spillovers of the knowledge and information contained in those works become out of their control. As long as there is no market dissemination (such as mechanical reproduction in the age of mass production or online sharing in the Internet age), copyright holders have no right to prevent the public from reading, appreciating, or orally sharing works in non-market contexts. Therefore, what type of 'welfare' is lost from overly broad copyright protection? The author argues that it is the loss results from increased costs associated with the creation of subsequent works.[80]

Since copyright originates from the market, it is only meaningful to discuss copyright issues within the market context, so we must return to the market considerations when answering the above questions. On this premise, the motivations for using others' works can be categorized into two: first, profiting from the dissemination of others' works (if unauthorized then it is called an infringement of 'piracy'); second, using others' works to create new works and profiting from the dissemination of the new works (if unauthorized then it is called as an infringement of 'plagiarism'). Clearly, only the latter relates to the boundaries (breadth) of copyright. If copyright protection is relatively broad, it implies a tendency to categorize 'information combinations' in the critical area as expressions, which would obviously increase the creation costs for cumulative innovation. Although the producer surplus for prior copyright holders may increase,[81] the producer surplus for subsequent creators will decrease—resulting in reduced net gains due to higher expression costs when the total demand remains unchanged, or a failure in maximizing the benefits of those prior works due to a withdrawal from utilizing prior works. Meanwhile, the surplus for end consumers (the public who reads and appreciates the works) is reduced (or at least not increased) in most cases. Therefore, deploying an 'expression cost -- copyright revenue' analytical framework can better reveal how the breadth of copyright protection affects cumulative innovation and, consequently, social welfare.

---

[79] The author's reputation and goodwill are not protected by copyright. While respecting and maintaining the connection between a work and its author can serve to protect the author's reputation, in other words, the reputation of the author and the work are interrelated, copyright protection plays an indirect role in the former. Although copyright includes moral rights, also known as author's personal rights, those familiar with the history of copyright law will know that these personal or moral rights stem from the concept of *authorship*, a term whose root indicates an identity, signifying that the author has the right to sell their work in the market. Therefore, copyright is fundamentally a property right. Relevant studies can refer to *supra*. Rose, Chapter 3, pp. 31–48.

[80] Landes, W. & Posner, R. (1989). 'An economic analysis of copyright law'. *The Journal of Legal Studies*, 18(2), 325–363. 348.

[81] In fact, it may not necessarily increase. An overly broad scope of copyright means that the 'grey area between ideas and expression' is more likely to be classified as 'expression'. However, since it is a grey area, it indicates that the originality of the related expression is not of a high degree. As a result, the market demand may decrease under the influence of broader protection, meaning that later creators are more likely to avoid these expressions to circumvent copyright infringement. Therefore, overly broad copyright protection for prior works that "lie" at the public–private boundary may not necessarily increase the copyright holder's producer surplus.

Table 2.1 Thought experiment of breadth of copyright protection

	The breadth of copyright protection	Amy	Work A	Bob	Work B
Scenario I	α_1	Rent-seeking incentives	High market value	Hard to circumvent A	High expression cost
Scenario II	α_1	Small space for rent-seeking	Average market value	Lack of incentives to use A	Low expression cost
Scenario III	α_2	Small space for rent-seeking	High market value	Substantial incentives to use A	Low expression cost
Scenario IV	α_2	Small space for rent-seeking	Average market value	Lack of incentives to use A	Low expression cost

We may conduct a thought experiment to illustrate this relationship. Assume Amy owns the copyright of prior work A, and Bob prepares to create work B and then introduce work B into market. At this point, Bob has two options: first, to derive work B from A; second, to complete the creation of B without infringing the copyright of A. The breadth of copyright protection is denoted by α, where α_1 represents broader protection and α_2 represents narrower protection. The behavioral choices of Amy and Bob, as well as the impact on the subsequent work under different breadths of α, can be categorized as in Table 2.1.

In scenario I, due to broader copyright protection, subsequent creators find it increasingly difficult to circumvent prior works, resulting in a higher expression cost.[82] Therefore, broader copyright protection may inhibit cumulative creation but encourages investment in the market of original works, thereby leading to the creation of original works with high market demand and value.

In scenario II, although copyright protection is broader, the limited value of prior works results in lower incentives for subsequent creators to create derive works based on them despite that the expression cost is lower. Consequently, broader copyright protection cannot maximize the economic benefits of such prior works, and the market for cumulative creation remains inactive.

In scenario III, copyright protection is narrower but the value of prior works is significant, thus subsequent creators will both 'actively' engage in free-riding and can circumvent prior works more easily. At this point, due to a lower expression cost, subsequent creations become more active; however, the rent of prior works is dissipated.[83]

---

[82] Landes & Posner, *supra* note 11, p.338.

[83] For an analysis of the rent dissipation problem, please refer to two classic papers: Gordon, H. S. (1954). 'The economic theory of a common property resource: The fishery'. *Journal of Political*

In scenario IV, copyright protection is relatively narrow and the value of prior works is insignificant. Due to the low cost of expression, subsequent creators will basically 'ignore' prior works, therefore the derivative work market is extremely inactive. But at the same time, precisely because of the low risk of infringement, the market for original works is very active.

In summary of the above thought experiment, broader copyright protection has positive effects only for works with extremely high market value and large market demand (where marginal utility increases), while it will lead to a decrease in utility for works with high demand substitutability. For most types of works, a narrower copyright protection is more appropriate. In short, similar to the issue of copyright duration, the most effective choice of breath of protection is not a one-size-fits-all approach; instead, it should involve different judicial policies tailored to different works (specifically, public policy choices in individual cases). Broader protection encourages investment in the creation of high-value works, thereby receives higher market returns, while narrower protection reduces the costs of using works with high demand substitutability so that 'one can freely use information that has already been produced without the need to confirm the right to each use'.[84]

2.2.2.2 Optimal Patent Protection Breadth

Compared to the creation of literary and artistic works, the characteristic of 'standing on the shoulders of giants' is more obvious in technological R&Ds, especially in industries such as communications, electronics, and computer software which occupy an important position in the current economic structure and involve highly active R&D activities. Such industries also incurred a large number of patent infringement disputes (including those involving trade secrets) and antitrust disputes. While technological innovation inherently follows the pattern of 'the new generation surpasses the old', prior technologies can serve as inspiration and promotion for the next generation of technologies, and the social value generated by the former is an essential component of the incremental social value created by the latter.

Similar to the previous discussion on the duration of patent protection, the breadth of protection also pertains to the issue of the cost of cumulative innovation. Regardless whether it is in the context of duration or breadth of protection, subsequent developers need to compare the 'cost of paying licensing fees' with the 'cost of circumventing prior patents' to choose the optimal path. For instance, if new entrants seek to avoid being constrained by technologies of the incumbents, they must strive to bypass the coverage of the patent rights of incumbents and develop fully substitutable technological solutions. The difference between the issues of duration and

Economy, 62(2), 124–142; Cheung, S. (1970). The structure of a contract and the theory of a nonexclusive resource. *Journal of Law and Economics*, 13(1), 49–70.

[84] Jiang, G. (2021). 'Lun zhuzuoquanfa de 'kuan jin kuan chu' jiegou' ['On the 'wide in and wide out' structure of Copyright Law']. *Zhongwai Faxue* [*Chinese and Foreign Law Studies*], 2, 339.

breadth is that, when considering in the dimension of duration, the cost of cumulative innovation relates to the payment cycle of using prior patents. It means that the longer the remaining cycle and the lower the technological advancement of the prior patents are, the more the latecomers should opt for independent R&D to circumvent the patents. In contrast, when considering in the breadth dimension, the threshold for patent infringement is 'identical or equivalent', therefore, subsequent developers need to analyze the scope of patent coverage to assess the cost and difficulties in developing substitute technologies. Clearly, this cost is influenced by the judicial policies surrounding the application of the doctrine of equivalence; if the application is flexible (indicating broader protection), the cost for subsequent developers to circumvent patents is higher, if the application is rigid (indicating narrower protection) such cost is relatively lower. As for the level of licensing fees, it depends on the specific context of intellectual property transactions: the more competitive the industry and the more symmetrical the information between the parties, the more transparent the pricing of licensing fees, thus reducing the rent-seeking (leverage) space for patent holders.

The breadth of patent protection primarily affects horizontal competition. On one hand, the breadth of patent protection affects the 'survival' space for differentiated substitutes in horizontal competition. From the perspective of consumers in the end market, there are no completely identical products or services, and this is the prerequisite for new entrants to enter the market occupied by existing patent holders. Even among similar products, the reason they can coexist on a differentiated basis is due to varying consumer preferences, which dictate that they made discrete choice over products and services.[85] Therefore, market participants engage in horizontal competition by choosing both geographical location and price[86]; otherwise, they would choose locations that are sufficiently distant from each other. When the breadth of patent protection is broad, the 'survival' space for differentiated substitutes is smaller. Thus, in industries where product differentiation is crucial, such as the smart terminal manufacturing industry, the constraints imposed by patent rights on horizontal competition will be significant. And if there is a lack of freedom in geographical location selection, it becomes challenging for latecomers to enter the relevant market. In this circumstance, new entrants may find it more efficient to enter the market through purchase rather than developing substitute technologies or via licensing. Conversely, when the breadth of patent protection is narrow, differentiated substitutes may find it easier to 'survive' regardless of whether it is a differentiation-sensitive industry, the constraints imposed by patent rights on horizontal competition are generally weaker. Hence, in industries with high fixed costs and R&D costs, such as the pharmaceutical industry, it can be readily understood why there are strong oppositions to a narrower approach on the protection of patent breadth.

On the other hand, the impact of the breadth of patent protection on horizontal competition can also be observed from the perspective of sequential innovation. The

[85] For meanings of discrete choices, see Small, K. & Rosen, H. (1981). 'Applied welfare economics with discrete choice models', *Econometrica*, 49(1), 105–130, 111.

[86] To simplify the issue, the impact of brand factors has been excluded here.

broader the protection, the higher the cost for the outcome of cumulative innovation to enter into the market—it is more difficult for later developers to engage in innovation outside the scope of patent protection, and easier for patent owners to gain greater competitive advantages. The following analysis distinguishes three scenarios[87]: First, we assume that the latecomer is homogeneous with the prior patent owner. In order to compete with the patent owner, the latecomer either enters the market through licensing, or search for substitute technologies outside the scope of patent protection. It should be noted that the latter approach has nothing to do with whether the technology is advanced or not, because even if the latecomer develops more advanced technology, as long as it uses the prior patent, paying the patent owner a license fee is a cost that the latecomer must bear. Whether the latecomer enters the market through licensing or finding substitute technologies, it will cause price erosion to patented products in horizontal competition.[88] Therefore, if the scope of the patent right is broad, the best choice for the patent owner is to refuse licensing, and because the patent owner is homogeneous with the latecomer, there is no need for the patent owner to worry about the risk of antitrust violation; but if the scope is narrow and the latecomer can easily find substitute technologies, the best choice for the patent owner is to offer for licensing, preferably with proper regional segmentation of the market. Secondly, let us assume that the production efficiency of the latecomer is lower than that of the patent owner. Since the latter has advantages both in efficiency and owning the patent, the latecomer cannot afford the patent licensing fee nor being capable of developing substitute technologies, so it is impossible for the latecomer to engage in horizontal competition with the patent owner. At this time, no substantial impact will be created no matter how broad the patent right is. Finally, let us assume that the production efficiency of the latecomer is higher than that of the patent owner. This is the most complex scenario, because once the latecomer enters the relevant market, the issue is not merely concerning price erosion to the existing patented product, but the subsequent entrants have a cost advantage over the patent holder which allowing them to further lower the product price. However, if the patent owner refuses to license, the latecomer is forced to develop substitute technologies, and the patent owner will also be put into a weak market position. Therefore, in the case of a wide patent protection breadth, the best choice for the patent owner is to open for licensing and reduce the production scale to a relatively low level to maximize its own interests; in the case of a narrow patent protection breadth, the best choice for the patent owner is to assign the patent right and completely withdraw from the relevant market, so as to avoid being forced to withdraw from the market later as a result of failure in competition.

Moreover, the breadth of patent protection also significantly impacts patent aggregation strategies, including well-known concepts like technical standards and patent pools. Individual or multiple patent holders may adopt various patent aggregation

---

[87] The analysis in this book assumes that competitors have sufficient information about each other. If this is not the case, asymmetric game theory analysis would be required.

[88] Scotchmer, S. (2006). *Innovation and incentives*. The MIT Press.108.

strategies based on the breadth of right according the manifestations of judicial policies. It is true that patent aggregation phenomena will exist in the market regardless of the issue on breadth, however, what matters is how the breadth of protection affects the specific patent combination methods and pricing strategies employed by patent holders (or groups). For example, in the communications sector, there is the H.265 standard, which includes two patent pools—'HEVC Advance' and 'MPEG LA'. Between the two patent pools, 50% of the patent rights overlap. As we know that the communications industry is characterized by active R&Ds and a high density of patents, and the breadth of patent protection in this industry is relatively narrow, this is a key reason for the aforementioned patent pool phenomenon. Therefore, similar to patent aggregation strategies, the breadth of patent protection cannot be viewed in isolation, it must be analyzed in conjunction with market structure, competition policies, and other factors. But what the author attempts to point out is that the breadth of patent protection is determined based on the interpretations of the judiciary and executive bodies over patent claims. When a country seeks to introduce a particular patent aggregation strategy as a guidance within a specific industry, it may do so by altering the understanding over the breadth of patent protection when interpreting the patent claims, thereby further influencing the self-regulation and even transformation of the industry structure.

Overall, the patent system should provide reasonable incentives for every innovator (market competitor). Although prior innovators already applied for patents, they simultaneously made their technological solutions public, subsequent innovators can engage in cumulative innovation thank to such contributions made by prior patent holders. Moreover, economists have long debated the relationship between innovation and the level of market competition, as evidenced by the well-known conflict between the doctrines of Schumpeter Hypothesis and Aghion Inverted U-shaped Relationship. Therefore, the complexity of cumulative innovation implies that it is impossible for an institutional design of general to exist. While some scholars have suggested that public policy choices for sequential innovation should entail a short while broad patent protection scheme,[89] however, if patent licensing frequently fails due to market failures, the benefits of such short and broad public policies for cumulative innovation would consequently be eliminated.

2.3 Summary of This Chapter

For a long time, both theoretical and practical circles in China have viewed the attributes of intellectual property rights from a static perspective, with little analysis of the behavior choices of the producers of knowledge property from a dynamic viewpoint. This chapter attempts to break away from established research paradigms by adopting a behaviorist perspective and using economic analysis as the methodology to interpret the principles of intellectual property entitlement.

[89] Ibid., 103–112.

Based on this notion, this chapter answers two questions: first, the initial entitlement of intellectual property is crucial, then how should individuals choose property claims that align with the specific intellectual property creation activity? Second, cumulative innovation is the primary form of economic activity in human society, and prior intellectual property inevitably impacts subsequent cumulative innovation, in constructing an intellectual property system aimed at maximizing overall societal welfare, how should the length (duration) and width (scope) of intellectual property protection be collaborated to achieve the dual incentive objectives—encouraging both originality and cumulative innovation?

The property claims over the creation of intellectual property should be understood on two levels: whether to invest in the activities of intellectual creation, and if so, what specific types of intellectual property to choose. The decision of market entities to invest in a particular technological R&D activity is certainly based on a 'cost–benefit' analysis, and the content included in such analysis is higly complicated and complex, for example, it requires an understanding on the R&D levels in relevant technological fields to assess the difficulty of technological advancement; an analysis on the competitive structure of relevant markets to evaluate the prospects for application of the innovation results; as well as an estimation on potential returns based on market demand and competitive intensity. Within specific technological fields or particular industries, choosing the most appropriate form of intellectual property to protect innovative results is crucial for intellectual creators. This chapter designates three topics—"patent vis-a-vis trade secret," "copyright vis-a-vis patent," and 'strategical choice on trademark registration'—to conduct thought experiments regarding the behavioral choices of market entities during the intellectual creation process. The aim is to reveal how the current legal framework for the entitlements of intellectual property rights affects business activities in pursuant to competitive advantage in the market.

In terms of the impact of intellectual property protection on cumulative innovation, the main focus is to answer the question of how to strike a balance between the rights holders' freedom to utilize their rights and public access. Looking from the perspective of the structure of rights, the institutional arrangements and legal applications for the duration and breadth of intellectual property protection are the two core aspects. Given the varying degrees of reliance on prior intellectual property by subsequent innovations, the effects of extending protection periods for copyright and patent rights are significantly different. The author believes that this chapter highlights a particularly meaningful finding that diverse institutional arrangements for patent protection duration are conducive in suppressing the motivations for negative market strategies. Regarding the issue of breadth, which pertains to the boundaries of intellectual property rights, an interesting discovery in this chapter is that whether it is for copyright or patent right, the most effective choice over breadth is never a 'one-size-fits-all' approach. It advocates that judicial decision-makers and law enforcement authorities should adopt a flexible public policy that adjusts the scope of protection based on the specific context of each case. This approach ensures that the scope of intellectual property protection is appropriate, which can avoid net losses for patent holders while fully harnessing the industry-adjustment function of cumulative innovation.

References

Arthur, B. (2018). *Jishu de benzhi [The nature of technology*] (D. Cao & J. Wang, Trans.). Zhejiang Renmin Chubanshe [Zhejiang People's Publishing House].

Belleflamme, P., & Peitz, M. (2010). *Industrial organization: Markets and strategies*. Cambridge University Press.

Bently, L., Sherman, B., Gangjee, D., & Johnson, P. (2018). *Intellectual property law* (5th ed.). Oxford University Press.

Bessen, J., & Hunt, R. (2007). An empirical look at software patents'. *Journal of Economics & Management Strategy, 16*(1), 157–189.

Cheung, S. (1970). The structure of a contract and the theory of a nonexclusive resource. *Journal of Law and Economics, 13*(1), 49–70.

Drahos, P. (1996). *A philosophy of intellectual property*. Dartmouth Publishing.

Gordon, H. S. (1954). The economic theory of a common property resource: The fishery'. *Journal of Political Economy, 62*(2), 124–142.

Hegel, G. (1961). *Fazhexue yuanli [The philosophy of right*] (Y. Fan & Q. Zhang, Trans.). Shangwu Chubanshe [The Commercial Press].

Hegel, G. (1996). *Mei Xue (Di Yi Juan)* [*Aesthetics (Vol. 1)*] (G. Zhu, Trans.), *Shangwu Chubanshe* [*Commercial Press*].

Jiang, G. (2021). Lun zhuzuoquanfa de 'kuan jin kuan chu' jiegou [On the 'wide in and wide out' structure of Copyright Law]. *Zhongwai Faxue [Chinese and Foreign Law Studies], 2*, 339.

Landes, W., & Posner, R. (1987). Trademark law: An economic perspective. *Journal of Law and Economics, 30*(2), 265–309.

Landes, W., & Posner, R. (1989). An economic analysis of copyright law. *The Journal of Legal Studies, 18*(2), 325–363.

Landes, W., & Posner, R. (2003). *The economic structure of intellectual property law*. Harvard University Press.

Li, X., MacGarvie, M., & Moser, P. (2018). Dead Poets' property—How does copyright influence price? *RAND Journal of Economics, 49*(1), 181–205.

Rose, M. (1993). *Authors and owners: The invention of copyright*. Harvard University Press.

Schwartz, P., & Treanor, W. (2003). Eldred and lochner: Copyright term extension and intellectual property as constitutional property'. *The Yale Law Journal, 112*(8), 2331–2414.

Scotchmer, S. (1991). Standing on the shoulders of giants: Cumulative research and the patent law. *The Journal of Economic Perspectives, 5*(1), 29–41.

Scotchmer, S. (2006). *Innovation and incentives*. The MIT Press.

Shavell, S. (2004). *Foundations of economic analysis of law*. The Belknap Press of Harvard University Press.

Small, K., & Rosen, H. (1981). Applied welfare economics with discrete choice models. *Econometrica, 49*(1), 105–130.

Stigler, G. (1961). The economics of information. *Journal of Political Economy, 69*(3), 213–225.

Su, L. (2006). Xifang de falv baohu he xianzhi——Cong <yi ge mantou yinfade xue'an> qieru ['Legal protection and limitations of parody—A case study of *A Bun Sparks a Bloodshed*]. *Zhongguo Faxue [China Legal Studies], 3*, 3–16.

Wang, Q. (2011). Moxing Zuopin Dingyi Chonggou [Reconstruction of the definition of 'model works']. *Huadong Zhengfa Daxue Xuebao [Journal of East China University of Political Science and Law], 3*, 22.

Williamson, O. (2010). Transaction cost economics: The natural progression'. *The American Economic Review, 100*(3), 673–690.

Yang, M., & Zhang, W. (2010). Gongyong mingcheng zhi shang chanquan zhengduo de jingjixue he faxue fenxi [An economic and legal analysis of the property rights struggle over 'shared names']. *Qinghua Faxue [Tsinghua Law Journal], 4*, 68–69.

Yu, L. (2020). Zhuzuoquan baohu qixian biaozhun de shenshen yu chonggou ['A review and reconstruction of the standards for copyright protection duration]. *Faxuejia [Jurist], 3*, 159.

Zhu, N. (2016). Yingguo Gongyepin Waiguan Sheji Baohu Zhidu De Bianqian Ji Pingjia [The evolution and evaluation of the industrial design protection system in the United Kingdom]. *Shanghai Zhengfa Xueyuan Xuebao [Journal of Shanghai University of Political Science and Law], 3*, 110–112.

Chapter 3
A Behavioural Analysis of Intellectual Property Transactions and Insufficient Supply of Legal Systems

3.1 Why Do Intellectual Property Transactions Occur?

Looking at the field of law both domestically and internationally, research on intellectual property systems primarily focuses on authorization, confirmation of rights, and infringement determinations and remedies, and the patent systems also designated a large part to antitrust issues. However, issues on intellectual property transactions - which are closely associated with the significance for the existence of intellectual property as a whole - are rarely studied by legal scholars, but are more emphasised in disciplines such as economics and management. This is an interesting 'division of labour', as we can see that such a situation has further affected intellectual property legislation. In terms of weighting, the legal norms regarding intellectual property transactions constitute a very small proportion of the overall legislation. In most views, intellectual property transaction are essentially issues to be addressed within contract law, company law, and property law,[1] and there is no need for extensive regulation on the adjustment of transactions within intellectual property legislation.

The author believes that there are different options for establishing a comprehensive intellectual property legal system at the legislative level. Given the enormous scope of property right system in civil law, and the fact that almost every property right involves transaction issues, the legislators must decide, first and foremost, whether the construction of intellectual property system is aiming at solving general issues systematically, or should it reflect individual characteristics of different types of intellectual property? If it is the former, a legislative model based on objectivism shall be chosen; if it is the latter, a legislative model based on behaviouralism should be adopted. Furthermore, when discussing the method of systematic construction, it

[1] The property law mentioned here mainly refers to the property law in continental law countries, where the relevant legal norms address issues such as the interests derived from the use of intellectual property and the issue of guarantee etc. In common law countries, legislations are enacted to address the same issues, but there is no individual 'Property Law' as a single branch of law. This legal term used here in this book is chosen based on the continental law nature of China.

© Intellectual Property Publishing House Co., Ltd. 2025

M. Yang, *Basic Theories of Intellectual Property Transaction*,
https://doi.org/10.1007/978-981-96-7039-0_3

merely refers to the forms of the overall legislative structure and the specific laws of intellectual property. But theoretical and practical research should not be constrained by such forms, as it may lead to the aforementioned biased 'division of labour'. In fact, the long disregard of intellectual property transaction issues within the legal field not only fails to provide adequate theoretical and methodological support for the industry, but often results in an inability to identify the deficiencies within the intellectual property legal system itself as well as the deviations in the application of certain specific legal systems.

The smooth implementation of intellectual property transactions is essential for ensuring the supply of knowledge products in the market, particularly the continuous supply of innovative products. In this regard, studying the relationship between intellectual property transactions and the supply of intellectual property legal systems from a behaviourist perspective has both theoretical and practical value. This approach allows for the examination of whether the entitlement of intellectual property rights violates the fundamental laws of technological, artistic, and industrial development, thereby providing a solid foundation for future legislative amendments.

As intellectual property originated in the background of the market, thus its discussion is only meaningful in the context of the market. In brief, there are two fundamental reasons for the occurrence of intellectual property transactions: one is to recover investments, and the other is the existence of market competition. Any inventions or creations in literature, art, or technology require investments. If someone made inventions or created works merely for the purpose of self-appreciation, they certainly would not be bothered to recover their investment, and the whole intellectual property system shows little significance to such creators.[2] For entities whose commercial purpose is the production of intellectual property, they would inevitably be concerned with investment recovering, and intellectual property entitlement serves as the starting point and foundation, especially for those with weaker preventative capacities. Market competition is both an objective condition for intellectual property transactions and its economic core. Competition compels resources to be allocated more efficiently among market participants. Even intellectual property holders themselves are not always the most efficient producers (especially true for authors or inventors of a natural person), they can only maximize the utility of their intellectual property through transactions. If there is no market exists or market competition cannot be formed, the value of intellectual property is meaningless, as the products of knowledge creation would not be treated as property at all.

As mentioned in the previous chapter, the creation of intellectual property is not always driven by the pursuit of economic interests from a logical perspective.

[2] Some may argue that copyright law can also play a role in protecting the moral rights of authors. However, prior to the establishment of the copyright system, there were already certain institutional arrangements for the protection of authorship. If the focus is solely on protecting the moral rights of authors, there is actually no need to create a new system. From the perspective of property rights, the interest distribution mechanism constructed for the dissemination of works is the original source of the copyright system, which can be clearly observed through historical examination.

However, the intellectual property system is designed to facilitate smooth transactions, thereby realizing interest distribution and ensuring its outcomes.[3] Even if the initial purpose of creation is purely for spiritual fulfilment, the intellectual property system ensures creators the possibilities to gain some economic benefits in the future. It should be noted that incentivizing creators to engage in intellectual property creation by ensuring they receive considerations is not limited to the intellectual property system alone. Other methods such as bonuses, subsidies, tax incentives, or franchises, can also be adopted.[4] Intellectual property entitlement is merely the most commonly used method, but is not necessarily the most efficient one in every case. Starting with the entitlement, intellectual property owners can either utilize the rights themselves (the significance of property rights lies in their right to refuse interference from others) or allow others to utilize their intellectual property through transactions, thus realizing the value of intellectual property.

Resources need to be allocated and transferred among different entities to meet various human needs. Consumer demand is the ultimate goal, although there are producer demands along the entire chain from raw materials to consumers, they ultimately aim at satisfying the needs of the final consumers. Therefore, consumer demand theory holds significant importance in understanding both static (i.e. the entitlement) and dynamic (mainly transactions) property relationships. It is not difficult to see that the process of resource circulation and demand satisfaction essentially reflects relationships between different entities, when designing a legal framework for such relationships, the key is to understand how the behaviour of one entity influences the behavioural choices of another. The marginalist school, which holds an important historical position in economics, contributed greatly to the formation and development of this theory. Economists such as Jevons, Marshall, and Menger provided systematic and thorough analysis over these thoughts, laying the foundation for further research on human interactions. For instance, Marshall, starting from an analysis of the basic factors that determine demand, proposed the famous marginal utility theory.[5] On this ground, the importance of interactions between different entities has been gradually emphasized. By analysing the utility functions of different entities, it helps to reveal the influencing factors and significance behind specific behavioural choices.

The vast majority of economic transactions occur through the market, as transactions and markets are fundamental elements of economic life in human society. Even before the establishment of intellectual property rights, intellectual assets were

[3] Lord Camden, the Chief Justice of the Common Pleas in Britain in the 1770s, had invoked Shakespeare, Bacon, Newton, Milton, and Locke to show that true geniuses had no view of personal gain in their works. "Macaulay discussed each of these writers to show that none was quite so disinterested as he represented. Shakespeare, for example, was plainly more concerned with filling the theater than with instructing mankind." See Rose, M. (1993), *Authors and owners: The invention of copyright*, Harvard University Press.106.

[4] In fact, different countries have adopted various methods to incentivize innovation, with awards and subsidies being the most common approaches.

[5] Regarding the marginalist utility theory of Marshall, see Blue, S. and Grand, R. (2008). *Jingji sixiang shi [History of economic thought]* (Di, X., et al. trans.), Peking University Press. 219–220.

already part of economic activities as production factors and significantly influenced pricing. For example, the production and sale of handicrafts made by skilled artisans commanded higher prices than those produced by ordinary individuals. Since intellectual assets were not as far entitled to protection, transactions and markets at that time revolved around tangible assets, artistic and skilled elements embodied in these tangible goods were considered only when setting prices. This is still true today for literary or artistic assets inseparable from their physical form, where transactions over their ownership and intellectual property rights are often mixed. With the emergence of modern intellectual property systems, intellectual assets themselves became objects of resource allocation, thus creating a market for intellectual property transactions (e.g., concepts like technology transfer, copyright markets, technology marketplaces, and IP-based business emerged consequently). The significance for the independent existence of the two concepts, i.e. 'market' and 'intellectual property transaction', allows us to understand how market participants make decisions and to identify the specific market conditions necessary to achieve targeted policy objectives.

In social life, entities interact with each other, even in static conditions, and this interaction forms the basis and rationale behind decision-making. Taking intellectual property as an example, the mere existence of a specific intellectual property right holder will prompt non-right holders to make related decisions in the market—whether to seek transactions with the right holder, and if so, what considerations they can bear for such transactions. In economics, such interactions are described and assessed by demand and utility. Demand differs between end consumers (consumers as we typically referred to in everyday life) and producers at different levels (for instance, downstream producers serve as consumers for upstream suppliers). The demand of end consumers relates to fundamental needs, such as health and desires etc. and the fulfilment of specific needs is determined by the maximum utility that a consumer's resources can afford in rational state. For instance, in the copyright field, when people have a need for reading, and both digital and high-quality print versions of a particular work are available in the market, what will consumers choose? The answer is straightforward—it is the same reason that explains why some consumers may opt for pirated versions. Utility theory addresses the priority that consumers would choose in decision-making, as individuals must allocate their expenditures under the constraint of total input in order to maximize utility. The resulted spending combination reflects their decision sequence. What we often refer to as consumer preferences is a direct manifestation of utility theory. Whether between consumers and producers or among producers at different levels, the 'demand-utility' theory provides a framework for analysing how various entities make sequential decisions.

Therefore, if we view the outcomes of intellectual property creation activities as consumer goods or production factors, it becomes clear how intellectual property transactions occur. The specific types of intellectual property, or the various subject matters of intellectual property, are often categorized into two main types:

creative results and distinctive marks.[6] From the 'demand--utility' perspective, the term 'creativity' and 'distinctiveness' show that different types of intellectual property serve to meet varying levels of human needs. The following section will analyse the three main categories of intellectual property rights separately.

Firstly, copyright represents an entitlement to specific expressions, where the protected works, as subject matters of rights, serve to satisfy people's high-level intellectual and cultural needs. In order for the content of works to reach consumers, it must rely on the activity of dissemination. Dissemination is an economic activity that requires investment, either by the creator themselves or by other entities entering the market to promote the work. If someone seeks to disseminate a particular work, he must first remove any obstacles of rights attached to the work, which inherently leads to copyright transactions.[7] Dissemination can be driven by several factors: first, when a work is well recognized and has substantial market demand, copyright holders or disseminators would then have incentives to invest in its distribution; second, when consumers have a strong demand for a specific type of work, someone would then invest in the creation of such work and introduce it into the market. In the first scenario, the utility of the work is so apparent that would influence the behavioural choices of the parties involved—both the copyright holder or non-right holders. In the second scenario, while the work is yet to be created and has not shown its actual utility at that time, but demand is an objective factor, it would guide parties to engage in relevant activities and thus create utility. In either case, when someone who does not hold the copyright acts as a disseminator of a work, a need for copyright transactions arises, with copyright licenses serving as essential production factors for such disseminations. In summary, copyright transactions provide disseminators with a path to market access.

Secondly, patent rights are entitlements to technological innovations, with the technological solutions as the subject matters of rights aimed at meeting human survival needs. Of course, survival needs to exist at various levels, and higher-level survival needs are essentially akin to spiritual needs. According to the substantive requirement of 'utility' upon patent grant, patented technologies must be complete technological solutions that can be applied in industrial production and yield positive effects. A successful patent application confirms the utility of the invention, whereas the utility of the patent directly corresponds to consumer demand. Therefore, the emergence of patent rights triggers a series of interrelationships: if the patent

[6] Classifying intellectual property subjects into creative works and distinctive identifiers originates from the 1992 guidelines set forth by the International Association for the Protection of Intellectual Property (AIPPI), which has since been widely adopted as a basis for defining intellectual property.

[7] Before the birth of copyright law, the book trade had already been very vigorous, with publishers, who could only enter the market with special approval, existing as commercial entities. However, since authors did not yet have copyright, there was no copyright barrier preventing publishers from entering the book market. Therefore, the advent of copyright law also marked the beginning of copyright transactions between authors and distributors. A depiction of the book trade before the birth of copyright law can be found in *supra*. Rose, M. (1993), 9–30.

holder engages in actual production, they typically refuse to engage in patent transactions to maintain their competitive advantage.[8] This exemplifies the dual nature of patent rights—they protect innovation while potentially hindering innovation.[9] Thus, a refusal to deal can also be deemed as a transactional state, but if such refusal is deemed a violation of antitrust laws, regulatory frameworks may compel the patent holder to engage in transactions. On the other hand, if a patent holder does not engage in actual production, it will become an inevitable choice for him to transact with implementors of the patent. Short-term failures in reaching agreements caused by the patent holder's attempt to set high prices or the implementor proposing low priced offers do not negate the incentive for the patent holder to engage in transactions. Negotiation for transaction is a complex process that may not always lead to successful agreements, but this outcome does not contradict the 'demand-utility' assessment of patent rights. This simply reveals the correlation issue, i.e. how the emergence of new patent rights in a particular technological field affects other entities in related industries and influences their future behaviours.

Finally, the basis for trademark[10] entitlement is a stable connection existed between a business operator and a specific symbol, such connection implies a capacity that helps reduce consumer search costs. The entitlement of property rights is essentially a 'reward' for this capacity—excluding others from establishing the same connection. For consumers, there are many means to identify goods or services, including trademarks, business names, product packaging and decorations, prices, advertisements, and places of origin etc. Legislation has chosen to confer property rights only to trademarks and business names, however, the entitlement to business names is not limited to their most distinctive part of the tradename but includes the entire name.[11] Among various identifying symbols, why did legislators choose trademarks? The reason lies in their capacity to convey information, i.e. the marginal utility of information. When consumers select goods or services, if they have developed clear and stable preferences, they can rely on any symbol that establishes a unique connection to a specific product or service. However, trademarks are the most efficient means of conveying information, as marginal utility of trademarks in conveying information is the highest. If consumers have yet to develop clear preferences among similar products, their initial choice will naturally incur higher recognition costs (related to price, product introductions, and even trial runs). Nevertheless, the outcome of that choice aids future selections of consumers. Trademarks represent the most efficient way to convey specific product information because

[8] It should be noted that the attitude of a patent holder towards patent transactions will vary depending on whether their production efficiency is higher or lower than that of their competitors.

[9] Taylor, T. (2015). *Sitanfu jijian jingjixue: Ruhe guoduan de quanheng liyi deshi [The Stanford guide to economics: How to make tough trade-offs]* (Lin, L., trans.) *Hunan renmin chubanshe* [Hunan People's Publishing House]. 87.

[10] Unless otherwise specified, the concept of 'trademark rights' used in this chapter refers to the exclusive rights of a registered trademark.

[11] Although a business name can be protected under the law against unfair competition to prevent others from free-riding, the most convenient way for a company to 'exclusively own' a particular business name is to simultaneously register it as a trademark (if the conditions are met).

their composition is relatively simple, thus incurring the lowest consumer attention costs for conveying the same amount of information. Thus, among various commercial marks, granting property rights to trademarks minimizes the costs of information transmission for non-rights holders. "[T]rademarks... are valuable because they denote consistent and stable quality of particular goods",[12] this feature enables trademark holders to introduce new goods under the same brand or allows other producers to enter relevant markets using that brand, saving on advertising and development costs (of course, the consistency and stability of quality are prerequisites for maintaining this feature). Consequently, the existence of trademark rights is beneficial for non-rights holders in terms of market entry, however, the goodwill accumulated from using someone else's trademark ultimately benefits the trademark holder and cannot be claimed by the user.[13] Therefore, for non-trademark holders, whether to use someone else's trademark to lower their market entry costs requires considerations of the utility of the trademark for their production and sales as well as its utility for consumers, leading them to adopt strategies that maximize their benefits. This explains why licensing in the trademark field is not as active as in the fields of copyright and patent rights. In practice, common approaches include franchising or forming commercial chains (where the trademark user does not aim to establish independent goodwill) or opting for 'free-riding' strategies that challenge the boundaries of trademark rights (avoiding licensing fees but risking infringement). Otherwise, once a business thrives and brand value increases, they may face disputes over profit distribution, similar to the disputes between *Wang Laoji* and *Jia Duo Bao* mentioned above.

In summary, the reason why intellectual property transactions take place is related to the market strategies of later entrants. In the fields of literature, art, or science and technology, later entrants consider the costs associated with cumulative innovation (if they merely seek to spread prior works or using earlier technologies for production, the problem is easier). And in commercial activities, there is no issue of cumulative innovation for later entrants, instead, they need to weigh the costs of establishing a new brand against the ability of prior trademarks in reducing consumer search costs. Regardless of the type of intellectual property involved, the 'demand-utility' analysis for later entrants must revolve around various factors, including the level of industry development and competitive structure in the relevant market, the comparative homogeneity and heterogeneity among competitors, the magnitude of potential market demand, and legal and judicial policies, thus allowing them to make behavioural decisions that maximize marginal utility (it is worth noting that from an objective perspective, there is no difference between the choices of infringing or challenging the boundaries of intellectual property rights).

[12] Landes, W. and Posner, R. (1987). Trademark law: An economic perspective. *Journal of Law and Economics*, 30(2), 265–309. 270.

[13] Even though people may notice the company name, they will still attribute the quality assurance to the trademark.

3.2 Behavioural Choice of Intellectual Property Right Holders

The discussion of 'why transactions occur' in previous section primarily examined the perspective of non-rights holders (i.e. those deciding to use prior intellectual property or to create intellectual property by themselves). However, a transaction involves both parties, only when the decisions of non-rights holders can match with those of intellectual property rights holders (when the wills expressed by both parties align) that a transaction can be successfully concluded. Thus, both parties establish transaction terms that maximize their own utility based on all available information each can collect. The relative bargaining positions, the sufficiency and symmetry of information between the parties (especially whether the information is sufficient for the other party) determine not only whether the transaction can succeed but also the terms under which it will occur. In view of this, the following discussion shifts to the perspective of intellectual property holders, analysing their thinking processes in making strategic choices in intellectual property transactions.

Intellectual property rights lie under the property rights model, its significance is to prohibit unauthorized use by others—infringement represents a form of forced transaction without considerations. The right to refuse is crucial for protecting the market position of intellectual property holders, enabling them to decide whether to exploit their intellectual property themselves or to authorize others to do so, thereby maximizing their benefits. In pursuit of this objective, and in consideration of overall social welfare, legislators issue corresponding guidance on decision-making for different entities, in which the responsibilities for violating prohibitive regulations are clarified as well. These legal instruments collectively form the intellectual property system we are familiar with. Since intellectual property is market-related, based on the assumption of rational economic actors, the reason why intellectual property holders refuse to authorize is typically caused by low price levels. Specifically, two distinct scenarios can be identified: first, the right holders do not exploit their intellectual property themselves, and they refuse to authorize because the implementer offers a price that is below the rights holder's subjective valuation of their property; second, if the intellectual property right holders exploit their intellectual property themselves in competitive industries, their refusal to authorize may be due to the same reason as the first scenario or a complete unwillingness to grant authorization. In both cases, the purpose of refusal is clearly to control the relevant market. Based on the distinctions between these two scenarios, the applicability of the intellectual property remedy system should also differ when infringement occurs.

3.2.1 *The Pricing of Intellectual Property and Its Impact on Transactions*

Pricing is a critical issue for intellectual property transactions to proceed smoothly, and it is very different from transactions involving tangible assets since the pricing of intellectual property is particularly challenging. In transactions involving tangible assets, price is usually not a key factor affecting the ultimate success of the transaction.[14] Even if the parties do not agree on the price clause in a contract, it may not substantially affect the establishment, validity, or performance of the contract, as the existence of indifferentiated market prices will allow the transaction to proceed smoothly. In contrast, intellectual property transactions are different. The reason for this lies in the peculiar nature of intellectual property compared to tangible assets. Whether it is copyright, trademark rights, patent technology, or trade secrets, there lacks undifferentiated market prices. Using an example to illustrate this point: when the same group of people evaluate a work, the results of assessment are different when the identity of the author is disclosed or concealed. Within the intellectual property system, rights related to technology are those of highest degree of objectivity in value, because valuation is primarily related to the maturity of the technology and normally not influenced by subjective factors. Although the methods used for valuing intellectual property are also commonly employed in asset valuation, such as the cost-based method, market-based method, income-based method, and relief from royalty method, however, due to the inherent characteristics of intellectual property rights (such as the ambiguity of rights boundaries, the instability of rights, and the existence of various rights limitation schemes), as well as factors influenced by market competition and public policy, the valuation of intellectual property is much more complex than that of tangible assets and other types of intangible assets (such as equity, debt, credit, etc.) in terms of data collection, model selection, and quantitative calculations etc.

The lack of undifferentiated market prices means that intellectual property transactions need to rely on either intangible asset evaluation or negotiation between the two parties. However, both approaches are fraught with significant disputes. Regarding intangible asset evaluation, its application in judicial practice is rather chaotic, primarily due to information asymmetry, unequal knowledge levels, and mutual distrust between the two parties and the judges. In addition, the lack of effective related mechanisms (including the credibility and credit constraints of the evaluation agency, the initiation of the evaluation procedure and the selection of the evaluation agency, the transparency and audit of the evaluation method, how the evidence system solves the problem of the acceptance of the evaluation report, etc.)

---

[14] This refers to tangible property with a clear market value. In civil law, there is a concept called 'generic goods' to describe it, where the price and value are consistent during transactions, determined by production costs, demand, and supply relations. However, there are also some special tangible properties, which lack a unified trading market (or are traded through personalized transactions), and thus do not have a general market price. The value of these items is not entirely composed of objective factors. In civil law, the corresponding concept for this is 'specific goods'.

is also an important contributing factor. In a litigation where the author has personally participated, both the plaintiff and defendant commissioned legally registered accounting firms to assess the intellectual property in suit. The results submitted to the court were vastly different—while the valuation of the plaintiff reached hundreds of thousands, the valuation of the defendant amounted to zero. Ultimately, the adjudication panel had to reject both of the valuation reports submitted. It is even more problematic when come to the pricing method negotiated by the two parties. Some may question that if transacting parties are facing so many obstacles when negotiating the pricing method, why there still exist a substantial amount of licenses being vigorously used in practice, such as publishing contracts, authorization agreements (platform dissemination, adaptation of works), patent licenses, and franchise licenses? The author believes that there is no direct logical relationship between whether negotiated pricing is problematic and its vigorous in practice. A failure in obtaining a consideration for optimal utilization will not necessarily inhibit the intellectual property holders from entering a transaction with others, especially when a particular intellectual property is being licensed for the first time. Moreover, factors such as the negotiating positions of the two parties, whether the information is symmetrical, and whether there existed government incentive policies will also have significant impacts on the results of negotiated pricing. Taking the standard essential patents (SEPs) as an example which have been the focus of attention in recent years, if the negotiated pricing mechanism works smoothly, different countries as well as international organizations around the world would not have to put in so much efforts to provide guidance for their licensing negotiations.[15]

Properties that lack of undifferentiated market price can be divided into two parts: (1) Subjective property. This type of property has value for the rights holder, but such value is meaningless to others, such as commemorative items. Therefore, conducting transactions involving subjective property is very difficult, as this part of value cannot be factored into pricing. While people can easily reach a consensus based on common sense about whether something has subjective value, they cannot derive a monetary transaction price based on that common sense. (2) Objective property lacking an undifferentiated market price. A fundamental difference between subjective property and objective property is that objective property has value for everyone. As to why there lacks an undifferentiated market is because the value of such objective property varies for the rights holder and others, examples include intellectual property and personal information, which share this characteristic. The absence of an undifferentiated market price for intellectual property is one of the main reasons that causes information asymmetry in the intellectual property transaction market.

[15] Recently, the United States, the European Union, Japan, South Korea, and the United Kingdom have introduced relevant policies to provide recommendations and guidance for the effective negotiation of SEP licensing fees. Relevant documents can be downloaded from the special topic *Global Consultation Drafts and Final Texts on Standard Essential Patents* on the 'Intellectual Property Finance' platform. See the 'Intellectual Property Finance' WeChat public account, published on August 12, 2022.

Intellectual property transactions are indeed developing in a contradicting dilemma. On one hand, traditional pricing mechanisms struggle to function effectively; on the other hand, the value of intellectual property in society today is increasingly emphasised, leading to more and more active transactions. Incentivized by the industrial development, the first-time transaction of intellectual property can usually be successfully concluded due to a common understanding that intellectual property management is mutually beneficial. However, when the contract for the first transaction expires and the parties start to negotiate upon renewal issues, disagreements often arise that make consensus difficult.[16] Another phenomenon observed in practice is that pricing issues are solved in specific intellectual property transactions through standardization, with the publishing contracts being the most typical example. However, it must be pointed out that the pricing clauses that are usually incorporated as the 'royalties' or 'fees' clauses in publishing contracts are merely drafted to facilitate the transaction and are often unilaterally determined, which cannot reflect the real market value of intellectual property, thus cannot be deem as an application of the price theory nor the result of a functioning price mechanism. For instance, the joint announcement made by the National Copyright Administration of China and the National Development and Reform Commission of China in 2014 on the *Method for Paying Remuneration for the Use of Literary Works* exemplifies this issue.[17] Therefore, the existence of standardized pricing practices in intellectual property transactions cannot indicate that the pricing problem has been effectively resolved. It should be understood that standardization is often unilateral, and such unilateral actions frequently imply that the party involved has improperly leveraged its advantageous position in the transaction, thereby causing harm to the interests of the other party.

The difficulty in determining the value of intellectual property and the resulted challenges in establishing transaction prices significantly impact whether intellectual property holders choose to engage in transactions and the specific methods they adopt. Due to the uncertainty of value, there is a high likelihood of information asymmetry between intellectual property holders and potential transacting parties, leading the party with informational advantages to potentially coerce the other party into accepting unfavourable transaction terms.[18] On the other hand, the intangible nature and public availability of intellectual property rights (made accessible through registration systems) allow multiple parties to use the rights simultaneously. No matter whether the uses are legally authorized or constitute infringements, they will inevitably affect subsequent transaction prices, thus making such information crucial for the demand-side entities despite that the supply-side (intellectual property

[16] In recent years, many well-known disputes over SEP (Standard Essential Patent) licensing fees in the telecommunications industry show this characteristic. The results of renewal negotiations are often failed transactions, leading to patent infringement lawsuits and antitrust litigation. Of course, there are also a few cases where the SEP licensing fees were not agreed upon from the outset.

[17] See the Article 4 & 5 of the *Method*.

[18] If the intellectual property holder is the dominant party, they often demand high licensing fees (the 'rip off' phenomenon); if the non-rights holder has an informational advantage, they tend to push for as low a licensing fee as possible (the so-called 'big store bullying the customer').

holders) clearly possesses more information in this regard. Additionally, there are issues of uncertainty regarding the status of rights, such as patents and trademarks, which can potentially be declared invalid. Even if a procedure for declaring invalidity is initiated, the outcome remains uncertain. This uncertainty naturally influences the offering price from non-right holders during negotiations, possibly leading them to abandon the transaction altogether. Therefore, intellectual property holders must develop strategies to address this issue, such as including 'non-challenge clauses' in offers or combining patents (i.e. combining patents with a certain degree of uncertainty with those whose rights status are recognized as stable) etc. In practices, if the intellectual property transaction occurs in a seller's market (where intellectual property holders are in an advantageous position), the uncertainty issue may not substantially impact the transaction.

In summary, whether caused by various challenges in value assessment or the inherent risks on stability of intellectual property, these uncertainties surrounding the value of rights often leads to the failure of intellectual property transactions or significantly increases transaction costs. Unlike the information asymmetry present in tangible property transactions, the information issues in intellectual property transactions are more related to inaccuracies, improper transmission, and a lack of verification systems, making it difficult for parties to establish mutual trust in pricing. When dealing with the price offered by intellectual property holders, non-right holders may easily perceive the other party as attempting to 'gouge' them and thus try to drive the price down. Conversely, intellectual property holders often find the price offered by non-right holders to be excessively low and difficult to accept. This manifests the difficulties in reaching agreements in intellectual property transactions, in practice, it is common to see the following situations: an intellectual property holder walked away from a transaction because they could not accept the low price, or he had to accept an unreasonable consideration for that transaction forced by the stronger market position of the other contracting party; the party using intellectual property may risk in moral hazard due to unsuccessful price negotiations, such as direct infringement or the imitation of intellectual property that challenges the boundaries of the rights involved (this means users would intentionally test the infringement standards by using knowledge acquired through imitation without concern for potential infringement lawsuits). Over time, the adverse selection phenomenon in the market will become more and more prevalent, where intellectual property owners are unwilling to enter the transacting market, while the party with demand for intellectual property are hesitant to establish transactional relationships, apparently, such a situation is extremely inefficient.

3.2.2 *Transaction Choices for Intellectual Property Holders: Self-Use or Authorize (Assign to) Others to Use*

Regardless of the initial purpose behind the creation of intellectual property, once rights holders obtain these rights, they inevitably have the incentive to exploit their intellectual properties, especially when the rights holder is a corporate entity. Trademark holders even have an obligation to use their marks. However, the exploitation of intellectual property cannot simply be achieved at the discretion of rights holders. In reality, the difficulty of exploiting intellectual property rights increases progressively from copyright to trademark rights and eventually to patent rights. Nowadays in the digital age, the rise and development of social media have eliminated barriers for copyright holders to disseminate their works. However, this also means that while content is subject to scrutinization (works must not contain illegal content), and whether this dissemination generates revenue for the rights holder remains uncertain. Trademark holders as commercial entities themselves will naturally engage in business activities, but as previously mentioned, they typically lack the motivation to engage in transactions. The incentive to implement patents existed undoubtedly, as rights holders can either use them themselves or license the patents to others, so there is never a lack of motivation for patent transactions, whether through licensing or assignment. However, converting this motivation into reality is not so easy.[19] Data from 2021 indicates that the industrialization rate of invention patents in China is 35.4%, with a licensing rate of 10.4% and a transfer rate of 7.4%, and the PTI (Patent Transformation Indicator) is 52.2.[20] While China has retained the first place in the total volume of patent applications and patent maintenance in the world for many years, yet the level of its industrial transformation still requires improvement.

It can be seen that although different types of intellectual property are slight variations in their uses, a common point is that rights holders have the incentive to generate income through the exploitation of their intellectual property. Therefore, the approaches on how to exploit intellectual property become very important. The criteria for approach selection are clear—utility maximization. Of course, in order to successfully complete an intellectual property transaction, the interests claimed by both parties must be matched, which means the maximization of overall social utility. From the perspective of intellectual property holders, whether to exploit the

[19] If this were not the case, the government would not prioritize patent commercialization as a key area of support. The latest policy can be found in the *Notice on Implementing the Patent Commercialization Special Plan to Assist Small and Medium Enterprises' Innovation and Development*, jointly issued by the Ministry of Finance and the National Intellectual Property Administration in March 2021 (Cai Ban Jian [2021] No. 23).

[20] National Intellectual Property Administration, 2021 China Patent Survey Report, pp. 4–6, downloaded from https://www.cnipa.gov.cn/module/download/downfile.jsp?classid=0&showname=2021年中国专利调查报告.pdf&filename=e48c21fe444a4651a72901c95a763bcc.pdf, accessed on August 1, 2022. The PTI index is constructed by the National Intellectual Property Administration based on data such as industrialization rates and industrialization revenue, combining records of intellectual property royalty exports and patent pledge financing amounts, to reflect the activity level of patent transfer and transformation.

rights themselves or to license (or assign) to others is fundamentally depending on the economic characteristics of the rights holder and the industry in which they operate, this includes various factors such as the attributes and capital strength of the entity, the industry in which they currently are or planning to enter, the competitive landscape of the industry, their own production efficiency compared to competitors, and future market prospects (such as industry convergence and product substitutability). The following section will discuss copyright, patent rights, and trademark rights separately.

3.2.2.1 Work Disseminations and Copyright Exploitations

In the nearly three hundred years period since the birth of the copyright system until the advent of the Internet, works were primarily disseminated by regulated entities with specialized qualifications, apart from those can simply rely on primitive human-based information transmission method (such as word of mouth or manual copying). The oldest entities of this type, and yet remained unchanged in its fundamental nature until to today, were publishers and booksellers.[21] In the era of mechanical reproduction, the basic characteristics of the work dissemination industry were: licensed entry, limited competition, high fixed costs, and low marginal costs. Consequently, disseminators could gain high profits through the distribution of works. From the early eighteenth century to the end of the twentieth century, publishing and distribution remained the most important (or even the only) industrial means of work dissemination for over two hundred years. Thus, during this historical period, copyright holders[22] could only generate income from their works through publishers (with very few exceptions, such as authors selling their art works through auctions to generate income[23]).

The development of digital technology has changed the structure of the market for work dissemination, allowing copyright holders to exercise their rights to refuse

[21] The completion of the industrial revolution in publishing established the dominant position of publishers, a position that continued well into the second half of the twentieth century and beyond. Finkelstein, D. & McCleery, A. (2012). *Shushi daolun [The history of the book]* (He, C., trans.). Shangwu Yinshuguan [Commercial Press]. 109.

[22] Not only authors, but even if the copyright holder is a business entity rather than a vulnerable natural person author, due to industry regulations, they are unable to directly enter the publishing market and must rely on cooperation with publishers.

[23] In reality, authors of art works rarely profit directly from auction transactions. Many artists, due to financial difficulties, often sell their works before they enter the auction market, as was the case with the famous French realist painter Jean-François Millet. For a historical introduction on the 'imbalance of economic interests for artists after the decline of the sponsorship system', see Dai, Z. (2017). 'Faguo zhuixuquan lifa jiqi qishi yanjiu' ['Research on the French resale right legislation and its implications'], *Dianzi Zhishi Chanquan [Electronic Intellectual Property]*, 12, 22. This is why the 'resale right' system was created to protect the economic interests of authors (artists). Introduction to the birth of the resale right system, see Reddy, M. (1995). 'The droit de suite: Why American fine artists should have a right to a resale royalty', *Loyola of Los Angeles Entertainment Law Journal*, 15(3), 509–510. (And footnotes on these pages).

transactions on the premise of safeguarding their own trading opportunities. The fundamental change brought by digital technology is the diversification of methods that works can be disseminated, which has deconstructed the 'monopoly' of the publishing market over the dissemination of works, thereby significantly weakening the bargaining power of publishers in copyright transactions. The emergence of the concept of 'self-media' together with its subsequent industrialization serve as the best example of copyright holders (including authors) enhancing their proactive positions in copyright transactions. In fact, a more noteworthy issue regarding the behavioral choices of copyright holders is the game between firms. For instance, if the copyright holder is an individual, they must engage in copyright transactions to gain economic benefits. However, if the copyright holder is a firm, refusing to transact may be more beneficial for the firm in controlling the relevant market, as seen in cases between film companies and distributors, software developers and distributors (especially with hardware manufacturers), and between platforms. How corporate copyright holders should decide whether to engage in transactions can be analyzed from the following two perspectives:

First, the type of work involved and the nature of the copyright owner, that is, the industry to which the work and the copyright owner belong. Different types of works, such as audiovisual works, musical works, literary works, computer software, online games, etc., can develop different types of markets—including primary markets, aftermarkets, and derivative markets. Those markets are very different, accordingly, the business strategies adopted by copyright owners in these markets differ. The type of work and the type of copyright owner are often related, for example, the work of a software developer is computer software. In some cases, the copyright owner will focus on its management in the primary market,[24] so it often refuses to license in this market, while for the aftermarket and derivative markets in which it is not directly involved, the copyright owner will make a profit through licensing. The copyright owners of works such as computer software and online games tend to adopt the strategy of market differentiation and apply different treatments; for other types of works, the copyright owners do not even carry out businesses in the primary market themselves but operate completely through copyright transactions and handing over the works to specialized enterprises in the market, for example, cinematographic works are usually not distributed by film and television production companies themselves, rather by physical theaters, TV stations, Internet platforms and so on in the form of cooperation.[25] Of course, if a copyright owner has multiple business qualifications at the same time (such as film and television production, distribution, content platform, etc.), it is highly likely that it will adopt a vertical integration strategy in order to control the entire market from top to bottom.

[24] It should be noted that the primary market referred to here is the market where the copyright holder first introduces their work. However, the work of the copyright holder may itself be a derivative work, such as a film adapted from another person's novel. Therefore, the primary market referred to in this book is not the market for the first issuance of a completely original work.

[25] Of course, this situation is related to the regulatory system of the issuing market, where enterprises without the necessary qualifications are also unable to engage in related business activities.

Second, the creation costs of the work and its potential market value, as well as the operating costs associated with various methods for dissemination. It specifically involves numerous factors, including its popularity, market demand (market size), substitutability, as well as the cost structure and amounts of different dissemination methods, the degree of market competition, and the production efficiency of the copyright owner and competitors etc. Based on these considerations, the copyright owner can make decisions regarding whether to operate the work themselves, license it to others, or even assign the copyright. Another important issue is that the copyright owner must clearly understand the fundamental difference between 'self-managing' and 'licensing others to manage' their works, whereas the former allows for market control but also entails risks, while the latter guarantees income but relinquishes market control. Risk aversion is a typical characteristic of rational economic actors, thus, ensuring revenue through licensing can be a reasonable choice for copyright owners. After licensing, the copyright owner can at least secure certain incomes, with the business risks transferred to the licensee. Although the copyright owner might gain more profit if they choose to self-manage, however, if the market fails then it would leave them with nothing. In extreme cases of risk aversion, i.e. the copyright owner lacks confidence in the market prospects for their work and prioritizes risk avoidance over income maximization, then his optimal choice would be to assign the copyright to others, thereby preemptively and completely monetize the value of his work. Of course, risk and reward are proportionate. Regarding the utilization of the work, the decision to engage in copyright transactions and the terms of such transactions result from the game between the copyright owner and the counterparty. The design of copyright law merely seeks to stabilize the variables involved in this game as much as possible.

3.2.2.2 Market Competition and Technological Innovation Behind Patent Transactions

Research and development require certain investments, and if a patent right is obtained from the outcomes of a R&D, it establishes a foundation for recovering investments and potentially generating additional profits.[26] The fundamental distinction between an assignment and a license is that assignment represents a 'cash out and exit', while licensing is akin to 'collecting admission tickets'. Consequently, licensing can serve as a means for the patent holder to restrict the ability of the licensee to engage in cumulative innovation, whereas an assignment signifies that

[26] But it does not necessarily have feasibility in practice. The author once had a personal experience where an individual obtained a utility model patent, the content of which was 'a solar umbrella mounted on an electric bicycle'. The patent holder sought the author's assistance in finding market opportunities for patent commercialization. However, the eventual reality was that there were no market opportunities for the commercialization of this utility model patent. Of course, if someone initiates an invalidation procedure, this patent might be invalidated.

the original patent holder has abandoned their 'future'.[27] In simple terms, for patent holders, there are two key questions regarding patent transactions: first, whether to choose 'cash out and exit' or 'steady-and-long income'; second, regardless of the choice made in the first question, how to determine the price. This section explores the first question, while the latter question will be addressed later in Chapter 5.

The benefits of assignment are self-evident, the value of patents are monetized immediately, risks associated with unsuccessful patent commercialization are avoided, R&D costs are successfully recovered, and there is a potential profit. The protection period for patent rights is fixed and relatively short (compared to copyright and trademark rights), which means that the commercial value of patented technology is subject to diminishing marginal returns. In contrast, the protection period for trademark rights is theoretically perpetual, thus allowing an increasing marginal value; while the protection period for copyright is definite and relatively long, and there are numerous factors that can bring the value of copyright up or down during a period, thus making it difficult to establish a quantitative relationship between the protection period and copyright value. Furthermore, the market structure and competitive conditions of the industry to which the patented technology belongs are also critical factors. If the lifecycle of the patented product or products using the patented technology in production is short, together with the aforementioned diminishing marginal value effect of patents, it is quite reasonable for the patent holder to monetize the patent by a timely assignment.

However, the disadvantages of assignment are also obvious: it is impossible to fully realize the value of the patent, and the original patent holder loses the opportunity to participate in the distribution of benefits from cumulative innovation. In contrast, licensing can be used to overcome such disadvantages of assignment. From a legal perspective, licensing occurs when patent owner and the user reach a consensus on intention to create a legal relation. From an economic perspective, licensing arises for the following reasons: "...to produce proprietary products efficiently, to let others use the intellectual property as inputs to innovations (research tools), to resolve blocking rights or to enable development of complementary inventions."[28] On the one hand, such a way of licensing can fully utilize patent technologies, because the production efficiency of the patent owner is limited after all, and if the patent technology has a significant value, the patent owner alone may not be able to develop it sufficiently; on the other hand, licensing with a goal of production efficiency can also promote competition, because the licensee can 'stand on the shoulders of

[27] Intellectual property transactions not only include assignment and licensing, but also pledge, contribution, trust, and securitization. However, based on the standard of 'cash-out and exit', intellectual property transactions can be divided into assignment-based transactions and non-assignment-based transactions. All the specific forms mentioned above can be categorized into these two types. Through non-assignment-based transactions, regardless of the specific form, the patent holder can constrain subsequent cumulative innovation behaviour. Among various non-assignment-based intellectual property transactions, licensing is the most typical form of utilizing intellectual property with the goal of production efficiency. Therefore, this section will focus on licensing as a representative form for further discussion.

[28] Scotchmer, S. (2006). *Innovation and incentives*, The MIT Press. 162.

giants' to continue R&D, and can further develop the technology at a lower cost. With the promotion of cumulative innovation, the price of patented products or products made by using patented technologies can be driven down. Although it will lead to a decrease in the producer surplus of the patent owner, the producer surplus and consumer surplus of the licensee will increase, so the overall social welfare is still increased.

It should be noted that for patent holders, the benefits of licensing are not limited to a single form. Depending on the differences in technologies and the relevant industries, the specific forms of licensing in practice can be quite diverse. In addition to agreements reached on specific patents, patent holders may also engage in transactions with licensees through various mechanisms such as patent pools, technical standards, patent bundling, restricting raw material purchasing channels, and product-hopping. Of course, the overarching goal of all these forms of transactions is to maximize producer surplus and mitigate the possible competitive pressures from the licensee. In summary, when a patent holder make strategic choices, he needs to consider the following factors: the market value of the patented technology and its potential market value, market structure and competitive relationships, product lifecycle, etc. Generally speaking, if the patent holder is a non-implementing entity, the relationship with the licensee—whether horizontal or vertical—is irrelevant, given that licensing is a business action that the patent holder has to take (licensing is the lifeline for such entities). If the patent holder is an implementing entity, that means it is also a manufacturing company, then it must identify whether the licensee is in a horizontal or vertical competitive relationship with the patent holder when making a licensing strategy: if there is a horizontal competitive relationship, the patent holder needs to be cautious when dealing with licensing since licensing would introduce more suppliers into the relevant market. This leads to competition and could further lower product prices, which would not benefit the patent holder. Therefore, patent holders often choose cross-licensing agreements with horizontally related licensees to avoid a passive position in the technological competition in the relevant market. If there exists a vertical relationship between the patent holder and the licensee, licensing generally does not adversely affect the patent holder. However, if the patent holder considers the possibility of entering the downstream market in the future, they must prepare for competitive arrangements when signing licensing agreements.[29]

It is evident from the above that patent holders will do everything possible in the arrangement of licensing contents to maintain their competitive advantages, but this also exposes them to corresponding legal risks. From practice, we can summarize that common strategies employed by patent holders which include: excessively high licensing fees, patent bundling, tying patents with non-patent products, restricting

[29] For example, the holder of a communication patent may not originally produce terminal products (hardware), but several years later, the patent holder decides to enter the hardware market or acquires another company in the hardware market.

the scope of business, exclusive grant-back, limiting resale prices, post-sale restrictions, and asymmetric cross-licensing, among others.[30] These licensing practices can restrict competition in the technology market; some are directly related to the patent holder (largely horizontal), while others are more complex in the analysis of competitive effects (largely vertical). Therefore, when formulating licensing strategies, patent holders need to clearly understand the potential legal risks involved and distinguish between prohibitive provisions and those are protected by 'safe harbor'.[31]

3.2.2.3 Trademark Rights Transactions: 'A Century-Old Store' or 'Harvesting the Present'?

The main forms of trademark rights transactions are assignment and licensing, which differ significantly from each other. The former indicates a transformation in the trademark holder's business operations and at least signifies their exit from the original market. In contrast, licensing represents a transaction mode that involves both risk and income. On one hand, licensing not only provides the trademark holder with royalty income but also serves as a means to expand market at a lower cost. On the other hand, the trademark holder faces risks, as the activities of the licensee could potentially diminish the value of the trademark. The following sections discuss how trademark holders make choices between assignment and licensing:

First, assignment means exit. In practice, the assignment of trademark rights is not common, which runs contrary to the continuous accumulation of goodwill by business owners. Even if the trademark owner intends to exit the original market, it does not necessarily mean that he needs to assign the trademark. Regarding the principle of trademark assignment, the trademark laws of most countries around the world adopt the principle of free assignment, although the U.S. *Lanham Act*[32] adheres to the principle of 'combined assignment', its application is relatively flexible in judicial practice.[33] Some may wonder, since the principle of free assignment is the prevailing principle, why is there a saying of 'assignment means exit'? The author believes that the principle of free assignment is considered from a perspective of the transferability of property, while 'assignment means exit' is viewed from

---

[30] The relevant provisions in the *Antitrust Guidelines for the Intellectual Property Sector* issued by the State Council Anti-Monopoly Committee on January 4, 2019, are actually a good summary of such agreements.

[31] The 'safe harbor' referred here in this article refers to the provision in Article 13 of the *Antitrust Guidelines for the Intellectual Property Sector* issued by the State Council Anti-Monopoly Committee, and more generally to any situation where legal regulations leave room for discretion.

[32] In academic circles in China, the 'Lanham Act' is commonly translated as the '兰哈姆法案'. However, this is actually an inaccurate translation because the letter 'h' in 'Lanham' is not pronounced. The expression used in this book is based on the accurate pronunciation of 'Lanham'. This clarification is provided to avoid any misunderstanding.

[33] The introduction and legislative comparison on the principles of trademark assignment, see Peng X, (2011). Shangbiao zhuanrang de lilun jiangou yu zhidu sheji ['Theoretical construction and institutional design of trademark transfer'], *Falv Kexue* [*Legal Science]*, No. 3, 136–139.

the perspective of asset utility. In fact, the principle of combined assignment better declares the assignor's exit from the original market, which can avoid market chaos to a certain extent. Moreover, in practice, most well-known trademarks are identical to the business names of the company, why would anyone buy a trademark of no popularity? Even under the principle of free assignment, the commercial value of the trademark owner is largely embodied in the trademark itself.[34] Once the trademark is assigned, the goodwill associated with it is also transferred and enjoyed by the assignee. If goodwill could be separated from the trademark, why would the assignee purchase another's trademark at all? In short, a trademark holder is motivated to assign their trademarks only when they plan to exit the original market. Considering that the higher the popularity in the trademark, the greater the willingness of others to purchase it. However, if that is the case, the willingness of the trademark holder to assign the mark will be low. This illustrates why trademark assignments are rarely seen in practice (excluding the abnormal phenomenon of trademark 'trolls' that register numerous trademarks for resale).

Second, licensing: a fusion of free-riding and 'making a wedding dress for others'. The licensing of trademark rights differs from that of copyright and patent rights. The ultimate purpose of a non-right holder using the trademark of another is to sell their own goods or services, rather than those of the original trademark holder. In contrast, when copyright or patent rights are licensed, what the licensee utilizes is the intellectual property of the rights holder; even in cumulative innovation, the prior intellectual achievements are an organic constituent part of the subsequent results. To put it another way, trademark licensing is akin to 'riding on the coattails of a brand' (it is legal in this context), while licensing copyright or patent rights involves 'dividing the market' for intellectual achievements. Therefore, licensing of trademark rights is a double-edged sword for rights holders. On one hand, it allows trademark owners to expand their operational scope without additional investment, thereby increasing opportunities to enhance their goodwill. On the other hand, the business activities of the licensee may potentially diminish the goodwill associated with the trademark, then the trademark holder will have to invest in monitoring costs to ensure the quality of the operations of the licensee.[35] Moreover, if the scope of licensing is expanded to an extreme extent, the trademark faces the real risk of being diluted to a generic term for the goods or services. Thus, when deciding whether to grant a license, trademark holders must consider various factors, including market expansion, monitoring costs, opportunities for enhancing or diminishing goodwill, and the potential for trademark dilution, in order to choose a strategy that maximizes their utility. This helps explain why trademark licensing often takes the form of 'franchising (chain business)'. Although franchisees are independent legal entities in terms of

[34] The commercial value is directly related to the trademark holder's reputation in a specific industry. If the trademark is highly renowned, it can be assumed that the trademark holder's reputation extends across all commercial fields.

[35] The stronger the trademark holder's ability to maintain the consistency of product quality, the greater their incentive to invest in maintaining a strong trademark. See Landes, W. and Posner, R. (1987). 'Trademark law: An economic perspective', *Journal of Law and Economics*, 30(2), 265–309. 270.

their status, they act substantively as branches of the trademark holder. Additionally, while trademark holders still incur monitoring costs, the goods or services sold by franchisees are not their own but rather those of the trademark holder, therefore such monitoring costs are significantly reduced.

3.3 Insufficient Supply of Systems for Intellectual Property Transactions in China's Current Legislation

The intellectual property sector specific laws in China adhere to an 'subjective matters based legislation' approach, constructing specific systems following a logical sequence of 'authorization of rights - content of rights - limitations on rights - remedies'. In contrast to property rights, which are also exclusive, why there is no similar issues raised on the insufficient systems supply for property rights transactions in the property law? The author believes that the intellectual property legislation resembles to the property law, but the former lacks an important internal 'spirit': the structural framework of property law is built around 'creation of rights - content of rights - changes in title of rights - protection of rights',[36] which is very similar to the aforementioned framework of intellectual property system. But a closer examination on the legislative styles reveals a significant gap in the latter—namely, the absence of crucial provisions governing the changes in the title of rights. Intellectual property transactions fundamentally involve changes in the title of rights, covering areas such as assignment, modification (licensing, pledging, investment), and extinguishment of rights. This gap is the main aspect manifested by the insufficient supply of systems for intellectual property transactions. Furthermore, despite the special emphasis placed on the creation, extinguishment, as well as the limitation of rights in intellectual property legislation, there still remain several institutional flaws, which also create some difficulties for the smooth transactions of intellectual property.

By analyzing intellectual property transactions from a behavioral perspective and comparing them to the specific structures established by the current intellectual property laws in China, it becomes clear that intellectual property transactions cannot be adequately supported by the existing system. Following a behavioral research approach, the following discussion will analyze three key areas respectively: the creation and extinguishment of intellectual property rights, the protection of bona fide assignees in intellectual property transactions, and the limitations of rights, to highlight the issue of insufficient supply of systems for intellectual property transactions.

---

[36] See the legislative structure of the 'Property Rights Book' in the *Civil Code of the People's Republic of China*.

3.3.1 The System of Creation and Extinguishment of Intellectual Property Rights: Leading to Increased Transaction Costs

Intellectual property rights are exclusive property rights, however, when compared to property rights over tangible properties which share the same exclusivity attribute, there are significant differences on the issues of creation of rights and extinguishment between the two types of rights. Should these differences be attributed to the inherent differences in the natures of their respective subject matters? This question requires further thinkings: should the system governing the creation and extinguishment of rights be designed based on the natures of the rights (i.e. as an exclusive property right) or based on the characteristics of the subjective matters themselves? The author observes that legislators have taken the subjective matter-based approach and structuring the right creation and right extinguishment systems of intellectual property rights differently from property rights, but neglected to make the same institutional arrangements for the two. As a result, it brought difficulties to the protection of intellectual property rights and increased the transaction costs of intellectual property rights. This problem is particularly evident in the areas of copyright and patent rights.

3.3.1.1 When Does Copyright Arise?

This question may seem very amateurish for those who specialize in intellectual property law. 'It arises automatically when the creation is completed' has become a well-known truth.[37] However, it is also a common understanding that copyright is an exclusive property right, then how can exclusivity arises automatically? This is not the case in property law, so why is it permitted in copyright law? According to the relevant provisions of property law, property rights must be published to attain exclusivity (or the creation of a right that can be called a property right),[38] as exclusivity requires external recognition. However, the institutional arrangement for the entitlement of copyright does not follow this principle, instead it comes into existence when the creation is completed. Some may compare copyright with personality rights to explain the rationality of the automatic creation of copyright: personality rights are also exclusive rights that arise automatically—natural persons enjoy personality rights against the world upon their births, and the relationship between works and authors is alike the relationship between the interests of personality and natural

[37] The *Berne Convention* adopts the principle of automatic protection for works; Article 6 of China's *Regulations for the Implementation of the Copyright Law* also clearly stipulates this principle.

[38] The provisions on 'the establishment of property rights' in the 'Property Rights Book' section of the *Civil Code of the People's Republic of China* illustrate this point.

persons, just as the German transcendental idealist philosophers believed in copyright.[39] Thus, by analogy, copyright could be seen as arising automatically in the same way as personality rights. However, even if we compare personality rights with copyright, it should also be noted that they are actually different since personality rights are more consistent with property rights. Similar to 'possession' in the context of property right, personality interests are attached to a natural person in his biological existence, thus personality rights follow the same principle of publication as ownership of movable property and derives exclusivity from 'possession'. In contrast, copyright differs. German philosophers emphasized the personal attachment of the work to its author, a view that better justifies the protection of moral rights rather than the source of exclusivity, by reason that the completion of a work does not simultaneously make it known to the public, and moreover, the work may become detached from the author after its completion. By the time it is known to the external public, it may already be associated with another party other than the author, thus raising the question of who truly holds the copyright. If we adopt the view that 'copyright cannot arise without public notice', the issue becomes much simpler. To clarify, this discussion pertains specifically to the 'creation of copyright' as an exclusive right, distinct from the act of creation itself—similar to how the creation of ownership is distinct from the production of the subject matters.

The lack of a formal system for the creation of copyright exclusivity creates significant challenges for copyright protection (not to mention copyright transactions). Cases like the earlier 'One item sold to two' lawsuits over the song *Mice Love Rice* and copyright enforcement controversies of the *Visual China Group* in 2019 highlight these issues. Besides, defendants in copyright infringement lawsuits often set out an argument that the plaintiffs do not hold the alleged copyrights at all, this is a defense strategy that cannot be deployed in disputes concerning ownership, unless evidence of a false public registration are provided. The absence of a publication principle for establishing copyright means that copyright protection and exploitation often require burdensome costs in confirming ownership, such costs are in fact sunk costs which cannot be recovered by any potential profits. Copyright can be disclosed in multiple ways, such as publication or registration. Copyright exclusivity arises upon the first disclosure, although undisclosed works may not give rise to exclusive copyright, yet copyright law still provides a certain level of protection, similar to the protection afforded to trade secrets.

3.3.1.2 Patent Invalidity Declaration: When Do the Rights Extinguish?

Unlike copyright, the creation of patent rights in patent law is explicitly stipulated—'effective as of the date of announcement',[40] which clearly embodies the principle

[39] Philosophers such as Kant and Hegel, who represent this school of thought, emphasize the personal attributes of a work, viewing it as an extension of the author's personality. Drahos, P. (1996). *A philosophy of intellectual property*, Dartmouth Publishing Company Limited. 74–75.

[40] See China's *Patent Law (2020)*, Articles 39 and 40.

of publication.[41] However, this does not mean that issues do not arise regarding the status of rights under patent law, specifically, the issue of when patent rights extinguish. Patent rights extinguish in two ways: they may lapse upon expiry, or they may be invalidated. It is the latter that is problematic. According to Article 47 of the *Patent Law of China* 2020, when a patent is declared invalid, it is deemed as never having existed. But does a patent extingshes from the moment the review board issues a decision of invalidity? Given that the patent holder can still invoke a remedial procedure—filing a lawsuit to the court, if the court decision reversed the review decision, does that mean the validity of patent is resumed from the date the court issues the judgement? Even if it is, is the patent effective during the intervening period between the review decision and the final judgment of the court (a period that could be substantially long)? During this time, if someone implements the patented technology, can they be held liable for infringement? If the patent is presumed not to extinguish when the invalidity decision is announced and remain effective until the court judgment, yet this interpretation is still problematic: judicially, lawsuits against review decisions are classified as administrative cases. This would imply that the review decision, as an administrative act, should take effect immediately upon issuance. Thus, between the patent review board and the court, which body does the declaration of invalidity under Article 47 of the *Patent Law* refers to? Moreover, there is another question needs to be asked: when patent rights are granted, they must be formally announced. Then why no similar announcement required upon extinguishment? This seems unreasonable. If an announcement is indeed necessary, who should make the announcement? The court or the review board? And if it is the review board, should the announcement occur upon the initial invalidation decision or when receiving a final court judgment?

The deficiencies of the system regarding the extinguishment of patent rights create significant challenges for the protection (certainly including transactions as well) of patent rights. Once a patent ceases to exist, the technical solutions entailed become free for anyone to use, drastically impacting market competition in the relevant industries.[42] In cases where a patent license is already in effect, the timing of the patent termination by invalidation—whether it takes effect immediately upon the decision of the review board or only after a final judicial decision in administrative litigation—critically affects the interests of both parties because it creates uncertainties to

---

[41] This raises further questions. Why, when both are forms of intellectual property, does the creation of patent and trademark rights apply the principle of publication, while copyright does not? The earlier hypothesis made by the author, drawing an analogy with personality rights, may indeed be a relatively reliable reason.

[42] The introduction of a drug patent linkage system in the fourth revision of China's *Patent Law*, and how such a system should be implemented if introduced, has sparked intense discussions in academic, judicial, and industrial circles. A relevant introduction can be found in Zhang, H. (2019). 'Jingzheng shiye xia zhongguo yaopin zhuanli lianjie zhidu de jishou yu tiao shi'['The reception and adjustment of the drug patent linkage system in China from the perspective of competition'], *Zhishi Chanquan* [*Intellectual Property*], 4, 50–70. This illustrates the significant impact that the extinguishment of patent rights can have on industrial competition.

the formation, performance, or termination of the licensing agreements. This uncertainty may either enhance the rent-seeking abilities of the patent holders or provide the licensee with an opportunity to 'rip off', thereby substantially increasing transaction costs of patent rights. The author believes that eliminating this uncertainty is the priority. However, merely stipulating that 'patent rights extinguishes as soon as the review board issues its decision and resumes at the time a court subsequently overturns the decision' would exacerbate the unpredictability of the patent's status.

3.3.2 Lacks of Protection for Bona Fide Assignees in Intellectual Property Transactions

Intellectual property transactions are closely related to the changes in titles of such rights, including assignment, licensing, or pledge, which can all be collectively referred to as acts of disposition of intellectual property. When the intellectual property owners dispose their rights, transactions can naturally proceed smoothly. However, cases of unauthorized disposition are not uncommon. If the intellectual property is exploited without authorization and the change of ownership has been registered, shall the bona fide party who acquires the rights based on such disposition be protected? If the bona fide party subsequently disposes the intellectual property again, this time with proper authorization and registration, should the second bona fide party in the transaction be protected as well? If, up until this point, the original intellectual property owner eventually discovers the unauthorized disposition, can he claim the invalidities of both the first-time and second-time dispositions?

Let us first look at a real world case of *Chen, Li vs. Qingdao Marine Welding Materials Co., Ltd. on Disputes Regarding Trademark Ownership and Trademark Transfer Contract*'. The facts of this case precisely correspond to the questions posed earlier. *Qingdao Marine Welding Materials Co., Ltd.* filed a lawsuit, arguing that the trademark assignment did not reflect its genuine intention and claiming both trademark assignments invalid. Ultimately, both the first and second-instance judgments supported the its claims.[43] It is evident that the judgment was based on Article 40 of the *Answers to Several Issues Regarding the Trial of Civil Trademark Disputes* issued by the Beijing Higher People's Court in March 2006.[44] However, does this provision raise concerns? Allowing the original trademark owner to invalidate two layers of the 'registration effect on trademark right ownership' and 'retrieve' the trademark from the assignee in the second transaction seems to declare that the 'principle of publication' shall not apply to trademark law. Is this reasoning well-founded? Would

[43] Beijing Second Intermediate People's Court (2008) Civil Judgment No. 1064, Case No. 2nd Intermediate Civil Final.

[44] The provision states: "The act of assigning the registered trademark of the trademark holder without authorization constitutes trademark infringement, and the assignee cannot acquire the trademark rights as a result. If the assignees re-assign the registered trademark to a third party through normal commercial transactions and obtains approval and announcement, the third party also cannot acquire the trademark rights."

the conclusion be the same if a similar dispute occurred in the context of copyright or patent rights?

The above case highlights a difficulty in intellectual property transactions: how should the law balance the protection of transaction security against safeguarding the interests of the true rights holders? According to the Beijing Higher People's Court's approach, the court evidently chose to protect the true rights holder, even though the judge did not provide a reasoning in the judgment for prioritizing one of these values over the other. The author believes that the reason is likely to stem from the notion that if the true trademark owner does not receive protection, the goodwill value embedded in the trademark would be lost entirely, which would be unfair to the rights holder. However, beyond the lack of basis and rationality in explicitly declaring that the 'principle of publication' does not apply to trademark law, is the lost value of goodwill to the trademark owner necessarily ranks higher than the value of transaction security?[45]

For unauthorized dispositions of trademark rights, it is not necessary to compare the value between the trademark owner's interests and transaction security in all cases, rather, such a comparison is only needed when the assignee is in good faith. This is because transaction security concerns arise only when the assignee is in good faith. In essence, transaction security refers to the ability of parties in a transaction to trust each other's actions within the transaction, allowing them to satisfy their respective needs according to the design of transaction. If the actions of one party fail to correspond to the actual situation but the counterparty can still achieve their intended purpose under the original transaction design, this is the value orientation toward protecting transaction security. Conversely, if the counterparty cannot achieve their intended purpose under the original design, this reflects a value orientation toward protecting the true state of affairs. The issue may seem simple: either the true rights holder bears the loss, or the counterparty in an unreal state bears the transaction costs and loses the expected benefits, however, making a choice between the two is far from straightforward. In property law, several mechanisms are designed to protect the security of property transactions, such as the principle of publication and the bona fide acquisition system for movable property.[46] It can be seen that these institutional arrangements ensure that the party satisfying the requirements of publication of property right achieves their intended needs. Given the comparability between property rights and intellectual property rights, it raises the question of

---

[45] In the previous case, the bona fide assignee, who had completed the change of registration twice, has a legitimate interest in relying on the trademark registration. If the original trademark holder can invalidate the effect of these two registrations, the future reliability of trademark registration will inevitably be undermined. The assignee will constantly worry that their trademark transfer transaction might be declared invalid, even after the change of registration has been completed. This represents a devaluation of the transactional security value.

[46] See Zhang, S. G. (2019). 'Wuquan gongshi yuanze de lilun goucheng: Yi zhidu zhengdangxing wei zhongxin' ['Theoretical structure of the principle of property rights publicity: focusing on institutional legitimacy'], *Fa Xue [Legal Studies]*, 1, 55. 65; Ji, H. L., (2014). 'Jiegou dongchan gongshi gongxin yuanze'['Deconstructing the principle of movable property publicity and trust'], *Zhongwai Faxue [Chinese and Foreign Law Review]*, 3, 706–713.

whether it is appropriate to apply the logic of the institutional design for protecting the security of property transactions, i.e. the standard (or principle) of 'ensuring that the party satisfying the requirements of publication of rights achieves their intended needs', to trademark rights and by extension, to all intellectual property rights? Since the principle of publication has not yet been established in the field of intellectual property law, this analogy lacks practical grounding. However, the author believes such an institutional arrangement is justified. Compared to a blanket approach that indiscriminately protects the true rights holder regardless of the specific context, this arrangement offers a more logical value choice based on the appearances of rights and actions.

Moreover, in trademark transactions, applying the standard of 'ensuring that the party satisfying the requirements of publication of rights achieves their intended needs' does not mean that the interests of trademark owners are completely disregarded or the goodwill value embodied in the trademark is ignored. The consideration of this value is reflected in the assessment of 'whether the requirements of publication of rights are met', specifically through the determination of a 'bona fide assignee'. If the assignee is deemed to be in good faith, they should acquire the trademark right and become the new right holder. It is particularly worth noting that the level of good faith on the part of the assignee should be proportionate to the popularity of the trademark involved in the transaction. The more well-known the trademark, the higher the standard for establishing good faith of the assignee. The match of value and obligation can facilitate an effective choice between transaction security and the interests of the true rights holder. For instance, if the popularity of trademark is low, choosing to protect transaction security is unlikely to result in any significant loss of goodwill value. On the contrary, if the trademark is highly recognized, it becomes significantly more challenging for the assignee to establish good faith.

If the design for protecting bona fide assignees in trademark transactions as outlined above is deemed correct, then the same approach can be applied even more appropriately to issues concerning copyrights and patent rights. Since unlike trademarks, there is no issue of goodwill value of the right holders embodied in a work or patented technology. The property characteristics of these intellectual assets in transactions are closer to those of tangible property rights. Therefore, it is entirely reasonable to adopt the standard of 'ensuring that the party satisfying the requirements of public notice rights achieves their intended needs' to protect bona fide assignees in such cases.

3.3.3 *Intellectual Property Rights Limitation Regime: Failure to Fulfil the Role of Compulsory Transactions*

The limitation regime on rights was not part of intellectual property law at its inception. The institutional arrangements for limitations on rights began to appear in legislation only when people increasingly recognized the public policy aspect of intellectual property protection. However, for a long time, both domestic and international intellectual property law scholars provide justifications for the limitation regime from the perspective of promoting public interest or balancing interests. Some American scholars have even proposed a 'user rights theory'.[47] While safeguarding public interest and promoting a balance of interests are undoubtedly correct, these arguments are insufficient to resolve specific problems. Consider this: is there any specific intellectual property rule that is not aimed at balancing interests? Indeed, this reasoning holds true even when elevated to the level of private law as a whole.

It is precisely due to the influence of this perception, the specific application of the rights limitation regime in relevant judicial practices in China is not aimed at addressing the issue of the boundaries of rights, but rather a comparison between the alleged acts and the specific situations as listed in the statutes. As a result, this often gives an impression of strong subject or result-oriented approach. Moreover, the long-standing failure to interpret the rights limitation regime from a market perspective makes it difficult to distinguish between the exploitation of intellectual property that is detached from the market vis-a-vis uses in the context of market transactions,[48] moreover, actions that do not fundamentally touch upon the boundaries of rights are nevertheless viewed as cases of rights limitation sometimes.[49] Such a legislative style makes it difficult to recognize the true purpose of the intellectual property limitation regime. Taking copyright law as an example, do we really need to address whether sketching or photographing arts that are displayed in public places constitutes fair use on judicial level? If the person who sketches or photographs never publicly exhibits their work, why does it matter whether their behaviour constitutes fair use (how would it affect the copyright holder)? Clearly, what the fair use regime in copyright law truly needs to address is whether the person can freely exploit the sketched or photographed works without being constrained by the copyright holder.

Since it is a restriction scheme over intellectual property rights, it must be a restriction on the controlling behaviours arise from intellectual property rights. If a certain act is beyond the control of intellectual property right per se, then there is no need to deploy the limitation scheme to 'protect' that act. In other words, if a rights limitation scheme is needed to preclude the illegality of a particular act, it indicates that the act in its nature is essentially an infringement of intellectual property rights, it is precisely because the provision of the limitation scheme serves as a defence to justify the illegality of the act, such acts can be deemed non-infringing. This book has

---

[47] For example, some American scholars argue that fair use is 'the right of the user to enhance their knowledge by utilizing copyrighted works.' See Patterson, L. R. and Lindberg, S. (1991). *The nature of copyright: A law of user's right*. The University of Georgia Press. 207.

[48] For example, the situation described in Article 24, Paragraph 1, Item (1) of China's *Copyright Law* (2020), which pertains to actions that are detached from market utilization and do not need to be defined as fair use but should be considered purely legal actions.

[49] For example, the situation described in Article 24, Paragraph 1, Item (10) of China's *Copyright Law* (2020), which pertains to actions that do not infringe upon the boundaries of copyright; additionally, the situation described in Article 59, Paragraph 1 of China's *Trademark Law* (2019), which pertains to actions that do not infringe upon the boundaries of trademark rights. This is commonly recognized as a limitation on trademark rights in trademark laws worldwide—descriptive use.

repeatedly emphasised that intellectual property law is a legal system related to the market, hence, both the controls arise from intellectual property rights and limitations imposed on intellectual property rights must be associated to market as well. Acts that have no connection to the market are neither acts of intellectual property infringement nor acts covered under the rights limitation regime. With a clear understanding of the market feature in rights limitations, we can see that the legislative intent behind this system is to break the control of intellectual property overall market activities, allowing certain market behaviours to be conditionally or even entirely free from such control.[50] Therefore, the rights limitation regime addresses the issue of market access restrictions faced by the actors. The actors can rely on this regime to introduce products related to intellectual property (whether products derived directly from intellectual property or those produced by using intellectual property) into the market. In essence, this results in a redistribution of the market originally monopolized by the intellectual property holder, allowing both the actor and the rights holder to share the market space.

If the determination on whether an act falls under the limitation regime is merely reduced to a comparison between the conduct of the defendant with the listed acts in the statutory provisions and checking if they 'fit in perfectly', it deviates entirely from the original intent of the limitation regime. This approach, however, is the long-standing judicial support that favours the 'promotion of public interest doctrine' (i.e. using public interest as a benchmark to solve the grey area of whether the conduct 'fits in perfectly'). However, returning to the origin and examining the rights limitation regime from a market perspective, we need to understand why an act that is essentially an infringement should be excluded from being classified as such. As previously mentioned, the rights limitation regime serves to partially exclude the control exerted by intellectual property and address the issue of rights block-up. This indicates that in the absence of such a regime, the control exercised by intellectual property rights would make it excessively costly for non-right holders to access the relevant market, thereby reducing overall social welfare.[51] Thus, to determine whether a particular act qualifies as a rights limitation, the criterion (or method) should be whether the actor would face excessively high transaction costs when attempting to access the market controlled by the intellectual property holder through transactional means, to the extent that such a transaction would, in fact, lead to a decline in social welfare.

From the dimensions of transaction costs and the damage suffered by the intellectual property right holders, the relationship between the intellectual property right holder and the counterparty in intellectual property transactions can be categorized into four scenarios: high transaction cost, low damage; high transaction cost, high damage; low transaction cost, high damage; and low transaction cost, low damage. Regardless of the type of limitation scheme, such as exhaustion of rights, fair use,

[50] Conditional control refers to a situation where the intellectual property holder does not have the right to refuse, but has the right to claim a royalty for use. Free from control refers to a situation where the intellectual property holder neither has the right to refuse nor the right to claim a royalty.

[51] Whether entering the market through licensing or circumventing prior intellectual property through independent creation, the costs for later entrants are very high.

or compulsory licensing, the application of which are differentiated based on these four scenarios, for instance, a situation of 'high transaction cost and low damage' should fall under the scope of the fair use scheme, while a 'low transaction cost and high damage' scenario should be absolutely excluded from fair use. Similarly, in the case of compulsory licensing, scenarios of 'high transaction cost, regardless of damage level' should be eligible for compulsory licensing, as the licensee under such a scheme is required to pay a reasonable amount of licensing fees to the patent holder. As for determining the extent of damage, the 'market substitution effect' from economic analysis can be employed.[52] However, the challenge lies in setting different standards of the 'market substitution effect' for various limitation schemes, such as fair use and compulsory (statutory) licensing. Intuitively, the substitution effect in fair use should be significantly smaller than in compulsory (statutory) licensing, since the latter still involves payment. However, how to quantify the distinction between the two substitution effects and how much the gap should be set indeed requires a highly refined metrological approach.

In summary, the rights limitation regime in intellectual property aims to facilitate intellectual property transactions by addressing the issue of rights block-up. When the transaction costs between the intellectual property holders and potential users of the intellectual property are too high (an extreme scenario being the intellectual property holder refusing to grant a license under any circumstances), the rights limitation regime allows potential users to bypass the block-up of the intellectual property holders and use the intellectual property by paying a certain amount of consideration, thus avoiding a loss of social welfare. Different uses by potential users require different prices: zero cost constitutes fair use, a reasonable price constitutes compulsory (statutory) licensing, and exhaustion of rights only applies to mediums of the intellectual property that already existed in the market. It is evident that the rights limitation regime essentially forces intellectual property holders to transact (as mentioned earlier, forced transactions mean that the right holder loses the right to refuse). Different limitation schemes require different conditions of forced transactions. For a long time, the intellectual property community in China has not approached the rights limitation regime from this perspective, rather, the angle for perception of the legislative and judiciary have consistently stayed on the level of public interest, emphasizing the so-called balance of interests between intellectual property holders and users. Although this approach is not incorrect, it lacks practical significance and fails to realize the potential of the rights limitation regime to enforce compulsory transactions, and artificially restricting the functionality of such a regime. By applying a limitation scheme to achieve compulsory transactions can effectively break the market constrain without resorting to the costly tool of antitrust regulation, thereby promoting intellectual property transactions, fostering cumulative innovation, and enabling effective competition. In the case of *Huaduo Co.,Ltd. v. NetEase*

[52] In his famous paper on fair use, Professor William Fisher III provides a detailed introduction on how to measure the impact of the use of works on copyright holders using economic analysis. In addition to the 'market substitution effect' method, he also discusses various other economic analysis approaches. See detail in Fisher III, W. (1988). Reconstructing the fair use doctrine. *Harvard Law Review*, 101(8), 1659–1795.1698–1744.

Co.,Ltd. on Tort of Monopoly and Unfair Competition,[53] regarding the relationship between game developers and online game streaming platforms, almost all scholars and practitioners argued that online game developers should be able to control the entire horizontal and vertical markets based on their copyright. However, from the perspective of the 'compulsory transaction function of the limitation regime', why not add one more avenue to enhance overall social welfare beyond antitrust regulation?

3.4 Summary of This Chapter

There is rarely any analysis of intellectual property transactions within the intellectual property academia, likely because intellectual property transactions are considered merely as contractual issues. Given the existence of an extensive and comprehensive contract law system, there seems to be no need for 'redundant efforts' within the field of intellectual property law. However, the ignorance on intellectual property transaction issues fails to provide theoretical frameworks and methods to address practical problems faced by the industry. It also leads to oversight of deficiencies in the intellectual property legal system itself and inaccuracies in its specific application. For a system like intellectual property, which originates in the market and can only exist within the market, conducting isolated institutional research departs from the market is significantly flawed. Intellectual property systems and intellectual property transactions are mutually responsive. Only by adopting a behaviourist perspective and employing an analytical framework of 'institution—market—behaviour' to study this dual system of 'institution—transaction' can we better understand the observed effects of the overall operation of the system. This approach allows us to examine the rationality of the institutional design and lay a solid foundation for future legislative amendments.

In view of this, this chapter begins by examining why transactions occur from the perspective of users of intellectual property. Specifically, it explores why transactions take place in the context of copyright, patent rights, and trademark rights. The author argues that the market strategies of later entrants significantly impact intellectual property transactions. Whether it is cumulative innovation aiming at intellectual achievements or aiming at brand cultivation, the 'demand-utility' analysis conducted must surround factors such as the level of industry development in the relevant market and the competitive structure, the comparison of homogeneity and heterogeneity among competitors, the size of potential market demand, and legal frameworks and judicial policies, so as to make decisions that maximize marginal utility.

On the side of the intellectual property owner, their choice in a transaction is essentially reduced to whether to utilize the intellectual property themselves or to authorize others to use it. This chapter first explains that the key issue in determining the success of an intellectual property transaction is pricing. Factors such as the instability of intellectual property and the difficulty in assessing its value create

[53] Guangzhou Intellectual Property Court, 2015.*Yue Zhi Fa Shang Min Chu Zi No. 25* Judgment.

significant challenges for pricing, which are also major causes of moral hazard or adverse selection. From the perspective of the intellectual property owner, the fundamental decision of whether to use the intellectual property themselves or to license (or assign) it to others depends on the economic characteristics of the rights holders and the industries they are involved in. This includes elements like the nature and capital strength of the entity, the industry in which it operates (or intends to enter), the competitive landscape of the industry, the production efficiencies of both the intellectual property holders and their competitors, and the future market perspective (such as industry integration or product substitutability). The completion of the transaction depends on the alignment of the needs of the intellectual property holders and the potential transacting parties on such basis.

After analysing the economic implications of intellectual property transactions from the perspectives of both parties, it becomes evident that the current intellectual property legal framework in China cannot provide sufficient support for intellectual property transactions in practice and revealing a shortfall in systems supply. This chapter examines three aspects—creation and extinguishment of intellectual property right, protection of bona fide purchasers in intellectual property transactions, and limitations on intellectual property rights—to identify deficiencies in systems supply. While explores the impacts caused by these institutional flaws, it also suggests that when static rules of the system are insufficient, adopting a dynamic behavioural perspective is a scientific approach to enriching legal application. This method can effectively fill the legal gaps and also helps us gain a deeper understanding of the inherent meaning and purpose of the system.

References

Dai, Z. (2017). Faguo zhuixuquan lifa jiqi qishi yanjiu [Research on the French resale right legislation and its implications]. *Dianzi Zhishi Chanquan [Electronic Intellectual Property], 12*, 22.

Belleflamme, P., & Peitz, M. (2010). *Industrial organization: Markets and strategies* (p. 508). Cambridge University Press.

Blue, S., & Grand, R. (2008). *Jingji sixiang shi [History of economic thought]* (Di, X., et al., Trans.). Peking University Press.

Drahos, P. (1996). *A philosophy of intellectual property*. Dartmouth Publishing Company Limited.

Finkelstein, D., & McCleery, A. (2012). *Shushi daolun [The history of the book]* (He, C., Trans.). Shangwu Yinshuguan [Commercial Press].

Fisher, W., III. (1988). Reconstructing the fair use doctrine. *Harvard Law Review, 101*(8), 1659–1795.

Ji, H. L. (2014). Jiegou dongchan gongshi gongxin yuanze [Deconstructing the principle of movable property publicity and trust]. *Zhongwai Faxue [Chinese and Foreign Law Review], 3*, 706–713.

Landes, W., & Posner, R. (1987). Trademark law: An economic perspective. *Journal of Law and Economics, 30*(2), 265–309.

National Intellectual Property Administration, 2021 China Patent Survey Report, pp. 4–6. https://www.cnipa.gov.cn/module/download/downfile.jsp?classid=0&showname=2021年中国专利调查报告.pdf&filename=e48c21fe444a4651a72901c95a763bcc.pdf. Accessed August 1, 2022.

Patterson, L. R., & Lindberg, S. (1991). *The nature of copyright: A law of user's right*. The University of Georgia Press.

Peng, X. (2011). Shangbiao zhuanrang de lilun jiangou yu zhidu sheji [Theoretical construction and institutional design of trademark transfer]. *Falv Kexue [Legal Science], 3*, 136–139.

Reddy, M. (1995). The droit de suite: Why American fine artists should have a right to a resale royalty. *Loyola of Los Angeles Entertainment Law Journal, 15*(3), 509–510.

Rose, M. (1993). *Authors and owners: The invention of copyright*. Harvard University Press.

Scotchmer, S. (2006). *Innovation and incentives*. The MIT Press.

Taylor, T. (2015). *Sitanfu jijian jingjixue: Ruhe guoduan de quanheng liyi deshi [The Stanford guide to economics: How to make tough trade-offs]* (Lin, L., Trans.). Hunan renmin chubanshe [Hunan People's Publishing House].

Zhang, H. (2019). 'Jingzheng shiye xia zhongguo yaopin zhuanli lianjie zhidu de jishou yu tiao shi'['The reception and adjustment of the drug patent linkage system in China from the perspective of competition']. *Zhishi Chanquan [Intellectual Property], 4*, 50–70.

Zhang, S. G. (2019). Wuquan gongshi yuanze de lilun goucheng: Yi zhidu zhengdangxing wei zhongxin [Theoretical structure of the principle of property rights publicity: Focusing on institutional legitimacy]. *Fa Xue [Legal Studies], 1*, 55.

Chapter 4
Contract Theory in Intellectual Property Transactions

4.1 The Theory of Incentives

The essence of intellectual property transactions lies in the distribution of surpluses, where the potential transactional surplus is predetermined, and the core of negotiation revolves around how to distribute this surplus. In the process of distributing the surplus, it is inevitable for the parties involved to clarify their respective responsibilities and obligations, such a description of responsibilities and obligations is what we call a contract. Transactions are not merely problems of optimization, as the behaviour of the parties is constantly evolving, making transactions is inherently a form of game, a contract serves as a framework that describe the behaviors of this game. Traditional economics has focused primarily on the outcomes of these games, such as equilibrium prices, but often neglecting the gaming process involved in reaching such outcomes. However, solely focusing on the results does not provide a comprehensive understanding of intellectual property transactions. Therefore, this chapter examines various issues that may arise during the contractual process and their impact on the formation of contracts. Contract theory provides a systematic study of the formation process of agreements and can be broken down into three primary components: the theory of incentives, transaction costs theory, and incomplete contract theory.[1] This chapter begins with a discussion of the principles and framework of contract theory, then explores the application of contract theory in the context of intellectual property transactions, analysing its relevance from both legislative and judicial perspectives, while considering the distinctive characteristics of intellectual property transactions.

Incentive theory focuses on the design of rules that motivate agents to exert their maximum effort or to disclose all the information they possess. It is a more advanced

[1] The grounds for the distinction are the respective studies of Brousseau and Glachant, see Brousseau, E. & Glachant, J. M. (2002). *The economics of contracts: theories and applications*. Cambridge University Press. 9.

© Intellectual Property Publishing House Co., Ltd. 2025

M. Yang, *Basic Theories of Intellectual Property Transaction*,
https://doi.org/10.1007/978-981-96-7039-0_4

field of study compared to the theory of teams,[2] as it addresses the issue of information asymmetry in multi-agent scenarios. Unlike game theory, incentive theory does not emphasize strategic behaviours. From a theoretical perspective, incentive theory examines scenarios involving games with incomplete information, with the aim to enable the principal to craft rules that incentivize agents to engage in the game in a way that maximizes the utility of the principal. As a fundamental component of economic research, incentive theory underpins the concept of self-interested behaviour, which is a core element of microeconomic analysis. Numerous theories, including consumer theory, firm theory, behavioural studies, game theory, and principal-agent theory, are all built upon the principles of the incentive theory. This section will provide a brief overview of the development of incentive theory and its theoretical framework.

4.1.1 The Historical Development of Incentive Theory

The concept of incentive theory has long been reflected in economic research, originating from the division of labour and the emergence of exchange, and it is the division of labour that led to the principal-agent relationship. Adam Smith, highlighted the relationship between employers and employees in his studies, pointing out the inherent conflicts of interest between the two.[3] In his analysis, he identified the game-like interactions between employers and employees and made preliminary reveals on the importance of incentives. On one hand, Smith noted that employers motivate employees through wages,[4] which is equivalent to the constrains applied to agents in contemporary incentive theory. On the other hand, Smith observed that it was nearly impossible for employers to provide incentives to slaves.[5] Furthermore, Smith discussed incentive issues in agricultural societies, noting that allocating land to farmers could encourage them to work harder.[6] However, unlike scholars focusing on incentive theory who approach these problems from the perspective of maximizing social welfare and pay close attention to the trade-off between incentives and distribution, the research of Smith did not reflect such a trade-off. Building on Smith's work, Charles Babbage took this analysis a step further by focusing on the assessment of performance in contracting.[7]

Compared to Adam Smith and Babbage, Barnard placed greater emphasis on the principal-agent issues within the internal structure of a cooperation, and sought to

---

[2] On theory of teams, see Marschak, J. & Radner, R. (1972). *Economic theory of teams*. Yale University Press.

[3] Smith, A. (1776). *The wealth of nations*. The Modern Library. 66–67.

[4] Ibid., 67.

[5] Ibid., 365. Smith mentions that the pursuit of slaves is for more food and less work, and these pursuits are exactly contrary to the goals of the employer.

[6] Ibid., 366.

[7] Babbage, C. (1835). *On the economy of machinery and manufactures*. Charles Knight. 297.

establish an incentive system within the management framework. He argued that a fundamental element of any cooperative organization is the effort its members are willing to contribute, and if an organization fails to sufficiently motivate its employees, it would inevitably fail.[8] Barnard distinguished between specific inducement and general incentives in his research.[9] His most significant contribution was clarifying the importance of balancing various incentives, noting that this balance is influenced by an unstable external environment and internal changes within the organization. Moreover, Barnard highlighted that cooperations cannot rely solely on contractual incentives to motivate all activities, he emphasized that effective delegation of authority and good communication are also essential to fostering cooperative goals.[10]

The development of incentive theory in economic research has not been linear. Broadly speaking, it can be divided into two main research routes: one focused on public issues, and the other on private property issues. Both research lines have significantly contributed to the formation of incentive theory.

Market failures associated with pure public goods made scholars to deem intervention necessary. In such cases, the mechanisms for collective decision-making must address the incentive problem of obtaining the true preferences regarding public goods of the agents, which is commonly known as the 'free-riding' problem. Hume was one of the earliest thinkers to identify a problem similar to free-riding. He noted that the benefit gained by one party could increase the burden on another.[11] However, Hume did not delve deeply into the study of free-riding behaviours. In contrast, Wicksell and Lindahl provided a more in-depth analysis of the free-riding issue.[12] They proposed ideal solutions for public intervention that respecting individual interests while eliminating the abuse of power. These ideas laid the groundwork for the eventual development of incentive theory.

Social choice theory has played an enlightening role in the development of incentive theory,[13] focusing on how to extract social objectives from individual preferences. Bowen identified the challenges of strategic voting,[14] observing that voters are better served by voting in favour or opposition based on their true preferences at each step of the process. If voters consider only the incentives at each step, the election process collects the optimal level of public interest.[15] Arrow's contribution

[8] Barnard, C. (1938). *The functions of the executive.* Harvard University Press.139.

[9] Ibid., 144.

[10] Ibid.,184.

[11] Hume, D. (1740). *A treatise of human nature.* Oxford University Press. 538.

[12] Silvestre, J. (2003). 'Wicksell, Lindahl and the theory of public goods'. *The Scandinavian Journal of Economics*, 105(4), 527–553.

[13] Social choice theory studies whether social arrangements can reflect individual preferences, with voting theory being just one part of social choice theory.

[14] Strategic voting refers to the act of voting for a third party, whose stance may not fully align with the voter's preferences, in order to prevent another party from winning, despite the third party having the greatest chance of winning.

[15] Bowen, H. R. (1943). 'The interpretation of voting in the allocation of economic resources'. *The Quarterly Journal of Economics*, 58(1), 27–48.

to social choice theory was groundbreaking. He demonstrated that it is impossible to derive group preference orderings from individual preference orderings.[16] Building on this, Vickrey in his 1960 research elaborated on Arrow's Impossibility Theorem and introduced the issue of strategic misrepresentation of preferences in the social welfare function, which links social rankings to individual preferences.[17] In fact, Vickrey has hinted at the issue of incentive problems in both his 1960 and 1961 studies.[18] Subsequent research by Farquharson,[19] Gibbard,[20] Satterthwaite,[21] and others further contributed to the evolution of incentive theory to varying degrees.

From these studies, we can observe the primary distinction between social choice theory and incentive theory is that there is a clearly defined objective for the latter. Compared to the role that incentive theory plays in the study of public issues, its contributions to private property research are even more extensive. It incorporates numerous incentive factors in areas such as regulation of natural monopolies, the insurance industry, property redistribution, price discrimination, and auctions.

For private property, increasing returns to scale often result in natural monopoly. When monopolistic enterprises possess private information about their costs or demand, regulating them becomes a principal-agent issue. Loeb and Magat incorporated regulatory challenges into a principal-agent framework with adverse selection by emphasizing the lack of information available to regulators. They advocated using the Groves dominant strategy mechanism in the absence of social costs.[22] Baron and Myerson reframed the regulatory issue as a second-best choice problem.[23] Laffont and Tirole employed a social welfare function and introduced the social cost of public assets. Their model features elements of both adverse selection and moral hazard, but given the ex post observability of costs, it is essentially an adverse selection model.[24]

When the value of a purchased good is unknown to the buyer but known to the seller, the transaction can trigger incentive problems. This issue is particularly prominent in insurance markets. Knight identified scenarios where moral hazard or

---

[16] Arrow, K. J. (1951). *Social choice and individual values* (2nd ed.). Yale University Press.

[17] Vickrey, W. (1960). 'Utility, strategy, and social decision rules'. *The Quarterly Journal of Economics*, 74(4), 507–535.

[18] Vickrey, W. (1961). 'Counterspeculation, auctions, and competitive sealed tenders'. *Journal of Finance*, 16(1), 8–37.

[19] Farquharson, R. (1969). *Theory of voting*. Yale University Press.

[20] Gibbard, A. (1973). 'Manipulation of voting schemes: A general result'. *Econometrica*, 41(4), pp. 587–601.

[21] Satterthwaite, M. A. (1975). 'Strategy-proofness and arrow's conditions: Existence and correspondence theorems for voting procedures and social welfare functions'. *Journal of Economic Theory*. 10(2), 187–217.

[22] Loeb, M. & Magat, W. A. (1979). 'A decentralized method for utility regulation'. *Journal of Law & Economics*, 22(2), 399–404.

[23] Baron, D. P. & Myerson, R. B. (1982). 'Regulating a monopolist with unknown costs'. *Econometrica*, 50(4), 911–930.

[24] Laffont, J.-J. & Tirole, J. (1986). 'Using cost observation to regulate firms'. *Journal of Political Economy*, 94(3), 614–641.

adverse selection could lead to the collapse of insurance markets.[25] Arrow analysed this phenomenon and concluded that it could result in market failure, since certain insurance markets would disappear due to moral hazard, and he attempted to alter the moral issues in seeking for a solution.[26] However, Pauly criticized Arrow's perspective,[27] shifting the focus more directly onto moral hazard. In comparison, Spence and Zeckhauser provided a more comprehensive study on the problem of nonlinear pricing contracts, addressing both moral hazard and adverse selection.[28]

Incentive factors also play a significant role in the context of wealth redistribution. Sidgwick may have been the first scholar to recognize the issue of incentives within redistribution theory.[29] On the other hand, Mirrlees made groundbreaking contributions to the analysis and development of incentive theory. His work on optimal nonlinear income taxation introduced the 'revelation principle' method that fully described all 'incentive-compatible' or feasible policies under asymmetric information.[30] Dasgupta and others further explored the 'revelation principle', centering their discussions on incentive mechanisms within society.[31] In fact, the 'revelation principle' provides a normative analytical framework for economic agents operating under asymmetric information and contractual constraints, such a framework effectively helps us to further understand incentive theory.

When a monopolist implements price discrimination strategies, it also needs to employ incentive mechanisms. Since the monopolist lacks information of consumer preference, it must design various sales models to maximize profits. This constitutes a typical incentive mechanism aimed at encouraging consumers to reveal their own information, thereby enabling the monopolist to ascertain their preference types. Dupuit highlights the issue of incentives in his study of consumer surplus.[32] Edgeworth extended this discussion to price discrimination issues in the railway industry.[33] Pigou further refined the concept by distinguishing between different

---

[25] Knight, F.H. (1921). *Risk, uncertainty and profit*. Houghton Mifflin. 251, 284.

[26] Arrow, K.J. (1963). 'Uncertainty and the welfare economics of medical care'. *The American Economic Review*, 53(5), 941–973.

[27] Pauly, M.V. (1968). 'The economics of moral hazard'. *The American Economic Review*, 58(3), 531–537.

[28] Spence, M. & Zeckhauser, R. (1971). 'Insurance, information, and individual action'. *The American Economic Review*, 61(2), 380–387.

[29] Sidgwick, H. (1883). *The principles of political economy*. MacMillan.

[30] Mirrlees, J. A. (1971). 'An exploration in the theory of optimum income taxation'. *The Review of Economic Studies*, 38(2),175–208.

[31] Dasgupta, P., Hammond, P. and Maskin, E. (1980). 'On imperfect information and optimal pollution control'. *The Review of Economic Studies*, 47(5), 857–860; Green, J. and Laffont, J.-J. (1977). 'Characterization of satisfactory mechanisms for the revelation of preferences for public goods'. *Econometrica*, 45(2), 427–438; Gibbard, A. (1973). 'Manipulation of voting schemes: A general result'. *Econometrica*, 41(4), 587–601.

[32] Beard, T. R. and Ekelund, R. B., Jr. (1991). 'Quality choice and price discrimination: A note on dupuit's conjecture'. *Southern Economic Journal*, 57(4), 1155. 1159–1161.

[33] Edgeworth, F. Y. (1912). 'Contributions to the theory of railway rates'. *The Economic Journal*, 22(86), 198–218.

types of price discrimination.[34] Scholars such as Gabor, Spence, Mussa, and Rosen analysed nonlinear pricing problems across diverse scenarios.[35] These studies have significantly contributed to the formation of the modern incentive theory framework.

Incentive theory has made particularly notable contributions to auction mechanism design. Auctions represent a classic example of a principal leveraging competition among agents to minimize the informational rents it must provide. In auction design, the principal needs to create a mechanism that incentivizes agents to bid under conditions of incomplete information. Harsanyi made significant contributions to the development of auction theory,[36] building on his insights, Wilson and other scholars gradually developed more commonly used auction models.[37]

Moreover, team theory developed by Marschak and Radner also played a critical role in the advancement of incentive theory. This theory acknowledges the decentralization of information and focuses on how to coordinate the actions of team members through proper information management.[38] However, the theory of teams does not address incentive issues and assumes that there is a common goal within an organization. As scholars recognized that individuals within organizations may have divergent goals, the limitations of team theory became apparent. When each agent within a team has different goals and incomplete information about one another, delegating a task to such a team can lead to problems. Incentive theory was developed to address such issues.

Based on the above discussion, we can identify two fundamental elements in incentive theory—divergent goals and decentralized information. Divergent goals refer to each individual pursuing their own economic interests, while decentralized information means that each individual has different information, some of which is private and some public. In simple terms, incentive theory involves designing rules that take into account objectives of individuals and known information to gather more information and encourage agents to exert their utmost efforts in helping the principal achieve utility maximization.

---

[34] Pigou, A. C. (1920). *The economics of welfare*. McMillan.

[35] Gabor, A. (1955). 'A note on block tariffs'. *The Review of Economic Studies*, 23(1), 32–41; Spence, M. (1977). 'Nonlinear prices and welfare'. *Journal of Public Economics*, 8(1),1–18; Mussa, M. & Rosen, S. (1978). 'Monopoly and product quality'. *Journal of Economic Theory*, 18(2), 301–317.

[36] Harsanyi, J.C. (1987). 'Games with incomplete information played by 'Bayesian' players'. *Management Science*, 14(3), 159–182.

[37] Wilson, R.B. (1977). 'A bidding model of perfect competition'. *The Review of Economic Studies*, 44(3), 511–518; Wilson, R.B. (1969). 'Competitive bidding with disparate information'. *Management Science*, 15(7), 446–448. Rothkopf, M.H. (1969). 'A model of rational competitive bidding'. *Management Science*, 15(7), 362–373. Vickrey, W. (1961). 'Counter speculation, auctions, and competitive sealed tenders'. *Journal of Finance*, 16(1), 8–37.

[38] Marschak, J. & Radner, R. (1972). *Economic theory of teams*. Yale University Press.

4.1.2 *The Basic Framework of Incentive Theory*

Incentive theory typically begins with a simple scenario where the less-informed party (the principal) devises an incentive scheme to induce the informed party (the agent) either to disclose information (adverse selection model) or to take actions aligned with the principal's interests (moral hazard model). The incentive content includes rewards that are conditional on the signals generated by the agent's actions. Based on this, it is evident that incentive theory encompasses two fundamental issues: adverse selection and moral hazard.

Adverse selection and moral hazard both describe problems arising from information asymmetry. The former stems from ex ante information asymmetry, while the latter arises from ex post information asymmetry, with 'ex ante' and 'ex post' defined relative to the point of contract formation. The adverse selection model typically involves hidden information, where the agent knows their own type, but the principal does not. In such cases, the parties enter into a contract, and the principal must design a mechanism to incentivize the agent to take actions favourable to the principal. The moral hazard model, on the other hand, involves hidden actions,[39] meaning one party's actions cannot be perfectly observed by the other. In this model, the principal cannot know the specific actions of the agent and can only infer them from the outcomes.

The solution to the adverse selection problem relies on the design of a 'contract' that induces the agent to self-disclose their private information. The principal designs a set of optional contracts—a group of payment formulas linked to each possible type of agent. Although the principal does not know the private information of the agent, they are aware of the probabilities of the agent to adopt a certain set of choices. Since the principal also understands the agent's preferences, they can design a contract that renders the agent to maximize the utility of the value of each piece of private information. When facing with these options, the agent will naturally select the contract that maximizes their utility and allow the principal to infer their private information.

A typical moral hazard problem arises when the principal cannot observe certain actions of the agent. For example, an employer is concerned with efficiency and profitability of an enterprise, but cannot deduce the actual effort level of the employees from the observed productivity, nor can the employer ascertain whether the employee is shirking because individual productivity depends on numerous variables that are beyond the employee's control and unobservable to the employer. For example, these variables may include the efforts of other employees or random factors affecting the production process. To incentivize employees, the employer might choose an optimal remuneration mechanism, such as determining wages based on observable productivity indicators. However, if the employee is risk-averse, they may reject such a payment scheme due to the possibility of receiving lower remuneration. To avoid this risk, employees would prefer a fixed salary. Yet, under a fixed wage arrangement, employees lack the motivation to exert maximum effort. To address this dilemma, an

[39] There is also the possibility of hidden information in the moral hazard model.

optimal payment scheme needs to combine a fixed base salary with a variable bonus tied to observable performance indicators. From this example it can be seen that, in the moral hazard model, the principal's primary concern is designing an incentive contract that induces the agent to exert an optimal level of effort.

Incentive theory primarily studies contractual issues under asymmetric information, with moral hazard and adverse selection being just two most fundamental problems. Asymmetric information can be categorized from two perspectives: time and content. From the perspective of time, asymmetry can be divided into ex ante and ex post. Studies on ex ante information models are generally referred to as adverse selection models, while studies on ex post information models are known as moral hazard models. From the content perspective, asymmetric information can be divided into actions and information. The former is referred to as hidden action models, and the latter as hidden information models. Hidden action models can be viewed as principal-agent contracts, wherein the principal delegates a task to the agent, but the actions of the agent are unobservable. In such cases, the principal can link remuneration to performance to incentivize the agent to complete the task. Thus, hidden action models can also be understood as studies of incentive problems, and can also be called as moral hazard with hidden action model.

Hidden information includes four types: adverse selection models, moral hazard with hidden information models, screening models, and signalling models. Adverse selection models have been discussed earlier and will not be reiterated here. In moral hazard with hidden information models, the principal and agent have complete information at the time of signing the contract. The state is naturally determined and cannot be chosen by either party, but the agent can observe the state and select an action, while the principal can observe the action of the agent but not the state. In this case, the principal must design an incentive mechanism to ensure the actions of the agent are most beneficial to the principal. Screening model and signalling model are distinguished based on whether or not the contracting parties actually hold the information. The difference between these two models lies in who acts first. In screening models, the less-informed party acts first. The agent is aware of their own type, but the principal is not. The principal offers multiple contract options for corporation, and the agent selects the one most suitable for their own type. In signalling models, the better-informed party acts first. The agent is aware of their own type, but the principal is not. The agent initially sends a signal, and after observing the signal, the principal contracts with the agent.[40]

---

[40] Early academic research on adverse selection, moral hazard, signaling, and information screening was conducted independently. For example, studies using information screening models to address agency problems, see Stiglitz, J.E. & Weiss, A. (1981). 'Credit rationing in markets with imperfect information'. *American Economic Review*, 71(3), 393–410; The classic signalling model, see Spence, M. (1973). 'Job market signalling'. *Quarterly Journal of Economics*, 87(3), 355–374. And the application of moral hazard in theories such as insurance and efficiency wages, see Arrow, K. J. (1970). *Essays in the Theory of Risk-Bearing*. North-Holland. Shapiro, C. & Stiglitz, J. E. (1984). 'Equilibrium unemployment as a worker discipline device'. *American Economic Review*, 74(3), 433–444.

It is evident that the analytical frameworks for adverse selection and moral hazard have become increasingly complex with the deepening of theoretical research. Economic studies have not only combined adverse selection models with moral hazard models but have also expanded the single principal-agent model to a model involving one principal and multiple agents. This extension allows asymmetric information to apply to various variables which continuously change over time.

4.2 Transaction Cost Theory

Transaction cost theory is usually discussed within the framework of new institutional economics. It addresses the issues of formation of contracts in transactions by analysing the costs incurred during the transaction process. Transaction cost theory is based on the assumption of bounded rationality, wherein parties have limited foresight about the future, making it impossible for them to perfectly anticipate the optimal ex post coordination mechanisms. Consequently, parties require more flexible ex post constraints. Transaction cost theory aims to analyse how economic agents combine ex ante investment agreements with flexible ex post constraints. This section will outline the framework of the transaction cost theory through its development process.

4.2.1 The Background and Objectives of Transaction Cost Theory

Before understanding transaction cost theory, let us first consider a simple example: Suppose we go to a supermarket to buy a regular water cup. We only need to find the cup on the shelf, pay 10 yuan at the checkout counter, and take the cup away. The simplicity of this transaction is due to two reasons: First, we know the approximate retail price of a water cup. Even if we do not, we can ask the staff and the cost of such inquiry is negligible. This demonstrates that the price system benefits buyers in transactions. Second, we have a clear expectation of the quality of the water cup, or at least in most cases we do not worry about quality issues. On the one hand, this is because the production of water cups is regulated by relevant authorities, and on the other hand, it is because we can seek redress if a quality issue arises later. This shows that institutions like the regulatory systems also benefit buyers in transactions. Similarly, sellers benefit from this transaction system because lower transaction costs significantly increase the efficiency and success rate of transactions. Due to the above two reasons, the uncertainty associated with transactions is minimal, and the cost of the transaction itself is negligible.

The transaction of the water cup seems simple to us because it is underpinned by a price system and institutional framework. However, let us imagine a scenario where there is no appropriate price system or institutional framework, even the seemingly simple transaction like buying a water cup would become so complicated that we might avoid the transaction altogether. One of the main reasons for the high transaction costs in intellectual property transactions today is the lack of an appropriate price system. The right holders and implementers often fail to reach an agreement on the price, thus resulting in the failure of the whole transaction. This example illustrates market failure in economics. Market failure refers to a situation where, even when supply and demand exist, transactions do not take place. Market failure can lead to serious negative consequences, that is why economists typically pay special attention to price systems and institutional frameworks. In fact, 'making the institutional environment correct' logically takes precedence over 'making the transaction correct'.[41]

However, in some complex transaction systems, the parties may not be able to fully rely on the price system or institutional framework. For example, suppose an inventor develops a technology to improve the clarity of mobile phone screens and wishes to license it to an implementer at a certain price. Suppose the technology does not make reference to any other technologies, then the parties may be unable to determine the quality of the technology in advance or accurately ascertain its value or price. This means both parties in the transaction bear significant risks. The basic risks might involve price or quality issues, for example, the implementer may discover that the price is too high after implementing the technology, or the inventor may find the licensing fee is too low afterwards. These problems might be resolved through renegotiation, but if these issues lead to other safety concerns, it will be hard to determine subsequent liabilities between the parties. Assume we replace the screen technology with battery technology, and the newly invented battery has unknown safety risks that cannot be detected in advance. If such risks cause harm to consumers, then subsequent liability will be difficult to determine. In the case of the battery, we can observe that on one hand, the existing price system cannot support advance pricing for both parties, and on the other hand, the existing institutional framework may not be able to adequately resolve liability issues arising from safety hazards. Due to such risks, and the unwillingness of both parties to bear the risks, similar technology transactions become difficult to complete. The purpose of transaction cost theory is to solve these issues, i.e., how to help businesses complete complex transactions.

[41] Williamson, O.E. (2000). 'The new institutional economics: Taking stock, looking ahead'. *Journal of Economic Literature*, 38(3), 595–597.

4.2.2 The Historical Development and Framework of Transaction Cost Theory

Transaction cost refers to the costs generated by the transaction mechanism, which also constitute the costs of running the economic system.[42] Coase was the first to recognize the importance of transaction costs in new institutional economic analysis. He argued that firms and markets reflect two different governance mechanisms. In Coase's research framework, transaction cost refers to the costs required to complete a transaction, including information search costs, bargaining costs, contracting costs, enforcement costs, and so on. Coase's basic approach was to take transactions as the object of analysis, identify the factors that distinguish different types of transactions, and then analyse the institutional frameworks required to manage these transactions, with transaction cost being the core of this study.[43] Coase observed that inter-firm relationships are governed by market prices, whereas intra-firm decisions are made through internal coordination, which is different from the basis of profit-maximizing entities setting market prices. In other words, if a transaction is not determined by the price system, it must be completed within the firm.[44]

The research of Coase primarily made two significant contributions: first, he proposed an analytical framework centered on transaction costs; second, he distinguished between the two transaction modes of firms and markets. Next, we will discuss these two aspects in detail.

Coase did not further classify the types of transaction costs in his research. Building on Coase's work, Williamson conducted further studies on transaction cost theory. He posited that the purpose of transaction cost theory is to address the question of when transactions occur within the market and when they occur within firms.[45] Dahlman refined the classification of transaction costs, asserting that they should at least include search costs, information costs, bargaining costs, decision costs, and enforcement costs.[46] In 1985, Williamson further divided transaction costs into two categories: ex ante and ex post costs.[47] Within Williamson's framework, search costs, information costs, bargaining costs, and contracting costs are considered ex ante costs, while enforcement costs are classified as ex post costs.

---

42 Arrow, K.J. (1969). 'The organization of economic activity: Issues pertinent to the choice of market versus nonmarket allocation', in *The Analysis and Evaluation of Public Expenditure: The PPB System*, US Joint Economic Committee. 501–502.

43 Coase, R.H. (1937). 'The nature of the firm'. *Economica*, 4(16), 386–405.

44 Coase, R.H. (1988). 'The nature of the firm: Origin'. *Journal of law, economics, & organization*, 4(1), 3–17. 3–4.

45 Williamson, O.E. (1991). 'Comparative economic organization: The analysis of discrete structural alternatives'. *Administrative science quarterly*, 36(2), 269–296. 269–270.

46 Dahlman, C.J. (1979). 'The Problem of externality'. *Journal of Law & Economics*, 22(1), 141–162. 141–148.

47 Williamson, O.E. (1981) 'The economics of organization: The transaction cost approach'. *American Journal of Sociology*, 87(3), 548–577.

According to Williamson, transaction costs arise from six factors: bounded rationality, opportunism, uncertainty and complexity, small numbers, information asymmetry, and atmosphere.[48] Subsequently, he attributed these sources of transaction costs to three characteristics of the transaction itself: asset specificity, uncertainty, and frequency of transaction.[49] In fact, these causes and classifications of transaction costs continue to influence our analysis and research on related issues today.

Coase posed a question in his research: if firms can reduce costs, why do market transactions exist?[50] Coase analysed the reasons behind this: first, there is a relationship between the size of a firm and the costs of managing internal transactions. In larger firms, the cost of managing internal transactions might be higher and eventually equate to the cost of additional market transactions. Second, as transactions within a firm increase, entrepreneurs may fail to allocate production factors to their most valuable use, meaning they do not fully utilize these factors of production.[51]

Williamson also pointed out that transactions are not limited to market exchanges; they also occur within firms. Williamson may have been the first scholar to focus on the dimensions of transaction specifications and processes, such dimensions include: asset specificity, frequency, and uncertainty. He argued that these dimensions influence the level of transaction costs: increased transaction frequency reduces transaction costs, and the larger the asset scale, the higher the transaction costs.[52] According to Williamson's framework, whether a transaction occurs within a firm depends on the internalized transaction costs. When external transaction costs are significantly high, internalizing the transaction is an appropriate decision. Conversely, when external transaction costs are relatively low, transacting in the market with other businesses is preferred.

Klein also studied the issue of transaction costs within firms. He pointed out that in vertically integrated firms, internal transaction costs should operate at levels lower than those in the actual market. Firms can reduce internal transaction costs through self-coordination and contractual commitments. He further noted that internal transaction costs might include factors such as information flow, incentives, monitoring, and performance evaluation.[53]

In a general sense, transaction cost theory is a framework for understanding how to structure transactions in a challenging decision-making environment. It primarily focuses on complex transactions, which are often affected by uncertainty and involve

[48] Williamson, O.E. (1975). *Markets and hierarchies: Analysis and antitrust implications, a study in the economics of internal organization.* The Free Press.

[49] Williamson, O.E. (1985). *The economic institutions of capitalism, firms, markets, relational contracting.* The Free Press.

[50] Coase, R.H. (1937). 'The nature of the firm'. *Economica*, 4(16), 386–405. 394.

[51] Ibid., 394–395.

[52] Williamson, O.E. (1991). 'Comparative economic organization: The analysis of discrete structural alternatives', *Administrative Science Quarterly*, 36(2), 269–281.

[53] Klein, P.G. (1998). 'New institutional economics', p. 11. Available at: https://papers.ssrn.com/sol3/papers.cfm?abstract_id=115811, accessed 30 July 2022.

irrevocable commitments.[54] Particularly, the fundamental aim of early transaction cost theory was to examine the details of transactions between transacting parties. Some scholars believe that understanding such transactions lays the groundwork for analysing other transactional behaviours and ultimately sheds light on the nature of the firm, as well as the determination of its size and scope.[55] In this sense, transaction cost theory can also be regarded as a theory of the firm.[56] Moreover, its insights extend beyond delineating the boundaries of industrial organization—it also serves as a management theory, since it has significant meanings for the internal organizational planning of firms. Finally, transaction cost theory is not confined to the transactions themselves; it addresses a series of issues arising during the contractual process. Therefore, in certain contexts, it can also be viewed as a governance theory.

However, the framework of transaction cost theory remains similar, and in the course of intellectual property transactions, understanding the causes and types of transaction costs can address most of the problems. Transaction costs arise from asset specificity, uncertainty, and transaction frequency; and these costs can be divided into two main categories: ex ante and ex post costs. *Ex-ante* costs include information search costs, bargaining costs, and decision costs, while ex post costs mainly refer to enforcement costs.

4.3 Incomplete Contract Theory

The application of incomplete contract theory in the intellectual property transaction system is very broad. Due to the intangible nature of intellectual property assets, there exist a significant number of uncertainties in transactions involving intellectual property. Such uncertainties increase the incompleteness of contracts in intellectual property transactions.[57] Therefore, incomplete contract theory can help addressing issues related to the use, entitlement, and even remedies of intellectual property rights in such transactions. This section will begin with the establishment of incomplete contract theory and gradually outline its basic framework.

[54] Williamson, O.E. (1975). *Markets and hierarchies: Analysis and antitrust implications, a study in the economics of internal organization*. The Free Press; Williamson, O.E. (1985). *The economic institutions of capitalism, Firms, markets, relational contracting*. The Free Press.

[55] Santos, F.M. & Eisenhardt, K.M. (2005). 'Organizational boundaries and theories of organization'. *Organization Science*, 16(5), 491–508.

[56] Conner, K.R. (1991). 'A historical comparison of resource-based theory and five schools of thought within industrial organization economics: Do we have a new theory of the firm?'. *Journal of Management*, 17(1), 121–154.

[57] The incompleteness of a contract refers to the inability of both parties to consider all factors during the formation of the contract. Therefore, the theory of incomplete contracts suggests that contracts are usually incomplete.

4.3.1 *The Establishment of the Theory of Incomplete Contracts*

The incomplete contract theory is generally believed to be proposed by Grossman, Hart and Moore (also known as the GHM model). Its initial aim was to examine Williamson's issue on vertical integration[58]; however, subsequent research diverged from this focus and developed into a general model for property rights theory.[59] Since then, incomplete contract theory began to investigate how institutional frameworks affect contract designs, specifically, it studied the impact of the allocation of property rights entitlements on the distribution of surplus among investors as well as their investment incentives.

The development of incomplete contract theory began with the study of long-term versus short-term contracts in economics.[60] This research gradually extended to exploring the reasons that hinder a party from entering into long-term contracts. Some economists attempted to explain these issues using the assumptions of bounded rationality or transaction costs, believing that these factors lead to contract incompleteness.[61] Tirole further elaborated on the causes of incomplete contracts from a cost perspective, identifying three types of costs that contribute to contract incompleteness: foreseeable costs, contracting costs, and ex post verification costs.[62] In fact, in addition to the above reasons, many other factors can lead to contract incompleteness, such as information asymmetry, vagueness in language during contract formation etc.

In terms of its assumptions, incomplete contract theory is close to neoclassical theory. However, the key distinction from incentive theory lies in one fundamental assumption. Incomplete contract theory assumes that it is impossible to write all of the future actions of inventors into the contract when there is no third party that can 'verify' the true value of the variables ex post. The issue here is that the authorities who ultimately ensure contract enforcement—such as courts or judges—cannot observe or evaluate certain relevant variables. For example, they cannot evaluate the investor's effort or some investments. Therefore, regulating unverifiable variables through the contract is meaningless, and the court must find other means to ensure effective coordination of such actions. In other words, incentive theory is a

---

[58] Grossman, S. J. & Hart, O. D. (1986). 'The costs and benefits of ownership: A theory of vertical and lateral integration'. *Journal of Political Economy*, 94(4), 691–719.

[59] Hart, O. D. & Moore, J. (1990). 'Property rights and the nature of the firm', *Journal of Political Economy*, 98(6), 1119–1158.

[60] Crawford, V. P. (1988). 'Long-term relationships governed by short-term contracts'. *The American Economic Review*, 8(3), 485–499.

[61] Williamson, O. E. (1979). 'Transaction-cost economics: The governance of contractual relations'. *Journal of Law & Economics*, 22(2), 233–261; Grossman, S. J. & Hart, O. D. (1986). 'The costs and benefits of ownership: A theory of vertical and lateral integration'. *Journal of Political Economy*, 94(4), 691–719.

[62] Tirole, J. (1999). 'Incomplete contracts: Where do we stand?'. *Econometrica*, 67(4), 741–781.

study based on the assumption of contract completeness, where the rights and obligations of both parties are pre-defined in various situations. In contrast, incomplete contract theory posits that contracts are inherently incomplete, so it is impossible to define all situations in advance, and it advocates for resolving issues through ex post renegotiation. Thus, while incentive theory focuses on the design of ex ante rules and obligations, we should put emphasis on ex post oversight; given incomplete contract theory posits the inherent incompleteness of ex ante designs, the attention shall thus be placed on the arrangement of ex ante rights or the design of transaction mechanisms.

Incomplete contract theory focuses on issues arising from the unverifiability of information, assuming that there is no information asymmetry between the parties. Both parties observe all information during each transaction period, but the court is unable to verify some of the information, therefore we can deem such information unable to be described or governed by the contract. The uncertainty arises because each investor must operate on variables that cannot be constrained by an unverifiable contract, without having complete information about the outcomes of their actions. As they cannot predict the actions of others with certainty, therefore the contract remains uncertain. Formally, such contracts typically involve at least two stages. The first stage is the investment phase, during which the investor makes unverifiable investments. The second stage is the transaction phase, where the price and quantity of the transaction are the only verifiable variables.

This creates a dilemma: We assume that the parties are engaged in a repeated game model and the contract can only constrain verifiable variables, as a result, the investor can make commitments only to the characteristics of the transaction in the second stage. However, the level of investment made by both parties in the first stage depends on the transaction level set forth in the contract. Once both parties know the actual investment level and the potential natural states that may occur during the transaction at the end of the first stage, the pre-agreed transaction level is no longer optimal. Therefore, renegotiating the transaction level afterwards would be the best choice. However, if both parties understand that renegotiating in the future will yield a better outcome, they will have no ex ante incentives to make effective investments, because the ex ante transaction is unreliable.

This dilemma can also be resolved through contractual mechanisms. The parties can enter into an ex ante agreement to limit the scope of ex post negotiations and incentivize the parties to make optimal investments in advance. Such a design might grant one party the authority to determine the transaction level that will be effective post-negotiation, yet the parties can create default clauses regarding a minimum transaction level to protect the interests of the other party.[63] The economic field has developed two models based on this framework. The first model, proposed by Hart and Moore,[64] argues that the effective investment level is not determined by implied terms, since default clauses cannot incentivize both parties to reach an

---

[63] We can understand the default clause as the provision of rights and obligations for both parties.

[64] Hart, O. & Moore, J. (1988). 'Incomplete contracts and renegotiation', *Econometrica*, 56(4), 755–785.

optimal level in all cases. The second model, based on the research of Aghion, Dewatripont, and Rey,[65] assumes that default clauses can incentivize both parties to reach an optimal investment level and that courts are capable of verifying and enforcing highly complex situations of breach of contract.

In summary, incomplete contract theory directly links the observability, evaluability, or enforceability of a contract with its efficiency. When certain variables are unobservable, the contract is considered incomplete. Therefore, the capacity of courts and other judicial institutions determines the complexity of implied terms, which can incentivize the party not benefiting from renegotiation to act efficiently.[66]

4.3.2 The Basic Framework of Incomplete Contract Theory

Incomplete contract theory is an analytical framework established with the incompleteness of contracts as its starting point, and the optimal allocation of control rights (or residual rights of control) as its objective. The basic logic of incomplete contract theory is that: due to the incompleteness of contracts, both the contracting parties cannot fully determine the dedicated investments in the ex ante negotiation, meaning that such investments cannot be included in the contract. Once the transaction begins, the parties will inevitably face a situation of renegotiation. During this renegotiation, the investor may face the risk of being 'held up'. Due to the expectation of this risk, the investor may have insufficient incentives to make investments in advance. In other words, incomplete contract theory argues that, under symmetric information, there will inevitably be insufficient or ineffective investments.

There are several approaches to solve the issues outlined above, the first being legislative or judicial intervention. The default clauses discussed earlier are a typical means of legal intervention. The premise for creating such default clause is that their creation cost is less than the total cost of privately solving the incomplete contract problems by the parties themselves, otherwise the default clause would be inefficient. Another form of legal intervention is conducted through compensation, where the principle of full compensation can also reduce instances of underinvestment.[67] The second approach is to address the issue through property rights theory. Due to the incompleteness of contracts, the ex ante contract necessarily includes residual rights, which stem from ownership, the more ownerships, the greater the residual control

---

[65] Aghion, P., Dewatripont, M. & Rey, P. (1994). 'Renegotiation design with unverifiable information', *Econometrica*, 62(2), 257–282.

[66] The incomplete contract theory argues that the distribution of residual rights of control defines firms and markets. In market transactions, the distribution of residual rights of control is symmetric between the parties, while in internal firm transactions, it means that residual rights of control are asymmetrically distributed. Here, residual rights of control refer to ownership in the legal sense.

[67] The full compensation here should include not only the positive losses but also the negative losses.

rights. Therefore, balancing investment incentives can be achieved through the entitlements of property rights.[68] In the GHM model, property rights should be granted to the party with the greater importance. The third approach is government intervention, which advocates resolving incomplete contract issues by reducing transaction costs. In the framework of government intervention, contract governance should be based on the transaction costs it generates, and incomplete contracts should align with higher levels of government intervention.

It can be seen that the theory of incomplete contracts is developed based on incentive theory and transaction cost theory. Compared to the other two theories, the theory of incomplete contracts is closer to reality and provides a better understanding of real-world issues. After clarifying the basic framework of contract theory, we will further explore its application in intellectual property transactions.

4.4 The Reflection and Application of Contract Theory in Intellectual Property Transactions

The impact of contract theory on intellectual property transactions is mainly reflected in two aspects: first, from the market transaction perspective, intellectual property right holders and implementers can use contract theory to understand the design of contract frameworks, thus using specific clauses to incentivize the other party to take actions that benefit them; second, from the legal system perspective, the government can use legislative design or judicial measures to facilitate transactions between right holders and implementers based on contract theory, and ensure that the public benefits from such transactions. However, in the first aspect, the core of the contracts for transactions between right holders and implementers revolves around the issue of price. It is not possible to effectively analyse pricing problems without discussing price theory. Therefore, we will address the pricing issues in the transactions between right holders and implementers in Chapter 5. This section will primarily focus on the application of contract theory in intellectual property legal system. In fact, the application of contract theory in the development of legal systems is very broad, and it would be difficult to thoroughly discuss all aspects in one chapter. Therefore, this section will only focus on representative examples. Specifically, in the construction of intellectual property systems, the application of contract theory can be reflected at both legislative and judicial levels. We will now proceed to discuss the application of contract theory at these two levels.

---

68 This conclusion is based on the assumption that the more assets one has, the greater the investment incentives. However, some scholars disagree with this view, arguing that the assumption does not hold under certain conditions, and may even lead to the opposite conclusion, see Chiu, Y.S., (1998). 'Noncooperative bargaining, hostages, and optimal asset ownership'. *The American Economic Review*, 88(4), 882–901; De Meza, D. & Lockwood, B. (1988). 'Does asset ownership always motivate managers? Outside options and the property rights theory of the firm'. *The Quarterly Journal of Economics*, 113(2), 361–386.

4.4.1 Contract Theory at the Legislative Level

The application of contract theory at the legislative level can be reflected in two aspects. First, the design of systems for the protection of rights, including the method, scope and duration of protection, involves contract theory. The deployment of contract theory in these areas mainly pertains to macro-level transactions, that is, transactions between the public and right holders. In this transaction, the government needs to grant a certain period of monopoly rights to inventors in exchange for the disclosure of the inventions, such trade-offs can benefit the public. Second, the government can incentivize transactions within industries through specific intellectual property system designs, which are relatively micro-level transactions between right holders and implementers. In these transactions, the government primarily intervenes through the institutional mechanisms, either mandating or 'facilitating' the transaction process between right holders and implementers, in order to promote the completion of the transaction. In this section, we will explore these two aspects in turn.

4.4.1.1 Transaction Between the Public and Right Holders

The transaction between the public and right holders is primarily reflected in the design of intellectual property protection systems. The framework of the current intellectual property system can be traced back to the fourteenth century, rulers of the time began granting exclusive rights to inventors.[69] However, the first patent law was enacted in 1474.[70] At that time, many scholars had debated what kind of reward should be given to right holders, and the prevailing view was that exclusive rights should be granted instead of monetary rewards. For example, Adam Smith argued that while monopolies were generally harmful to society, granting exclusive rights for a certain period of time as a reward for inventors was nevertheless a good approach.[71] Jeremy Bentham also conducted a comparative study of the respective efficiencies of granting exclusive rights vis-a-vis monetary rewards, concluding that the former was clearly a more appropriate method.[72] Similarly, John Stuart Mill believed that rewarding inventors with exclusive rights was more efficient, as it reduced the need for the government to make determinations regarding the invention or its value, thus leaving those decisions to consumers.[73] However, some scholars have argued that other forms of rewards should replace monopoly rights. For instance, Johann

[69] Frumkin, M., (1945). 'The Origin of Patents'. *Journal of the Patent Office Society*, 27(3), 143.

[70] Yin, X. (2011). *Zhongguo zhuanlifa xiangjie* [*Detailed explanation of Chinese patent law*], Zhishi Chanquan Chubanshe[Intellectual Property Publishing House]. 1.

[71] Smith, A. (1901). *An inquiry into the nature and causes of the wealth of nations*, J.M. Dent. 471–474, 584.

[72] Bentham, J. (1843). 'A manual of political economy', in *McMaster University Archive for the History of Economic Thought*.

[73] Mill, J. S. (2004). *Principles of political economy*. Hackett Publishing. 271.

Friedrich Lotz questioned whether granting inventors monopoly rights was appropriate, arguing that state rewards for inventors were fairer and more economically advantageous.[74] Additionally, some scholars differentiated between types of inventions, suggesting that inventions which require substantial costs should be rewarded, but accidental discoveries should not necessarily be granted with such rewards.[75]

As research deepened, four theoretical foundations supporting the granting of exclusive rights for a certain period as a reward for inventors gradually emerged. Fritz Machlup summarized these viewpoints into four doctrines: the nature law thesis, the reward by monopoly thesis, the monopoly-profit-incentive thesis, and the exchange for secret thesis.[76] The nature law thesis posits that individuals have a natural right to their own ideas, and unauthorized use of these ideas constitutes theft.[77] Natural law grants everyone an inherent right to exclusivity, and therefore, the exclusive enforcement of patent rights is justified. The reward by monopoly thesis holds that an inventor's reward should be proportional to the level of usefulness of the invention to society, therefore the most effective form of reward is to grant exclusive monopoly rights for a limited period of time.[78] This approach helps avoid errors caused by subjective evaluation of patents, leaving the determination of value to the market. The monopoly-profit-incentive thesis is similar to the reward by monopoly thesis, but it examines the patent monopoly rights more from an incentive perspective. It argues that sufficient incentives are necessary to motivate inventors to continue to innovate, and monopoly rights are the most appropriate measure of incentive. The Exchange for Secret thesis views patents as a transaction between the inventor and society, where society provides a limited period of monopoly rights in exchange for the disclosure of the technologies from the inventors.

From the above discussion, we can see that the design of patent protection mechanisms takes into account both incentive and cost factors. On one hand, exchanging monopoly rights for the disclosure of inventions can motivate inventors to invest more time, effort, and financial resources into innovative activities. On the other hand, if the government were to adopt a monetary reward system, it would incur substantial costs in price settings, and the accuracy of such pricing would be difficult to ensure. In contrast, the cost of granting monopoly rights as a reward is much lower than the combined costs of individual pricing. Therefore, the government ultimately chooses to reward inventors with monopoly rights for a certain period as a means of incentivizing innovation.

After determining the method of intellectual property protection, the next step followed was a discussion on the patent protection period and scope. Nordhaus

---

[74] Machlup, F. & Penrose, E. (1950). 'The patent controversy in the nineteenth century'. *The Journal of Economic History*, 10(1), 24.

[75] Machlup, F. (1959). *An economic review of the patent system*, United States Government Printing Office. 20.

[76] Ibid.

[77] Murphy, M. C. (2006). *Natural law in jurisprudence and politics*, Cambridge University Press; Crowe, J. (2012). 'Clarifying the natural law thesis'. *Australian Journal of Legal Philosophy*, 37(8), 159–181.

[78] Mill, J. S. (2004). *Principles of political economy*. Hackett Publishing. 271, 279.

approached this issue from an algebraic perspective, and comprehensively described the methods for determining the patent protection period.[79] Scherer then supplemented this view from a geometric perspective.[80] Nordhaus subsequently acknowledged Scherer's geometric method but highlighted a series of issues related to the patent protection period and patent thresholds. He argued that a fixed patent protection period is not optimal, and a long-term patent protection period is preferable to short terms. Although this may lead to monopoly concerns, but monopoly can be addressed by raising the thresholds for granting patents.[81]

Subsequently, academic focus shifted to the scope of patent protection. Klemperer's research concentrated on the trade-off between the scope of patent protection and the duration of patent protection. He deployed a model explaining how to determine the appropriate level of reward for inventors with minimal social cost, thereby defining the reasonable scope of patent rights.[82] Gilbert and Shapiro's study focused on balancing the innovation incentives provided by patents with the deadweight loss caused by monopolies. Their paper pointed out that excessively long patent protection could hinder subsequent innovation.[83] Merges and Nelson also emphasized that the core of the patent system lies in balancing innovation incentives with the negative effects of monopolies. They argued that the industrial competitive environment should be maintained as best as possible without significantly reducing innovation incentives, rather than allowing patent holders to dominate the market.[84] Professor Manfredi M.A. La Manna also highlighted the shortcomings of solely focusing on discussions of patent protection duration, he believed that setting a reasonable threshold for patentability can provide a more significant meaning than simply determining the appropriate patent protection period.[85] Additionally, Lerner, through empirical research, examined the impact of patent protection scope on firms.[86] Lerner employed the international patent classification (IPC) scheme to assess the scope of patent rights by testing the relationship between the stock of intellectual property and firm value. Using 535 samples, Lerner found that the scope of patent protection had a significant impact on the evaluation of these firms. Lerner

[79] Nordhaus, W. D. (1969). *Invention, growth, and welfare: A theoretical treatment of technological change*. The MIT Press. 168.

[80] Scherer, F. M. (1972). 'Nordhaus' theory of optimal patent life: A geometric reinterpretation'. *The American Economic Review*, 62(3), 422–427.

[81] Nordhaus, W. D. (1972). 'The optimum life of a patent: Reply'. *The American Economic Review*, 62(3), 428–431.

[82] Klemperer, P. D. (1990). 'How broad should the scope of patent protection be'. *The RAND Journal of Economics*, 21(1), 113–130.

[83] Gilbert, R. & Shapiro, C. (1990). 'Optimal patent length and breadth'. *The RAND Journal of Economics*, 21(1), 106–112.

[84] Merges, R.P. & Nelson, R.R. (1990). 'On the complex economics of patent scope'. *Columbia Law Review*, 90(4), 868.

[85] La Manna, M.A.M. (1992). 'Optimal patent life vs. optimal patentability standards'. *International Journal of Industrial Organization*, 10(1), 81–89.

[86] Lerner, J. (1994). 'The importance of patent scope: An empirical analysis'. *The RAND Journal of Economics*, 25(2), 319–333.

then investigated the relationship between the scope of patent protection and the difficulty consumers face when switching to substitute products. He discovered that companies holding subclass patents place greater emphasis on the scope of patent protection, which is consistent with Klemperer's findings in 1990. Similar empirical studies include the work of O'Donoghue, Scotchmer, and Thisse, who found that, compared to patent protection duration, the scope of patent protection seemed to be more important. This is because only a small proportion of patents remain paid for until the end of the protection period, while most patent holders do not invest money to maintain the validity of their patents.[87]

After 2000, countries led by the U.S. further emphasized the scope of patent protection.[88] Jaffe summarized relevant research from previous decades and conducted in-depth empirical studies, but the results were unideal. Due to the difficulty in quantifying patent policies into parameters and the challenge of identifying statistical significance amidst dynamic variable changes, his study only yielded rough conclusions. Jaffe argued that expanding the scope of patent protection did not significantly impact the R&D process. He seemed to disagree with the further strengthening of patent protection in the U.S. at that time.[89]

Gallini also conducted research on the U.S. patent system reform. He believed that the reason Jaffe's empirical study in 2000 did not find the reason for strengthening of patent protection in the U.S. was that companies had not yet had enough time to respond to the policy change. Meanwhile, he pointed out that when designing effective rules, one should no longer simply rely upon trade-off principles, such as aiming to stimulate innovation at the cost of limiting the use of innovative products. The reason is that in a cumulative innovation environment, the patent system, instead of protecting the inventions it aimed to safeguard, actually hindered them. The impact of patent reform on the innovation process extended far beyond its effect on innovation incentives.[90] This can be seen as an early form of the 'patent thicket' theory. Subsequently, Chu attempted to use dynamic equilibrium theory to determine the scope of patent protection. He sought to address the dynamic distortion in capital accumulation models and hoped to eliminate the negative effects caused by patent barriers in order to expand the scope of patent protection. In his study, Chu found that as long as the long-term Total Factor Productivity (TFP) growth part is not negligible, the market investment in R&D would be insufficient. However, expanding the breadth of patents could be an effective solution to the problem of insufficient R&D

---

[87] O'Donoghue, T., Scotchmer, S. & Thisse, J.-F. (1998). 'Patent breadth, patent life, and the pace of technological progress', *Journal of Economics and Management Strategy*, 7(1), 1–32.

[88] At least from the cases at the time, the United States began to gradually emphasize patent holders' rights starting in 1980, reaching an unprecedented height around the year 2000. It was only after the eBay case that limitations were placed on the rights of patent holders.

[89] Jaffe, A. B. (2000). 'The U.S. patent system in transition: Policy innovation and the innovation process'. *Research Policy*, 29(4–5), 531–557.

[90] Gallini, N. T. (2002). 'The economics of patents: Lessons from recent U.S. patent reform'. *Journal of Economic Perspectives*, 16(2), 131–154.

investment. The resulting impact on consumption could be substantial.[91] Palokangas later simulated two industrial scenarios—one with a sole innovator in the industry, and the other with an innovator and a follower—aiming to establish the optimal scope of patent protection. He discovered that patent laws influence patent protection duration, while compulsory licensing systems and royalty fees affect inventors' expected returns. Governments could balance innovation and imitation through these two systems. The optimal patent strategy relies on two externalities: diversification and the spillover effect of R&D (which refers to the externality of R&D, i.e. how R&D conducted by Firm A affects Firm B). Diversification can increase consumer efficiency, when diversification exceeds the spillover effect of R&D, the patent protection period should be extended, but the scope of protection should be narrowed. Palokangas argued that as the scale of competition grows, there would be a conflicting effect: welfare increases due to the growth in diversification, but spillover effects also become stronger. However, spillover effects lead to increased R&D efforts and reduced productivity, which causes a decrease in consumption and a reduction in social welfare. To increase the scale of competition, the scope of patent protection should be reduced, large-scale competition can decrease the marginal returns on deposits, meanwhile, the discount factor as an objective of households needs to be reduced to the same extent, but this can only happen when the growth rate decreases. Therefore, the government must ensure a slow growth, in order to achieve this, innovation incentives for a duopoly should be reduced by extending the duration of patent protection. Ultimately, Palokangas proposed an early model for the optimal patent protection in an economy with non-divisible risk and product cycles.[92] Influenced likely by the view of Palokangas, or due to the ruling in the eBay case, U.S. courts gradually began to limit the scope of rights of patent holders.

The thinking of the duration and scope of intellectual property protection also reflects the application of contract theory in academic thought. From an incentive perspective, longer duration and broader scope of intellectual property protection are bound to stimulate innovation and investment. However, at the same time, monopolies increase competition costs in society, and when monopolists harm overall social welfare, breaking the monopoly incurs higher costs. Therefore, the determination of the duration and scope of intellectual property protection must balance both incentive and cost factors.

---

[91] Chu, A. C. (2007) 'Optimal patent breadth: Quantifying the effects of increasing patent breadth'. MPRA paper 3910. Available at: https://mpra.ub.uni-muenchen.de/id/eprint/3910 accessed 30 July 2022.

[92] Palokangas, T. (2011). 'Optimal patent length and breadth in an economy with creative destruction and non-diversifiable risk'. *Journal of Economics*, 102(1), 1–27.

4.4.1.2 Transactions Between Right Holders and Implementers

In addition to the transactions between the public and right holders, the government can also promote transactions between right holders and implementers by institutional designs. Typical systems include compulsory licensing of patents, statutory licensing of copyrights, and open licensing of patents etc. These systems share certain common characteristics while are different in some aspects, this section will discuss these three types of licensing systems respectively.

Compulsory licensing refers to the act where the implementer can use a patent without the consent of the patent holder. In China, compulsory licensing exists only in the patent system. The basic procedure for compulsory licensing is as follows: the implementer can submit a written application to the administrative department of the State Council, requesting the granting of a compulsory license. The administrative department needs to inform the applicant after making a decision, if the decision is to grant the compulsory license, it must be registered and announced to public. According to Article 53 to Article 57 of China's *Patent Law* (revised in 2020), the granting of a compulsory license must take into account the impact of the licensing behaviour on market competition, public health, and innovation. These considerations aim to safeguard public interest, prevent patent holders from profiting at the expense of public welfare, and to create deterrence when patent holders refuse to license, thereby incentivising patent holders to engage in licensing.

However, from a transaction cost perspective, compulsory licensing may not necessarily reduce transaction costs. The difference between compulsory licensing and voluntary licensing by patent holders lies in different forms of price settings: the former is judicially determined, while the latter is determined by the market. Since the costs associated with judicial pricing are not necessarily lower than those of market pricing, the purpose of the compulsory licensing system is more related to create incentives rather than reducing transaction costs.

Let us now look at the compulsory licensing system in the U.S. copyright law.[93] Under this system, the implementer may use the copyrighted work without the consent of the copyright holder, but they are required to inform the copyright holder, and if the copyright holder cannot be located, the implementer must notify the Copyright Office and pay the statutory fee or statutory rate. In terms of procedure, the U.S. compulsory licensing system for copyright differs from China's patent compulsory licensing system, as the U.S. copyright compulsory licensing does not require extensive review; instead, it categorizes certain types of works that can be compulsorily licensed. As long as the copyright falls within one of these categories, it can be used directly. Compared to China's patent compulsory licensing system, the U.S. compulsory licensing system for copyrights can effectively reduce the uncertainty in transactions, lower transaction costs for both copyright holders and implementers, thus improve the efficiency of their transactions.

---

[93] For the sake of consistency in this book we will use 'copyright' to refer to 'author's right' (*Zhu Zuo Quan*).

Although the copyright law of China does not provide a compulsory licensing regime, it does feature two limitation schemes on copyright: fair use and statutory licensing. The statutory licensing in China is similar to the compulsory licensing in the U.S., as they both adopt a typological approach by listing specific situations where statutory or compulsory licenses shall apply. However, the U.S. compulsory licensing requires prior notice or at least 'quasi-prior notice', while China's statutory licensing allows for post-notification. Furthermore, statutory licensing in China does not require the consent of the copyright holder, whereas in the case of compulsory licensing, the implementer must request permissions from copyright holders under reasonable conditions. If the copyright holder refuses the license without a legitimate reason, the implementer may apply for compulsory licensing. The fundamental difference between the two systems lies in the incentives they can provide. Prior notice, as required in the U.S. compulsory licensing system, can reduce the risk of hold-up. Whereas post-notification increases the risk of hold-up, mainly in terms of price. Therefore, such risk can be reduced by means of setting a statutory licensing fee rate. Thus, it can be seen that that the statutory licensing in copyright law in China can also lower transaction costs and improve transaction efficiency. Nonetheless, determining the appropriate statutory licensing fee rate requires great caution, as setting it too high or too low could create undesirable incentives.

The fair use rule is another limitation on copyright. Fair use allows the implementer to use a work without the permission of the copyright holder and does not require any payment of fees. There are two major differences between fair use and statutory/compulsory licensing: First, fair use does not require notification to the copyright holder or payment of any fees, whereas statutory licensing and compulsory licensing both require notification to the right holder and payment. Second, the conditions for statutory licensing are clearly outlined in the law both in China and the U.S. However, in China's *Copyright Law*, Article 24 lists 12 specific circumstances for fair use, but it also includes a catch-all clause, which creates uncertainty to the application of fair use.

The first distinction reflects a legal restriction on copyright, aiming to dismantle the monopolistic power of existing copyrights and reduce their adverse impact on innovation. The second distinction reflects how the fair use principle introduces additional uncertainty into transactions. In general, the greater the uncertainty is in a transaction, the higher the transaction costs will be, to an extent that may hinder the transaction between the parties. However, from an incentive perspective, the rational use of uncertainty may serve to incentivize transactions. Take fair use as an example. Without such system, the right holder will be in a relatively advantageous position when negotiating with the implementer. They could leverage their copyright to increase their bargaining power or even engage in hold-up behaviours. Fair use, however, increases the risk of bargaining and hold-up, as in some 'ambiguous' cases, a court might rule that the implementer's use qualifies as fair use. This could make the copyright holder more cautious when negotiating or attempting to engage in hold-up behaviours. In this case, the uncertainty created by the fair use system can lower the copyright holder's price expectations, which ultimately promotes the conclusion of the transaction. Therefore, the fair use system can serve as an incentive to facilitate transactions.

Similar to compulsory licensing, statutory licensing, and fair use, the open licensing system may also facilitate the completion of transactions. However, since the open licensing system is yet sufficiently practiced nor comprehensively refined, its exact effect in promoting transactions remains unknown. The open licensing system is a special licensing regime newly introduced in the amended *Patent Law* (amended in 2020) of China. Open licensing refers to a system where the right holdermakes a public statement through the patent licensing department, indicating that implementers can obtain a license to use the patent by paying a prescribed licensing fee. The essence of the open licensing system is that the government provides a platform for transactions, where the patent holder makes an offer, and the implementer can search for the patent holder on this platform and pay the price to use the patent technology. The core goal of open licensing is to reduce transaction costs and facilitate the completion of transactions between the parties. However, it overlooks the distinctiveness of the patent bargaining process.

In theory, if the open licensing system operates exactly according to its underlying principles, it could indeed reduce transaction costs. If implementers can find the right holderthrough the platform, it would reduce their information search costs. If the right holderand the implementer reach an agreement based solely on the patent pricing under the open licensing system, it would reduce negotiation costs and contracting costs. Additionally, if courts refer entirely to the prices established in the open licensing system when handling price disputes, it could also lower enforcement costs. However, in practice, whether the open licensing system will function as designed remains unknown.

First, implementers may not necessarily pay fees as envisioned by the open licensing system and may raise objections to the price or the patent itself. On one hand, patent open licensing is similar to a showcase product, where the patent licensing fee is clearly marked, and theoretically, it should be uniformly priced. However, unlike traditional tangible properties, uncertainties exist in terms of price, quality, validity, and scope of protection of a patent, all of which could increase the likelihood of disputes between the parties. In a sense, the open licensing system still involves bargaining issues, which are not so different from the negotiation process in ordinary patent licensing. On the other hand, although patents under the open licensing system can be searched through public channels, it cannot be assumed that the implementer will necessarily be aware of the existence of the patent. The implementer may still face relatively high search costs. Therefore, while the open licensing system can reduce search costs to a certain extent, the bargaining and contracting costs between the parties may still be high.

Second, when a dispute arises between the right holderand the implementer, the open licensing system does not specify the methods of remedy, meaning that the judicial remedies for open licensing patents would still follow the regular patent remedy framework. As a result, the enforcement cost will not change significantly. In the case of open licensing, the newly entered implementer may face two scenarios: (1) the implementer is unaware that he/she used the patented technology under the open license; (2) the implementer discovers that the claims of the patent cover features of their products. The first scenario concerns infringement. In the second scenario, further analysis is needed. When the implementer discovers the patent, they can either accept or reject the rights holder's offer. If the implementer accepts the offer, no remedy issue arises. If the implementer rejects the offered price, four possible scenarios may arise: (1) the implementer negotiates with the right holderand receives a royalty rate that is lower than the listed price; (2) the implementer choose not to negotiate with the right holder and uses the patent straightaway; (3) the implementer does not use the patent; (4) the implementer files a lawsuit, claiming the price is too high and requesting the court to determine a reasonable license fee. In scenario (1), the negotiation process between the implementer and the right holder is a market negotiation process, thus does not involve the issue of judicial remedy; in scenario (2), the act of the implementer constitutes an infringement; scenario (3) does not involve any pricing issues; and scenario (4) is in fact a claim to confirm the license fee.

It is not difficult to observe that in the case of open licensing, judicial pricing could lead to two types of claims: a claim on infringement and a claim to determine the reasonable license fee. The next question is how the court should address the pricing issue in these two types of 'claims'. When dealing with an infringement claim, the court can adopt the usual methods of judicial pricing used in patent infringement cases, such as the method of calculating the actual losses, the reasonable royalty compensation method, or statutory damages method, or it could choose to directly use the price set by the right holder in the open license as the amount of damage. If the court directly adopts the right holder's listed price, it would imply that the court has recognized the reasonableness of the offer made by the rights holder. If the price is reasonable, there should be no problem, but if the price is excessively high, should the court correct it? If the court does correct it, how would this differ from the usual judicial pricing for patent licensing? Would judicial pricing in the open licensing system eventually revert to the regular patent licensing model? If the court does not correct the price in such circumstances, right holders will likely demand higher prices in the open license in the future, using the system as a tool for patent hold-up and extracting excessive profits. If the court recalculates the damages using the infringement damage calculation method, then there would be no difference to judicial pricing in regular patent infringement cases, which would make the listed price of patent holder in the open license meaningless. If the calculated damage amount is lower than the price offered by the right holder, it could lead to hold-out by the implementer—where they use the patent first and pay later—thus undermining the open licensing system. Similarly, the court faces a similar dilemma in cases where they need to determine the reasonable royalty fee, whereas redetermining the rate would be the same as judicial pricing in regular patent licensing, thus undermining the open licensing system. Yet directly adopting the rights holder's price could incentivize patent hold-up behaviour. When the right holderand the implementer renegotiate, it may give rise to a litigation for breaching of contract, in which the implementer claims that the price set in the open license is too high. At this point, the court faces the same dilemma. If the court agrees with the implementer and chooses to reset the price, this would also undermine the open licensing system, and at that point, judicial pricing in open licensing would be no different from regular patent licensing. If the court accepts the price set by the right holder, it increases the bargaining power of the right holderand the likelihood of hold-up behaviour.

Thus, it can be seen that in the case of open licensing, there are no special remedies whether it is the first license or subsequent licenses. From the perspective of legal remedies, the open licensing system does not reduce the enforcement cost of transactions. In general, compulsory licensing, statutory licensing, and fair use regimes can reduce transaction costs to varying degrees and incentivize right holders and implementers to engage in complete transactions. However, the open patent licensing system can merely reduce information search costs to a small extent, it may lower bargaining and contracting costs only in special circumstances. Yet the open licensing system cannot reduce enforcement costs, as it applies the ordinary remedies model in judicial remedies. From the open patent licensing system, it is evident that while the legislative design of such a system may have good intentions, there remains significant uncertainty during the implementation phase, leading to results that may not be entirely 'satisfactory'. Therefore, the legislative design of the system is only one part of legal intervention, with judicial intervention being another crucial component.

4.4.2 Contract Theory at the Judicial Level

The application of contract theory in the judiciary is primarily manifested on the issue of remedies. In China, remedies for intellectual property infringement are mainly concering two types: monetary remedies and injunctive reliefs. These two types of remedies serve different purposes and yield different outcomes. This section will examine the differences between these two forms of remedies, starting with monetary remedies and injunctive reliefs, and discuss their distinctions within the framework of contract theory, thereby revealing their impact on the behavioural choices of the contracting parties.

4.4.2.1 Contract Theory in Monetary Compensation and Injunctive Relief

Monetary compensation and injunctive relief are two commonly used remedies in China. Both of these remedies embody the economic principles of contract theory. We will discuss each of them in turn.

Monetary compensation has diversified functions, including compensatory, preventive, and punitive functions.[94] Among those, the compensatory function is

[94] Wang, L. (2010). *Qinquan zerenfa yanjiu* [*Research on Tort Liability Law* (Vol. 1)](2nd ed.). Zhongguo Renmin Daxue Chubanshe [China Renmin University Press]. 676.

the fundamental function of monetary compensation, and its essence is to make up for the damage that has already occurred.[95] The preventive and punitive functions serve as supplements to the compensatory function. For example, the purpose of the punitive damages system is to punish malicious infringers and, to some extent, to warn others against engaging in similar behaviours.

The compensation system for damage caused by intellectual property infringement takes monetary compensation as the primary form of remedy. To achieve the compensatory function, the monetary compensation system adheres to the principles of full compensation and prohibition of unjust enrichment.[96] These two principles represent the bottom line and cap of the amount of compensation respectively, and together determine the reasonable range for monetary compensation.

In traditional damage compensation, determining the value of tangible property may not be difficult. However, in the case of damages for intellectual property infringement, the issue of pricing is often the most challenging and contentious. Right holders often expect to receive higher compensation, while implementers tend to seek lower amounts. In the absence of incentives, the parties can hardly reach an agreement through negotiation in a short period of time. In such cases, the court needs to be involved to set the price, which is undoubtedly inefficient. On the contrary, having the court directly determine the amount of damage compensation through judicial pricing can save the time spent on inefficient negotiations, allowing the right holders to be compensated more quickly for their losses.

Although the shortcomings of judicial pricing have been widely criticized—many argue that the amount of compensation determined by judicial rulings are too low,[97] and some scholars question the burden of proof system[98]—this does not negate the

[95] Busneli, F. et al. (2005). *Principles of European Tort Law: Text and Commentary*. Springer. 102.

[96] Cheng, X. & Wang, D. (2013). 'Sunhai peichang de fangfa' ['Methods of damage compensation'], *Faxue Yanjiu [Legal Studies]*, 3, 55. The principle of full compensation is upheld in civil law, but the principle of prohibition of unjust enrichment remains controversial, with few scholars considering it as a fundamental principle of damage compensation, see Wang, L. (1993). *Minfa:Qinquan Xingwei Fa [Civil Law: Tort Law]*. Zhongguo Renmin Daxue Chubanshe [China Renmin University Press], 561; Yang, L. (2010). *Qinquan Sunhai Peichang [Tort Damage Compensation]*. Falv Chubanshe [Law Press], 233.

[97] Lü, L. (2016). 'Zhuanli qinquan sunhai peichang de shizheng yangjiu' ['Empirical study on patent infringement damage compensation'], *Dianzi Zhishi Chanquan [Electronic Intellectual Property]*, 11, 19–26; Standing Committee of the National People's Congress. (2014). 'Guanyu jiancha zhonghua renmin gongheguo zhuanlifa shishi qingkuang de baogao'['Report on the inspection of the implementation of the *Patent Law of the People's Republic of China*'], 23 June. Available at: http://www.npc.gov.cn/npc/c12491/201406/1fa592eaddef4bd190bfaf2df40d8f74.shtml accessed 10 January 2022; Li, M. (2016). Zhishi chanquan qinquan lvjinbuzhi yuanyin zhiyi shi sunhai peichang de shu'e guodi ['One of the reasons for the persistent infringement of intellectual property rights is the low amount of damages']. *Henan Keji [Henan Science and Technology]*, 8, 6; Zhan, Y. & Zhang, H. (2015). 'Woguo zhishi chanquan qinquan sifa panli shizheng yanjiu yi weiquan chengben he qinquan daijia wei zhongxin' ['An empirical study of intellectual property infringement judicial cases in China: Focusing on enforcement costs and infringement costs'], *Keyan Guanli [Science Research Management]*, 7, 150.

[98] Wu, H. (2014). 'Zhishi chanquan qinquan sunhai peichang zhong de juzheng zeren daozhi' ['Burden of proof reversal in intellectual property infringement damage compensation'], *Zhongguo*

efficiency of monetary compensation. As long as appropriate pricing methods are used, monetary compensation can be more reasonable.

In practice, the compensatory function is regarded as the fundamental purpose of monetary compensation because, in theory, it effectively incentivizes right holders to innovate and invest, ensuring that they are not deterred from further innovation by the acts of infringement. However, relying solely on the compensatory function is insufficient to deter infringement because it does not make the infringer 'worse off' due to their infringing actions. Consequently, under a monetary compensation system based solely on the compensatory function, implementers may still have an incentive to engage in infringing activities. For this reason, monetary compensation must also serve preventive and punitive functions to address the shortcomings of the compensatory function. For example, if courts consistently apply punitive damages to malicious infringers, this could serve as a deterrent to future malicious infringers.

Compared to monetary compensation, injunctive relief can better apply incentive theory to realize the preventive and punitive functions, while also facilitating the completion of transactions. It not only addresses the transaction issue in the current case but can also encourage future negotiations between other implementers and right holders. Injunctive relief is typically seen as a remedy that is more conformed to the nature of patent rights, as it effectively prevents the possibility of future infringement. In some cases, injunctive relief can also motivate both parties to negotiate, thereby improving social welfare. However, this does not necessarily mean that injunctive relief always has better economic effects compared to directly setting a royalty rate in intellectual property licensing. However, injunctive relief is not suitable for every situation, and different types of injunctive relief can have varying effects. If applied incorrectly, it may lead to negative consequences. Therefore, before adopting injunctive relief as an incentive, its impact needs to be carefully considered and evaluated.

Many scholars have long discussed whether courts should grant injunctive relief or determine future royalty rates after ruling on intellectual property infringement.[99] The main arguments in favour of injunctive relief can be summarized as follows: (1) Injunctive relief can reflect the value of intellectual property more accurately, preventing the imposition of unreasonable royalty rates by the court that could

Shenpan [*China Trial]*, 5, 14; Li, Y. and Chen, X. (2020). 'lun zhuzuoquan chengfaxing peichang zhidu jianping minfadian zhishi chanquan chengfaxing peichang tiaokuan' ['On the punitive damages system for copyright: A discussion on the punitive damages provisions for intellectual property in the *Civil Code*']. *Zhishi Chanquan* [*Intellectual Property]*, 8, 34–45; He, P. and Jiang, Q. (2018). 'Lun zhuanli qinquan sunhai peichang shu'e rending de zhengming zeren fenpei' ['On the allocation of the burden of proof in determining the amount of damages for patent infringement'], *Zhishi Chanquan* [*Intellectual Property]*, 7, 48–59.

[99] Ogus, A.I. & Richardson, G.M. (1977). 'Economics and the environment: A study of private nuisance'. *Cambridge Law Journal*, 36(2), 284–325; Tromans, S. (1982) 'Nuisance—Prevention or payment?'. *Cambridge Law Journal*, 41(1), 87–109; Lemley, M. A. (2011). 'The ongoing confusion over ongoing royalties', *Missouri Law Review*, 76(3), 695–707; Sidak, J. G. (2016). 'Ongoing royalties for patent infringement', *Texas Intellectual Property Law Journal*, 24(2), 161–214.

have negative impacts on innovation[100]; (2) Injunctive relief encourages negotiations before infringement occurs and avoids post-infringement negotiations, which is more aligned with the social value of intellectual property.[101] (3) Injunctive relief can help prevent hold-out situations.[102]

On the other hand, the main arguments against injunctive relief are based on the its potential to increase the bargaining power of right holders, thereby raising the likelihood of patent hold-up.[103] Undoubtedly, both sides of arguments provide solid legal and economic reasoning. Therefore, injunctive relief should not be completely granted nor completely prohibited, but should instead be determined on a case-by-case basis.

The primary significance of injunctive relief can be summarized into two key points: First, injunctive relief can raise the cost of infringement for the implementer, thereby creating additional risks and disincentivizing future infringement; Second, injunctive relief can influence the behaviour of both rights holders and infringers by intervening in their decision-making processes. The first point of significance of injunctive relief is quite clear: if the implementer is permanently prohibited from using the intellectual property, their prior investments may not be recovered, and they will be excluded from future market competition. Therefore, injunctive relief effectively serves a preventive and punitive function by raising the costs and risks of infringement for the implementer. The second significance of injunctive relief involves the issues of hold-up and hold-out, which will be discussed in detail in the next section.

4.4.2.2 Contract Theory and the Behavioural Choices of Parties

The application of contract theory in the judicial context is primarily reflected in its influence on the behavioural choices of the contracting parties. Any policy will have an impact on the contracting parties, thereby altering their behavioural choices to some extent. Judicial remedies also influence the decisions and choices of the right holders and implementers, with hold-up behaviour being a typical reflection

[100] Mulligan, C. and Lee, T.B. (2012). 'Scaling the patent system'. *NYU Annual Survey of American Law*, 68(2), 289–318. Sterk, S.E. (2008). 'Property rules, liability rules, and uncertainty about property rights'. *Michigan Law Review*, 106(7), 1304.

[101] Merges, R.P. (1994). 'Of property rules, Coase, and intellectual property'. *Columbia Law Review*, 94(8), 2655–2673. Schoenhard, P.M. (2008). 'Who took my IP—Defending the availability of injunctive relief for patent owners'. *Texas Intellectual Property Law Journal*, 16(2), 289. Heald, P.J. (2008). 'Optimal remedies for patent infringement: A transactional model'. *Houston Law Review*, 45(4), 1175.

[102] The incentive for the implementer in a hold-out situation lies in delaying negotiations or demanding a lower price, which typically occurs in the absence of adequate remedies. However, injunctive relief can deter hold-out parties by increasing costs.

[103] Lemley, M. A. & Shapiro, C. (2007). 'Patent holdup and royalty stacking'. *Texas Law Review*, 85(7), 1991–2049.

of such choices. Hold-up behaviour can be divided into two types: positive hold-up and negative hold-out. Positive hold-up refers to the behaviour where the right holder takes advantage of the implementer, while negative hold-out refers to the behaviour where the implementer takes advantage of the right holder. Although hold-up behaviours also occur in copyright law, it is generally more common in the patent field, which is related to its underlying causes. This section will discuss the formation and impact of both hold-up and hold-out behaviours, primarily within the context of patents.

There is no unified definition of hold-up behaviours. According to past academic research, hold-up can be divided into two categories: broad hold-up and narrow hold-up. Broad hold-up refers to the pricing behaviour of a right holder where he/she sets a price above their marginal contribution rate.[104] Narrow hold-up refers to the behaviour where the right holder forces the implementer to pay an ex post license fee which is higher than the previously determined amount.[105]

Discussions over hold-up behaviour are generally based on network effects. Network effects, also known as network externalities, refer to the phenomenon where a user's valuation of a product depends on the total number of users of that product.[106] The more users there are, the higher the valuation of the product by each individual user.[107] It can be considered that 'under the same conditions, it is better to be

[104] For example, Yi Jiming and Hu Xiaowei argue that patent hold-up refers to the behaviour in which the patent holder forces the implementer to accept unreasonable licensing fees or licensing terms, see Yi. J. & Hu, X. (2021). 'Biaozhun biyao zhuanli shishi zhong de jingzheng zhengce—— 'Zhuanli jiechi' Yu 'Fanxiang jiechi' de sifa hengliang'['Competition policy in the implementation of standard-essential patents: judicial measurement of patent 'hold-up' and 'hold-out'']. *Shaanxi Shifan Daxue Xuebao (Zhexue Shehui Kexue Ban) [Journal of Shaanxi Normal University (Philosophy and Social Sciences Edition)]*, 2. 84. Ding Maozhong defines patent hold-up as the phenomenon where the rights holder forces the collection of a license fee higher than the reasonable amount, see Ding, M. (2016). 'Lun zhuanli gaojia xuke de fanlongduan guizhi' ['On the antitrust regulation of high patent licensing fees'], *Zhishi Chanquan[Intellectual Property]*, 3, 72. These studies all mention the term 'reasonable', which can be interpreted as meaning that the licensor's licensing fee income should be proportional to the contribution rate of their patent. According to the aforementioned reasoning, pricing above the marginal contribution rate can be considered unreasonable.

[105] Farrell, J., et al. (2007). 'Standard setting, patents, and hold-up'. *Antitrust Law Journal*, 74(3), 608–610. Farrell, et al. (2007). 'Standard setting, patents, and hold-up'. *Antitrust Law Journal*, 74(3), 603. 608–610. Cotter, T.F., Hovenkamp, E., Siebrasse, N. (2019). 'Demystifying patent holdup'. *Washington & Lee Law Review*, 76(4), 1501. Luo, J., (2015). 'Lun biaozhun biyao zhuanli susong de 'Gongping, heli, wu qishi' Xuke——Neihan, feilv yu shiyong'['On the 'fair, reasonable, and non-discriminatory' licensing in standard essential patent litigation—Connotation, rate, and application']. *Faxuejia [The Jurist]*, 3, 86.

[106] Shapiro, C. & Varian, H.R. (1999). *Information rules: a strategic guide to the network economy*, Harvard Business School Press.13. Belleflamme, P. & Peitz, M. (2014). *Chanye zuzhi: Shichang he celue [Industrial organization: Markets and strategies]* (Chen, H., Xu, L. et al.trans.). Gezhi Chubanshe, Sanlian Shudian, Shanghai Renmin Chubanshe [Gezhi Publishing House, Sanlian Bookstore, Shanghai People's Publishing House]. 477.

[107] Some scholars have defined network effects in the form of increasing functions.

connected to a larger network'.[108] Network effects can be divided into direct network effects and indirect network effects. Direct network effects refer to the utility that users derive directly from the number of other users, while in indirect network effects, users do not care about how many other users there are on the network, but do care about the functions provided by the network. Direct network effects are commonly found in network markets, such as *Weibo*, *WeChat*, and *Dianping*, where the more users on the network, the higher the utility obtained by each user. Indirect network effects are more common in system markets for complementary goods, such as the Apple iOS system and software available in its app store, or the Android system and the software available in its app store. In these system markets, users do not care about the number of other users, rather about the quantity of softwares available on the Apple or Android systems. Network effects are often accompanied by switching costs,[109] which consequently create lock-in effects,[110] making it more difficult for implementers to switch.

Some scholars argue that hold-up behaviour is based on sunk costs.[111] Cotter points out that it is precisely because of the existence of sunk costs that the right holder can 'ambush' the implementer to obtain higher licensing fees.[112] Siebrasse and Cotter advocate for distinguishing between transfer costs and sunk costs. They argue that transfer costs are future costs, while sunk costs are costs that have already been incurred. Therefore, the influence of transfer costs on hold-up behaviour is minimal, and attention should instead be placed on sunk costs and opportunity costs.[113] However, other scholars believe that sunk costs are positively correlated with switching costs, as the investment in sunk costs increases the future switching costs.[114] Although some scholars argue that sunk costs have no impact on choices or

---

[108] Belleflamme, P. & Peitz, M. (2014). *Chanye zuzhi: Shichang he celue* [*Industrial organization: Markets and strategies*] (Chen, H., Xu, L. et al.trans.). Gezhi Chubanshe, Sanlian Shudian, Shanghai Renmin Chubanshe [Gezhi Publishing House, Sanlian Bookstore, Shanghai People's Publishing House]. 477.

[109] Some scholars have further examined the relationship between switching costs and network effects, pointing out that direct network effect is a cause of increased switching costs, while indirect network effect is indeed a result of the switching costs. Belleflamme, P. & Peitz, M. (2014). *Chanye zuzhi: Shichang he celue* [*Industrial organization: Markets and strategies*] (Chen, H., Xu, L. et al.trans.). Gezhi Chubanshe, Sanlian Shudian, Shanghai Renmin Chubanshe [Gezhi Publishing House, Sanlian Bookstore, Shanghai People's Publishing House]. 479. However, whether it is direct or indirect network effect, switching costs are always present.

[110] Shapiro, C. & Varian, H. R. (1999). *Information rules: A strategic guide to the network economy*. Harvard Business School Press.11.

[111] See e.g. Farrell, J., Hayes, J., Shapiro, C. & Sullivan, T. (2007). 'Standard setting, patents, and hold-up'. *Antitrust Law Journal*, 74(3), 604.

[112] Cotter, T.F., (2009). 'Patent holdup, patent remedies, and antitrust responses'. *Journal of Corporation Law*, 34(4), 1151–1208.

[113] Siebrasse, N.V. & Cotter, T.F., (2015). 'Why switching costs are irrelevant to patent holdup'. *Comparative Patent Remedies*, 24 September. Available at: http://comparativepatentremedies.blogspot.com/2015/09/why-switching-costs-are-irrelevant-to_24.html, accessed on 30 July 2022.

[114] Gilbert, R. (2011). 'Deal or no deal? Licensing negotiations by standard setting organization'. *Antitrust Law Journal*, 77(3), 862.

decisions,[115] from a behavioural choice perspective, it seems that sunk costs always influence decision-making.[116]

In addition, another issue that is often considered in hold-up situations is the apportionment problem. Apportionment occurs primarily in patent hold-up cases, where the contribution of an individual patent to an implementer's product may be low when the product incorporates multiple patents. However, if each patent holder threatens with injunctions or litigation, they can all demand higher licensing fees.[117] Compared to the first two types of hold-ups, the apportionment problem resembles the issue of collective hold-up. Some scholars believe this is caused by externalities, as each patent holder, by increasing the price of their respective components, imposes an externality on other patent holders, resulting in the patent royalty being charged higher than the effective patent royalty.[118]

Compared to patent hold-up, the issue of hold-out has also garnered significant attention. Hold-up and hold-out are relative concepts, and discussions of hold-up are insufficient without considering the issue of hold-out at the same time.[119] There is no unified definition of hold-out itself. Miceli and Segerson argued that hold-out is related to factors such as high transaction costs, imperfect information, and unequal bargaining power etc.[120] Menezes and Pitchford explained hold-out as an act of delaying negotiations.[121] Cadigan et al. defined hold-out as strategically delaying negotiations to obtain a higher surplus.[122] Collins and Isaac, based on previous studies, suggested that hold-out manifests in at least three ways: unequal surplus distribution, costly negotiation delays, and failure to complete an effective transaction.[123] All the above arguments are reasonable, and combining them, hold-out can be understood as the behaviour of the implementer using the systematic rules to obtain a lower licensing fee by refusing to pay or delaying negotiations.

---

[115] See e.g. Frank, R.H. & Bernanke, B.S. (2009). *Principles of Microeconomics* (4th ed.). McGraw-Hill, 11. Mankiw, N.G. (2009). *Principles of microeconomics* (5th ed.). Thomson South-Western. 297.

[116] Friedman, D. et al., (2007). 'Searching for the sunk cost fallacy'. *Experimental Economics*, 10(1), 79–104. Kanodia, C. et al. (1989). 'Escalation errors and the sunk cost effect: An explanation based on reputation and information asymmetries'. *Journal of Accounting Research*, 27(1), 59–77.

[117] Lemley, M.A. & Shapiro, C. (2007). 'Patent holdup and royalty stacking'. *Texas Law Review*, 85(7), 1991–2049.

[118] Boldrin, M. & Levine, D.K. (2013). 'The case against patents'. *Journal of Economic Perspectives*, 27(1), 8.

[119] Chien, C.V. (2014). 'Holding up and holding out'. *Michigan Telecommunications & Technology Law Review*, 21(1), 1.

[120] Miceli, T.J. & Segerson, K. (2012). 'Land assembly and the holdout problem under sequential bargaining'. *American Law & Economics Review*, 14(2), 373.

[121] Menezes, F. & Pitchford, R. (2004). 'A model of seller holdout'. *Economic Theory*, 24(2), 231–253.

[122] Cadigan, J. et al. (2009). 'An experimental study of the holdout problem in a multilateral bargaining game'. *Southern Economic Journal*, 76(2), 444.

[123] Collins, S.M. & Isaac, R.M., (2012). 'Holdout: existence, information, and contingent contracting'. *Journal of Law & Economics*, 55(4), 794.

Similar to hold-up behaviour, hold-out essentially leverages the costs incurred by the right holderin creating the invention to seize the rights holder. The way right holders recover these costs is either by using the intellectual property themselves or by collecting licensing fees. In cases where the right holder does not use the intellectual property, licensing income may be their only source of revenue. Faced with the pressure of litigation costs, the right holder is highly likely to compromise and agree to a lower price proposed by the implementer.[124] The motivation for hold-out arises from the insufficiency of legal remedies. In short, if the implementer is not made worse off by hold-out, they will be motivated to engage in it. In reality, hold-out is more likely to occur in standard-essential patents (SEPs), because it is always harder to obtain injunctions or punitive damages for SEPs, so implementers typically face no punishment for hold-outs in such circumstances.

From a risk perspective, hold-out can essentially be seen as a form of risk-shifting behaviour by the implementer. When the implementer pre-pays for the patent, the right holder can recover the costs they invested in patent development in advance. However, when the implementer delays payment, the right holder not only fails to recover their investment in research and development but also bears the risk of the implementer's business failure. If the implementer ultimately fails in their business, the right holder may never recover their licensing fees.

In fact, the hold-out behaviour of a single implementer may not be particularly troublesome, but once an implementer profits from hold-out behaviour, it is inevitable that more implementers will follow suit. When most of the implementers engage in hold-out, the income of licensing fee of right holders will no longer be secured, which undoubtedly affects the R&D incentives of other right holders within the industry. For this reason, Delarhaim argues that the impact of hold-out is more severe than that of hold-up.[125] Galasso and Schankeman also approach the issue from the perspective of patent disputes and settlements, explaining the need of speed for settlement and resolution of the right holders.[126] This indirectly proves that hold-out can have a negative impact on right holders, thereby leading to a reduction in their R&D incentives.

---

[124] Hold-out is a typical form of opportunism, similar to the speculative behavior of patent hold-up. See Merges, R.P., & Kuhn, J.M. (2009). 'An estoppel doctrine for patented standards'. *California Law Review*, 97(1), 11–15. In the absence of punitive measures, the speculation of hold-out not only does not harm the implementer but also benefits the implementer.

[125] Delrahim, M. (2017). 'Take it to the limit: Respecting innovation incentives in the application of antitrust law'. Remarks at USC Gould School of Law (November 10, 2017), available at: https://www.justice.gov/opa/speech/assistantattorney-general-makan-delrahim-delivers-remarks-usc-gould-school-laws-center, accessed on Jul 30 2022.

[126] Galasso, A. & Schankerman, M. (2010). 'Patent thickets, courts, and the market for innovation'. *The RAND Journal of Economics*, 41(3), 472–503.

The resolution of hold-up and hold-out can be approached through judicial remedies. Specifically, injunctive relief can help balance hold-up and hold-out.[127] Hold-up allows a right holder to obtain a price higher than the actual contribution of their patents, while hold-out allows the implementer to evade payment, delay payment, or pay less than the actual contribution made by the patent. Hold-up and hold-out represent the extreme cases in intellectual property licensing, while reflecting two kinds of unreasonable pricing: too high (hold-up) or too low (hold-out). Therefore, resolving hold-up and hold-out issues can ensure that both parties reach an agreement at a reasonable price. However, it is not easy to address these issues as they are both influenced by judicial decisions. If judicial relief is overly generous, it can lead to hold-up; on the contrary, inadequate relief can lead to hold-out. Therefore, courts need to define clear boundaries for relief.

Based on the above analysis, it is evident that the motivation for hold-up stems from demanding high prices. When there are alternative technologies for the implementers, the pricing space leveraged by right holders in a hold-up scenario is the switching cost of the implementer. In the absence of alternative technologies, the leverage extends to the expected future profits of the implementers. Conversely, one of the motivations for hold-out arises from fee evasion, a form of opportunism wherein the implementer hopes that the right holders will not detect the infringement or, upon detection, will forgo enforcement because the cost of enforcement is higher than its benefits. Another motivation for hold-out is demanding lower prices, premised on court-determined rates being lower than those established through market negotiations. Thus, injunctive relief is particularly effective in incentivizing implementers to negotiate. Regardless of the reason why implementers engage in hold-out, injunctive relief can effectively curb it. However, injunctive relief cannot inherently encourage right holders to carry out negotiations. Therefore, the effective use of injunctive relief to incentivize negotiations relies on the strong willingness of right holders to license.

Although injunctive relief will inevitably enhance the bargaining power of right holders, and consequently enable them to engage in hold-up behaviours, the extent of such an increase of power is limited. The licensing revenue of the right holder is based on the actual sales volume of the implementer,[128] meaning that sales loss suffered by the implementer due to an injunction will also affect the licensing income of the right holder. Consequently, the right holder has a certain incentive to minimize the sales loss of the implementer so as to secure higher licensing fees. Moreover, the impact of preliminary and permanent injunctions on negotiation willingness differs. For firms

[127] Hold-up reflects the rights holderss strong bargaining power, while hold-out reflects the implementer's strong bargaining power. Therefore, injunction relief can also be seen as a mechanism for balancing the bargaining power between the rights holder and the implementer.

[128] The rights holder may opt for a 'one-price' system, where the patent fee remains fixed regardless of how many products the rights holder produces. Alternatively, there could be a tiered payment structure, where the rights holder establishes different production and sales quantity thresholds, with varying fees for each tier. Another possibility is a per-unit fee, where the cost of using the patent is determined by multiplying a fixed rate by the actual sales volume, with the total royalty calculated accordingly. In the latter two scenarios, the rights holder's royalties are both linked to the implementer's sales volume.

with products or technologies characterized by longer life cycles, only permanent injunctions possess sufficient influence to incentivize negotiations. In contrast, for firms with shorter product or technology life cycles, both preliminary and permanent injunctions can effectively stimulate negotiation.[129]

In the long run, if implementers, after multiple cases, come to realize that offering excessively low prices is highly likely to result in injunctive relief granted by courts, their speculative mindset will consequently diminish. To avoid the loss of expected profits or the payment of switching costs, implementers will proactively reach out to right holders for negotiations from the outset, thereby engaging in pre-emptive negotiations.

4.5 Summary of This Chapter

Contract are the guarantees of intellectual property transactions, and contract theory explains various issues that may arise in intellectual property transactions. Its purpose is to facilitate the completion of the final transaction between the parties. Studies of contract theory not only help us to better understand the original intent behind the establishment of a system but also enable us to recognize which remedy is most conducive to intellectual property transactions when facing difficult issues in judicial practice. Although the intellectual property transaction system contains numerous principles of contract theory, contract theory cannot explain all the issues in intellectual property transactions. Rather, it can only assist us in analysing the root causes that hinder transactions, the conflicts of interest between parties during the contracting process, as well as their corresponding solutions. Nevertheless, it cannot explain another core issue in intellectual property transactions—the price.

References

Aghion, P., Dewatripont, M., & Rey, P. (1994). Renegotiation design with unverifiable information. *Econometrica, 62*(2), 257–282.

Arrow, K. J. (1951). *Social choice and individual values* (2nd ed.). Yale University Press.

Arrow, K. J. (1970). *Essays in the theory of risk-bearing*. North-Holland.

Arrow, K. J. (1963). Uncertainty and the welfare economics of medical care. *The American Economic Review, 53*(5), 941–973.

[129] Of course, in most countries, when granting injunctive relief, the issue of incentivizing negotiations is not usually considered. Instead, the focus is more on whether granting an injunction would harm the public interest and whether the absence of such relief would cause the rights holder irreparable harm. The author does not argue that injunctive relief should ignore these factors, but rather suggests a different perspective—understanding injunctive relief from the angle of incentivizing transactions.

Arrow, K. J. (1969). The organization of economic activity: Issues pertinent to the choice of market versus nonmarket allocation. In *The analysis and evaluation of public expenditure: The PPB system*. US Joint Economic Committee.

Babbage, C. (1835). *On the economy of machinery and manufactures*. Charles Knight.

Barnard, C. (1938). *The functions of the executive*. Harvard University Press.

Baron, D. P., & Myerson, R. B. (1982). Regulating a monopolist with unknown costs. *Econometrica, 50*(4), 911–930.

Beard, T. R., & Ekelund, R. B., Jr. (1991). Quality choice and price discrimination: A note on Dupuit's conjecture. *Southern Economic Journal, 57*(4), 1155.

Belleflamme, P., & Peitz, M. (2014). *Chanye zuzhi: Shichang he celue* [*Industrial organization: Markets and strategies*] (H. Chen, L. Xu, et al., Trans.). Gezhi Chubanshe, Sanlian Shudian, Shanghai Renmin Chubanshe [Gezhi Publishing House, Sanlian Bookstore, Shanghai People's Publishing House].

Bentham, J. (1843). A manual of political economy. In *McMaster University archive for the history of economic thought*.

Boldrin, M., & Levine, D. K. (2013). The case against patents. *Journal of Economic Perspectives, 27*(1), 8.

Bowen, H. R. (1943). The interpretation of voting in the allocation of economic resources. *The Quarterly Journal of Economics, 58*(1), 27–48.

Brousseau, E., & Glachant, J. M. (2002). *The economics of contracts: Theories and applications*. Cambridge University Press.

Busneli, F., et al. (2005). *Principles of European Tort Law: Text and commentary*. Springer.

Cadigan, J., et al. (2009). An experimental study of the holdout problem in a multilateral bargaining game. *Southern Economic Journal, 76*(2), 444.

Cheng, X., & Wang, D. (2013). Sunhai peichang de fangfa [Methods of damage compensation]. *Faxue Yanjiu [Legal Studies], 3*, 55.

Chien, C. V. (2014). Holding up and holding out. *Michigan Telecommunications & Technology Law Review, 21*(1), 1.

Chiu, Y. S. (1998). Noncooperative bargaining, hostages, and optimal asset ownership. *The American Economic Review, 88*(4), 882–901.

Chu, A. C. (2007). Optimal patent breadth: Quantifying the effects of increasing patent breadth. MPRA paper 3910. https://mpra.ub.uni-muenchen.de/id/eprint/3910. Accessed 30 July 2022.

Coase, R. H. (1937). The nature of the firm. *Economica, 4*(16), 386–405.

Coase, R. H. (1988). The nature of the firm: Origin. *Journal of Law, Economics, & Organization, 4*(1), 3–17.

Collins, S. M., & Isaac, R. M. (2012). Holdout: Existence, information, and contingent contracting. *Journal of Law & Economics, 55*(4), 794.

Conner, K. R. (1991). A historical comparison of resource-based theory and five schools of thought within industrial organization economics: Do we have a new theory of the firm? *Journal of Management, 17*(1), 121–154.

Cotter, T. F. (2009). Patent holdup, patent remedies, and antitrust responses. *Journal of Corporation Law, 34*(4), 1151–1208.

Cotter, T. F., Hovenkamp, E., & Siebrasse, N. (2019). Demystifying patent holdup. *Washington & Lee Law Review, 76*(4), 1501.

Crawford, V. P. (1988). Long-term relationships governed by short-term contracts. *The American Economic Review, 8*(3), 485–499.

Crowe, J. (2012). Clarifying the natural law thesis. *Australian Journal of Legal Philosophy, 37*(8), 159–181.

Dahlman, C. J. (1979). The problem of externality. *Journal of Law & Economics, 22*(1), 141–162.

Dasgupta, P., Hammond, P., & Maskin, E. (1980). On imperfect information and optimal pollution control. *The Review of Economic Studies, 47*(5), 857–860.

De Meza, D., & Lockwood, B. (1988). Does asset ownership always motivate managers? Outside options and the property rights theory of the firm. *The Quarterly Journal of Economics, 113*(2), 361–386.

Delrahim, M. (2017, November 10). *Take it to the limit: Respecting innovation incentives in the application of antitrust law*. Remarks at USC Gould School of Law. https://www.justice.gov/opa/speech/assistantattorney-general-makan-delrahim-delivers-remarks-usc-gould-school-laws-center. Accessed on 30 July 2022.

Ding, M. (2016). Lun zhuanli gaojia xuke de fanlongduan guizhi [On the antitrust regulation of high patent licensing fees]. *Zhishi Chanquan [Intellectual Property], 3*, 72.

Edgeworth, F. Y. (1912). Contributions to the theory of railway rates. *The Economic Journal, 22*(86), 198–218.

Farquharson, R. (1969). *Theory of voting*. Yale University Press.

Farrell, J., Hayes, J., Shapiro, C., & Sullivan, T. (2007). Standard setting, patents, and hold-up. *Antitrust Law Journal, 74*(3), 603–670.

Frank, R. H., & Bernanke, B. S. (2009). *Principles of microeconomics* (4th ed., p. 11). McGraw-Hill.

Friedman, D., et al., (2007). Searching for the sunk cost fallacy. *Experimental Economics, 10*(1), 79–104.

Frumkin, M. (1945). The origin of patents. *Journal of the Patent Office Society, 27*(3), 143.

Gabor, A. (1955). A note on block tariffs. *The Review of Economic Studies, 23*(1), 32–41.

Galasso, A., & Schankerman, M. (2010). Patent thickets, courts, and the market for innovation. *The RAND Journal of Economics, 41*(3), 472–503.

Gallini, N. T. (2002). The economics of patents: Lessons from recent U.S. patent reform. *Journal of Economic Perspectives, 16*(2), 131–154.

Gibbard, A. (1973). Manipulation of voting schemes: A general result. *Econometrica, 41*(4), 587–601.

Gilbert, R. (2011). Deal or no deal? Licensing negotiations by standard setting organization. *Antitrust Law Journal, 77*(3), 862.

Gilbert, R., & Shapiro, C. (1990). Optimal patent length and breadth. *The RAND Journal of Economics, 21*(1), 106–112.

Green, J., & Laffont, J.-J. (1977). Characterization of satisfactory mechanisms for the revelation of preferences for public goods. *Econometrica, 45*(2), 427–438.

Grossman, S. J., & Hart, O. D. (1986). The costs and benefits of ownership: A theory of vertical and lateral integration. *Journal of Political Economy, 94*(4), 691–719.

Harsanyi, J. C. (1987). Games with incomplete information played by 'Bayesian' players. *Management Science, 14*(3), 159–182.

Hart, O., & Moore, J. (1988). Incomplete contracts and renegotiation. *Econometrica, 56*(4), 755–785.

Hart, O. D., & Moore, J. (1990). Property rights and the nature of the firm. *Journal of Political Economy, 98*(6), 1119–1158.

He, P., & Jiang, Q. (2018). Lun zhuanli qinquan sunhai peichang shu'e rending de zhengming zeren fenpei [On the allocation of the burden of proof in determining the amount of damages for patent infringement]. *Zhishi Chanquan [Intellectual Property], 7*, 48–59.

Heald, P. J. (2008). Optimal remedies for patent infringement: A transactional model. *Houston Law Review, 45*(4), 1175.

Hume, D. (1740). *A treatise of human nature*. Oxford University Press

Jaffe, A. B. (2000). The U.S. patent system in transition: Policy innovation and the innovation process. *Research Policy, 29*(4–5), 531–557.

Kanodia, C., et al. (1989). Escalation errors and the sunk cost effect: An explanation based on reputation and information asymmetries. *Journal of Accounting Research, 27*(1), 59–77.

Klein, P. G. (1998). *New institutional economics* (p. 11). https://papers.ssrn.com/sol3/papers.cfm?abstract_id=115811. Accessed 30 July 2022.

Klemperer, P. D. (1990). How broad should the scope of patent protection be. *The RAND Journal of Economics, 21*(1), 113–130.

Knight, F. H. (1921). *Risk, uncertainty and profit*. Houghton Mifflin.
La Manna, M. A. M. (1992). Optimal patent life vs. optimal patentability standards. *International Journal of Industrial Organization, 10*(1), 81–89.
Laffont, J.-J., & Tirole, J. (1986). Using cost observation to regulate firms. *Journal of Political Economy, 94*(3), 614–641.
Lemley, M. A. (2011). The ongoing confusion over ongoing royalties. *Missouri Law Review, 76*(3), 695–707.
Lemley, M. A., & Shapiro, C. (2007). Patent holdup and royalty stacking. *Texas Law Review, 85*(7), 1991–2049.
Lerner, J. (1994). The importance of patent scope: An empirical analysis. *The RAND Journal of Economics, 25*(2), 319–333.
Li, M. (2016). Zhishi chanquan qinquan lvjinbuzhi yuanyin zhiyi shi sunhai peichang de shu'e guodi [One of the reasons for the persistent infringement of intellectual property rights is the low amount of damages]. *Henan Keji [Henan Science and Technology], 8*, 6.
Li, Y., & Chen, X. (2020). Lun zhuzuoquan chengfaxing peichang zhidu jianping minfadian zhishi chanquan chengfaxing peichang tiaokuan [On the punitive damages system for copyright: A discussion on the punitive damages provisions for intellectual property in the *Civil Code*]. *Zhishi Chanquan [Intellectual Property], 8*, 34–45.
Loeb, M., & Magat, W. A. (1979). A decentralized method for utility regulation. *Journal of Law & Economics, 22*(2), 399–404.
Lü, L. (2016). Zhuanli qinquan sunhai peichang de shizheng yangjiu [Empirical study on patent infringement damage compensation]. *Dianzi Zhishi Chanquan [Electronic Intellectual Property], 11*, 19–26.
Luo, J. (2015). Lun biaozhun biyao zhuanli susong de 'Gongping, heli, wu qishi' Xuke——Neihan, feilv yu shiyong [On the 'fair, reasonable, and non-discriminatory' licensing in standard essential patent litigation—Connotation, rate, and application]. *Faxuejia [The Jurist], 3*, 86.
Machlup, F. (1959). *An economic review of the patent system*. United States Government Printing Office.
Machlup, F., & Penrose, E. (1950). The patent controversy in the nineteenth century. *The Journal of Economic History, 10*(1), 24.
Mankiw, N. G. (2009). *Principles of microeconomics* (5th ed.). Thomson South-Western.
Marschak, J., & Radner, R. (1972). *Economic theory of teams*. Yale University Press.
Menezes, F., & Pitchford, R. (2004). A model of seller holdout. *Economic Theory, 24*(2), 231–253.
Merges, R. P. (1994). Of property rules, Coase, and intellectual property. *Columbia Law Review, 94*(8), 2655–2673.
Merges, R. P., & Nelson, R. R. (1990). On the complex economics of patent scope. *Columbia Law Review, 90*(4), 868.
Merges, R. P., & Kuhn, J. M. (2009). An estoppel doctrine for patented standards. *California Law Review, 97*(1), 1.
Miceli, T. J., & Segerson, K. (2012). Land assembly and the holdout problem under sequential bargaining. *American Law & Economics Review, 14*(2), 373.
Mill, J. S. (2004). *Principles of political economy*. Hackett Publishing.
Mirrlees, J. A. (1971). An exploration in the theory of optimum income taxation. *The Review of Economic Studies, 38*(2), 175–208.
Mulligan, C., & Lee, T. B. (2012). Scaling the patent system. *NYU Annual Survey of American Law, 68*(2), 289–318.
Murphy, M. C. (2006). *Natural law in jurisprudence and politics*. Cambridge University Press.
Mussa, M., & Rosen, S. (1978). Monopoly and product quality. *Journal of Economic Theory, 18*(2), 301–317.
Nordhaus, W. D. (1969). *Invention, growth, and welfare: A theoretical treatment of technological change*. The MIT Press.
Nordhaus, W. D. (1972). The optimum life of a patent: Reply. *The American Economic Review, 62*(3), 428–431.

O'Donoghue, T., Scotchmer, S., & Thisse, J.-F. (1998). Patent breadth, patent life, and the pace of technological progress. *Journal of Economics and Management Strategy, 7*(1), 1–32.

Ogus, A. I., & Richardson, G. M. (1977). Economics and the environment: A study of private nuisance. *Cambridge Law Journal, 36*(2), 284–325.

Palokangas, T. (2011). Optimal patent length and breadth in an economy with creative destruction and non-diversifiable risk. *Journal of Economics, 102*(1), 1–27.

Pauly, M. V. (1968). The economics of moral hazard. *The American Economic Review, 58*(3), 531–537.

Pigou, A. C. (1920). *The economics of welfare*. McMillan.

Rothkopf, M. H. (1969). A model of rational competitive bidding. *Management Science, 15*(7), 362–373.

Santos, F. M., & Eisenhardt, K. M. (2005). Organizational boundaries and theories of organization. *Organization Science, 16*(5), 491–508.

Satterthwaite, M. A. (1975). Strategy-proofness and arrow's conditions: Existence and correspondence theorems for voting procedures and social welfare functions. *Journal of Economic Theory., 10*(2), 187–217.

Scherer, F. M. (1972). 'Nordhaus' theory of optimal patent life: A geometric reinterpretation. *The American Economic Review, 62*(3), 422–427.

Schoenhard, P. M. (2008). Who took my IP—Defending the availability of injunctive relief for patent owners. *Texas Intellectual Property Law Journal, 16*(2), 289.

Shapiro, C., & Stiglitz, J. E. (1984). Equilibrium unemployment as a worker discipline device. *American Economic Review, 74*(3), 433–444.

Shapiro, C., & Varian, H. R. (1999). *Information rules: A strategic guide to the network economy*. Harvard Business School Press.

Sidak, J. G. (2016). Ongoing royalties for patent infringement. *Texas Intellectual Property Law Journal, 24*(2), 161–214.

Sidgwick, H. (1883). *The principles of political economy*. MacMillan.

Siebrasse, N. V., & Cotter, T. F. (2015, September 24). Why switching costs are irrelevant to patent holdup. *Comparative Patent Remedies*. http://comparativepatentremedies.blogspot.com/2015/09/why-switching-costs-are-irrelevant-to_24.html. Accessed on 30 July 2022.

Silvestre, J. (2003). Wicksell, Lindahl and the theory of public goods. *The Scandinavian Journal of Economics, 105*(4), 527–553.

Smith, A. (1776). *The wealth of nations*. The Modern Library.

Smith, A. (1901). *An inquiry into the nature and causes of the wealth of nations*. Dent.

Spence, M. (1973). Job market signalling. *Quarterly Journal of Economics, 87*(3), 355–374.

Spence, M. (1977). Nonlinear prices and welfare. *Journal of Public Economics, 8*(1), 1–18.

Spence, M., & Zeckhauser, R. (1971). Insurance, information, and individual action. *The American Economic Review, 61*(2), 380–387.

Standing Committee of the National People's Congress. (2014, June 23). Guanyu jiancha zhonghua renmin gongheguo zhuanlifa shishi qingkuang de baogao [Report on the inspection of the implementation of the *Patent Law of the People's Republic of China*]. http://www.npc.gov.cn/npc/c12491/201406/1fa592eaddef4bd190bfaf2df40d8f74.shtml. Accessed 10 January 2022.

Sterk, S. E. (2008). Property rules, liability rules, and uncertainty about property rights. *Michigan Law Review, 106*(7), 1304.

Stiglitz, J. E., & Weiss, A. (1981). Credit rationing in markets with imperfect information. *American Economic Review, 71*(3), 393–410.

Tirole, J. (1999). Incomplete contracts: Where do we stand? *Econometrica, 67*(4), 741–781.

Tromans, S. (1982). Nuisance—Prevention or payment? *Cambridge Law Journal, 41*(1), 87–109.

Vickrey, W. (1960). Utility, strategy, and social decision rules. *The Quarterly Journal of Economics, 74*(4), 507–535.

Vickrey, W. (1961). Counter speculation, auctions, and competitive sealed tenders. *Journal of Finance, 16*(1), 8–37.

Wang, L. (1993). *Minfa:Qinquan Xingwei Fa [Civil Law: Tort Law].* Zhongguo Renmin Daxue Chubanshe [China Renmin University Press].

Wang, L. (2010). *Qinquan zerenfa yanjiu [Research on Tort Liability Law (Vol. 1)]* (2nd ed.). Zhongguo Renmin Daxue Chubanshe [China Renmin University Press].

Williamson, O. E. (1979). Transaction-cost economics: The governance of contractual relations. *Journal of Law & Economics, 22*(2), 233–261.

Williamson, O. E. (1975). *Markets and hierarchies: Analysis and antitrust implications, a study in the economics of internal organization.* The Free Press.

Williamson, O. E. (1981). The economics of organization: The transaction cost approach. *American Journal of Sociology, 87*(3), 548–577.

Williamson, O. E. (1985). *The economic institutions of capitalism, firms, markets, relational contracting.* The Free Press.

Williamson, O. E. (1991). Comparative economic organization: The analysis of discrete structural alternatives. *Administrative science quarterly, 36*(2), 269–296.

Williamson, O. E. (2000). The new institutional economics: Taking stock, looking ahead. *Journal of Economic Literature, 38*(3), 595–597.

Wilson, R. B. (1969). Competitive bidding with disparate information. *Management Science, 15*(7), 446–448.

Wilson, R. B. (1977). A bidding model of perfect competition. *The Review of Economic Studies, 44*(3), 511–518.

Wu, H. (2014). Zhishi chanquan qinquan sunhai peichang zhong de juzheng zeren daozhi [Burden of proof reversal in intellectual property infringement damage compensation]. *Zhongguo Shenpan [China Trial], 5*, 14.

Yang, L. (2010). *Qinquan Sunhai Peichang [Tort Damage Compensation].* Falv Chubanshe [Law Press].

Yi, J., & Hu, X. (2021). Biaozhun biyao zhuanli shishi zhong de jingzheng zhengce——'Zhuanli jiechi' Yu 'Fanxiang jiechi' de sifa hengliang [Competition policy in the implementation of standard-essential patents: judicial measurement of patent 'hold-up' and 'hold-out']. *Shaanxi Shifan Daxue Xuebao (Zhexue Shehui Kexue Ban) [Journal of Shaanxi Normal University (Philosophy and Social Sciences Edition)], 2*, 84.

Yin, X. (2011). *Zhongguo zhuanlifa xiangjie [Detailed explanation of Chinese patent law].* Zhishi Chanquan Chubanshe [Intellectual Property Publishing House].

Zhan, Y., & Zhang, H. (2015). Woguo zhishi chanquan qinquan sifa panli shizheng yanjiu yi weiquan chengben he qinquan daijia wei zhongxin [An empirical study of intellectual property infringement judicial cases in China: Focusing on enforcement costs and infringement costs]. *Keyan Guanli [Science Research Management], 7*, 150.

Chapter 5
Price Theory in Intellectual Property Transactions

5.1 Development and Framework of Price Theory

The facilitation of price theory in intellectual property transaction is primarily manifested in the process of. Price is an indispensable component of intellectual property transactions, reflecting a relationship realized by the exchange goods. Determining the price is the key to concluding a transaction, yet it is often the most challenging aspect of transactions. In intellectual property licensing, the licensee needs to communicate with the right holder to obtain the right for authorized use, but this communication is not always smooth. Intellectual property, as a gateway to certain fields or as a critical element for improving efficiency, is of immense importance. Right holders often expect to collect higher licensing fees based on their intellectual property, conversely, licensees typically aim to pay lower fees to reduce production and operational costs. When these conflicting interests cannot be resolved, disputes arise. Price theory is a theoretical study targeting most directly to pricing issues. It not only reveals the formation process and fluctuation patterns of prices but also systematically summarizes the impact that price produces. By studying price theory, we gain a deeper understanding of the process of price formation in intellectual property transactions, and are better equipped to deal with judicial pricing issues. This chapter will first outline the basic framework of price theory and then discuss its specific application in intellectual property transactions.

Price theory serves as a crucial tool in facilitating intellectual property transactions. On one hand, it helps in understanding the negotiation process between right holders and implementers; on the other, it provides a foundation for judicial pricing. Price theory can be categorized specifically into three subfields: perfect competition price theory, monopolistic price theory, and monopolistic competition price theory. Among these, perfect competition price theory is the most significant, and this section will focus primarily on its application. Yet, this section does not aim to exhaustively explore all methodologies within price theory but will emphasize only the issues relevant to intellectual property transactions. Given that price theory spans multiple

© Intellectual Property Publishing House Co., Ltd. 2025

M. Yang, *Basic Theories of Intellectual Property Transaction*,
https://doi.org/10.1007/978-981-96-7039-0_5

schools of thought, this section will first provide an overview of the background and current framework of price theory, and further discuss demand theory and equilibrium theory within this framework. Finally, a brief discussion on pricing in monopoly market as well as monopolistic competition market will be included.

5.1.1 History and Significance of Price Theory

Price theory serves as an indispensable methodological foundation in intellectual property transactions. From the perspective of schools of thought, early price theory can be divided into four main schools: the school of labour theory of value, the school of marginal utility theory, the equilibrium price school, and the Sraffa price school.

Adam Smith, representing the school of labour theory of value, attributed the increase in wealth and income to labour input and regarded labour as the foundation of price formation.[1] Ricardo further refined the labour theory of value based on the work of Smith.[2] The school of labour theory of value views the cost of producing goods as the basis for price. In contrast, the marginal utility school rejects this view, asserting that marginal utility determines the price of goods.[3]

The Sraffa price school examines price from the perspective of the relationship between inputs and outputs, as well as labour-capital distribution.[4] Scholars have noted that the Sraffa price school focuses on 'the calculation for the exact value of a production price which is based on specific forms of the exchange value or direct basis of price'.[5] The equilibrium price school, represented by Alfred Marshall, advocates using the equilibrium price formed by the supply and demand of products to assess value.[6] The equilibrium price school remains the dominant school today, with its theories widely applied in microeconomics[7] and adopted by subsequent Chicago School of price theory.[8]

In fact, the aforementioned four schools of thought on price theory differ significantly from the modern price theory as we know. Strictly speaking, the former sounds

---

[1] Smith, A. (1901). *An inquiry into the nature and causes of the wealth of nations*. J.M. Dent. 41.

[2] Ricardo, D. (2001). *On the principles of political economy and taxation*. Batoche Books.

[3] Jevons, W. S. (2013). *The theory of political economy*. Palgrave Macmillan; Menger, C. (2007). *Principles of economics*. Ludwig von Mises Institute.

[4] Sraffa, P. (1960). *Production of commodities by means of commodities: Prelude to critique of economic theory*. Cambridge University Press.

[5] Bai, B. & Bai, R. (2011). 'Silafa jiage tixi fenxi'['*Sraffa price system analysis*']. Dangdai Jingji Yanjiu [*Contemporary Economic Research*], 1, 9–17.

[6] Marshall, A. (2013). *Principles of economics* (8th ed.). Palgrave Macmillan.

[7] Mas-Colell, A., Whinston, M.D., & Green, J.R. (1995). *Microeconomic theory*. Oxford University Press. 733; Frank, R.H. & Bernanke, B., (2009). *Principles of microeconomics* (4th ed.). McGraw-Hill. 11; Jiang, D. (2017). Gaoji weiguan jingjixue [*Advanced microeconomics*] (2nd ed.).Beijing Daxue Chubanshe [Peking University Press].

[8] Friedman, D. D. (1990). *Price theory: An intermediate text*. Cincinnati. South-Western Publishing Co.; Jaffe, S. et al. (2019). *Chicago price theory*. Princeton University Press.

more like 'value theory' than price theory, or put it another way, the former did not distinctly separate value theory from price theory in research. Following the equilibrium price school, the focus of economics shifted to understanding how market processes determine the efficient allocation of scarce resources. This emphasis on allocating sales volume led economists to pay close attention to the role of competition. With further research into market competition, the modern conception of price theory emerged, and the term 'price theory' came to specifically refer to the mechanisms for determining prices of goods. The early usage of the term 'price theory' largely aimed at distinguishing it from traditional value theory, highlighting the increasing attention of economists on the mechanisms of price formation and fluctuation pattern.[9] However, this distinction also reveals a prominent feature of price theory: its recognition of various types of competition that influence price determination, coupled with its focus on factors specific to different market competition types.

In the process of refining price theory, economists have demonstrated their diverse approaches. Scholars like Hotelling and Samuelson introduced a large number of mathematical tools into economics, further enriching Marshall's theories.[10] On the other hand, Friedman placed greater emphasis on Marshall's traditional theory, integrating theoretical analysis of economics with practical applications. This approach laid the foundation for the Chicago price theory[11] while broadened the scope of the theory as a whole.[12]

It can be said that today, the Chicago price theory not only studies the formation of prices but also examines the impact of prices. Price theory is an economic analytical tool[13] that not only describes the pricing behaviour of individuals but also analyses the effects of pricing behaviour on issues such as welfare and optimization.[14] As Hammond aptly put it: "Price theory is a tool to solve problems rather than a set of problems to be solved".[15]

Price theory is intended to explain the behaviours of both buyers and sellers, analysing the price of intellectual property from both the supply and demand sides.

---

[9] Stigler, G. J. & Boulding, K. E. (1952). *Readings in price theory*. Association by R.D. Irwin; Bain, J. S. (1972). *Essays on price theory and industrial organization*. Little, Brown.

[10] Hotelling, H. (1931). 'The economics of exhaustible resources'. *Journal of Political Economy*, 39(2), 137–175; Samuelson, P. A. (1947). *The foundations of economic analysis*. Harvard University Press; Hicks, J. R. (1939). *Value and capital*. Oxford University Press; Arrow, K. J., & Debreu, G. (1954). 'Existence of an equilibrium for a competitive economy', *Econometrica*, 22(3), 265–290; Debreu, G. (1959). *The theory of value*. J. Wiley and Sons.

[11] Becker, G. S. (1991). 'Milton Friedman', in E. Shils (ed.), *Remembering the University of Chicago: Teachers, Scientists, and Scholars*, University of Chicago Press. 142.

[12] Snowdon, B. & Vane, H. R. (1998). 'Transforming macroeconomics: An interview with Robert E. Lucas Jr.'. *Journal of Economic Methodology*, 5(1), 120–121.

[13] Weyl, E. G. (2014). A Short Summary of Price Theory as commissioned by the *Journal of Economic Literature*, p. 3. Available at: https://hope.econ.duke.edu/sites/hope.econ.duke.edu/files/Price_Theory_Summary_6_14.pdf, accessed on 30 Jul. 2022.

[14] Ibid., 5.

[15] Hammond, D. J. (2010). 'The development of post-war Chicago price theory', in Emmett, R. B. (ed.), *The Elgar Companion to the Chicago School of Economics*, Edward Elgar Publishing. 6.

Supply and demand can determine the equilibrium price, so price theory can also be seen as the process of exploring prices on the basis of equilibrium. Therefore, the framework of price theory mainly includes demand theory and equilibrium theory, with equilibrium theory covering the supply issue. On this ground, the subsequent research framework in this section follows the same logic: we will first start from the perspective of the demand the implementers, and then introduce the pricing behaviour of the right holders to study the market equilibrium problem.

Before the formal discussion, it is necessary to distinguish between supply and supply quantity to avoid unnecessary confusion during the discussion. In simple terms, changes in price do not affect the supply of products by firms, but they do affect the quantity of supply. Similarly, there is a difference between demand and demand quantity; changes in price do not affect people's demand for a product, but they do affect the quantity of demand.

5.1.2 Demand Theory

Demand theory describes the impact of changes in consumer demand on market prices, reflecting the relationship between consumer demand and market prices. The demand for a product at a certain price reflects the expected satisfaction of consumers from consuming that product, referred to as utility. Utility varies among consumers, and the demand for a product or service depends on two factors: (1) the utility derived from satisfying the demand; and (2) the ability of consumers to pay for the product or service. Under given conditions, consumers can maximize their benefit in two ways: first, by maximizing utility under a fixed budget; second, by minimizing costs for a given level of utility. We will begin by examining the first situation.

5.1.2.1 Utility Maximization

The concept of utility maximization was first proposed by Bentham and Stuart Mill.[16] Utility maximization is a core component of consumer theory, which explores how consumers allocate their wealth within a given budget. The theory of utility maximization is based on the assumption of rational consumers, because consumers are rational, they would seek to achieve the highest possible utility with their limited budget.[17] In traditional utility maximization theory, consumers would spend their entire income to make the marginal utility of each good purchased equalling to its

[16] Welch, C. (1987). *Utilitarianism.* The Macmillan Press Limited. 772; Mill, J. S. (1836). 'Essay on the definition of political economy', in Robson, J. M. (ed.), *The Collected Works of John Stuart Mill*, Vol. 4, University of Toronto Press. 321–322.

[17] Stigler explained the three attributes of rational consumers. (See Stigler, G. (1987). *The theory of price.* Macmillan Publishing Company, 52).

price. However, this theory fails to explain the paradox of value.[18] Consequently, economists attempted to introduce the concept of marginal utility.[19] Utility can be further divided into total utility and marginal utility. Total utility refers to the overall satisfaction derived from the consumption of a good or service, while marginal utility refers to the additional satisfaction gained from consuming an additional unit of a good or service.

The law of diminishing marginal utility is consistent with demand theory. If consumers experience diminishing marginal utility as they consume more of a good, they will only continue to purchase the good when its price is lower. In other words, consumers will only be willing to purchase an additional unit of a good when its price falls, as the additional unit provides less satisfaction than the previous unit consumed. The law of diminishing marginal utility also seems to align with the price elasticity of demand, as the price elasticity of demand decreases along a linear demand curve.

The law of diminishing marginal utility tells us how each consumer responds to the consumption of additional goods, but it does not provide much information about consumer choices. Consumers typically consume more than one good, and they must purchase these goods at constant prices with limited income. To understand the quantity of each good a consumer chooses to purchase, we need a framework to assist our analysis. To create an environment where a single consumer decides the quantity of each good to purchase, we will assume that the consumer's goal is to maximize total utility, that the consumer has complete preferences for the two goods available in the market, and that the consumer adheres to the law of diminishing marginal utility. Lastly, we must assume that the consumer faces constant income and fixed prices of the two goods. The assumption of complete preferences means that the consumer knows exactly how much utility they will gain from consuming a specific quantity of goods or services. These assumptions are sufficient for us to analyse the consumer's utility maximization.

Early neoclassical economists assumed that utility is quantifiable and measurable. When utility can be quantified and measured, it is referred to as cardinal utility.[20] In the twentieth century, neoclassical economists realized that this assumption should be abandoned, and their goal was to replace the less reliable hypothesis of measurable satisfaction with simpler assumptions. In other words, they rejected cardinal utility and introduced another form of utility in their consumer behaviour models: ordinal

---

[18] The value paradox refers to the phenomenon where many goods, despite their high prices, seem to have little practical use, such as diamonds and other luxury items. In contrast, the most useful goods are typically the cheapest, such as rice, water, salt, and so on.

[19] Jevons, W.S. (2013). *The theory of political economy*. Palgrave Macmillan; Menger, C. (2007). *Principles of economics*. Ludwig von Mises Institute; Fisher, I. (1892). *Mathematical investigations in the theory of value and prices*. Yale University Press; Forsythe, R., Nelson, F., Neumann, G.R. & Wright, J. (1992). 'Anatomy of an experimental political stock market'. *The American Economic Review*, 82(5), 1142–1143.

[20] Strotz, R. (1953). 'Cardinal utility'. *The American Economic Review*, 43(2), 384–397.

Kauder, E. (1953). 'Genesis of the marginal utility theory: From Aristotle to the end of the eighteenth century'. *The Economic Journal*, 63(251), 638–650.

utility.[21] Ordinal utility means that consumers derive satisfaction from consuming goods, but it can only rank their preferences.

On this basis, economists further studied the problem of utility maximization, examining it from the perspectives of budget and preferences.[22] The budget line is a tool used to study budget constraints, and the slope of the budget line represents the ability of consumers to switch from one good to another at current prices in the market. A change in prices causes the budget line to rotate (changing of slope), while a change in income results in a parallel shift of the budget line (with the slope remaining unchanged). The indifference curve is a tool used to study preferences, in simple terms, an indifference curve represents the consumption combinations that provide the consumer with the same level of utility, and its slope is generally negative. The slope of the indifference curve is typically the marginal rate of substitution between two goods. Utility maximization requires that the slope of the budget line equals the marginal rate of substitution. The Marshall demand function is also a key tool in solving the utility maximization problem.[23]

5.1.2.2 Cost Minimization

Next, we can shift our standing point and examine the cost minimization problem under the condition of constant utility. Cost minimization is the dual problem to utility maximization. The Hicksian demand function is a commonly used tool for studying the cost minimization problem, as it shows the relationship among demand, price, and utility. The objective is to calculate consumers' minimum expenditure required to achieve a given level of utility at specific prices. The partial derivatives of the cost function of consumers yield the Hicksian demand function. The significance of studying the Hicksian demand function lies not only in cost minimization but also in the analysis of the Hicksian substitution effect. The Hicksian substitution effect refers to the situation where, when prices change proportionally, the consumption bundle remains unchanged and the cost would not change, furthermore, utility also remains unchanged. In other words, the new budget of implementers is just sufficient to satisfy the original level of utility at the new prices of the products. The Hicksian substitution effect can help to explain the issue of renegotiating higher prices in intellectual property pricing, particularly when right holders and implementers need to set new terms after the expiration of the initial license. In the renegotiation process, the product revenue or budget of the implementers might change, leading to a potential price increase of the products. Consequently, the prices of other intellectual properties within the intellectual property bundle may also change.

---

[21] Stigler, G. (1937). 'The economics of carl menger'. *Journal of Political Economy*, 45(2), 240; Hicks, J. and Allen, R. (1934). 'A reconsideration of the theory of value'. *Economica*, 1(1), 52–76.

[22] Suppes, P. and Winet, M. (1955). 'An axiomatization of utility based on the notion of utility difference'. *Management Science*, 1(3–4), 197–281; Fuchs-Seliger, S. (1983). 'Budget preferences and direct utility'. *Journal of Economic Theory*, 30(1), 188–190; Mas-Colell, A., Whinston, M. D. and Green, J. R. (1995). *Microeconomic theory*. Oxford University Press.

[23] Nicholson, W. (1978). *Microeconomic theory*. Dryden Press. 90–93.

Similar to the Hicksian substitution effect, the Slutsky substitution effect describes the impact of price changes on the quantity demanded of a good assuming the budget remains unchanged. The key difference between the Hicksian substitution effect and the Slutsky substitution effect lies in the definition of real income, or more specifically, the definition of the budget. In the Slutsky framework, the budget is defined in terms of purchasing power, meaning that after a price change, it is assessed whether the new budget allows the consumer to purchase the same quantity of the good as before. In contrast, the Hicksian substitution effect focuses on whether the consumer can return to the same indifference curve as before the price change at the new price level. Both effects can bc used to analyse the different characteristics of intellectual property products. This includes understanding whether a particular INTELLECTUAL PROPERTY product is a normal good or an inferior good, a luxury good or a Giffen good.[24]

5.1.3 Market Equilibrium: From the Perspective of Supply Behaviour of Rightsholders

A market requires at least one buyer and one seller. After understanding the demand function of the implementer, the next step is to bring in the pricing behaviour of right holders and analyse the market. Market demand is essentially a distribution function, and discussing market prices is essentially analysing the process where individuals go from being unwilling to trade to being willing to trade. When the supply of sellers balances with the demand of buyers, the market reaches an equilibrium price.

We begin with the most basic assumption—assuming that the intellectual properties offered by two right holders in the market are heterogeneous. In the case of a single implementer, they will certainly engage in transactions with the right holder offering the better deal (lower price or higher quality). The rightsholder unable to offer a better deal will not be able to earn revenue. Now, consider expanding the scenario of having two rightsholders to two groups of rightsholders, each offering intellectual property of different quality, while the implementer also changes from an individual to a group. If the demand quantity of the implementers matches the supply of one group of rightsholders, the transaction outcome will be the same as before, where the implementers would engage in transactions with the group of rightsholders that offering the better deal. If the combined supply from the two groups of rightsholders is sufficient to meet the demand of the implementers, but the supply from any single group is insufficient to meet the total demand of the implementers, then some implementers will trade with the rightsholders offering the higher quality intellectual property, while other implementers will be forced to trade with the other group of rightsholders that offering lower quality.

[24] For the meanings of 'Giffin Goods', see Jaffe, S., Minton, R., Mulligan, C. B., & Murphy, K. M. (2019). *Chicago price theory*. Princeton University Press. 38–41.

In a market where there are two groups of rightsholders and two groups of implementers, and each group of implementers has different consumption preferences—some implementers prefer high-quality intellectual property, while others prefer low-quality intellectual property—each group of rightsholders will be able to trade with at least one group of implementers. This quality difference in the market is referred to as vertical differentiation, which contrasts with horizontal differentiation. Horizontal differentiation refers to the scenario where different consumers have different preferences for various brands or types of products, whereas vertical differentiation refers to the scenario where different consumers share the same preference for a particular feature of a product. Both vertical and horizontal differentiation can be collectively referred to as product differentiation, and they play a key role in explaining why rightsholders are motivated to increase their research and development (R&D) investments. Product differentiation is commonly observed in the operation of intellectual property markets, particularly vertical differentiation, which is essentially the core issue in many cases where different intellectual properties serve as substitutes for one another. If horizontal differentiation can explain why rightsholders of homogenous intellectual properties are motivated to distinguish their intellectual property from others (e.g., through design features or appearance), vertical differentiation can explain why rightsholders are more motivated to offer intellectual property of varying quality levels.

For research coherence, we first start with horizontal differentiation. In horizontal differentiation pricing, the simplest model is the location differentiation model, which is also called the classic Hotelling model. It explains that firms will try to distinguish product differences in order to make profits. However, due to the discontinuity of its demand function, this model has certain limitations. If the distance cost is converted into a quadratic function, the discontinuity problem can be solved. The quadratic Hotelling model can sufficiently explain on the argument that product differentiation is the source of corporate pricing, which can also explain why many firms would deliberately differentiate their products from those of competitors in practice, such as Wifi technology and WAPI technology.

In vertical differentiation, consumers generally agree on the same standard, that is, a certain product must be of better quality than another product. The difference among consumers lies on the different degrees of attention they placed on quality, and each consumer has his or her own quality preference. For example, even in the 5G era, some consumers will continue to choose 4G technology because of budget. Although consumers generally prefer high-quality products, they are limited by budget. If the price of high-quality products is excessively high, consumers will choose to substitute them with low-quality products. This part has been discussed in the section on cross-price elasticity of demand and will not be repeated here.

In the vertical differentiation of intellectual property rights, the right holder will face two choices, one is the quality choice and the other is the price choice. We can infer that the only way for right holders of low-quality intellectual property rights to license their intellectual property rights is to lower the price. The right holder needs to let the implementer use the price difference to make up for its poor quality. The price of high-quality intellectual property rights will increase with the improvement of quality, but if the quality of low-quality intellectual property rights is improved, its price difference to high-quality intellectual property rights will be narrowed. In the vertical differentiation model, the larger the gap between low-quality intellectual property rights and high-quality intellectual property rights, the stronger its pricing power would be. Therefore, if the right holder of low-quality intellectual property rights takes the initiative to widen the quality gap with the high-quality intellectual property right holder, the pricing power of both parties will be improved. The reason why this phenomenon arises can be understood as when the right holder of low-quality intellectual property rights improves its quality, the intensity of competition between it and high-quality intellectual property rights will increase. In order to alleviate the intensity of this competition, both parties have the motivation to further differentiate the qualities of their products so as to improve their pricing powers respectively.

Of course, the above strategy of expanding profits through vertical differentiation may be feasible for ordinary products, but it remains unknown whether it will work in the field of intellectual property. In theory, the right holder of low-quality intellectual property cannot further reduce the quality of its intellectual property. Then, the options left are either to increase R&D efforts to surpass high-quality intellectual property, or to give up R&D and wait for other right holders to further improve the quality of intellectual property. Obviously, no matter what categories the intellectual property right holder falls into, he would never give up on R&D. Therefore, the right holder can only work hard to improve the quality of its own R&D, or develop as many intellectual property rights as possible, so that to cover all levels of quality.

Intellectual property differentiation can also be called 'the relative advantage of intellectual property', and its relative advantage is an essential consideration in the pricing of intellectual property transactions. Horizontal differentiation can explain why right holders have the motivation to differentiate their intellectual property horizontally. However, the only way to achieve vertical differentiation seems to be to increase research and development investment. Although the behaviour of vertically differential pricing may not be perfectly applicable to the field of intellectual property, its pricing principle can help us understanding the impact that product differences of intellectual property rights bring to prices.

5.1.4 Pricing in Monopoly Markets and Monopolistic Competition Markets

It is not difficult to find that in the analytical framework of the above price theory, the right holder and the implementer are actually price takers rather than the price makers, and the price is determined by the market equilibrium. In other words, the right holder and the implementer each has their own functions about the combination of price, supply and demand. When the two function curves intersect, an equilibrium point will appear, which reflects the price at market equilibrium.

The premise of the above price theory is that intellectual property rights are substitutable. When intellectual property rights are completely non-substitutable or have low substitutability, right holders can enforce monopoly pricing or price discrimination. At this time, the right holder is no longer a price taker, but a price maker. Generally speaking, monopoly unified pricing will be higher than the equilibrium price in a perfectly competitive market. Therefore, when there is monopoly unified pricing, the monopolist can obtain excess profits greater than normal profits. This excess profit will lead to unnecessary losses, thereby reducing the overall welfare of society. Therefore, monopoly unified pricing always attracts the attention of antitrust enforcement agencies. Meanwhile, price discrimination is another pricing method commonly used by monopolists, which can also be called differential pricing. Price discrimination is a sales strategy in which customers are charged with different prices for the same product or service based on how the seller thinks they can satisfy the customer. In the case of first-degree discrimination, a firm charges each consumer the highest price they are willing to pay, which can 'squeeze' the surplus value of each consumer to the greatest extent. Second-degree price discrimination means that a firm charges different prices for different consumption quantities. Second-degree discrimination includes discounts for products or services purchased in bulk etc. Third-degree price discrimination refers to the situation where a firm groups customers according to certain attributes and charges different prices to each group. Third-degree discrimination reflects different prices for different consumer groups. For example, an amusement park groups adults and children, and sets different ticket prices for different groups. Since price discrimination does not necessarily lead to a reduction in social welfare, its illegality is still open to question.

Similarly, the pricing methods in a monopolistic competition market will also differ. In a monopolistic competition market, there are both large enterprises and numerous small businesses. In the short term, the monopolistic competition market is similar to a purely monopolistic market, where there may be excess profits or losses. However, in the long term, the total revenue in a monopolistic competition market will equal total costs, achieving a break-even point. In a monopolistic competition market, firms can also price above marginal cost, which may lead to deadweight loss.

5.2 The Application of Price Theory in Intellectual Property Transactions

There are many applicable scenarios for price theory in intellectual property transactions. It not only can be reflected in conventional market transactions, but also assist judicial institutions in judicial intervention or judicial remedy. Since the prices in free market transactions conform with the price formation mechanism itself, we will not elaborate here. However, when right holders and licensees cannot reach an agreement by themselves, the court may need to determine the royalty price to facilitate the completion of the transaction. Moreover, when the market is monopolistic, the reasonableness of the price set by the right holders may be questioned, and judicial intervention may be required to maintain the order in the intellectual property market. Therefore, this section primarily explores how price theory can be applied in judicial interventions and remedies so as to assist completions of intellectual property transactions. This section will first discuss the application of price theory in determining reasonable royalty rates, then combine price theory with contract theory, exploring the impact of price theory on transaction prices as in a negotiation scenario. Finally, the section will examine the application of price theory in antitrust judicial interventions in intellectual property.

5.2.1 *Price Theory in Intellectual Property Licensing*

Licensing is an essential component of intellectual property transactions which represents the contract between the parties. The core of a license is the price, and the most important aspect in a licensing agreement for both right holders and implementers is to define the royalty rate. However, in some cases, right holders and licensees may fail to reach an agreement on the price. In this circumstances, the court may need to assist the parties in determining a reasonable royalty fee to facilitate the completion of the transaction. In this process, the court faces two key issues: The first issue is the difference between judicial pricing and market pricing. Price theory describes the price formation mechanism in the market, but in judicial practice, there is no such market. Therefore, the court needs to clarify whether it should consider market factors in judicial pricing. The second issue is the design of the pricing mechanism. Price theory is based on a perfectly competitive market, but due to the exclusivity and irreplaceability of intellectual property right (especially patent right), it does not meet the conditions of a perfectly competitive market. As a result, the court cannot simply and fully apply price theory, instead, it must consider various factors to determine a reasonable royalty fee. This section will discuss these two issues respectively.

5.2.1.1 Market Pricing and Judicial Pricing

Market pricing and judicial pricing are two set of concepts frequently discussed in intellectual property pricing. Market pricing refers to the method where the price is voluntarily determined by the parties themselves according to the principles of market operation, and price theory is the study of such market pricing mechanism. Judicial pricing, on the other hand, refers to the process by which the price is determined through judicial intervention.[25] Market pricing and judicial pricing used to be mentioned frequently in legal academia, despite they appear to be opposing concepts,

---

[25] Wu, H. (2018). 'Zhishi chanquan sunhai peichang de shichang jiazhi fenxi: Lilun, guize yu fangfa' ['An analysis of market value in intellectual property damages: Theory, rules, and methods'], *Faxue Pinglun* [*Law Review*], 1, 65–74; Jiang, H. (2017). 'Zhishi chanquan sunhai peichang de shichang jiazhi' ['Market value of intellectual property damages'], *Zhishi Chanquan* [*Intellectual*

they are in fact not entirely incompatible. Judicial pricing usually considers market factors and often simulates market negotiation methods. Similarly, market pricing can also be influenced by judicial pricing. Different approaches and outcomes of judgments in individual cases would inevitably affect the negotiation strategies and expectations of the parties in the market, thereby influencing the overall market pricing process. Because the boundaries between market pricing and judicial pricing are not clear-cut, they should be viewed as different pricing processes within a transaction scenario, rather than as distinct paradigms. They represent different pricing processes, not different methodologies. In practice, there is hardly any difference in the methodologies of judicial vis-à-vis market pricing[26]; the key difference lies in the variables considered and the information adopted in respective methods. Therefore, judicial pricing should be grounded in the market, and courts should take into account the market attributes of intellectual property when engaging in judicial pricing.

In the process of intellectual property operation, right holders usually aim for utility maximization. They can find the optimal price solution that maximizes utility through profit functions, and use this optimal price solution as a reference for formulating pricing strategies. Several factors will influence the profit function of a right holder, such as cost, supply, demand, and substitutability etc. Among these, the substitutability of intellectual property plays a significant role. The substitutability of intellectual property determines market segmentation and directly impacts supply and demand. In theory, each intellectual property right could constitute a separate market, because each of them is unique. However, since there are usually multiple intellectual property rights that can achieve the same or similar outcomes, intellectual property rights are usually substitutable to a certain extent, therefore, intellectual property markets will influence each other and cannot operate entirely independently. As a result, each right holder is both a monopolist and a competitor, and the degree of

Property], 7, 60–67; Kong, W. (2020). 'Lun ziyou maoyi beijingxia jishu biaozhun de sifa dingjia guize-Yi shichang zhudao wei qierudian' ['On judicial pricing rules for technical standards under the background of free trade: From the perspective of market dominance'], *Zhongguo Zhuanli Yu Faming* [*China Invention and Patent*], 1, 29–34.

[26] It can be seen from previous judicial practices that when courts use the hypothetical negotiation method to calculate reasonable royalty fees, they need to refer to the negotiation elements in market pricing. (See Georgia-Pacific Corp. v. U.S. Plywood Corp. (1970) 318 F. Supp. 1116 (S.D.N.Y.)). The related pricing research also shows that when scholars provide judicial pricing ideas for courts or explain intellectual property pricing issues, they often choose methods based on market pricing. For example, Contreras and Eixenberger, in their study of jury pricing models, introduced various factors considered in market pricing. (See Contreras, J. L. & Eixenberger, M. A. (2016). 'Jury instructions for reasonable royalty patent damages'. *Jurimetrics*, 57(1), 1–24). Love also incorporated the market pricing factors to be considered in judicial pricing research, and pointed out that when non-infringing substitutes exist, a reasonable royalty should not be supported. (See Love, N.C. (2008). 'Reasonable royalties for patent infringement'. *University of Chicago Law Review*, 75(4), 1749–1772) Michel also took the negotiation methods in market pricing as a starting point in his research on reasonable royalty issues in standards. (See Michel, S. (2011). 'Bargaining for RAND royalties in the shadow of patent remedies law'. *Antitrust Law Journal*, 77(3), 889–911) Ayres and Parchomovsky also based their solution to the patent thicket problem on price and sales factors. (See Ayres, I. & Parchomovsky, G. (2007). 'Tradable patent rights'. *Stanford Law Review*, 60(3), 863–894).

competition is determined by the substitutability between their intellectual properties. Consequently, their pricing ability will also be affected.

When the intellectual property of a right holder is highly substitutable, its pricing is constrained by other competing intellectual properties. If it operates in a market closes to perfect competition, the right holder cannot set the price autonomously and becomes a price taker rather than a price maker.[27] In such a scenario, the determining factors for the price are supply and demand,[28] and in this case, judicial pricing should align with market pricing, using the market price that is established when supply and demand reach equilibrium. In other words, when intellectual property is in a perfectly competitive market, the implementation of any intellectual property would incur similar costs for the implementer. Therefore, the court only needs to assess the royalty fee based on market standards.

When the intellectual property of a right holder is not fully substitutable, its pricing must take into account the pricing of substitute intellectual property. However, in this case, the right holder is not entirely a price taker; they have some degree of autonomy in setting the price. This situation can be further subdivided into two market competition scenarios: monopolistic competition and oligopoly.

In a monopolistic competition market, there may be one or several large right holders with significant market shares, along with many smaller right holders with minor market shares. The reason that a right holder may take a larger market share may due to the significant advantage in cost-effectiveness of their intellectual property, or because their intellectual property is a recommended standard.[29] In this case, the profit function of right holders includes three factors: price, licensing quantity, and costs. The licensing quantity can be seen as a function of the licensing price and the quality or characteristics of intellectual property. The primary competition among right holders in monopolistic competition is the competition for licensing quantities. Because intellectual property rights are substitutable, if the implementer chooses another right holder, the unchosen right holder will not receive licensing fees. Therefore, unless transaction costs are too high, right holders are generally willing to license their intellectual property in exchange for higher returns, because in a market with many substitutable intellectual properties, a right holder cannot maintain a monopoly position in the downstream market by refusing to license their intellectual property. Since whether to license does not affect their position in the downstream market, therefore, while refusing to license cannot provide any advantage to the right holder, it also means that their revenue will be captured by other right holders. Hence, in a monopolistic competition scenario, right holders are incentivized to license their intellectual property until their licensing quantity reaches the point of profit maximization.

[27] Jiang, D. (2017). *Gaoji weiguan jingjixue* [*Advanced microeconomics*] (2nd ed.). Beijing Daxue Chubanshe [Peking University Press].13.

[28] Marshall, A. (1890). *Principles of economics*. Macmillan. 194.

[29] Mandatory standards generally do not form monopolistic competition markets, but rather lead to either a pure monopoly or an oligopoly market.

When judicial pricing involves a monopolistic competition market, the court needs to consider the right holder's position within the monopolistic competition market and comprehensively evaluate the profit function and licensing quantity function of the right holder to determine the appropriate licensing fee.

In an oligopolistic market, there are only a few right holders, and the market price is jointly determined by these few right holders. The most typical oligopoly models are the Bertrand model and the Cournot model. The Cournot model is less likely to occur in reality because right holders in an oligopoly market are price setters rather than price takers, and they are unlikely to accept excessively low prices. Therefore, the assumptions of the Bertrand model are closer to reality. The Bertrand model is a typical model of price competition between two oligopolists, in which both parties set prices at their marginal costs. It is easy to imagine that when the intellectual properties offered by several right holders in the market are perfect substitutes, a price reduction by one right holder means they will gain more licensing quantity, while a price increase will result in a greater loss of market share. The Bertrand model reflects that, in an oligopoly, the pricing of right holders is based on their estimation of the prices of their competitors. A sudden change in price would trigger a price war, which is unfavourable for any party involved. Therefore, in an oligopoly, right holders must speculate on the profit functions and licensing quantity functions of their rivals, and estimate their possible prices in order to set their own price. Judicial pricing for an oligopoly is relatively straightforward. The court can simply refer to the prices set by the competitors to determine the price, which is similar to the comparable agreement pricing method.

However, the assumption of the Bertrand model is that the intellectual properties provided by right holders and their competitors are perfectly homogeneous, which is nearly impossible in the field of intellectual property. This is because intellectual properties cannot be absolutely homogeneous, even if different intellectual properties can achieve the same effect, their methods and costs will inevitably differ. For heterogeneous intellectual properties, the Hotelling model can better explain the relationship between product differentiation and pricing. According to the Hotelling model, product differentiation is the source of pricing power. The greater the differentiation of intellectual properties, the stronger the pricing power of the right holder.[30] Therefore, when considering the pricing of heterogeneous intellectual properties, courts need to take the substitution rate of intellectual properties into account. The court can refer to the utility provided by intellectual properties to the implementer in order to determine the marginal rate of substitution between intellectual property rights. Although it is difficult to make direct comparisons between intellectual property rights, they can be uniformly transformed into utility, and the substitution relationship between intellectual property rights can be measured in terms of utility.[31]

---

[30] Belleflamme, P. & Peitz, M. (2014). *Chanye zuzhi: Shichang he celue* [*Industrial organization: Markets and strategies*], (Chen, H., Xu, L. et al. trans.). Gezhi Chubanshe, Sanlian Shudian, Shanghai Renmin Chubanshe [Gezhi Publishing House, Sanlian Bookstore, Shanghai People's Publishing House]. 95–104.

[31] In neoclassical economics, consumers obtain different levels of utility by purchasing different combinations of products, and along the same indifference curve, consumers derive the same level

When the intellectual property of a right holder is completely non-substitutable, they can freely set prices above marginal cost, either by implementing unified monopoly pricing or through price discrimination to obtain greater profits. In theory, under market pricing, a purely monopolistic right holder does not need to consider their actual contribution to the implementer when setting prices and can virtually deprive the implementer of all surplus. In such cases, judicial pricing cannot fully adhere to market pricing standards because the market is already in a state of failure.[32] Thus, in judicial pricing, the court must base its pricing on the actual contribution rate made by the intellectual property to the product.

5.2.1.2 Pricing Mechanism Design in the Judiciary

There exist many pricing mechanisms in intellectual property transactions, and various fields have discussed the pricing methods in intellectual property. One of the most commonly used methods is the hypothetical negotiation method, which simulates the negotiation process between the right holder and the implementer before infringement and determines the price on that basis. This method is widely applied in the United States. In the *Georgia Pacific* case, the U.S. court proposed 15 factors[33] that need to be considered in a hypothetical negotiation, which are referred to as the 'bottom-up approach'.[34]

When establishing a hypothetical negotiation, attention is typically given to the timing and information issues. The 'timing issue' refers to the point of time when the negotiation takes place, and the 'information issue' refers to the information that both parties hold at that time which influences the negotiation. In contrast, the 'top-down approach' is also frequently adopted in certain cases.[35] The top-down approach involves the court first determining an appropriate base royalty rate, then calculating the total royalty payment based on the revenue attributable to that base, and finally determining the portion of the total royalty attributable to the intellectual property in question based on its relative importance. In addition, methods such as the decomposition method,[36] established royalty, ECPR (Efficient Cost of Production

of utility. Therefore, utility is often used to observe consumer behaviour. See Jiang, D. (2017). *Gaoji weiguan jingjixue* [*Advanced microeconomics*] (2nd ed.). Beijing Daxue Chubanshe [Peking University Press]. 45–46.

[32] For more explanations on market failure, see Jiang, D. (2017). *Gaoji weiguan jingjixue* [*Advanced microeconomics*] (2nd ed.). Beijing Daxue Chubanshe [Peking University Press]. 271–272.

[33] Georgia-Pacific Corp. v. U.S. Plywood Corp., (1970). 318 F. Supp. 1116 (S.D.N.Y.).

[34] Contreras, J. et al. (2019). 'The Effect of FRAND commitments on patent remedies', in C.B. Biddle (ed.), *Patent remedies and complex products*. Cambridge University Press. 162.

[35] In re Innovatio IP Ventures, LLC Patent Litig.(2013) MDL Docket No. 2303 (N.D. Ill. 27) (U.S.). Samsung Elecs. Co. v. Apple Japan LLC, IP High Ct., 2014, paras. 132–138 (Japan).Unwired Planet Int'l Ltd. v. Huawei Techs. Co., [2017] EWHC 711 (Pat), paras. 475–480 (UK).

[36] TWM Manufacturing Co. v. Dura Corp., (1986) 789 F.2d 895, 899 (Fed. Cir.).

Rule),[37] and Shapley value[38] are also commonly used. These methods can all assist in judicial pricing mechanisms.

Furthermore, prices can be determined through an auction mechanism. Daniel Swanson and William Baumol used an incomplete information static game model—the pre-emptive bidding model—in patent pricing.[39] The basic idea is that before a patent enters a standard, the right holders of competing patents bid for their licensing fees to the standard-setting organization, which then selects the patent with the lowest bid and incorporates it into the standard. High-quality patents provide greater cost advantages to implementers, so that they have more room to offer lower quotations. The advantage of this method is that it can lower the price of SEPs.

However, the disadvantages of this method are also obvious. First, it only considers the substitutability between technologies, but ignores their complementarity.[40] Additionally, the method reduces the profit margin for right holders, especially when there is high substitutability or small technological differences between competing patents, leaving the right holders with almost no profit.[41] Furthermore, the method overlooks the fact that the contribution rate of SEPs varies for each product, as a result, a uniform pricing approach will inevitably neglect the contribution rate issue. However, this method can provide another pricing approach—sealed bid auctions. This method achieves the goal of lowering the licensing fee by having the right holders submit sealed bids. The price determined by this method would indeed be closer to the marginal contribution rate of the intellectual property. Vice-versa, we could observe the price of the competitive portion of the intellectual property by having implementers place bids.

Sealed bid auctions are also a typical incomplete information static game model. First, assume there are n implementers participating in the bidding auction for the right holder. The type of participant i is the valuation of the object V_i, which only the participant knows, but other participants can estimate the range of the type based on existing experience. The behaviours of participant i is its bidding strategy B_i (•) and its actual bid b_i is only known to itself before made public. Then, we can write the payoff function π_i of participant i as:

$$\left[\begin{cases} \pi_i = V_i - B_i & \text{if awarded the bid,} \\ \pi_i = 0 & \text{if not awarded the bid.} \end{cases}\right]$$

[37] Rude v. Westcott, (1889).130 U.S. 152, 164–165 (U.S.); Fulta Elec. Machinery Co. v. Watanabe Kikai Kogyo K. K. (IP High Ct. 2015) (Japan).

[38] Layne-Farrar, A., Padilla, J. & Schmalensee, R. (2007). 'Pricing patents for licensing in standard-setting organizations: Making sense of FRAND commitments', *Antitrust Law Journal*, 74(3), 671–706.

[39] Swanson, D.G. & Baumol, W.J. (2005). 'Reasonable and nondiscriminatory (RAND) royalties, standards selection, and control of market power', *Antitrust Law Journal*, 73(1), 15–21.

[40] Layne-Farrar, A., Padilla, J. & Schmalensee, R. (2007). 'Pricing patents for licensing in standard-setting organizations: making sense of FRAND commitments'. *Antitrust Law Journal*, 74(3), 688–689.

[41] Siebrasse, N.V. & Cotter, T.F. (2017). 'The value of standard'. *Minnesota Law Review*, 101(3), 1187–1188.

In the highest price bidding model, the implicit assumption is that the higher the participant's valuation of the intellectual property, the higher their bid. Therefore, the bidding strategy of the participant is reversible. The condition for participant i to win can be expressed in probability form: $\Pr\{B_j(V_i) < b_i\} = F_j\left(B_j^{-1}(b_i)\right), i \neq j$, where $F(\bullet)$ is the cumulative distribution function used to measure probability. For the sake of discussion, we assume that all participants have the same bidding strategy, meaning that the optimal strategy functions are identical, but with different valuations. Thus, we can derive the expected utility of the participant as: $E_{-i}\left[u_i(b_i, B_{-i}(V_{-i}); V_i)|V_i\right] = \left[F\left(B^{-1}(b)\right)\right]^{n-1}(V_i - b)$, where u_i represents the utility function. The condition for maximizing the expectation of the participant is that the first derivative of their function equals zero. By differentiating, we obtain the bidding strategy function of the participant as: $B(V) = \frac{V(n-1)}{n}$. This strategy function indicates that when the number of participants is sufficiently large, the offer made by the implementer will be infinitely close to the valuation of the intellectual property by that implementer.

The above model is also known as the first-price sealed-bid auction model. In this model, the final auction price of the intellectual property is the upper limit of the valuation of the intellectual property by the implementer in the relevant market. As the number of participants in the auction increases, the price of the intellectual property will also rise, which can reflect the maximum price for the licensing of intellectual property to some extent. Since only one participant ultimately wins the auction, this model is more suitable for pricing in exclusive or sole licenses. In the case of non-exclusive licensing, this model can only serve as a reference for the upper limit of judicial pricing by the court. However, if combined with the pre-auction bidding model of Swanson and Baumol, theoretically, it can determine both the upper and lower limits of the licensing price of intellectual property.

Through the design of judicial pricing mechanisms, we can identify a very important set of concepts in the pricing process, namely ex ante and ex post. *Ex-ante* and ex post typically affect the final price, reflecting the influence of contract theory on price construction.

5.2.2 *The Impact of Contract Theory on Licensing Prices: From a Negotiation Perspective*

In the previous section, we discussed common pricing mechanisms in intellectual property transactions, but the discussion did not address the contracting issue. To provide a more comprehensive perspective, this section will combine contract theory and examine how contract theory and pricing theory jointly play a role in intellectual property transactions from the perspective of negotiation. Ex-ante negotiation and ex post negotiation are two basic types of intellectual property licensing negotiations, and the prices determined in these two negotiation scenarios differ. In fact, both ex ante and ex post negotiations not only involve pricing theory but also reflect the impact of contract theory on pricing. In this section, we will follow the framework of contract theory to explore its influence on price formation. In both ex ante and ex post negotiations, three main factors influence the price: (1) information factors; (2) changes in the bargaining power of the right holder and the implementer; and (3) differences in transaction costs. The following discussion will explain how these three factors influence the outcomes of ex ante and ex post negotiations.

5.2.2.1 Differences in Information Factors

The biggest difference between ex ante negotiation and ex post negotiation lies in the level of information accessibility. Information in ex ante negotiations typically has higher uncertainty. Theoretically, negotiations before the implementation of intellectual property can all be considered as ex ante negotiations, which inherently contain uncertainty, but the uncertainty in the first ex ante negotiation is usually higher. In ex ante negotiations, when the right holder and the implementer determine the future royalty rate, they typically rely on estimates of relevant data, which introduces uncertainty. This uncertainty exists whether in uniform pricing or differentiated pricing. On one hand, the implementer generally cannot be sure that the contribution of the intellectual property to the product will truly align with its price. Although this uncertainty can be reduced through repeated games, even after numerous iterations, it cannot be entirely eliminated. On the other hand, the implementer cannot fully ascertain whether the intellectual property is truly effective.[42] These uncertainties can also be understood as informational asymmetries regarding the quality of intellectual property during ex ante negotiations,[43] which directly affect the transaction price between the two parties.

In ex ante negotiations, implementers typically use price reduction strategies to mitigate the negative effects of information asymmetry.[44] Specifically, this may involve the implementer requesting a corresponding discount factor in the royalty rate to reduce the adverse impact of uncertainty. For the right holder, their ultimate goal is to maximize their own interests, and including a discount factor clearly does not align with their interests. However, because the right holder is also uncertain about the value of their intellectual property during ex ante negotiations, especially in the first ex ante negotiation, they may agree to a reasonable price reduction. As the number of repeated transactions increases, the right holder and the implementer will gradually adjust the royalty rate. That is, both parties will observe the implementation effects from the previous stage and determine the royalty rate for the next stage. Although this is an ex ante negotiation for the next stage, it is essentially based

[42] Trademark and copyright rights have higher certainty, whereas patent rights have lower certainty. Even if a right holder obtains a patent, the patent could be invalid, and the implementer's product does not necessarily fall within the scope of the patent's protection.

[43] Of course, in such cases, the right holder may not necessarily have a better understanding of the quality of their intellectual property. In other words, the right holder's estimation of the quality of intellectual property may also be uncertain.

[44] Akerlof, G.A. (1970). 'The market for 'lemons': quality uncertainty and the market mechanism'. *Quarterly Journal of Economics*, 84(3), 489.

on ex post information from the previous stage. At this point, the effects of ex post negotiations in the previous stage may be similar to those of ex ante negotiations in the next stage.

In ex post negotiations, both parties are aware of the implementing behaviours that have already occurred to a certain extent, which can reduce some of the uncertainties of ex ante negotiations. For example, after using the intellectual property, both the right holder and the implementer can estimate the value of the intellectual property more accurately, thus determining the price attributable to the contribution rate more clearly. However, ex post negotiations do not necessarily eliminate all uncertainties. For instance, in the ex post negotiations that are related to market pricing, the implementer still cannot ascertain the validity of the intellectual property or the potential infringement of their use. These issues can be determined only during judicial pricing. In contrast, ex post negotiations imply that the implementer has used the intellectual property for a period of time and has gained a more comprehensive understanding of different aspects of the intellectual property such as the contribution rate etc. Therefore, in theory, ex post negotiations can determine a price that reflects the actual contribution of the intellectual property more accurately.[45]

5.2.2.2 Changes in Bargaining Powers

Bargaining power is a frequently mentioned concept in negotiations, distincts from the concept of bargaining itself. Bargaining power theory focuses solely on the impact on the formation of agreement terms, while bargaining theory encompasses a broader scope.[46] In a sense, bargaining is a process, whereas bargaining power is simply a factor that influences the process. Commons defined bargaining power as the ability to withhold products or production capabilities before negotiations on ownership transfer.[47] Slichter defined bargaining power as the cost of A causing harm to B.[48] Lindbloom considered bargaining power as the ability of both buyers and sellers to set or maintain prices.[49] Building on earlier works, Chamberlain and Kuhn defined

---

[45] Of course, the right holder may leverage the competitiveness of intellectual property to obtain excess profits, but—a pricing at least allows both parties to be more certain about the price attributable to the contribution portion.

[46] Mabry, B.D. (1965). 'The pure theory of bargaining'.*Industrial & Labor Relations Review*, 18(4), 479.

[47] Commons, J.R. (1934). *Institutional economics: Its place in political economy*. Macmillan. 331.

[48] Slichter, S.H. (1940). 'Impact of social security legislation upon mobility and enterprise'. *American Economic Review*, 30(1), 57.

[49] Lindbloom, C.E. (1948). 'Bargaining power in price and wage determination'. *Quarterly Journal of Economics*, 62(3), 402–403.

bargaining power as the ability to have one's own proposal accepted by the other party,[50] a concept that has been widely accepted and applied.[51]

Chamberlain's definition of bargaining power originated from his proposed method of calculating bargaining power. He defined A's bargaining power as the cost of B rejecting A's proposal, and B's bargaining power as the cost of A rejecting B's proposal. Under this definition, if the cost of B rejecting A's proposal is higher than the cost of accepting it, B will accept A's proposal; otherwise, B will reject it. Similarly, if the cost of A rejecting B's proposal is higher than the cost of accepting it, A will accept B's proposal; otherwise, A will reject it.[52]

Based on Chamberlain's calculation method, it can be observed that bargaining power changes between ex ante and ex post negotiations. In ex ante negotiations, both parties focus more on the value of intellectual property and the respective substitutability of the buyer and seller. In contrast, in ex post negotiations, the implementer also takes into account sunk costs.

The application of Threat Points in game theory is the most direct manifestation of bargaining power in ex ante negotiations. A threat point refers to the utility that a party receives if negotiations fail, and it can be understood as the opportunity cost for both parties.[53] A transaction will occur only if the benefit from a successful deal exceeds the threat points of both parties. However, what we focus on is not the absolute value of the threat points, but the utility differences between different choices.

For example, assume the patent holder values the exclusive license of their patent at 600,000 yuan, the implementer has 1,000,000 yuan and needs the patent or a similar technology of the patent holder, and the implementer values the exclusive license of the patent at 700,000 yuan. If the transaction does not occur, the patent holder will receive their patent, and the implementer will receive 1,000,000 yuan. Therefore, the patent holder's threat point is 600,000 yuan, and the implementer's threat point is 1,000,000 yuan. If the transaction is completed, the additional benefit is 100,000 yuan (the difference between 700,000 yuan and 600,000 yuan). This additional benefit also represents the increase in social welfare from the successful transaction, and the bargaining can be seen as the division of this additional benefit.

Assuming that both parties have equal bargaining powers, they may choose to split the 100,000 yuan equally, setting the price at 650,000 yuan. After the deal is made, the utility of the patent holder is equal to their threat point minus their valuation of the patent, plus the transaction price, i.e. 650,000 yuan. When the transaction is

---

50 Chamberlain, N.W. & Kuhn, J.W.(1965). *Collective bargaining* (2nd edn.). McGraw-Hill Book Co., Inc. 162–190.

51 Of course, subsequent research has also presented other perspectives. For instance, some scholars believe that bargaining power is a function of the relative willingness and ability to strike. (See Livernash, E.R. (1983). 'The relation of power to the structure and process of collective bargaining'. *Journal of Law & Economics*, 6, 18) Nonetheless, it is evidence that Chamberlain's concept can be accepted more easily.

52 Chamberlain, N.W. & Kuhn, J.W. (1965). *Collective bargaining* (2nd edn.). McGraw-Hill Book Co., Inc. 222.

53 If bargaining is successful, both parties need to abandon their respective threat points (interests).

completed, the implementer's utility is their threat point minus their valuation of the patent, then plus the transaction price, i.e. 1,050,000 yuan. The patent holder's bargaining power is the cost to the implementer of rejecting the patent holder's proposal, or the loss the implementer would incur if the transaction does not occur, which is 50,000 yuan. Similarly, the patent holder's bargaining power is also 50,000 yuan. Thus, bargaining power in the game is directly reflected in how the additional profit is distributed between both parties.

It is not difficult to see that, in the distribution process, the differences in valuation between the two parties are more important than the absolute values of their threat points. The difference in valuations determines the bargaining range and the size of the profits that can be allocated. In the example above, the patent holder's valuation of 600,000 yuan may be because there are other implementers who are willing to pay 600,000 yuan. Similarly, the implementer's valuation of 700,000 yuan will certainly be influenced by the substitutability of the patent. If a perfect substitute of the patent worths 500,000 yuan, the implementer's valuation of the patent will decrease. On the contrary, if the patent holder's technology cannot be substituted, the implementer's valuation of the patent may be higher of the implementer must enter into the market. It can be said that bargaining power increases when the degree to which the other party relies on the negotiation relationship increases.[54] The dependency on the negotiation of both parties is influenced, on one hand, by the availability of other products or technologies, and on the other hand, by the intrinsic value of the patent technology itself.

In ex post negotiations, both parties' valuations of the intellectual property become more accurate. For the implementer, choosing other intellectual property not only means paying a licensing fee, but also results in the existing investments becoming sunk costs, which increases the cost of choosing alternative technologies. For the right holder, ex post negotiations do not affect the cost of refusing to grant a license. Therefore, ex post negotiations merely increase implementers' the rejection costs and reduce their bargaining power, whereas the relative bargaining power of the right holder increases.[55]

5.2.2.3 Changes in Transaction Costs

Ex-ante and ex post negotiations also have impacts on transaction costs. Transaction costs typically include search costs, negotiation costs, and enforcement costs.[56]

[54] Bacharach, S.B. & Lawler, E.J. (1981). *Bargaining: Power, tactics, and outcomes*. Jossey-Bass. 59–79.

[55] In the model, we typically substitute bargaining power with price, but in reality, bargaining power is not only reflected in price; it also includes non-price factors.(See Choi, A. & Triantis, G. (2012). 'The effect of bargaining power on contract design'. *Virginia Law Review*, 98(8), 1667). For example, some additional agreements or terms. However, these non-price factors are interpreted narrowly by some scholars, while broadly speaking, these factors can all be seen as manifestations of price.

[56] Cooter, R. & Ulen, T. (2012). *Law & Economics* (6th edn). Pearson. 88.

Search costs refer to the costs incurred in locating potential trading partners, which may include monetary costs, but more often refer to the costs of time spent. Negotiation costs refer to the costs incurred during the negotiation process between the right holder and the implementer. These costs may include the human, material, and financial resources invested by both parties in the negotiation. Negotiation costs can include both monetary costs and time costs. Enforcement costs refer to the costs involved in ensuring that both parties fulfil the terms of the transaction, in general, enforcement costs arise in cases of breach of contract. If one party breaches the contract after the agreement is reached, the other party incurs enforcement costs to protect its rights.

In terms of search costs, the implementer needs to search for intellectual property that may cover the attributes of their product, while the right holder also needs to search for potential infringing implementers. In ex ante negotiations, since the implementer has not yet begun to implement the intellectual property, the right holder always finds it difficult to locate target implementers. Therefore, in ex ante negotiations, the search costs are mainly borne by the implementer. In ex post negotiations, the implementer typically does not proactively search for the right holder. Instead, it is usually the right holder who identifies the infringing implementers. As a result, in ex post negotiations, the search costs are typically borne by the right holder.

In terms of negotiation costs, the implementer first needs to assess whether the right holder's intellectual property is valid and estimate the probability of their actions constituting an infringement, ultimately deciding whether to enter negotiations with the right holder, as well as determining the negotiation strategy and reasonable price range. On the other hand, the right holder also needs to assess the relatedness between the implementer's product and their intellectual property, and formulate an appropriate negotiation strategy. Ex-ante and ex post negotiations usually do not significantly change the negotiation costs. During negotiations, both parties will still base their pricing on the substitutability and value of the intellectual property. However, in ex post negotiations, there is a more straightforward understanding of the value of the intellectual property, which may help reduce some of the negotiation costs.[57]

In terms of enforcement costs, the implementer generally does not need to worry about the breaching of contract of the right holders. On the contrary, the right holder needs to prevent the implementer from breaching of contract. Therefore, enforcement costs are typically borne by the right holder. Ex-ante and ex post negotiations do not significantly affect enforcement costs, once the implementer breaches the contract, the right holder needs bear the associated costs. However, compared to ex post negotiations, ex ante negotiations may have a higher likelihood of breach. If after implementing the intellectual property, the implementer realizes that the intellectual property was overvalued in the ex ante negotiations, they may refuse to pay or request a lower fee in the ex post phase.

---

[57] However, when the implementer's product contains multiple intellectual properties, and the right holder's intellectual property is only one of them, using the smallest saleable unit method to calculate the contribution rate may even increase negotiation costs.

Overall, the impacts of ex ante and ex post negotiations on transaction costs are typically manifested on the switching of transaction costs. From the perspective of transaction costs transfer, right holders generally prefer ex ante negotiations, as they can reduce the search costs paid in ex post negotiations. On the other hand, implementers typically prefer ex post negotiations, as this allows them to delay payments, switch search costs, and obtain a more accurate valuation of the intellectual property, which helps reduce negotiation costs.

5.2.3 Price Theory in Antitrust of Intellectual Property

The previous discussion addresses pricing from a positive perspective, but when market failure occurs, it is necessary to view the transaction from a negative perspective—namely, antitrust regulation on intellectual property transactions. When an intellectual property right holder abuses their rights, causing adverse effects on market competition, consumer interests, and overall social welfare, antitrust law must regulate their behaviours to maintain market order and protect the trading environment. Again, antitrust analysis of intellectual property can be framed within the context of price theory. On its appearance, antitrust cases mostly involve analysis on economic effects, such as the impact of the alleged behaviour on market competition, consumer welfare, and overall social welfare and efficiency. However, after careful analysis, it is evident that most of the contested behaviours are competitive behaviours, which can largely be categorized as pricing issues. The term 'price' here is not necessarily monetary; it refers broadly to any valuable considerations. Therefore, in the context of intellectual property antitrust and judicial pricing, not only the monetary pricing should be looked at, but also the pricing issues related to non-monetary considerations. Many scholars advocate for converting antitrust enforcement into a pricing issue. For example, some propose using the Efficient Component Pricing Rule (ECPR) to address refusal-to-deal issues.[58] However, some scholars disagree with ECPR.[59] For instance, Salop argues that ECPR has shortcomings and proposes the Protected Profits Benchmark (PPB) standard as an alternative.[60] The PPB standard is essentially another form of price analysis. Therefore, transforming

[58] Ordover, J.A. & Willig, R.D., (1981). 'An economic definition of predation: pricing and product innovation'. *Yale Law Journal*, 91(1), 8–53; Baumol, W.J. & Sidak, J.G. (1994). 'The pricing of inputs sold to competitors'. *Yale Journal on Regulation*, 11(1), 171–202; Albon, R. (1994). 'Interconnection Pricing: An analysis of the efficient component pricing rule', *Telecommunications Policy*, 18(5), 414–420.

[59] ECPR is a pricing method that addresses pricing by emphasizing the opportunity costs of monopolists. These opportunity costs will depend on market conditions, specifically including product differentiation, bypass, and substitute possibilities, among others. In the most basic case, if the monopolist's profit from interconnection and access is equal to the profit derived from retail product sales, then new entrants can only enter the market if they are more efficient than the monopolist. ECPR has also become a mainstream method for testing the legality of refusal to deal.

[60] Salop, S.C. (2010). 'Refusals to deal and price squeezes by an unregulated, vertically integrated monopolist'. *Antitrust Law Journal*, 76(3), 709–740.

intellectual property antitrust analysis into pricing problems is justified and price theory can significantly facilitate this analysis. This section will discuss the issues of price theory in intellectual property antitrust.

5.2.3.1 Excessive Monopoly Price

Monopoly pricing is generally divided into two main pricing models: uniform pricing and price discrimination. In uniform pricing, the right holder sets a single price for different implementers, with the pricing strategy aimed at maximizing profits. In traditional monopoly uniform pricing models, compared to the price in a perfectly competitive market, the monopoly price leads to deadweight loss on the one hand, meaning the total surplus is not maximized, which reduces efficiency. On the other hand, monopoly pricing also implies that the right holder is depriving the implementer of their surplus. Overall, monopoly uniform pricing is generally considered a violation of antitrust laws, unless it can be shown that the monopoly price is similar to the price in a perfectly competitive market. However, this conclusion cannot necessarily be applied into intellectual property monopoly pricing.

The reason traditional monopolistic pricing can maximize profits is because the firm sets the price where marginal revenue equals marginal cost. In the case of intellectual property licensing, the marginal cost for the right holder is zero. The total revenue for the right holder is equal to the price multiplied by the quantity of licenses (number of licenses granted) minus the total fixed costs (costs incurred in developing the intellectual property). At this point, the right holder only needs to decide the number of licenses to issue in order to maximize revenue.

Sometimes, the price set by the right holder may not be affected by the number of licenses issued, meaning the prices for exclusive licenses, sole licenses, and non-exclusive licenses are identical. In this case, the more licenses the right holder grants before the secondary market (the market between the implementer and consumers) becomes saturated, the higher their revenue will be.[61] However, in most of the cases, the price of the license is related to the number of licenses granted, and the licensing

[61] The premise here is that intellectual property is necessary for the implementer to enter the market. Once the number of implementers is saturated, allowing one more implementer into the market may mean that other implementers will leave, and their departure would lead to a corresponding reduction in the licensing fee. When intellectual property is not necessary for entering the market but only serves to improve efficiency or reduce costs, even if the secondary market is saturated, the right holder can still allow more implementers to enter through licensing, as long as the licensing fee for the intellectual property is slightly lower than the efficiency improvement or cost reduction it provides, and there are no alternative technologies. Implementers with licensing agreements with the right holder will have the opportunity to squeeze out those who do not use the intellectual property from the market. If the substitutability of the intellectual property is high, further examination of the substitutability between the intellectual property and its alternatives, as well as the differences in licensing fees, is needed to determine when the right holder can maximize their profits. However, since this section focuses on the study of intellectual property monopoly pricing, all discussions should be based on the assumption of monopoly. Therefore, the author assumes that intellectual property is necessary for the implementer to enter the market.

price set by the right holder can be expressed as a function of the number of licenses (P(Q)), that is, the rates for exclusive licenses, sole licenses, and non-exclusive licenses vary. Also, even the number of implementers may influence the price of the license, for example, if the right holder licenses to 4 implementers, the rate for each implementer is 50,000 per year; if licensing to 6 implementers, the rate drops to 40,000 for each implementer per year; and if licensing to 10 implementers, the rate is further reduced to 30,000 per year.

In this case, the court cannot hastily conclude that the uniform pricing by the right holder is inefficient, nor can it be assumed that the uniform monopolistic pricing necessarily leads to inefficiency. The court must assess whether the uniform monopolistic pricing constitutes an excessive monopoly price. The distinction between 'high' and 'low' prices is relative, and the judgment of 'high' is essentially an effect-based analysis. In antitrust in intellectual property, excessive monopoly pricing can be defined as pricing that leads to a reduction in efficiency or an unequal distribution. Conversely, if pricing does not lead to a reduction in efficiency or an unequal distribution, it should be regarded as reasonable pricing. Meanwhile, the determination of efficiency can be made by observing changes in overall social welfare, while the judgment of distribution can be made by examining changes in consumer surplus and producer surplus.[62] In the framework of price theory, the analysis of efficiency issues is aimed at observing whether monopolistic high pricing leads to deadweight loss, while the analysis of distribution issues is focused on assessing the reasonableness of price gouging or wealth transfer.

If the right holder adopts a monopolistic uniform pricing strategy in the pricing process, the court must split the price into two parts: the portion attributable to the intellectual property contribution rate and the portion attributable to the competitive strength of the intellectual property.[63] The court should then observe the implementer's willingness to accept the price attributable to the competitive strength and assess the impact of this competitive pricing on the market. For example, if the right holder sets the price at 300,000 per year, and within the relevant market, the income attributable to the average contribution rate of the intellectual property is 100,000, with the remaining 200,000 attributable to its competitive strength. When the transaction cost is zero, consumers may be willing to pay more to encourage the monopolist to increase output to meet market demand.[64] If the intellectual property is an essential facility for the implementer to enter the market, some implementers may also be willing to pay more. The court must then observe the abilities of implementers

[62] The concepts of 'welfare' and 'surplus' are most closely related, and scholars often equate 'welfare' with 'surplus' when discussing welfare. (See Lande, R.H. (1999). 'Wealth transfers as the original and primary concern of antitrust: The efficiency interpretation challenged'. *Hastings Law Journal*, 50(4), 871–958; Farrell, J. & Katz, M.L. (2006). 'The economics of welfare standards in antitrust'. *Competition Policy International*, 2, 3).

[63] The price attributable to the contribution rate is equivalent to the marginal cost. The monopolist will always price above the marginal cost, and we only need to observe whether the price above the marginal cost is reasonable.

[64] Calabresi, G. (1968). 'Transaction costs, resource allocation and liability rules'. *Journal of Law & Economics*, 11(1), 67.

in accepting the excess profits of 200,000 of the right holder. If this excess profit prevents most implementers from entering the market, the court should consider the pricing behaviours of the right holder as unreasonable. On the contrary, if the pricing only involves distribution issues, the court can evaluate it from the perspective of distribution. If the intellectual property is not essential for the implementer to enter the market, then regardless of whether the pricing is reasonable, it should not be considered as a violation of antitrust law, because the granting or refusal of the intellectual property license would not affect efficiency.

When the court assesses whether a price is high or low, it should refer to the average level of price within the industry. This is because the same intellectual property can generate different levels of efficiency in the hands of different implementers. Continuing with the previous example, in the case of a product made by a high-efficiency implementer, the contribution-based income might reach 150,000, while for a low-efficiency implementer, it could be as low as 50,000. In such a case, the court needs to consider the average contribution rate of the intellectual property within the industry. If the contribution-based income would reach 100,000 in light of the average level of the industry, then even if the price might prevent some implementers from entering the market, it should still be considered reasonable.

5.2.3.2 Price Discrimination

Compared to uniform monopoly pricing, price discrimination is a more common pricing strategy in intellectual property licensing. Price discrimination refers to the practice where a right holder demands different prices from different implementers for the same technology at the same time. This pricing strategy stems from the right holder's pursuit of utility maximization. When implementers are homogeneous, the right holder will not engage in differentiated pricing. However, because implementers are heterogeneous, with each willing to pay a different price to obtain the intellectual property license, the right holder can maximize their utility by capturing the entire surplus of each implementer.

The premise for price discrimination is that the right holder to have market power, as it is not feasible in a perfectly competitive market. In other words, if the intellectual property is highly substitutable, the right holder would be unable to implement a price discrimination strategy. Another possible prerequisite for price discrimination is that the right holder needs to have access to the demand function of the implementer or obtain information about their demand. However, this is not always essential. Even without knowledge of the demand information of the implementer, the right holder can still implement price discrimination. Over the course of repeated transactions, the right holder can gradually gather information about the preferences of the implementer and adjust their pricing strategy accordingly. Price discrimination generally occurs at three degrees.[65] We will now discuss each of these degrees in detail.

[65] Belleflamme, P. & Peitz, M. (2014). *Chanye zuzhi: Shichang he celue* [*Industrial organization: Markets and strategies*]. (Chen, H., Xu, L. et al. trans.). Gezhi Chubanshe, Sanlian Shudian,

First-Degree Price Discrimination First-degree price discrimination refers to the practice where the right holder sets different prices for different implementers, which is a commonly used pricing strategy in intellectual property licensing. From an efficiency perspective, first-degree price discrimination is highly efficient. Theoretically, the equilibrium point of first-degree price discrimination is the same as that in a perfectly competitive market, and it can maximize total surplus. Therefore, first-degree price discrimination does not reduce efficiency and may even achieve Pareto optimality. From a distributional perspective, although first-degree price discrimination does not affect efficiency, but it does impact the distribution of surplus. First-degree price discrimination transfers consumer surplus into producer surplus. The right holder can convert the implementer's surplus into their own surplus through first-degree price discrimination. However, in practice, the right holder cannot know the reserved prices of each implementer, as a result, they cannot fully implement first-degree price discrimination. Nonetheless, the right holder can still obtain part of the implementer's surplus through a form of near-first-degree price discrimination.

Next, it is necessary to determine whether this surplus transfer violates antitrust law. As mentioned earlier, the price composition of intellectual property includes two parts: the portion attributable to the contribution rate and the portion attributable to competitiveness. The court should first separate the part related to the contribution rate and then analyse whether the portion related to competitiveness is reasonable. This judgment on distribution involves a high degree of subjectivity and is also influenced by the national policy direction. If the country is currently focused on technological development, then the right holder should be allowed to retain a larger portion of the surplus. Conversely, if the policy is not aligned with such goals, then the right holder should not be allowed to retain excessive surplus.

Second-degree price discrimination The most common form of second-degree price discrimination is nonlinear pricing, where different prices are charged based on different quantities. First-degree price discrimination requires the right holder to have complete knowledge of the consumption preferences of implementers. However, in most cases, the implementer's consumption preferences are not immediately obvious, especially in the first transaction, when the right holder may not have access to the implementer's preference information. In this situation, second-degree price discrimination allows the implementer to choose their own consumption preferences, and this provides the right holder with information about the implementer's preferences.

Second-degree price discrimination is also common in intellectual property transactions, which is mainly manifested in the form of discounts. Some right holders would set prices according to the production volume of the intellectual property products. The times of usage of the intellectual property is often related to the production and sales volume of the product, and the right holder can indirectly determine the level of intellectual property usage by calculating the production and sales volume of the product. Based on different usage levels, the right holder can categorize the pricing into tiers. For example, the right holder might set the price for usage under

Shanghai Renmin Chubanshe [Gezhi Publishing House, Sanlian Bookstore, Shanghai People's Publishing House]. 169–171.

1,000 units at 10 yuan per use, for sales between 1,000 and 10,000 units at 8 yuan per use, and for sales exceeding 10,000 units at 5 yuan per use.

The efficiency in the form of discount has the potential to reach an optimal state. It offers more pricing options than uniform pricing, making it possible to approach the marginal cost. When the minimum price equals the marginal cost, the total surplus under the discount pricing system is the same as the total surplus in both first-degree price discrimination and a perfectly competitive market. Therefore, an assessment of efficiency in the form of discount requires an analysis of its minimum price. If the minimum price is equal to the marginal cost, it is efficient; however, if it exceeds the marginal cost, it would lead to deadweight loss. In the context of intellectual property licensing, the price that reflects the contribution rate should be used as a substitute for the marginal cost, since the marginal cost in intellectual property licensing is zero. From a distributional perspective, the discount does not completely extract the surplus of the implementer. Its advantage over first-degree price discrimination is that it leaves some consumer surplus, making it more favourable for the sake of distribution. The author believes that the form of discount is generally more acceptable than first-degree price discrimination and should, in most cases, not be considered a violation of antitrust law.

In addition to the discount form, two-part tariff pricing is another form of nonlinear pricing. A two-part tariff involves the right holder setting a total licensing fee that combines a fixed base fee and a variable fee based on the quantity. Its general expression can be written as: $T(q) = T + pq$, where $T(q)$ is the total licensing fee, T is the fixed fee, p is the per-unit price, and q is the quantity of production or sales. Alternatively, the two-part tariff can be expressed as: $T(q) = T + p_1q_1 + p_2(q_2 - q_1) + \cdots + p_k(q_k - q_{k-1})$. This expression can explain most nonlinear pricing issues. In this context, the base fee T can be used to differentiate among target consumers. If the right holder only wishes to deal with implementers who are less price-sensitive, they can set a higher base fee; if they are willing to accept some price-sensitive implementers, they can lower the base fee; if they wish to engage with any implementer, they can set the base fee to zero. When the base fee is set at zero, the two-part tariff model is very similar to the form of discount. For example, the right holder can adopt a membership fee model, selecting implementers who are willing to pay the membership fee and only entering into licensing agreements with this group of members. This approach effectively prevents low-efficiency implementers from entering the market because they may not even be able to recover the base fee. The implementers who remain in the market at least demonstrate that they can generate enough revenue to cover the base fee.

Although it is unclear whether such a licensing model exists in practice, it seems to be a feasible approach. From an efficiency perspective, this model can, in certain circumstances, achieve total surplus maximization equivalent to that in a perfectly competitive market. Consider this: if the minimum total licensing fee price $(T + p_1q_1)$ is set equal to the marginal cost (attributable to the income from the contribution rate of intellectual property), total surplus can be maximized. Therefore, this model is more efficient than uniform monopoly pricing. From a distributional perspective, two-part tariff converts some consumer surplus into producer surplus. Compared to first-degree price discrimination, it does not fully extract consumer surplus. The distributional effect of the two-part tariff is similar to that of discount pricing. The key to determining whether the two-part tariff model violates antitrust law lies in evaluating whether the minimum licensing fee ($T + p_1 q_1$) and the subsequent breakdown ($p_2(q_2 - q_1) + \cdots + p_k(q_k - q_{k-1})$) are reasonable. The minimum licensing fee can be considered as the market entry barrier. If the entry barrier is too high and leads to deadweight loss, it should be deemed unreasonable. The subsequent breakdown concerns distribution, and when it is sufficiently detailed, it becomes equivalent to first-degree price discrimination. In this case, the distribution issues mentioned in first-degree price discrimination should be applied to evaluate whether the two-part tariff violates antitrust law.

Third-Degree Price Discrimination Third-degree price discrimination refers to the practice of dividing the implementers into different groups and charging each group a different price. In practice, right holders may not have enough information to fully understand consumer preferences or demand functions, in such circumstances, it is difficult to implement first-degree price discrimination. However, right holders may have partial information about the demand of the implementer. In such cases, rather than applying second-degree price discrimination, the right holder can choose to divide implementers into different groups based on this information and then apply differentiated pricing to each group. For example, the right holder of Wi-Fi technology may classify implementers into categories such as computers, mobile phones, and printers, and charge different prices for each category. Third-degree price discrimination essentially distinguishes among different markets, charging different prices for the implementers in each market segment. In third-degree price discrimination, the right holder will set lower prices for implementers with more elastic demand and higher prices for those with less elastic demand. In the above example, if third-degree price discrimination is applied, the licensing fee for Wi-Fi technology in mobile phones will be higher than in computers, and also higher than in printers. Of course, such ‘high’ or ‘low’ refers to relative prices rather than absolute prices, as the licensing fee is also influenced by the overall price of the product.

From an efficiency perspective, the total surplus in third-degree price discrimination needs to be assessed on a case-by-case basis. This is because it is equivalent to implementing a uniform monopoly pricing strategy across different markets, if the pricing is symmetric to the contribution rate, then no deadweight loss will be caused. However, if the pricing exceeds the base price that corresponds to the contribution rate, deadweight loss will occur. In monopoly pricing, the factor that influences the profit maximization of the right holder is the implementer’s demand function. When the substitutability of the technology is low, the right holder will set prices entirely based on the demand function of the implementer. Therefore, whether third-degree price discrimination harms efficiency needs to be assessed on a case-by-case basis. From a distributional perspective, third-degree price discrimination may also lead to the exploitation of implementers. The process for determining this aspect can be referenced from the evaluation of first-degree price discrimination.

Antitrust enforcement addresses the issue of abuse of rights from an external perspective for the purpose of promoting transactions, however, the enforcement costs are often high. In contrast, addressing abuse within the internal structure of rights is more effective. When the right holder and the implementer cannot reach an agreement, the court may, in certain cases, directly determine a reasonable royalty rate to facilitate the transaction. This is particularly relevant in situations such as the licensing of SEPs. In the next section, we will discuss the application of price theory in intellectual property licensing.

5.3 Summary of This Chapter

Price theory studies the mechanisms of price formation, and determining a price is the core of intellectual property transactions. Once the parties reach an agreement on the price, that means the transaction is essentially completed. However, in many cases, the right holder and the implementer cannot agree on a unified price, and in such situations, the court may need to facilitate both parties in determining a reasonable royalty. A clear understanding of price theory can assist the court in setting prices that are more in line with market realities. Furthermore, when the price set by the right holder is excessively high and potentially triggers antitrust concerns, the court can use price theory to assess the reasonableness of the price set by the right holder. In fact, the above two scenarios are merely the most common applications of pricing theory in intellectual property transactions, yet its actual scope of application in intellectual property transactions is much broader than this.

References

Akerlof, G. A. (1970). The market for 'lemons': Quality uncertainty and the market mechanism. *Quarterly Journal of Economics, 84*(3), 489.

Albon, R. (1994). Interconnection Pricing: An analysis of the efficient component pricing rule. *Telecommunications Policy, 18*(5), 414–420.

Arrow, K. J., & Debreu, G. (1954). Existence of an equilibrium for a competitive economy. *Econometrica, 22*(3), 265–290.

Ayres, I., & Parchomovsky, G. (2007). Tradable patent rights. *Stanford Law Review, 60*(3), 863–894.

Bacharach, S. B., & Lawler, E. J. (1981). *Bargaining: Power, tactics, and outcomes*. Jossey-Bass.

Bai, B., & Bai, R. (2011). Silafa jiage tixi fenxi [Sraffa price system analysis]. *Dangdai Jingji Yanjiu [Contemporary Economic Research], 1*, 9–17.

Baumol, W. J., & Sidak, J. G. (1994). The pricing of inputs sold to competitors'. *Yale Journal on Regulation, 11*(1), 171–202.

Becker, G. S. (1991). Milton Friedman. In E. Shils (Ed.), *Remembering the University of Chicago: Teachers, scientists, and scholars*. University of Chicago Press.

Belleflamme, P., & Peitz, M. (2014). *Chanye zuzhi: Shichang he celue [Industrial organization: Markets and strategies]* (H. Chen, L. Xu, et al. Trans.). Gezhi Chubanshe, Sanlian Shudian, Shanghai Renmin Chubanshe [Gezhi Publishing House, Sanlian Bookstore, Shanghai People's Publishing House].

Calabresi, G. (1968). Transaction costs, resource allocation and liability rules'. *Journal of Law & Economics, 11*(1), 67.

Chamberlain, N. W., & Kuhn, J. W. (1965). *Collective bargaining* (2nd ed.). McGraw-Hill Book Co.
Choi, A., & Triantis, G. (2012). The effect of bargaining power on contract design. *Virginia Law Review, 98*(8), 1667.
Commons, J. R. (1934). *Institutional economics: Its place in political economy*. Macmillan
Contreras, J., et al. (2019). The effect of FRAND commitments on patent remedies. In C. B. Biddle (Ed.), *Patent remedies and complex products*. Cambridge University Press.
Contreras, J. L., & Eixenberger, M. A. (2016). Jury instructions for reasonable royalty patent damages. *Jurimetrics, 57*(1), 1–24.
Cooter, R., & Ulen, T. (2012). *Law & Economics* (6th ed.). Pearson.
Debreu, G. (1959). *The theory of value*. Wiley.
Farrell, J., & Katz, M. L. (2006). The economics of welfare standards in antitrust. *Competition Policy International, 2*, 3.
Fisher, I. (1892). *Mathematical investigations in the theory of value and prices*. Yale University Press.
Forsythe, R., Nelson, F., Neumann, G. R., & Wright, J. (1992). Anatomy of an experimental political stock market. *The American Economic Review, 82*(5), 1142.
Frank, R. H., & Bernanke, B. (2009). *Principles of microeconomics* (4th ed.). McGraw-Hill.
Friedman, D. D. (1990). *Price theory: An intermediate text*. Cincinnati. South-Western Publishing Co.
Fuchs-Seliger, S. (1983). Budget preferences and direct utility. *Journal of Economic Theory, 30*(1), 188.
Hammond, D. J. (2010). The development of post-war Chicago price theory. In R. B. Emmett (Ed.), *The Elgar companion to the Chicago School of Economics*. Edward Elgar Publishing.
Hicks, J. R. (1939). *Value and capital*. Oxford University Press.
Hicks, J., & Allen, R. (1934). A reconsideration of the theory of value. *Economica, 1*(1), 52–76.
Hotelling, H. (1931). The economics of exhaustible resources. *Journal of Political Economy, 39*(2), 137–175.
Jaffe, S., Minton, R., Mulligan, C. B., & Murphy, K. M. (2019). *Chicago price theory*. Princeton University Press.
Jevons, W. S. (2013). *The theory of political economy*. Palgrave Macmillan.
Jiang, D. (2017). Gaoji weiguan jingjixue [*Advanced microeconomics*] (2nd ed.).Beijing Daxue Chubanshe [Peking University Press].
Jiang, H. (2017). Zhishi chanquan sunhai peichang de shichang jiazhi [Market value of intellectual property damages]. *Zhishi Chanquan [Intellectual Property], 7*, 60–67.
Kauder, E. (1953). Genesis of the marginal utility theory: From Aristotle to the end of the eighteenth century. *The Economic Journal, 63*(251), 638–650.
Kong, W. (2020). Lun ziyou maoyi beijingxia jishu biaozhun de sifa dingjia guize-Yi shichang zhudao wei qierudian [On judicial pricing rules for technical standards under the background of free trade: From the perspective of market dominance]. *Zhongguo Zhuanli Yu Faming [China Invention and Patent], 1*, 29–34.
Lande, R. H. (1999). Wealth transfers as the original and primary concern of antitrust: The efficiency interpretation challenged'. *Hastings Law Journal, 50*(4), 871–958.
Layne-Farrar, A., Padilla, J., & Schmalensee, R. (2007). Pricing patents for licensing in standard-setting organizations: Making sense of FRAND commitments. *Antitrust Law Journal, 74*(3), 671–706.
Lindbloom, C. E. (1948). Bargaining power in price and wage determination. *Quarterly Journal of Economics, 62*(3), 402.
Livernash, E. R. (1983). The relation of power to the structure and process of collective bargaining. *Journal of Law & Economics, 6*, 18.
Love, N. C. (2008). Reasonable royalties for patent infringement'. *University of Chicago Law Review, 75*(4), 1749–1772.

Mabry, B. D. (1965). The pure theory of bargaining. *Industrial & Labor Relations Review, 18*(4), 479.
Marshall, A. (1890). *Principles of economics*. Macmillan.
Marshall, A. (2013). *Principles of economics* (8th ed.). Palgrave Macmillan.
Mas-Colell, A., Whinston, M. D., & Green, J. R. (1995). *Microeconomic theory*. Oxford University Press.
Menger, C. (2007). *Principles of economics*. Ludwig von Mises Institute.
Michel, S. (2011). Bargaining for RAND royalties in the shadow of patent remedies law. *Antitrust Law Journal, 77*(3), 889–911.
Milgrom, P. (2020). *Jiage lilun [Discovering prices]* (C. Han, Trans.). CITIC Publishing Group [Zhongxin Chubanshe].
Mill, J. S. (1836). Essay on the definition of political economy. In J. M. Robson (Ed.), *The collected works of John Stuart Mill* (Vol. 4). University of Toronto Press.
Nicholson, W. (1978). *Microeconomic theory*. Dryden Press.
Ordover, J. A., & Willig, R. D. (1981). An economic definition of predation: Pricing and product innovation. *Yale Law Journal, 91*(1), 8–53.
Ricardo, D. (2001). *On the principles of political economy and taxation*. Batoche Books.
Salop, S. C. (2010). Refusals to deal and price squeezes by an unregulated, vertically integrated monopolist. *Antitrust Law Journal, 76*(3), 709–740.
Samuelson, P. A. (1947). *The foundations of economic analysis*. Harvard University Press.
Siebrasse, N. V., & Cotter, T. F. (2017). The value of standard. *Minnesota Law Review, 101*(3), 1187.
Slichter, S. H. (1940). Impact of social security legislation upon mobility and enterprise. *American Economic Review, 30*(1), 57.
Smith, A. (1901). *An inquiry into the nature and causes of the wealth of nations*. Dent.
Snowdon, B., & Vane, H. R. (1998). Transforming macroeconomics: An interview with Robert E. Lucas Jr. *Journal of Economic Methodology, 5*(1), 120.
Sraffa, P. (1960). *Production of commodities by means of commodities: Prelude to critique of economic theory*. Cambridge University Press.
Stigler, G. (1937). The economics of carl menger. *Journal of Political Economy, 45*(2), 240.
Stigler, G. (1987). *The theory of price*. Macmillan Publishing Company.
Stigler, G. J., & Boulding, K. E. (1952). *Readings in price theory*. Association by R.D. Irwin; Bain, J. S. (1972). *Essays on price theory and industrial organization*. Little, Brown.
Strotz, R. (1953). Cardinal utility. *The American Economic Review, 43*(2), 384–397.
Suppes, P., & Winet, M. (1955). An axiomatization of utility based on the notion of utility difference. *Management Science, 1*(3–4), 197–281.
Swanson, D. G., & Baumol, W. J. (2005). Reasonable and nondiscriminatory (RAND) royalties, standards selection, and control of market power. *Antitrust Law Journal, 73*(1), 15–21.
Welch, C. (1987). *Utilitarianism* (p. 772). The Macmillan Press Limited.
Weyl, E. G. (2014). A Short Summary of Price Theory as commissioned by the *Journal of Economic Literature* (p. 3). https://hope.econ.duke.edu/sites/hope.econ.duke.edu/files/Price_Theory_Summary_6_14.pdf. Accessed on 30 Jul. 2022.
Wu, H. (2018). Zhishi chanquan sunhai peichang de shichang jiazhi fenxi: Lilun, guize yu fangfa [An analysis of market value in intellectual property damages: Theory, rules, and methods]. *Faxue Pinglun [Law Review], 1*, 65–74.

Chapter 6
Theoretical Manifestations in Specific Types of Intellectual Property Transactions

6.1 Market, System and Behaviour in Intellectual Property Transactions

When examining the operation of market economies, economic study places a central focus on price as the key element. The emphasis on the result (i.e. equilibrium price) of a transaction has surpassed the focus on the behaviours themselves. It is almost a common understanding that economic analysis must address 'market' and its 'equilibrium' from the outset because, in most of those authors' views, it is difficult to define the cost (consideration) of any item without clarifying its market equilibrium (price).[1] However, this research takes a different approach by shifting the focus to the behavioural process of market transactions, specifically the game-theoretic formation of the equilibrium price, aiming to clarify the internal logic of 'institutions', 'markets', and 'behaviours'. Deconstructing transactions is not merely an optimization problem, the behaviours of market participants change as the transaction progresses. At its core, this is a behaviour of gaming, and the eventual agreement (such as a contract) is the concrete manifestation of this gaming behaviour. Based on contract theory and price theory discussed in the previous chapters, this chapter analyses the specific behaviours in intellectual property transactions, focusing on the behavioural choices of market participants under the existing system. In this chapter, intellectual property transactions are categorized into voluntary and involuntary behaviours, typical transactional behaviours such as intellectual property licensing, assignment, and capitalization are selected as the objects for this analysis.

Intellectual property transactions facilitate the circulation of market resources by adjusting the residual value. The construction of the intellectual property transaction market involves not only the game over interests between the market participants but also considerations of transaction cost and benefits. Contract theory focuses

[1] Wang, D. (2015). *Xingwei jingjixue yaoyi [The essentials of behavioural economics]*. Shanghai Renmin Chubanshe [Shanghai People's Publishing House]. 12.

© Intellectual Property Publishing House Co., Ltd. 2025

M. Yang, *Basic Theories of Intellectual Property Transaction*,
https://doi.org/10.1007/978-981-96-7039-0_6

on the gaming behaviours in intellectual property transactions as well as institutional design as key issues in these transactions. It concerns the efficient operation of the behaviours of market participants and the achievement of high-quality market outcomes. In intellectual property transactions, the market serves as the venue where transactions take place, with the aim of providing convenience for market participants to engage in market activities, and the goal to promote the effective allocation of market resources and the maximization of interests of market participants through a fair and orderly operating environment. Regarding the institutional framework for intellectual property transactions, it essentially reflects the application of incentive theory in the design of market rules. Whether it is public policy or legal norms for intellectual property protection, the essence lies in the design of rules to incentivize both parties in intellectual property transactions to make their utmost efforts to engage in the game, so as to maximize the utility of the transaction behaviours.

The behaviours in intellectual property transactions are essentially the manifestations of the content of market operation onto the transaction participants. Market participants, based on factors such as information asymmetry and transaction costs, conduct gaming behaviours through contracts, aiming to reach an equilibrium price and achieve the optimal solution for the allocation of market resources.

6.1.1 A Trading Market Centered on Intellectual Property Rights

6.1.1.1 Understanding of the Market Attributes of Intellectual Property

The academic understanding of the nature of intellectual property in China can be categorized from three levels: political attributes, legal attributes, and market attributes. The market value of intellectual property was not initially recognized when China first introduced the intellectual property system. In the 1970s, when China introduced the intellectual property system for the first time, the primary goal was to align with international developments and meet global demands. At this time, China was eager to join the World Trade Organization (WTO), and in response to the demands of developed countries, it was necessary to establish an intellectual property protection system in line with the overall international trend of intellectual property protection. Therefore, the establishment of the intellectual property system at the first stage in China was heavily influenced by political factors.

The second stage occurred during the period of rapid development of China's market economy. In this stage, Chinese scholars increasingly emphasized the private law attributes of intellectual property to effectively enhance public recognition of intellectual property and improve the operational capabilities of enterprises intellectual property. This perspective emphasized that intellectual property is a private right, and intellectual property works would be strictly protected by law while generating economic value for the owner.

The third stage emerged with the development of the era of technological innovation. Scholars recognized that intellectual property should not only be seen as a form of private protection but should also focus on the role of intellectual property in promoting social innovation and its impact on market competition.[2] It was at this stage that the market attributes of intellectual property became more evident.

6.1.1.2 The Role of Intellectual Property Rights in Economic Growth

On October 28, 2021, the State Council issued *the 14th Five-Year Plan for National Intellectual Property Protection and Utilization*, which clearly outlined the strategic plan for the future of national intellectual property work in its 'Guiding Ideology'. It specifically emphasized the need to 'comprehensively improve the level of intellectual property creation, utilization, protection, management, and services', with the aim of promoting high-quality economic and social development through strengthening the application of intellectual property in all its aspects. This indicates that in the construction of a strong nation of intellectual property, the 'utilization' of intellectual property has become as important as 'creation' and 'protection'. The premise of effective intellectual property utilization is the establishment of a sound intellectual property transaction market. In this regard, some scholars have conducted empirical analysis on the degree of impact of intellectual property in the market economy, in these analysis, the contribution of the intellectual property system to economic growth can be divided into two parts: the promotion of economic growth by the quantity of intellectual property itself, and the driving effect of the intellectual property market on the economy. A calculation of the data from 2001 to 2015 shows that the contribution rate of intellectual property accumulation to economic growth was 4.4%, while the contribution rate of the intellectual property market to economic growth was 4.1%.[3] Function analysis of the specific data reveals that in the long term, the contribution of the intellectual property market to economic growth will eventually surpass that of intellectual property accumulation. Improving the level of contribution of intellectual property to economic growth will increasingly depend on the continuous improvement of the intellectual property market system, rather than the mere increase in the quantity of intellectual property itself.

---

[2] Zhang, X. '*From the State Council institutional reform to the market-oriented operation of enterprise intellectual property*', *IPRdaily Chinese Network*. Available at: http://www.iprdaily.cn/article_18536.html, accessed on 23 July 2022.

[3] Ji, P., Sun, F. & Zhao, X. (2018). 'Zhishichanquan dui jingji zengzhang zuoyong de shizheng yanjiu' ['*An empirical study on the role of intellectual property in economic growth'*]. *Honguan Jingji Yanjiu [Macroeconomic Research]*, 12, 54.

6.1.1.3 Main Types and Development Trends of Intellectual Property Transaction Markets

In recent years, China's intellectual property transaction market has begun to take shape. Intellectual property transaction markets with names such as 'transaction platforms', 'exchanges', 'transaction networks', 'transaction centers', and 'public service platforms' have been established and are now in operation. Based on their establishment methods, these markets can be divided into two types: those established voluntarily by enterprises and those approved by the government. In terms of business scope, they can generally be categorized into four types: comprehensive property transaction markets, patent property transaction markets, trademark property transaction markets, and copyright transaction markets.[4] The operational models of these four types of markets are relatively similar, involving information sharing and connection between the parties to the transaction, which facilitates the conversion of intellectual property into tradable and exchangeable products in a market-oriented manner. From the perspective of the current types of intellectual property transactions in China, based on traditional classifications, transactions on intellectual property rights can be divided into licensing, assignment, and capitalization methods centered around intellectual property pledges, trusts, and securitization.

Among these, the comprehensive intellectual property transaction market is characterized by government support, enterprise participation, rational layout, and the largest scale. The patent and copyright intellectual property transaction markets are more policy-driven, with an early start, wide regional distribution, clear hierarchy, and complete functions. The trademark property transaction market has been in operation for a longer time and is mainly enterprise-driven, with more matured online operations.[5] However, there are still prominent issues in the construction of China's intellectual property market, including imbalances in competition, security fraud, low efficiency, a single format, and an unreasonable market structure etc. These problems still require further governance and coordination.

6.1.2 Institutional System Related to Intellectual Property Transactions

In 2008, the State Council promulgated and implemented the *National Intellectual Property Strategy Outline*, marking the elevation of intellectual property to a national strategy. Following this, a series of policies and legal regulations were introduced,

[4] Chen, L. & Xu, Q. (2018). 'Zhishi chanquan jiaoyishichang jianshe taishi yu lujing zhaoxun' [*'The construction trend and path search of the intellectual property transaction market']. Gaige [Reform]*, 5, 122.

[5] Xue, X. & Peng, C. (2019). 'Zhishi chanquan jiaoyi shichang de jianquan yu wanshan' [*'The improvement and perfection of the intellectual property transaction market']. Renmin Luntan [People's Forum]*, 7, 85.

leading to the rapid development of the intellectual property sector. However, despite the large scale of China's intellectual property market, it remains relatively weak, and the low quality of R&D and innovation products remain core issues in China's intellectual property development and innovation capability enhancement. To address this, the State Council released the *Several Opinions on Accelerating the Construction of a Strong Intellectual Property Nation in the New Situation* in 2015, which clearly emphasized the goal of accelerating the establishment of a strong intellectual property nation. The concept of a strong intellectual property nation involves establishing a complete legal system and regulatory framework that can clearly define and protect the operation of intellectual property rights while fully considering the background of science, technology, economic and social development, and dynamically adjust it on a relatively stable basis.[6] In 2021, the Central Committee of the Communist Party of China and the State Council issued the *Outline for the Construction of a Strong Intellectual Property Nation (2021–2035)* to further promoting the progress of building a strong intellectual property nation. Therefore, to address the issues arising in China's intellectual property development, it is imperative to establish a complete institutional frameword for systematic regulation, thereby achieving a significant leap in intellectual property development and innovation. This is undoubtedly an essential requirement for building a strong intellectual property nation.

Legal operation refers to the movement or process of law following a certain intent and specific manner, from its creation to implementation and ultimately its realization.[7] Specifically, the process of legal operation consists of three essential stages: the creation of law, the implementation of law, and the realization of law. Intellectual property operation, as a special form of legal operation, also includes multiple stages such as the creation, operation, management, protection, and service of intellectual property.[8] Therefore, the institutional framework related to intellectual property transactions can be divided into two main components: policies on intellectual property protection and the legislative system for intellectual property. These two components are further explored in the following discussion.

6.1.2.1 Public Policy on Intellectual Property Protection

Public policy refers to the normative documents formulated by public authorities concerning the management of public affairs. These documents mainly take the form of decrees, regulations, rules, plans, strategies, measures, and projects, forming

---

[6] Liang, Z., Luo, Y. & Deng, X. (2016). 'Jiyu jiazhilian shijiao de zhishi chanquan qiangguo jianshe lujing yanjiu' [*'Research on the path of building a strong intellectual property country from the perspective of the value chain'*]. *Zhongguo kexueyuan yuankan [Bulletin of the Chinese Academy of Sciences]*, 9, 1011.

[7] Zhang, W. (2003). Falixue (Di er ban) [*Jurisprudence (2nd ed.)*]. Gaodeng jiaoyu chubanshe [Higher Education Press]. 213.

[8] Wu, H. (2018). 'Zhongguo zhishi chanquan falv bianqian de jiben mianxiang' [*'The basic aspects of the evolution of China's intellectual property law'*]. *Zhongguo shehui kexue [Social Sciences in China]*, 8, 112.

a cohesive and interrelated system of institutional norms. Within the intellectual property policy system, there are three main categories of concepts: core policies, related policies, and supportive policies. Core policies are directly related to the innovation, utilization, protection, and management of intellectual property. They include development plans, strategic outlines, annual implementation plans, and so on. Related policies are those associated with the commercialization of innovative achievements, industrialization of intellectual property, and the 'intellectualization' of foreign trade. Examples include science and technology development plans, measures for technology transfer, industrial development catalogues, and enterprise promotion methods. Supportive policies include financial, fiscal, tax, and talent support policies, such as tax incentives, pledge financing, and talent rewards.[9] Specifically, the development of China's public policy system on intellectual property can be divided into four periods: the initial period, the development period, the enhancement period, and the strategic period.[10]

The 1980s was the initial stage, during which the main task was to establish a framework for intellectual property management under the guidance of relevant laws and regulations. The key policy documents during this period include the *Regulations on Strengthening Enterprise Patent Work* jointly issued in 1986 by the State Economic and Trade Commission, the State Science and Technology Commission, the Ministry of Finance, and the Patent Office, which called for the adoption of administrative and fiscal measures to establish a framework for intellectual property management in enterprises; the *Decision on Deepening the Reform of the Science and Technology System* issued by the State Council in 1988, and the *Notice on Strengthening Patent Management Work* issued by the State Science and Technology Commission and the Patent Office in 1990. These two policy documents clarified the law enforcement and management functions of the patent management authorities and established the framework for government intellectual property management.

The 1990s was the development period, emphasizing the promotion of intellectual property creation, utilization, protection, and management under the intellectual property management framework. During this development stage, laws and regulations such as the *Science and Technology Progress Law* and the *Law on Promoting the Transformation of Scientific and Technological Achievements* were successively enacted. Policy documents such as the *National Medium- and Long-Term Science and Technology Development Outline*, the *Decision on Accelerating Technological Innovation, Developing High-Tech, and Achieving Industrialization*, and the *Key Points of the Implementation Opinion on Strengthening Current Intellectual Property Protection Work* were issued successively.

---

[9] Liu, H. & Meng, Q. (2009). 'Zhishi chanquan gonggong zhengce de moshi xuanze yu tixi goujian' [*'Model selection and system construction of intellectual property public policy']. Zhongguo Ruankexue [China Soft Science]*, 7, 11.

[10] Zhang, P. (2014). 'Zhishi chanquan gongong zhengce tixi de lilun kuangjia, goucheg yaosu he jianshe fangxiang yanjiu' [*'Research on the theoretical framework, components, and construction directions of the public policy system for intellectual property']. Zhishi chanquan [Intellectual Property]*, 12, 70.

After the twenty-first century, the intellectual property public policy system entered the enhancement period. In 2001, the State Intellectual Property Office issued two policy documents, the *National Patent Work 10th Five-Year Plan* and the *National Patent Workforce Construction and Human Resources Development 10th Five-Year Plan*, marking the gradual formation of intellectual property core policies.

The *National Intellectual Property Strategy Outline* issued by the State Council in 2008 marked the entry of China's intellectual property public policy system into the strategic period. During that time, intellectual property work began to be integrated into the national development strategy, with documents such as the *12th Five-Year Plan for the Development of National Strategic Emerging Industries* and the *Opinions on Deepening the Reform of the Science and Technology System and Accelerating the Construction of the National Innovation System* that both contained content on intellectual property. In 2021, the Central Committee of the Communist Party of China and the State Council issued the *Outline for Building a Strong Intellectual Property Nation (2021–2035)*, which again emphasized the comprehensive improvement on the level of intellectual property protection and further advanced the process of building a strong intellectual property nation. An important experience in China's intellectual property operation lies in establishing a relatively systematic and more effective public policy system.[11] In the construction of the public policy system, China continuously strengthens the guiding role of intellectual property in various economic and social livelihood policies, while also focusing on enhancing the effective connection between intellectual property policies and other policies.

6.1.2.2 Legal Norms of Intellectual Property Protection

There has always been a debate in China regarding the 'codification' and 'de-codification' of intellectual property law. Codification refers to the creation of a unified intellectual property code or a model similar to the *Tort Liability Law* or *Debt Law* being included as an independent section in the *Civil Code*.[12] However, due to considerations of legislative techniques and costs, China has not yet codified intellectual property law. Instead, it has formed an intellectual property legislative system consisting 'intellectual property provisions in the general principles of the *Civil Code* + intellectual property provisions in various parts of the *Civil Code* + individual intellectual property laws'.[13]

---

[11] *National Intellectual Property Strategy Outline*, Guo Fa [2008] No. 18, released on June 5, 2008.

[12] Wu, H. (2003). 'Zhishi chanquan lifa tili yu minfadian bianzuan' [*'The legislative framework of intellectual property and the compilation of the Civil Code']. Zhongguo Faxue [Chinese Law Review]*, 1, 50.

[13] Liu, Q. & Sun, Q. (2020). '<Minfadian> Zhishi chanquan tiaokuan lifa yanjiu – jianlun 'minshang zhiheyi' lifa tili de goujian' [*'Legislative study on intellectual property provisions in the Civil Code: A discussion on the construction of the 'unified civil and commercial law' legislative system'*]. *Zhongnan Daxue Xuebao(Shehui Kexue Bao) [Journal of Central South University (Social Science Edition)]*, 6, 62.

First, the provisions on intellectual property in the *Civil Code*. The relationship between intellectual property law and the *Civil Code* has always been a focus of academic attention. Before the formal publication of the *Civil Code*, there was intense debate in academic circles on how intellectual property law should be regulated within the *Civil Code*. Specifically, there were four viewpoints emerged: separation form, inclusion form, linkage form, and blending form.[14] In the *Civil Code* promulgated in 2020, the rules on intellectual property are presented in the form of linkage clauses, which include two types: narrow linkage and broad linkage clauses.[15] Narrow linkage clauses refer to provisions that do not establish rights and obligations regarding the creation, use, and protection of intellectual property, but merely serve the function of linking to specific intellectual property laws. Article 123 of the *Civil Code* lists the scope of intellectual property under the '7 + N'[16] approach. Broad linkage clauses, on the other hand, serve dual functions: they link to specific intellectual property laws and also establish specific rights and obligations, such as provisions on intellectual property pledges and punitive damages for intellectual property infringement.

Second, individual legislation for intellectual property. A review of the legislative history of the intellectual property system reveals that the intangible nature of intellectual property is closely related to the legalism in intellectual property rules. It is also noteworthy that both common law and civil law countries generally adopt an individual legislation model to regulate intellectual property systems.[17] Currently, in China, the individual legislation approach for intellectual property mainly focuses on patents, trademarks, copyrights, and other types of intellectual property. Additionally, judicial authorities have issued specialized and targeted interpretations or normative documents based on the development of practical situations, gradually enriching the legal system for intellectual property.

Meanwhile, along with the progress and development of times, China's intellectual property legal system has also been continuously updating and iterating. Especially in the past two years, China has begun to intensively amend laws in the field of intellectual property, gradually forming a more complete protection system.[18] However,

---

[14] Cao, X. (2005). 'Zhishi chanquan yu minfadian lianjie moshi zhi xuanze - <zhishi chanquan fadian> de bianzuan wei shijiao'[*'The choice of connection model between intellectual property and the Civil Code: A perspective on the compilation of the 'Intellectual Property Code"]. Fashang Yanjiu [Legal and Business Studies]*, 1, 27.

[15] Liu, Q. & Sun, Q. (2020). '<Minfadian> Zhishi chanquan tiaokuan lifa yanjiu – jianlun 'minshang zhiheyi' lifa tili de goujian' [*'Legislative study on intellectual property provisions in the Civil Code: A discussion on the construction of the 'unified civil and commercial law' legislative system*']. *Zhongnan Daxue Xuebao(Shehui Kexue Bao) [Journal of Central South University (Social Science Edition)]*, 6, 62. 63.

[16] Yi, J. (2017). 'Zhishi chanquan fading zhuyi jiqi huanhe——Jian dui <Minfa Zongze> Di 123 tiao tiaowen de fenxi' [*'Intellectual property legalism and its moderation: An analysis of Article 123 of the General Principles of Civil Law']. Zhishi Chanquan [Intellectual Property]*, 5, 9.

[17] Zhu, Y. (2020). 'Lun zhishi chanquan fading zhuyi cunzai de quexian jiqi kefu' [*'On the defects of the legalism of intellectual property law and its remedies']. Sifa [Private Law]*, 2, 279.

[18] On April 23, 2019, China revised the *Trademark Law* for the fourth time, with the amended provisions coming into effect on November 1, 2019. On the same day, the *Anti-Unfair Competition Law* was revised for the third time, with the amended provisions also taking effect on November

the current individual legislation model is still criticized by scholars. Academics, represented by Professor Wu Handong, argue that the individual intellectual property regulations often conflict and contradict one another.[19] A series of single norms lack harmonization and unity, making it difficult to achieve 'good governance' in the field of intellectual property by merely amending a single norm during implementation.[20] Therefore, to reduce contradictions and conflicts between different types of individual legislation, and to ensure the integrity of the legal system, it is necessary to consider the institutional arrangements for intellectual property from a holistic perspective. By integrating and addressing the intellectual property related rules and issues, a general set of norms shall be formulated that can address the essences in the field of intellectual property law.[21] In 2021, the National Intellectual Property Administration, expressed support for the proposal to 'formulate an intellectual property code' in its response[22] and stated that since 2009, relevant legislative work focusing on the feasibility, necessity, and content of unified legislation has made initial progress, and the work on unified legislation is ongoing.

6.1.3 *Typology of Intellectual Property Transactions*

The operating mechanism of intellectual property refers to the way intellectual property operates to achieve specific goals, usually manifested as the method of exercising rights, thereby realizing its economic value and social functions.[23] If classified based on different subject matters, it can be divided into the operation of patents, copyrights, trademarks, and other intellectual property; if classified based on the subjects, it can be divided into operations by government agencies, commercial entities, and research organizations; and according to the actual operating (transaction) methods, the main modes include assignment, licensing, and capitalization.

Although the 'strong intellectual property nation' policy emphasizes the broad role of intellectual property in promoting innovation and enhancing public welfare,

---

1, 2019. On October 17, 2020, China revised the *Patent Law* for the fourth time, with the new law coming into effect on June 1, 2021. On November 11, 2020, China revised the *Copyright Law* for the third time, with the amended provisions taking effect on June 1, 2021.

[19] Wu, H. (2009). 'Guoji biange dashi yu zhongguo fazhan daju zhong de zhishi chanquan zhidu' [*'Intellectual property system in the context of international changes and China's development']. Faxue Yanjiu [Legal Studies]*, 2, 16.

[20] Lin, W. (2022). 'Lun minfadian shidai <Zhishi chanquan fa tongze> de zhiding' [*'On the formulation of the General Principles of Intellectual Property Law in the era of the Civil Code']*. Chongqing guangbo dianshi daxue xuebao *[Journal of Chongqing Radio and Television University]*, 1, 45.

[21] Ibid.

[22] National Intellectual Property Administration, (2021). *Reply to the proposal No. 1632 of the fourth session of the 13th National People's Congress*, Guo Zhi Jian Ti Fa Han [2021] No. 17, published on July 15, 2021.

[23] Wu, L. (2005). 'Lun zhishi chanquan de kuozhang yu xianzhi' [*'On the expansion and limitation of intellectual property']*. Master's thesis, Shanxi University, 17.

it is important to recognize that intellectual property is a private right, showing the same exclusivity, exclusionary and monopolistic characteristics as property rights. This means that the operating rules of intellectual property must also adhere to the principle of autonomy of will, with offer and acceptance of both parties as a necessary process.[24] The use of intellectual property works of another party must be based on the precondition that there exist consent or authorization of the other party. However, based on the principle of balancing interests or considering public interest and reducing transaction costs from the legislative perspective, there are also special rules that allow the works to be used without the need for consent. Such special rules can be classified into voluntary transactions and involuntary transactions based on whether the consent of the right holder is required.

6.1.3.1 Voluntary Transactions

Voluntary transactions refer to legal actions carried out by both parties based on mutual consent. The autonomy of will as the core of freedom of contract is the fundamental attribute and institutional advantage of voluntary transactions. The autonomy of private rights reflects the basic principles of modern private law—self-determination, self-restraint, and self-responsibility. In economics, the freedom of contract becomes an important means for individuals to realize their interests because everyone has an inherent tendency to seek profit and avoid harm. Therefore, in the intellectual property transaction market, adhering to freedom of contract as the basic principle is conducive to the realization of the interests of all parties and also facilitates the full functioning of market mechanisms.[25]

In intellectual property operations, explicit consent and authorization through contracts are the conventional modes of voluntary transactions. However, a transaction model based on implied licenses also exists widely in practice. The implied license system first appeared in case law under the *Patent Act 1911* of the UK.[26] Later, with the evolution of technology in information communication on the Internet and the updates to online community rules, the implied license model gradually began to be applied to copyright as well.

However, there has been ongoing debate in academia regarding how to define the legal nature of implied licenses and whether they should be classified as 'voluntary transactions' or as a form of 'involuntary transaction' within the rights limitation regime. Some scholars support the rights limitation view, arguing that implied

[24] Dai, F. (2022). 'Zhishi chanquan lanyong guizhi de lilun jichu ji zhidu wanshan' ['*Theoretical foundation and institutional improvement of intellectual property abuse regulation*']. *Zhishi Chanquan [Intellectual Property]*, 3, 112.

[25] Zhao, R. (2021). Hulianwang huanjing xia banquan xuke zhidu yanjiu [*Research on copyright licensing system in the internet environment*]. Zhishi chanquan chubanshe [Intellectual Property Publishing House], 107.

[26] Chen, Y. (2018). 'Zhuanli moshi xuke yanjiu' ['*A study on patent implied licenses*']. Ph.D. thesis, Southwest University of Political Science and Law, 54.

licenses involve legally prescribed rules similar to compulsory licensing for patents.[27] Others believe that an implied license could serve as a defence against infringement, akin to the fair use doctrine in copyright law.[28] However, some scholars are skeptical, noting that while an implied license may not involve explicit an authorization from the right holder, however, it still allows for the presumption of the fact that the right holder has permitted others to use the intellectual property based on other actions or provisions within the licensing agreement. Furthermore, if implied licenses fall into the category of rights limitation, the interests of right holders would undoubtedly be further limited, which could essentially damage the exclusivity of intellectual property rights.[29] In light of the practical applications of implied licenses, it should be classified as a form of voluntary licensing. This is not only because courts introduce implied licenses into contracts for reasons of fairness, reasonableness, and policy,[30] but also because it serves as an optimized institutional design to facilitate smooth transactions in the intellectual property market.

6.1.3.2 Involuntary Transactions

From a static perspective, the determination of a certain right decides the interests of a specific subject. However, the exercise of rights is dynamic, and the operation of rights is also a process of distributing benefits. Essentially, rights should be seen as a social mechanism for balancing interests, with the fundamental purpose of its establishment as being to achieve social justice.

The content of intellectual property rights has gradually expanded with the changing times, from trade secrets[31] and plant varieties[32] to the currently debated data. If the essence of intellectual property contains attributes of social public resources, then the process of expanding the subject matters of intellectual property is actually a process of continuously incorporating social public resources into the realm of private interests in the form of rights subject matters. Based on this, how

[27] Drexl, J. (2003). *Zhishi chanquan xuke: Shang [Intellectual Property Licensing: Volume 1]*. (Wang, C. trans.). Beijing: Qinghua Daxue Chubanshe [Tsinghua University Press]. 181–183.

[28] Lü, B. (2009). 'Wangluo shidai de banquan moshi xuke zhidu: Liangqi Google an de fenxi' [*'The implied copyright licensing system in the internet age: Analysis of two Google cases']. Dianzi zhishi chanquan [Electronic Intellectual Property]*, 4, 74.

[29] Zhao, R. (2021). *Hulianwang huanjing xia banquan xuke zhidu yanjiu [Research on copyright licensing system in the internet environment]*. Zhishi chanquan chubanshe [Intellectual Property Press]. 108.

[30] Chen, J. (2016). 'Zhishi chanquan moshi xuke lilun yanjiu' *['Theoretical research on implied licensing of intellectual property']. [Jinan Journal (Philosophy and Social Sciences Edition)]*, 10, 84.

[31] On March 15, 2017, the Fifth Session of the Twelfth National People's Congress approved the *General Principles of Civil Law of the People's Republic of China* with a majority vote, officially incorporating 'trade secrets' into the scope of intellectual property protection.

[32] On May 28, 2020, the Third Session of the Thirteenth National People's Congress approved the *Civil Code*, which lists plant varieties alongside works, patents, trademarks, and trade secrets as subject matters of intellectual property.

to balance these two attributes becomes a key issue. If intellectual property is treated like real property and confer it with absolute protection, it could potentially harm the social interests of the public: for example, technology patents would control the markets, pharmaceutical patents would undermine justice, and gene patents would shake ethical concepts. Therefore, when intellectual property is merely regarded as a subject matter for 'deciding' and distributing benefits, it would be instrumentalized by the right holder and completely governed by the market, leading to the abuse of intellectual property.

Intellectual property law, as a product of the legal system, can be limited through institutional design in order to achieve social benefits. The involuntary transaction rules in the operation of intellectual property essentially aim to exclude certain behaviours from being identified as infringements by legal provisions, so as to expand the free use of social information and intellectual property. The involuntary transaction rules in intellectual property law are mainly concentrated in licensing systems, such as the statutory licensing and fair use regimes in copyright law, and the compulsory licensing and open licensing regimes in patent law.

Although owning intellectual property does not necessarily mean that it will lead to behaviours that restrict social competition, it is easily subjectivized in the process of its operation. Therefore, in an era where intellectual property is continuously developing and expanding in scope, the limitations scheme should also be comprehensive and kept in time.

6.2 Basic Theories and Systems of Intellectual Property Licensing and Its Future Improvements

The emergence of intellectual property licensing stems from the need of right holders to pursue economic value. Essentially, intellectual property licensing serves as a connection between the interests of property rights and the utilization of its economic value, involving games of interests and value trade-offs among market participants. In an intellectual property licensing model, the licensor grants permission to the licensee through a contractual agreement, which not only involves the duration, type, and mode of the license based on the value of the intellectual property, but also includes the valuation of the intellectual property being licensed. The purpose of the valuation is to provide a market judgment of the value of the licensed intellectual property. However, this judgment involves subjective assessments and a comprehensive game of interests, which varies at different stages of the transaction. In the early stages of market transactions, the licensor often holds an advantageous position in negotiation over the licensee due to information asymmetry. At the same time, due to factors such as the intangibility of intellectual property and the uncertainty in its market value assessment, market participants can hardly form stable expectations over the price of transactions. In the circumstances where the market value of an intellectual property is uncertain, the licensee may lack sufficient information resources to assess the value of the intellectual property, resulting in higher transaction costs for the intellectual property licensing deal. Furthermore, even if the uncertainties in intellectual property transactions are explained or clarified, this may still lead to additional transaction costs or unexpected conflicts.[33] In the later stages of the market transaction, as intellectual property is further exploited and implemented, the market will develop a set of corresponding standards for assessing the value of the licensed intellectual property, thus reducing the information asymmetry between the licensor and the licensee. Then on theory, the licensing fee for intellectual property will align with the actual market contribution value, and the uncertainty in value assessment decreases.

6.2.1 The Nature of Intellectual Property Licensing Rights

6.2.1.1 The Origin and Development of Intellectual Property Licensing

There is no standardized conceptual interpretation of the 'intellectual property licensing system' in the current legal framework in China. As the intellectual property law of China follows an individual legislation model, there exist more common expressions include 'copyright licensing', 'patent implementation licensing', and 'registered trademark usage licensing'.[34] Therefore, there is no unified definition of intellectual property licensing in the academic field, also there are different views regarding its attributes. This section will first review the historical background and development of intellectual property licensing in order to better define the attributes of rights of intellectual property.

Intellectual property first appeared in Europe during the feudal period in the thirteen to fourteenth centuries. It has a relatively short history compared to property rights and moral rights. However, as an extension of property rights in intellectual achievements, intellectual property has been closely tied to the market since its inception, with economic benefits becoming an important manifestation of its value. In this context, intellectual property licensing serves as the main link between property rights and the market. The closer the connection between intellectual property and the factors of production in the market, and the more urgent their mutual demand in the market, the more apparent the value and function of licensing will be.

For copyright, it was believed that the right holder was the publisher rather than the author early in the UK. Publishers were granted exclusive printing privileges and royal charters by the government or monarch, but this system of privilege did not reflect the free will between equal parties, nor was it licensing in the modern sense. In

---

[33] Weber, L. & Mayer, K. (2014). 'Transaction cost economics and the cognitive perspective: Investigating the sources and governance of interpretive uncertainty'. *AMR*, 39, 344–363.

[34] Liu, J. (2016). *Zhishi chanquan xuk xianzhixing tiaokuan fanlongduan guizhi yanjiu [Research on the antitrust regulation of restrictive clauses in intellectual property licenses]*, Zhishi chanquan chubanshe [Intellectual Property Publishing House]. 2.

1710, the UK enacted the first modern copyright law in the world, the *Statute of Anne*, which abolished the previous feudal monopoly system on intellectual works and recognized the author as the right holder of their intellectual achievements. It was then that the interests of authors began to be protected. In this law, the licensing provisions of copyright began to take shape: "[W]hereas printers, booksellers, and other persons have of late frequently taken the liberty of printing, reprinting, and publishing, or causing to be printed, reprinted, and published, books and other writings, without the consent of the authors or proprietors of such books and writings, to their very great detriment, and too often to the ruin of them and their families: for preventing therefore such practices for the future, and for the encouragement of learned men to compose and write useful books... that the author of any book or books already composed, and not printed and published, or that shall hereafter be composed, and his assignee or assigns, shall have the sole liberty of printing and reprinting such book and books for the term of fourteen years." From the text of the *Statute of Anne* it can be seen that publication of content of the work within the statutory period must be authorized by the author who holds the exclusive right.

For patent rights, the patent system not only granted the patent holder exclusive monopoly rights from its inception but also explicitly established the 'licensing' system. In 1474, the first patent law in the world- the *Venetian Patent Statute*-was enacted. It stipulated: "...[e]very person who shall build any new and ingenious device in this City, not previously made in our Commonwealth, shall give notice of it to the office of our General Welfare Board when it has been reduced to perfection so that it can be used and operated. It is prohibited for anybody in any land or place of ours, making any other similar contraption, and those must obtain the consent and license of the author for ten years. If the tribunal says he has counterfeited, he is forced to pay hundred ducats and the aforementioned contraption shall be destroyed."

From the above background it can be seen that there are licensing rules for both copyright and patent rights that appeared alongside the protection rules for the right holders. In common law countries, the concept of 'property' is used instead of 'rights over objects', so the content of intellectual property rights as 'intangible property' mainly includes possession, use, and disposal. To encourage more inventions and creations, it is necessary to protect the legitimate interests of right holders by law, granting them exclusivity over their inventions and creations. At the same time, in order to realize and expand the social benefits of inventions and creations, the rule-makers generally encourage intellectual property to enter the market and realize its economic value. Therefore, we can reasonably infer from historical development that intellectual property licensing is essentially a way for right holders to dispose their private rights, which is also a form of property transaction.[35]

It is important to emphasize that the intellectual property licensing mentioned above can be viewed as a form of property transaction, but it must be clearly distinguished from the transaction of tangible goods. In a transaction over tangible goods, once the buyer acquires the product, they have full rights of possession, use, benefit,

[35] Dong, M. (2013). *Zhishi chanquan xuke yanjiu [Research on intellectual property licensing]*. Falv Chubanshe [Law Press]. 18.

and disposal. However, in intellectual property licensing, what is being traded is intangible intellectual property, and the right holder only allows the licensee to exercise or implement the intellectual property. The licensee does not have the right to dispose of the intellectual property.

6.2.1.2 Types and Legal Nature of Intellectual Property Licensing

Types and legal nature of copyright licensing The copyright owner has three ways to exploit their rights: self-implementation, assignment, and licensing. However, self-implementation and realization of value are often restricted by other production factors, and the assignment of copyright causes the loss of the key economic rights, preventing the original owner from continuing to control their work. Therefore, in practice, copyright licensing has become the most common mode of implementation. Copyright licensing is primarily divided into two types: direct licensing and licensing by collective management organizations.

First, direct licensing is divided into general licensing and exclusive licensing. Existing civil rights are classified into static (entitlement) and dynamic (exercise) categories based on their form. In German civil law theory, dynamic exercise of rights refers to legal actions taken by the right holder based on their intent regarding the right itself. These are mainly divided into acts of disposition and acts of encumbrance.[36] An act of encumbrance refers to 'a legal act in which one person undertakes an obligation to do or refrain from doing something towards another person or several persons'.[37] The legal effect of an act of encumbrance does not change the ownership of the right itself, but merely imposes a restriction on the exercise of the right. Whereas an act of disposition refers to 'a legal act that directly affects an existing right, such as changing the title of a right or assigning a right, as well as imposing encumbrance on a certain right or terminating the right, etc. The object of disposition is always a right or a legal relationship'.[38] The consequence of exercising a right of disposition is 'directly resulting in the acquisition, loss, or changes in the title of a right'.[39]

Currently, China follows the classification of the German Civil Code to adjust and define exclusive licensing and non-exclusive licensing: Exclusive copyright licensing is an act of disposition in which the copyright holder assigns the specific economic rights of a work to another party for exercise; however, non-exclusive licensing is an

36 Dong, M. (2011). 'Yingmei faxi yu dalu faxi Zhong banquan bei xukeren su wenti bijiao yanjiu-Yi <Qinquan zerenfa wei chufadian>' ['A comparative study of the rights of copyright licensees in the common law and civil law systems: From the perspective of the tort liability law'], *Zhishi Chanquan [Intellectual Property]*, 8, 90.

37 Larenz, K. (2003). *Deguo minfa tonglun [General Theory of Civil Law]* (Wang, X., et al., trans.). Falv Chubanshe [Legal Publishing]. 435.

38 Larenz, K. (2003). *Deguo minfa tonglun [General Theory of Civil Law]* (Wang, X., et al., trans.). Falv Chubanshe [Legal Publishing]. 436.

39 Gao, F. (2009). *Minfa xue [Civil law studies]*. Falv Chubanshe [Legal Publishing]. 192.

act of encumbrance in which the copyright holder imposes a burden on the specific economic rights of the work. This is the fundamental distinction between the two.[40]

Second, copyright collective management organization licensing. The content of copyright economic rights is diverse, in practice, it is always difficult for right holders to fully exercise these rights by themselves, and more often, they are collectively managed by copyright collective management organizations. Common examples include the Film Copyright Association, Music Copyright Association, etc. Intellectual property authorization includes three types: delegated authorization, authorization by trust, and authorization by licensing. The nature of copyright collective management organizations should be considered as authorization by trust.

According to the definition in Article 2 of the *Trust Law* of China,[41] it can be seen that the trustee is entitled to the ownership of the property and may manage and dispose of the property in his own name within the effective period of a trust. Hence, the 'right holder' and the 'interests holder' can thereby be separated while ensuring the independence of decision-making of the trustee. Based on the characteristics of a trust, the authorization provided by a copyright collective management organization to copyright users is not as complete as the authorization provided by the right holder themselves. Its characteristics are as follows: First, the collective management organization can only grant ordinary licenses and cannot grant exclusive licenses; Second, when the copyright holder requests the collective management organization to manage their economic rights, the collective management organization cannot refuse if the request is made under reasonable conditions; Third, the license granted by the copyright collective management organization cannot exceed two years at a time; Fourth, after the right holder enters into a management contract with the collective management organization, the right holder cannot himself grant licenses for the rights managed by the organization to other users during the term of the contract. Similarly, before signing the management contract with the collective management organization, the right holder cannot assign or grant exclusive licenses for the copyright to external parties.

Types and legal nature of trademark licensing A trademark, unlike creative works and patents, is closely tied to the commercial reputation of its owner and contains certain personal attributes. However, unlike the moral rights in copyright, which cannot be assigned or licensed, trademarks can be licensed and assigned under the *Trademark Law* of China. Trademark rights and patent rights are referred to as industrial property rights, and their value lies in their utilization. In practice, trademark holders often license their trademarks to local enterprises in other regions to expand market share, as well as to enhance the reputation and influence of their trademarks, with internationally famous trademarks being typical examples. Trademark licenses can be divided into sole licenses, exclusive licenses, and general (ordinary)

---

[40] Dong, M. (2013). *Zhishi chanquan xuke yanjiu [Research on intellectual property licensing]*. Falv Chubanshe [Law Press]. 30.

[41] *Article 2 of the Trust Law provides*: "The trust referred to in this Law means that the trustor, based on trust in the trustee, entrusts their property rights to the trustee, who, in their own name and according to the trustor's wishes, manages or disposes of the property for the benefit of the beneficiary or for a specific purpose."

licenses. The difference between exclusive licenses and sole licenses lies in whether the trademark holder himself can continue to use the trademark.

Regarding the legal nature of trademark licensing, general (ordinary) trademark licensing is similar to general licensing in copyright, and is also an act of encumbrance. In principle, the licensee of a general license cannot obtain exclusive rights or the right to prohibit (the right to file infringement lawsuit in his own names) in relation to the trademark. However, Article 4, Paragraph 2 of the *Supreme People's Court's Interpretation on Several Issues Regarding the Application of Law in the Trial of Civil Disputes Involving Trademarks* stipulates that a general trademark licensee, upon receiving clear authorization from the trademark owner, may file an infringement lawsuit in his own name. Such rule does not exist in the general licensing of copyrights or patents. In fact, the reason can be inferred from the interface between trademark law and the anti-unfair competition law. Trademark infringement lawsuits stem from the passing off action in common law systems or the action for unfair competition in civil law systems. Even though trademark law is separately legislated, it still reflects the potential damage to competition rules. When a trademark holder files an infringement lawsuit, it is based on the civil remedy for rights protection. The exercise of litigation by a general licensee effectively performs a function of combating unfair competition. The ability of a general trademark licensee to file a lawsuit under authorization is based on the unique attributes of trademark rights, and this rule cannot be applied to other types of intellectual property.

Types and legal nature of patent licensing Similar to trademark licensing, patent licensing can be categorized into sole licenses, exclusive licenses, and general licenses. According to the civil law disposition rules of Germany as well as the different definitions of licenses and exclusive licenses in common law systems, a general license is merely an act of encumbrance in which the patent holder waives their exclusionary rights within the scope defined in the licensing agreement. Sole licensing and exclusive licensing, on the other hand, are acts of disposition of the patent right by the patent holder, with the aim of excluding any other entities and individuals, even the right holder himself, from exercising the patent, except for the licensee.

The difference between exclusive licensing and sole licensing lies in the fact that, under a sole license, the patent holder retains the right to use the patented technology themselves. However, the legal nature of this reservation requires separate discussion. Logically, since patent rights entail the 'right to exclude any unit or individual' from using the patented technology, whether it is exclusive licensing or sole licensing, the rights granted must be the 'right to exclude any unit or individual' from using the patented technology, due to the indivisibility of the patent. Therefore, if the patent holder retains the right to use the technology within the scope of the sole license, they should separately obtain the consent of the licensee, rather than leaving the exclusionary right granted by the patent incomplete. However, since the patent holder is often in an advantageous negotiating position, the licensee will naturally agree at the offer stage to allow the patent holder to retain the right to use the patented technology. Thus, the nature of this reservation can be regarded as a contractual claim on the patent.

6.2.2 *Basic Issues in the Conclusion of Licensing Agreements*

An intellectual property licensing agreement is a contract in which specific capacities of intellectual property rights are taken as the subject of the contract and authorizations are granted to others for reasonably use of the intellectual property within the agreed scope. As a type of civil contract, intellectual property licensing agreement is basically subject to the relevant provisions of contract law. However, due to the inherent characteristics of intellectual property, there are sui-generis legal rules dedicated to intellectual property licensing agreement.

6.2.2.1 Elements of Licensing Agreements

Forms of licensing agreement The licensing agreement should be understood as a formal contract. Article 496 of the *Civil Code* stipulates that contracts can be in oral form, written form, or other forms. However, the *Civil Code* also explicitly requires that technology licensing agreements, which include patent licensing agreements, must be in written form.[42] For copyright licensing agreements, the *Regulation on the Implementation of the Copyright Law* requires a written form only for exclusive copyright licenses but not for general licenses,[43] in principle, general license for copyright can be granted either in written or oral forms. As for trademark licensing agreements, there is no mandatory requirement in law regarding the form of the contract. However, it is important to note that the *Regulation on the Implementation of the Copyright Law*, the *Rules on the Implementation of the Patent Law*, and the *Rules on the Implementation of the Trademark Law*[44] contain provisions regarding the filing of licensing agreements. In practice, oral contract can hardly meet the documentation requirements for filing. Therefore, to avoid unnecessary legal risks and disputes in practice, contracting parties of copyright, patent, or trademark rights licenses usually prefer to sign the licensing agreements in a written form.

Offer and acceptance The signing of a contract includes two stages: offer and acceptance. Due to the complexity of the subject matters and ownership of intellectual property licensing agreements compared to general civil rights and their subject matters, as well as the complex and lengthy process of intellectual property productization—commodification—commercialization which requires substantial support in terms of personnel, equipment, technology, and funds, therefore, licensee should conduct a comprehensive evaluation of the intellectual property before signing the

[42] *Article 863, Paragraph 3 of the Civil Code provides*: "Technology transfer contracts and technology licensing contracts must be in writing."

[43] *Article 23 of the Regulations on the Implementation of the Copyright Law provides*: "The use of another person's work should be subject to a licensing agreement with the copyright owner. If the licensed use is an exclusive right, it must be in writing, except for the publication of works by newspapers and periodicals."

[44] *Article 25 of the Regulations on the Implementation of the Copyright Law, Article 14, Paragraph 2 of the Implementation Rules of the Patent Law*, and *Article 69 of the Implementation Rules of the Trademark Law* all stipulate that licensing should be recorded within the statutory time frame.

licensing agreement. The evaluation should include the validity of the licensed subject matter, whether the license fee and the technical value align, the degree of difficulty in implementing the technology, the possibility of future improvements to the technology, market sales forecasts after commercialization of the intellectual property, the presence of substitute intellectual property (the intensity of market competition), and the financial capacity to bear the costs etc. During the contract signing process, the relevant terms should be negotiated comprehensively, particularly the price and payment methods, the subject matter (the licensed rights and the subject matters of those rights), the nature of the license (whether it is an exclusive license, sole license, or general license), the publication of the license, and essential clauses such as the warranty for the licensed rights provided by the licensor, together with any other terms that require special agreements.[45]

Terms of the licensing agreement The content of an intellectual property licensing agreement mainly includes two aspects: the scope and manner of using the rights by the licensee, and the licensing fees to be received by the licensor. The intellectual property contract must first comply with Article 470 of the *Civil Code*, which requires the inclusion of the main provisions of a general contract. At the same time, due to the complexity and professionalism of intellectual property licensing agreements, the terms of the contract may vary depending on the type of license.

First, the warranty clause of the licensor. The validity and stability of the licensed intellectual property is the prerequisite and foundation for the contract to be effective, maintained, and performed. Since the legal stability of different types of intellectual property is not always the same, the warranty clause should also differ. Moreover, especially for intellectual property related to technology, even though the rights are validity, it is not always clear whether the rights can be commercially applied as expected. Such risks can thus be the distributed between both parties by way of the warranty clauses. Therefore, these clauses include the warranty of the validity of the rights as well as the warranty of commercial feasibility from the licensor. The warranty of the validity of the rights primarily includes two aspects: first, a warranty of the authenticity and validty of the rights; and second, a warranty that the licensor holds the licensed intellectual property and that this intellectual property does not infringe upon the rights of any third parties, i.e., its legality.

Second, the subject of the licensed use and its object. The subject of the licensing agreement should be distinguished from its object. The subject refers to the specific rights of intellectual property, such as the right to reproduce or the right to distribute in the case of copyright. Whereas the object of the licensing agreement refers to the work itself. Since intellectual property encompasses a wide range of economic rights, the specific rights to be licensed should be clearly defined or reserved in the contract. In the United States, there is also a distinction regarding the source of the licensed object, such as the differentiation between internally developed patents and externally acquired patents. This distinction allows a group of companies using specific technologies to purchase the exclusive rights to patents developed by an

---

[45] Dong, M. (2013). *Zhishi chanquan xuke yanjiu [Research on intellectual property licensing]*. Falv Chubanshe [Law Press]. 98.

emerging competitor, and agreeing not to assign them to anyone, thereby protecting their own technology from competition.[46] Therefore, due to the intangible nature of intellectual property, it is particularly important to specify details such as the name, copyright registration number, or trademark registration number in the contract.

Third, the type of license. In the section of 'Legal Nature of Intellectual Property Licenses' above, the types of intellectual property licenses were systematically introduced and distinguished between two or three types based on exclusivity. Additionally, the licensing agreement should not only specify the type of license granted but also address whether the licensee is allowed to sublicense.

Fourth, the scope of the license. The scope of the license includes the scope of rights, the scope of usage methods, the geographical scope, and the technical scope, among others. The scope of usage methods is relatively rare; for example, the parties can agree whether the usage is for commercial or non-commercial purposes, and can even define more specifically as to the product scope, such as whether a pharmaceutical patent is used for clinical treatment or medical research.

Fifth, the duration of the license. Temporality is a typical characteristic of intellectual property. The usage duration stipulated in the licensing agreement should not exceed the protection period of the intellectual property; otherwise, the part exceeding the protection period will be invalid due to the violation of mandatory legal provisions. However, for trademark licensing agreements, a different approach should be taken. The protection period of trademark rights is ten years, but as long as the trademark owner applies for renewal within the statutory period, the protection period can be extended indefinitely. Therefore, in a trademark licensing agreement, any provisions regarding a period beyond the protection term should be treated as conditional contracts. If the protection period is extended through renewal, such provisions regarding the extended period in the agreement remains valid.

Sixth, licensing fees. The licensing fee for intellectual property is often a focal point of dispute in intellectual property licensing agreements. Before negotiating the licensing fee, the licensor should properly assess the value of the intellectual property.

Seventh, other clauses. In addition to the main contract clauses mentioned above, depending on the type and use of the intellectual property, the licensing agreement generally includes the following clauses: interpretation of technical terms and terminology; technical information (such as patent design drawings, user manuals, data); ownership and sharing of improvements (Article 875 of the *Civil Code*[47]); confidentiality clauses; liability for breach of contract, etc.

[46] Bohannan, C., & Hovenkamp, H. (2010–2011). 'Concerted refusals to license intellectual property rights'. *Harvard Business Law Review Online*, 1, 23.

[47] Article 875 of the *Civil Code* provides: "The parties may agree in the contract on the sharing method of technical achievements resulting from the implementation of patents or the use of trade secrets, based on the principle of mutual benefit. If there is no agreement or the agreement is unclear, and it still cannot be determined according to Article 510 of this Law, the technical achievements resulting from subsequent improvements by one party shall not be shared by the other parties."

6.2.2.2 Effectiveness of Licensing Agreements

According to Book Three on Contract in the *Civil Code* of China, the effectiveness of contracts can be classified into three categories: valid, with pending validity, and void.

Valid intellectual property licensing agreements According to the provisions of the *Civil Code* on contracts, a contract becomes effective upon its establishment, but if approval or other formalities are required, the contract shall be subject to those requirements. This rule explicitly states that whether the requirement for registration or filing procedures is a sine qua non for the effectiveness of certain contracts. Under the current rules, filing is required for all copyright, trademark, and patent licenses; however, whether the filing procedure affects the effectiveness of the contract has always been a topic of dispute. Article 19 of the *Measures on Filing for Patent Implementation Licensing agreement* issued by the State Intellectual Property Office on June 27, 2011, stipulates that: "The types, terms, calculation methods or amounts of the license fees for the filed patent implementation licensing agreements can be used as a reference by the patent managing authorities in mediating the amount of compensation for infringement." According to this rule, the filing of a patent licensing agreement is primarily for the purpose of fixing evidence and using the agreed licensing fee as a basis when dealing the case in court. Therefore, whether or not a patent licensing agreement is filed does not, and should not, affect the validity of the contract.

Regarding the filing of trademark licensing agreements, Article 19 of the *Interpretation on Several Issues Concerning the Application of Law in the Trial of Trademark Civil Dispute Cases* stipulates that whether or not a trademark licensing agreement is filed does not affect the validity of the trademark licensing agreement itself.[48] However, the filing of the trademark licensing agreement has the effect of protecting bona fide third parties. The reason for this is that filing effectively makes the relationship between the trademark owner and the trademark user public, thereby protecting the interests of consumers.

Intellectual property licensing agreements with pending validity The uncertainty of market transactions as well as the high transaction costs within the existing legal framework resulting from the intellectual property licensing agreements with pending validity are also key concerns for foreign scholars.[49] Intellectual property licensing agreements with pending validity often arise in three situations: First, conditional contracts or contract with time limitations, trademark licensing agreements discussed above is a typical example; Second, situations provided by civil law that render the contract pending in effect, such as when the contracting parties lack full civil capacity, act beyond the scope of their agency authority, or engage in the acts of unauthorized

[48] Article 19 of *Interpretation on Several Issues Concerning the Application of Law in the Trial of Trademark Civil Disputes* provides: "The validity of a trademark license contract is not affected by the failure to file for recordation, unless the parties have other agreements."

[49] Tosato, A. (2018). 'Intellectual property license contracts: Reflections on a prospective UNCITRAL project'. *U. Cin. L. Rev.*, 86, 1251, 1272.

disposition of rights. The most peculiar situation is the unauthorized disposition of rights, with the specific issue being whether the bona fide third party can invoke the doctrine of good faith acquisition and continue using the licensed intellectual property (the third part of this chapter will focus on the system of good faith acquisition in intellectual property law); Third, licensing agreements entered during the temporary protection period of invention patents.

Since the China adopts the early publication system of patents and deferred examination system for invention patent applications, when the patent office receives an invention patent application and determines that it meets the requirements after the review on formality, it should be published within 18 months from the application date for public opposition review. From the date of publication, the invention enters a provisional protection period. Within three years from the application date, the applicant can request a substantive examination at any time. Then the question can be summarized as: should a license agreement for an invention patent during its provisional protection period be considered valid or the validity is pending (subject to conditions)? During the provisional protection period, the invention is in a state of public, and the public can access the invention while the opposition review is taking place. If the invention is not protected during this period, it creates the potential for infringement once the patent is granted. However, considering the possibility that the patent application may not be granted eventually, the law thus chooses to provide appropriate protection. Article 18 of the *Supreme People's Court's Interpretation on Several Issues Concerning the Application of Law in the Trial of Patent Infringement Cases (II)* issued by the Supreme People's Court of China in 2016 essentially rebuts the nature of infringement during the provisional protection period.[50] For individuals or organizations attempting to implement the invention during this period, even if the patent is granted afterwards and the scope of implementation falls within the protected scope, they are merely required to pay the appropriate fees in accordance to relevant statutory provisions. Nevertheless, there are still licensing agreements entered during the provisional protection period in practice, primarily due to considerations on the economic costs. On one hand, prior to patent grants, judicial interpretations do not clarify the 'appropriate fees' to be paid by the implementers, instead suggesting that 'the people's courts may reasonably determine the patent license fees'. However, with an existing licensing agreement, the licensee can clarify the implementation fee before implementation, thus avoiding the risk of post-grant infringement litigation. On the other hand, even though implementing the invention before patent grant is

[50] *The Supreme People's Court's Interpretation on Several Issues Regarding the Application of Law in the Trial of Patent Infringement Cases (II)*, Article 18(1): "If the right holder requests payment from the units or individuals who implemented the invention between the publication date of the invention patent application and the date of the grant notice, based on Article 13 of the Patent Law, the People's Court may reasonably determine the patent license fee." Article 18(2): "If the scope of protection requested by the applicant at the time of the publication of the invention patent application is inconsistent with the scope of the patent right at the time of the grant notice, and the accused technical solution falls within both scopes, the People's Court shall recognize that the defendant implemented the invention during the period specified in the previous paragraph; if the accused technical solution falls within only one scope, the People's Court shall recognize that the defendant did not implement the invention during the period specified in the previous paragraph."

not considered an infringement, once the patent is granted, the implementer must stop using the invention or it will constitute an infringement. Given the consideration of sunk costs, the implementer is likely to sign a license agreement with the patent holder eventually. However, there are significant differences on the range of the pricing game between the two stages of licensing for the licensee. On this basis, entering into a licensing agreement for an invention during its provisional protection period allows the licensee to secure a lower licensing cost. In terms of determining the legal nature of such contracts, reference can be made to Article 29(2) of the *Supreme People's Court's Interpretation on Several Issues Concerning the Application of Law in the Trial of Technology Contract Disputes*: "The licensing agreement entered into by the parties concerning the technological achievements of a patent application, before the patent application is published, shall be subject to the relevant provisions of the technology secret transfer contract; after the publication of the invention patent application but before the grant of the patent, shall be subject to relevant provisions of the patent implementation licensing agreement; after the patent is granted, the original contract shall be deemed a patent implementation licensing agreement and shall be subject to the relevant provisions of the patent implementation licensing agreement." Paragraph 3 states, "People's courts shall not invalidate a contract on the grounds that the parties entered into a patent implementation license agreement for technology that has been patented but has not yet been granted." Therefore, a licensing agreement for an invention patent entered during its provisional protection period should be considered a valid contract in principle.

Void intellectual property licensing agreements The grounds for the voidness of intellectual property licensing agreements are essentially the same as those in civil law, including: lack of civil capacity, false declaration of intent, violation of mandatory provisions in laws and administrative regulations, contravention of public order or good morals, and malicious collusion.

At the same time, there is another special ground, which is the non-existence of the licensed rights, which mainly give rises to two subsequent situations: the contract does not exist from the beginning, and the contract ceases to exist after it is formed.

First, contract does not exist from the beginning. In the field of intellectual property licensing, it is a common situation where the subject matter does not exist objectively from the outset. Examples include: licensing a registered trademark beyond the approved goods category, or signing a licensing agreement for a non-existent trade secret. There are two theoretical views on the validity of such licensing agreements: one view holds that because the subject matter of the contract does not exist from the outset, the contract was never formed, and the licensee can claim *culpa in contrahendo*. The other view holds that the contract should be deemed void. In this case, the licensee can claim rights against the licensor based on *culpa in contrahendo* or breach of contract.

Second, contract ceases to exist after formation. This refers to situations where the intellectual property was valid at the time of signing the licensing agreement but extinguished during the term of the licensing agreement. There are many reasons for the extinguishment of intellectual property rights, such as the expiration of the protection period, the abandonment of the rights by the holder, the rights being declared invalid, or the loss of the secrecy of a trade secret. First, expiration of the protection period: Since the validity period of the licensing agreement generally does not exceed the protection period of the intellectual property, in most cases, the expiration date of the protection period is also the termination date of the contract; Second, abandonment of rights: If the right holder voluntarily declares abandonment of rights during the term of the contract, the rights are extinguished from the date of abandonment, and the licensing agreement terminates; Third, loss of secrecy of technical secrets: A technical secret must be confidential in nature. If the technical secret loses its confidentiality due to legitimate disclosure by a third party, the subject matter of the contract extinguishes, and the contract terminates.

6.2.2.3 Licensing Fees

Intellectual property licensing agreements, as typical bilateral and onerous contracts, in which the licensing fees is one of the primary ways for licensors to generate revenue from property rights, it is also one of the most concerning and contentious issues in practice.[51] Key points regarding licensing fees mainly include payment methods and calculation methods: On the one hand, payment methods of licensing fees are diverse. In practice, payment methods of licensing fees are not limited to money, but may also include cross-licensing, equities, stock options, and other methods. On the other hand, calculation methods of licensing fees are closely tied to the specific circumstances of transactions. Since the economic value of an intellectual property is unclear before its actual production, and despite the licensee is required to conduct a diligent evaluation of the utility and value of the intellectual property before requesting the license, however, in order to reduce risks, it is common to make partial payments in advance and adjust the fees according to the actual situation after the production and implementation process begins. Therefore, this section will discuss and summarize different types of payment and calculation methods of licensing fees.

Payment methods First, advance payment (prepayment). When the licensing fee is paid in this way, the licensee effectively assumes a lower duty of care and does not need to conduct a detailed assessment of the creditworthiness, business condition, or the patent of the licensor. The essential characteristic of this payment method is simplicity and ease of operation. The process involves the licensee first making a prepayment, and then paying the full amount once the intellectual property is put into production and generates actual benefits. The licensor can use the prepayment received to cover the costs of earlier research and development, thereby capitalizing the intellectual property more efficiently. On this basis, both parties should clearly specify in the agreement that under what circumstances the prepayment can be refunded, and whether it can be used to offset part of the future licensing fees.

[51] Fu, H. & Tan, H. (2017). *Zhishi chanquan yunyin guangli falv shiwu yu zhongdian wenti quanshi [Intellectual property operation management legal practice and interpretation of key issues]*. Zhongguo Fazhi Chubanshe [China Legal Publishing House]. 19–22.

Second, instalment payment. This method is more commonly used in patent licensing agreements, where the licensee can pay the licensing fees based on the development progress of the technology. Since the long development cycle of technology and the potential technical barriers faced by the technicians during the research phase can create instability, the licensee typically avoids paying the entire amount of fee at once. Instead, they opt to pay in stages or at the time when significant progress is made in the technological research. It not only provides an incentive for the licensor on technical development while motivates researchers, but can also mitigate the financial pressure faced by the licensee.

Calculation methods The calculation of licensing fees is always closely related to the actual sales of the intellectual property. More specifically, it is very common to set the licensing fee rate based on the sales performance. This method links the actual operating situation (the licensee's revenue) with the licensing income of the licensor, similar to the IP-backed equity transaction where both parties share the risks and benefits. The specific factors in determining licensing fees are typically considered through the following three methods:

First, based on product quantity. Using the sales quantity of the product as the calculation basis is relatively easy and is not affected by fluctuations in price or exchange rates.

Second, based on product sales revenue. This method is more flexible and variable, depending on the price set by the licensee and the quantity of the product sold. This means that the licensee has more space to adjust the selling price of the product, thereby maintaining their market position and protecting the licensor from market fluctuations. When using this method, attention needs to be placed on the scope of net sales price, whether it includes tariffs, freight, insurance, and other handling fees, etc.; if the intellectual property is used only on some components of the product, whether net sales should be calculated based on the price of the components or the price of the finished product; and whether sales from affiliated enterprises, which are often priced lower than the market price, should also be included, etc. These types of issues must be clearly stipulated in the licensing fee calculation method.

Third, based on net profit. This method can better reflect the economic benefits of the licensee, but from the licensor's perspective, it should be avoided as much as possible. This is because determining net profit involves the actual amount of costs. While sales revenue is relatively easy to determine, the 'costs' directly associated with sales is a vague concept. It is difficult to distinguish such costs from the general operating costs of the company, and ensuring that the licensee does not manipulate, falsify, or overstate the data is a major challenge, which will bring uncertainties to the licensor.

Due to the complexity of the calculation methods for licensing fees, and in order to protect the interests of both parties, the parties to the license agreement often take various measures, such as including calculation templates in the agreement and stipulating minimum and maximum licensing fees. The minimum licensing fee ensures that the licensor is protected from the licensee's poor performance, meaning that even if the licensee does not achieve good economic results, they are still required to pay the minimum licensing fee to the licensor. If no minimum licensing fee is specified, the licensor should at least stipulate in the contract that if the licensee fails to meet performance requirements, the licensor has the right to terminate the contract, preventing the licensee from neglecting to implement the license and thereby making it difficult to realize the value of the intellectual property. The contracting parties to the license should also agree on the payment date of the licensing fee, the type of currency, the date of financial audit, and related expenses.

6.2.3 Special Types of Intellectual Property Licenses

6.2.3.1 Copyright Statutory Licenses

Statutory licensing regime refers to a system directly stipulated by law where works that have already been published can be used in certain ways without the permission from the copyright owners, but the user must pay a fee to the copyright owner.[52] The purpose of this system is to limit the absolute rights of copyright owners, preventing the copyright holder from exerting absolute control over the work in a way that would prevent socially beneficial works from realizing their value, thus avoiding a waste of resources. However, as the legal right holder, the results of labour of the copyright owner yet to be respected by law, therefore the right holder shall receive appropriate remuneration.

The *Berne Convention 1886* allows member countries to make special provisions to limit the rights of copyright holders, such as the right to reproduction, broadcasting rights, and the right of recording of musical works. The relevant provisions are mainly Article 9, paragraph 2, on 'limitations of the right of reproduction', Article 11, paragraph 2, on 'limitations of the right of broadcasting', and Article 13, paragraph 1, on 'limitations of the right of recording musical works'. The Berne Convention does not specifically define the circumstances under which statutory licenses may apply; it simply summarizes the 'three-step test' principle for copyright limitations, which states that whether it is fair use, statutory licenses, or compulsory licenses, a limitation on copyright should be deemed a special circumstance, which should not conflict with the normal exploitation of the work, and should not unreasonably prejudice the legitimate interests of the author.

Currently, the copyright law of China provides for six situations for statutory licensing, which are listed in different provisions in the *Copyright Law*, including: statutory licenses for compiling textbooks, statutory licenses for newspaper and periodical reprints, statutory licenses for making sound recordings, statutory licenses for broadcasting published works, statutory licenses for producing courseware, and statutory licenses for supporting online dissemination in impoverished rural areas.

---

[52] Liu, C. (2014). *Zhishi Chanquanfa [Intellectual property law]*. Renmin Daxue Chubanshe [Renmin University Press]. 122.

6.2.3.2 Trademark Licensing in Franchising

Franchising, as a business model for marketing goods and services, originated in the 1880s in the U.S. and has since gradually spread worldwide, with over a century of history. However, the concept of 'franchising' has not yet been harmonized. Definitions from international organizations such as the International Franchise Association and the World Intellectual Property Organization, as well as the Federal Trade Commission of the United States, the European Franchise Federation, and the Japan Franchise Association all differ.[53] In China, the *Regulations on the Administration of Commercial Franchising* issued in 2007 defines franchising in Article 3 as follows: "Commercial franchising refers to a business activity in which an enterprise (the franchisor) that owns registered trademarks, business logos, patents, proprietary technologies, and other business resources licenses these resources to other operators (the franchisees) in the form of a contract, and the franchisee operates under a unified business model as agreed in the contract and pays franchise fees to the franchisor." At the same time, the franchisee must maintain consistency with the franchisor in both business and operational models, typically manifesting in the acceptance of the guidance and control of the franchisor, thereby forming a franchising system.

One of the most valuable assets in all franchising models is the original trademark used in operations. A trademark essentially serves as the medium of the public's impression of the quality of goods and services offered by the operator. If a franchisee gains the right to use a trademark that are influential and highly recognized, they can obtain a significant market advantage from the beginning of their business operations. Therefore, the trademark becomes a key element in the franchising system.

In a franchise agreement, to ensure that the value of the trademark is not diminished by the operations of the franchisees, proper supervision and control over the trademark must be implemented. During the negotiation process, both parties should clarify the obligations of the franchisee regarding the trademark. When drafting the franchise agreement, the provisions related to trademarks must include specific terms for the use of the mark, quality standards, and uniformity standards. Consequently, the franchisee will have a detailed usage guide or manual therefrom.

The franchisor should also pay attention to available sources of information, including trademark registries and domain name registries, to prevent the infringement of identical or confusing trademarks. Conflicting use can lead to a reduction in legal protection, the inability to protect the trademark, or the technical abandonment of the trademark. In fact, the franchisee may sue the franchisor claiming that the failure of the franchisor to supervise and protect the trademark has led to a reduction in the value of the trademark and the franchising system. The franchisor must also supervise its franchisees to ensure they do not infringe upon other trademark rights,

---

[53] Zhang, S. & Liang, Z. (2010). 'Lun shangye texu jingyingquan Zhong de zhishi chanquan falv baohu' ['On intellectual property legal protection in commercial franchising']. *Jingji Yu Fazhi [Economics and Law]*, 6, 234.

or the franchisor will bear joint liability.[54] When the franchise agreement terminates or expires, the agreement should specify that the franchisee loses its economic interests in the franchised goods, including the rights and obligations related to trademarks, packaging, and other intellectual property licenses. After the termination of the franchise agreement, the franchisee should consciously fulfil the corresponding subsidiary obligations according to the principles of good faith and business practices, such as removing the brand logos and adhering to confidentiality and non-compete clauses specified in the agreement.

6.2.3.3 Open Licensing and Compulsory Licensing of Patent Rights

Patent open licensing The operation process for patent open licensing includes declaration and application. Specifically, the patent holder first declares the open licensing to the State Intellectual Property Office and registers, while clearly stating the licensing fees, payment methods, and other conditions. Then the patent is made available for licensing to the public. When the public requests to use the patent, they only need to meet the conditions previously published by the patent holder and notify them. Compared to regular licensing, open licensing essentially standardizes and simplifies the process, transforming what would have been a negotiation between both parties into a more convenient transaction method.[55]

The patent open licensing system was introduced in the fourth amendment of China's patent law, officially passed in June 2021, and is formally stipulated in Article 50 of the *Patent Law*.[56] Subsequent provisions also address the implementation, acquisition, effectiveness, and dispute resolution of patent open licensing. The purpose of this system is to promote the social application of patented technologies by reducing licensing costs. From a comparative law perspective, the patent open licensing system has been recognized in many countries, with the UK and Germany achieving positive results in its implementation.[57] Statistics show that in the UK, over 3% of patent licenses granted each year are through the 'license of right' (same as 'open licensing'), while in Germany, about 5%-7% of patents registered annually with the German Patent and Trade Mark Office are granted through license of right,

[54] Fu, H. & Tan, H. (2017). *Zhishi chanquan yunying guanli falv yu zhongdian wenti quanshi [Intellectual property operation management legal practice and interpretation of key issues]*. Zhongguo Fazhi Chubanshe [China Legal Publishing House]. 128–129.

[55] Chen, C. (2022). 'Lun zhuanli kaifang xuke zhidu zai woguo shishi Zhong de wenti yu jiejue fangan' ['On the issues and solutions in the implementation of the patent open licensing system in China']. *Dongnan Daxue Xuebao (Zhexue Shehui Kexuebao) [Journal of Southeast University (Philosophy and Social Sciences Edition)]*, Supplement, 106.

[56] Article 50, Paragraph 1 of *Patent Law* provides: If a patent holder voluntarily declares in writing to the State Intellectual Property Office (SIPO) that they are willing to license any entity or individual to use their patent, and specifies the payment method and standards for the license fee, the SIPO shall announce the open license. For utility model and design patents, a patent evaluation report must be provided when declaring open licensing.

[57] Zhang, Y. (2019). 'Zeren guize shijiao xia de zhuanli kaifang xuke zhidu' ['Patent open licensing system from the perspective of liability rules']. *Qinghua Faxue [Tsinghua Law Review]*, 5, 187.

with a generally increasing trend.[58] This shows that the patent open licensing system has certain institutional value for market participants.

Since October 2021, provinces such as Zhejiang, Hubei, and Sichuan have gradually released the first batch of patents for open licensing in pilot programs.[59] However, the patent open licensing system in China has only been established recently and is still in the process of improvement. Whether it can achieve its intended goal of promoting technological innovation needs to be further verified by data.

Patent compulsory licensing Currently, the compulsory licensing system for intellectual property in China is limited to the field of patent law. In the following situations, a patent can be implemented by the government or a third party authorized by the government, without the consent or agreement of the patent holder, and the third party must pay a reasonable royalty for their use, i.e. patent compulsory licensing.

First, compulsory licenses for the purpose of preventing abuse of patent rights. According to Article 53 of the *Patent Law* of China, there are two types of compulsory licenses to prevent abuse, the first is general compulsory license. "If the patent holder has not implemented or fully implemented the patent without justifiable reasons, three years after the patent is granted or four years after the patent application is filed.", this provision is based on Article 5A(4) of the *Paris Convention*: "A compulsory license may not be applied for on the ground of failure to work or insufficient working before the expiration of a period of four years from the date of filing of the patent application or three years from the date of the grant of the patent, whichever period expires last; it shall be refused if the patentee justifies his inaction by legitimate reasons."; Second, antitrust compulsory license: "When the patent holder's exercise of patent rights is legally recognized as monopolistic behaviours, and the compulsory license is granted to eliminate or reduce the adverse effects of such behaviours on competition." This provision is based on Article 31(11) of the *Trade-Related Aspects of Intellectual Property Rights Agreement (TRIPS)*: "Members are not obliged to apply the conditions set forth in subparagraphs (b) and (f) where such use is permitted to remedy a practice determined after judicial or administrative process to be anti-competitive." Subparagraph (b) provides the circumstances for compulsory licensing.

[58] Yi, J. (2017). 'Zhuanlifa de zhuanxing: cong eryuan jiegou dao sanyuan jiegou' ['*The transformation of patent law: From a dual structure to a triadic structure']. Faxue Zazhi [Legal Studies Journal]*, 7, 46.

[59] Zhejiang Provincial Government. (2022). 'Zhejiang tuijin 'zhuanli kaifang xuke'zhidu' ['Zhejiang promotes the 'patent open licensing' system']. *Democracy and Law Net*. Available at: http://www.mzyfz.com/html/1993/2022-04-26/content-1561214.html, accessed on 20 July 2022; *China National Intellectual Property Administration*. (2022). 'Hubeisheng zhishi chanquanju zhaokai zhuanli kaifang xuke shidian gongzuo tuijian zuotanhui' ['Hubei Provincial Intellectual Property Office holds a seminar to promote the patent open licensing pilot project']. Available at: https://www.cnipa.gov.cn/art/2022/7/28/art_57_176884.html, accessed on 20 July 2022. Sichuan Provincial Intellectual Property Service and Promotion Center. (2022). 'Sichuansheng zhuanli kaifang xuke shidian gongzuo jinru quanmian tuijin jieduan' ['Sichuan's patent open licensing enters full promotion phase'], *Sichuan Provincial Intellectual Property Service and Promotion Center*. Available at: http://scipspc.sc.gov.cn/ztzl/cycj/202207/t20220705_30705.html, accessed on 20 July 2022.

Therefore, when abuse of patent rights leads to illegal monopolistic behaviours, compulsory licensing can serve as a regulatory tool.

Second, compulsory licensing for dependent patents. This system is stipulated in Article 56 of the *Patent Law* of China. Paragraph 2 of this article also mentions that, after granting a compulsory license, the holder of the earlier patent can apply to the State Intellectual Property Office for a compulsory license for the later patent. This is essentially similar to a compulsory cross-license.

Third, compulsory licensing for public interest. Article 54 of the *Patent Law* of China stipulates that in the event of a national emergency or exceptional circumstances, or for public interest purposes, the State Intellectual Property Office may grant a compulsory license for the implementation of an invention patent or a utility model patent.

Fourth, compulsory licensing for pharmaceutical patents. This system is stipulated in Article 55 of the *Patent Law* of China. Under Chinese legal framework, compulsory licensing of pharmaceutical patents should apply to the needs of public health for the prevention and treatment of both infectious and non-communicable diseases, with the key focus on the accessibility of medicines. The applicable standards can be borrowed from the more mature experiences of developing countries such as South Africa, Brazil, and India.[60] The pharmaceutical patent system is an inevitable requirement to realize the concepts of modern human rights, and it also aligns with the inherent logic for the development of the patent system. During the pandemic, the specific application standards of this system have become a focal point of academic attention.

6.3 Institutional Deficiencies and Supplements for Intellectual Property Assignments

The absence of the intellectual property assignment system is mainly reflected in the lack of the design of an incentive system. Given that intellectual property shows market attributes, its circulation by way of assignment can better promote its market value. Currently, the absence of relevant systems in intellectual property assignment leads to situations where market participants cannot effectively obtain protection when disputes arise. This lack of institutional arrangement makes it difficult for market participants to have reasonable expectations that their rights can be protected in transactions, which in turn reduces the transaction rate of intellectual property assignments. A typical example is the lack of a bona fide assignee system in intellectual property assignments. When intellectual property is disposed without authorization and the change of ownership is registered, the bona fide assignee, due to lack of necessary information and subjective good faith, is unlikely to receive all the

[60] Li, Z. (2021). 'Lun gonggong jiankang xuqiu xia de yaopin zhuanli qiangzhi xuke' ['On the compulsory licensing of pharmaceutical patents under public health needs']. Zhongguo Faming Yu Zhuanli [*China Invention and Patent*], 8, 71.

information of the transaction. In such cases, should the bona fide party be protected? The uncertainties surrounding the rights being assigned increase transaction costs for both parties in the market,[61] and the disparity in information and the uncertainty of the assigned rights further exacerbate transaction risks.

Contract theory serves as the theoretical basis for explaining the various issues that arise in intellectual property transactions, aiming to facilitate the smooth realization of the transaction between the parties and improve transaction efficiency. However, intellectual property assignment differs from other forms of intellectual property disposal, as it involves not only the assignment of rights but also the potential involvement of bona fide third parties. Due to the lack of a design for market incentive system, there is no motivation for both parties to disclose transaction information, as a result, the parties involved in the transaction cannot distinctively select a contract design that maximizes utility. This undermines the stability and security of the rights assignments. Therefore, it is necessary to clarify the specific issues that arise in intellectual property assignments in order to accurately assess the practical problems that the parties may face, and explore possible solutions.

6.3.1 Specific Issues Regarding Intellectual Property Assignment

Intellectual property assignment, as a key stage in promoting the circulation and utilization of intellectual property, involves balancing the interests of multiple parties and the allocation of rights and obligations. Unlike the detailed provisions on the assignment of property rights in the *Civil Code*, there is still no comprehensive legal and regulatory framework for intellectual property assignment. In judicial practice, issues such as unauthorized disposal of intellectual property rights, protection of bona fide counterparts and so o have led to inconsistent judicial attitudes, making it difficult to form a unified and coherent approach to rulings. One significant reason for this inconsistency is the particularity of the subject matters of intellectual property as well as the differences in the way how titles of rights can be changed regarding different types of intellectual property rights. Therefore, it is necessary to explore the issues currently present in intellectual property assignment, clarify the potential coordination and conflicts between intellectual property assignment and the existing property law system, and provide references for improving the intellectual property assignment system.

[61] Celtekligil, K. (2020). 'Transaction cost theory', in Dincer, H. and Yüksel, S. (eds.), *Strategic priorities in competitive environments*. Springer. 141–154.

6.3.1.1 Theoretical Controversies

Intellectual property, as a right with both personal and economic characteristics, fundamentally falls within the category of civil rights. Although the law legislates separately for different types of intellectual property, in cases of intellectual property disputes where no specific applicable provisions can be found in the intellectual property laws, the relevant provisions of the *Civil Code* can still apply.[62] Similar to the transfer of property rights, the assignment of intellectual property, as a legal act in civil law, also involves the disposition of rights, and thus the relevant provisions for property rights are often referred to in judicial practice. However, due to the intangible nature of intellectual property and the differences in the modes of change in titles for various types of intellectual property rights, the issues related to intellectual property assignment cannot be easily aligned with the provisions for property rights transfer, causing the 'inapplicability' of certain traditional civil law systems in the field of intellectual property.[63] Therefore, clarifying the distinctions and connections between intellectual property assignment and property rights transfer has certain referential value for understanding and addressing the specific issues in intellectual property assignment.

The difference between intellectual property assignment and property right transfer In the traditional civil law system, the transfer of rights involves changes in the subjects, objects, and content of the rights, as well as the methods for changing the title of rights and the effects of such changes. The same applies to the assignment of intellectual property rights. Due to the diversity of different types of intellectual property, the law makes different provisions regarding changes in the title of rights accordingly, which results in differences between the assignment of intellectual property rights and the transfer of property rights. Currently, academic debates on the distinctions between intellectual property assignment and property rights transfer mainly focus on the following areas: the subject matter of the rights, the methods for changing the title of rights, and the legal effects of changes in titles, as outlined below:

The subject matter of rights is different. Unlike the subject matters of property rights, which is a 'thing', the subject matter of intellectual property rights is intellectual achievements, which are 'non-material' in nature. This is one of the main features distinguishing intellectual property from property rights. In the transfer of property rights, such as the case concerning movable properties, the transferor can effect a change in ownership of the property simply by delivering the material object. However, in the assignment of intellectual property, what is assigned is not the material object itself, but the intangible intellectual achievements that the material

---

[62] Wang, L. et al. (2020). Minfa Xue (Di Liu Ban) [*Civil Law Studies (6th ed.)*]. Falu Chubanshe [Law Press China]. 164.

[63] Shi, S. (2000). Wuquanfa lun [*The theory of property law*]. Zhongguo Zhengfa Daxue Chubanshe [China University of Political Science and Law Press]. 8.

object 'carries'.[64] For example, in the assignment of copyright, the assignee does not acquire the physical object of the work itself after signing the copyright assignment agreement with the assignor. Instead, the assignee obtains the economic rights associated with the copyright, which represents the intangible intellectual achievements reflected in the work. Conversely, acquiring ownership of the work does not automatically grant the assignee the copyright to the work. Therefore, the differences in the subject matter of rights lead directly to the distinction between intellectual property and property rights, which in turn causes the differences between the assignment of intellectual property rights and the transfer of property rights.

The ways in which the titles of rights are changed differ. According to Articles 209(1)[65] and 224[66] of the *Civil Code* of China, Chinese law generally requires registration or delivery as the conditions for the effective transfer of property rights based on legal actions. Specifically, the transfer of real property rights requires registration to be effective; in principle, it has no effect without registration. For movable property rights, delivery is the condition for effectiveness, meaning that the transfer is effective upon delivery. In contrast, the conditions for the assignment of intellectual property rights vary depending on the type of intellectual property involved. Taking copyright, patent rights, and trademark rights as examples: for the assignment of copyright, according to Article 27 of the *Copyright Law*[67] and Article 25 of the *Implementing Regulations of the Copyright Law*[68] in China, the assignment of the economic rights of copyright should be made by a contract, and while 'it is possible to file with the copyright administrative department', there is no explicit provision regarding the legal effect against third parties of such filing; Regarding patent rights: according to Article 10(3) of the *Patent Law*,[69] the assignment of a patent application or patent rights becomes effective upon the date of registration. This is similar to the transfer of real property rights, where registration is the condition for effectiveness; As to trademarks, according to Article 42(4) of the *Trademark Law*,[70] a trademark assignment requires an assignment agreement, and the effectiveness of the assignment is subject to publication. Thus, the diversity of intellectual property types leads to more complex requirements for the conditions under which intellectual property rights are assigned compared to property rights. This complexity is a key difference between the assignment of intellectual property rights and transfer of property rights.

---

[64] See Wang, Q. (2021). *Zhishi chanquan fa jiaocheng (Di qi ban)* [*Intellectual property law textbook (7th Edition)*]. Zhongguo Renmin Daxue Chubanshe [China Renmin University Press]. 5.

[65] See Article 209, Paragraph 1 of the *Civil Code of the People's Republic of China*: "The establishment, change, transfer, and termination of real property rights take effect upon registration according to law; without registration, they do not take effect, unless otherwise stipulated by law."

[66] See Article 224 of the *Civil Code of the People's Republic of China*: "The establishment and transfer of rights in movable property take effect upon delivery, unless otherwise stipulated by law."

[67] Article 27. *Copyright Law of the People's Republic of China.*

[68] Article 25. *Regulations for the Implementation of the Copyright Law of the People's Republic of China.*

[69] Article 10. *Patent Law of the People's Republic of China.*

[70] Article 42. *Trademark Law of the People's Republic of China.*

The legal effects between rights transfer and assignment differ. The legal effects of the transfer of property rights differ from the assignment of intellectual property rights. Taking ownership as an example, when a transferor transfers ownership of a movable or real property to the transferee through delivery or registration, the transferee enjoys full and permanent control over the property. However, the assignment of intellectual property rights operates differently. When the assignee acquires intellectual property rights, the rights obtained may not be comprehensive. A typical example is the assignment of copyright, where only the economic rights can be assigned, while the moral rights in the copyright cannot be transferred. The primary reason for this difference lies in the distinct nature of the two types of rights. Property rights are purely economic rights, whereas intellectual property rights encompass both economic and personal (moral) components. Unlike tangible property such as movable or real property, which exists in a material form that can be fully transferred, intellectual property is intangible, and its subject matter not only includes the economic rights but also carries personal value specific to the right holder.[71] This means that although an assignment of intellectual property right gives the assignee a right to dispose the intellectual property, they are also limited by the 'intangible' connotation of moral rights. Therefore, the differences in the nature of property rights and intellectual property rights lead to significant differences in their transfers and assignments.

The relationship between assignment of intellectual property rights and property rights transfer After explaining the differences between the assignment of intellectual property rights and the transfer of property rights, it is important to note the connections between the two. As part of the traditional civil law system, the differences in the subject matters as well as nature of intellectual property rights from property rights do not mean that there is no connection between the two. In fact, there are similarities between the assignment of intellectual property and the transfer of property rights. Specifically, these include the following aspects:

First, both are inseparable from the traditional civil legal system. In social life, there are numerous connections between individuals, which together shape social and economic life.[72] The complex social relationships need to be regulated and adjusted by law, thus giving rise to civil legal relationships. As the rights and obligations relationships of civil subjects, civil legal relationships are structured around three elements: subjects, objects, and content, which forming the overall framework of the civil legal system. This allows for the regulation and adjustment of personal and proprietary relationships of civil subjects within a unified and clear system. As parts of the civil legal system, intellectual property and property rights naturally have a 'bloodline' connection. The reason for dividing intellectual property law, property law, and other branch laws is mainly due to the considerations of legal jurisprudence

[71] Wu, H. (2009). *Zhishi chanquan zhidu jichu lilun yanjiu [Research on the Basic Theories of Intellectual Property System]*. Zhishi Chanquan Chubanshe [Intellectual Property Publishing House]. 25.

[72] Zheng, Y. (1997). *Minfa xue [Civil Law Studies]*, Zhongguo Zhengfa Daxue Chubanshe [China University of Political Science and Law Press]. 224.

and systematization.[73] In applying the laws, attention should be placed on their interaction and connection within the civil legal system to avoid detachment from real-life practices.[74]

Second, the content of rights in the transfer of intellectual property and property rights is interconnected. It is worth noting that, like property rights, intellectual property shows a strong property-rights character. Intellectual property law primarily regulates the proprietary relationships between equal entities based on intellectual achievements or other non-material results.[75] The moral rights aspects of intellectual property, due to its personal nature, is not transferable. The *Copyright Law* of China also explicitly limits the transfer of copyright to the part of economic rights. Although there are significant differences between intellectual property and property rights in terms of their subjective matters, they place the same emphasis on proprietary value, which undoubtedly reduces this disparity. With the development of the economy and society, there is even a trend of integration among various property rights regarding different forms of subject matters.[76]

From the perspective of the legislative system, same as the German legal system, China's civil law system limits the subject matters of property rights to tangible items, and intellectual property, due to the intangible nature of its subject matter, is naturally excluded from the scope of the subject matter of property rights. However, with the development of the economy and the increasing complexity of proprietary relationships, the emergence of various intangible assets has greatly impacted the existing legal system of property. Some scholars believe that the subject matters of intellectual property have, through their material carriers, acquired a fixed form, making them a 'tangible' existence.[77] Meanwhile, other scholars argue that the existing property law has already accommodated the existence of intangible property, and the relevant institutional systems should promptly respond to the needs of economic and social

---

[73] Gu, D. (2015). 'Zhishi chanquan susong zhong wuquanfa guifan de leitui shiyong' ['The analogical application of property law norms in intellectual property litigation'], in He, R. (ed.), *sifa tizhi gaige yumin shangshi falv shiyong wenti yanjiu: quanguo fayuan di 26 jie xueshu taolunhui huojiang lunwenji [Research on Judicial System Reform and the Application of Civil and Commercial Laws: Award-Winning Papers from the 26th National Court Academic Seminar]*, Renmin Faxue Chubanshe [People's Court Press]. 1161.

[74] Zhou, J. and Shen, Y. (2008). 'Hetongfa zai zhishi chanquan qinquan anjian zhong de shiyong moshi chutan —— yi fali shengsi ji shili kaocha wei yanjiu yituo' ['An initial exploration of the application model of contract law in intellectual property infringement cases—based on legal reflections and case studies'], in Gong, P. (ed.) *Sikao Yu Tansuo [Thinking and Exploration, The Path We Have Taken]*, Zhongguo Fazhi Chubanshe [China Legal Publishing House]. 1427.

[75] Wang, Q. (2021). *Zhishi chanquanfa jiaocheng (Di qi ban) [Intellectual Property Law Textbook (7th ed.)]*. Zhongguo Renmin Daxue Chubanshe [Renmin University of China Press].13.

[76] Wang, G. (2012). 'Zhishi chanquan shanyi qude de helixing fenxi- Jianlun zhishi chanquan zhidu yu wuquan zhidu de jianrongxing' ['Analysis on the rationality of good faith acquisition of intellectual property—Also discussing the compatibility of intellectual property system and property rights system'], *Hainan Daxue Xuebao(Renwen Shehui Kexueban) [Journal of Hainan University (Humanities and Social Sciences Edition)]*, 4, 88.

[77] Sun, X. (2009). Zhongguo wuquanfa zonglun (Di 2 ban) [*General Theory of Chinese Property Law (2nd ed.)]. Falv Chubanshe* [Legal Publishing House]. 205.

development.[78] Therefore, intellectual property rights and property rights cannot simply be separated based on the differences in their subject matters; the content of their rights being transferred actually reflects the trends of contemporary economic and social development.

6.3.1.2 Practical Problems

After discussing the theoretical controversies surrounding the assignment of intellectual property rights and property rights, attention should also be given to the specific issues in judicial practice regarding intellectual property assignment, primarily including unauthorized disposition of rights, protection of bona fide counterparties, and market risks in assignments. Currently, the existing intellectual property laws of China have provided comprehensive regulations on the assignment of intellectual property. However, with the increasing complexity of economic and social development, the assignment of intellectual property is not simply a 'one sale for a single right' process, rather, there are situations such as the assignment of one right to multiple buyers or unauthorized agency, where the issue of how to protect the legitimate rights and interests of bona fide counterparties and balance the interests between the true right holder and the bona fide counterparty becomes a challenge in judicial practice. Therefore, it is necessary to deeply investigate and address the practical issues in intellectual property assignments to provide a stable and secure legal environment for promoting the application of intellectual property.

The criteria for determining unauthorized disposal in intellectual property assignment is unclear In the traditional civil law system, an unauthorized disposition refers to an act where a person disposes of another's property and enters into a contract for the transfer of the property without having the right of disposition.[79] The concept and essential elements of unauthorized disposition in intellectual property assignments are similar to those in the traditional civil law system. Specifically, it refers to an act in which a person without the right to dispose of intellectual property disposes of another's intellectual property and enters into a corresponding contract. The constituent elements include two factors: first, the person without the right to dispose of the intellectual property performs the act of disposition; and second, the person enters into a corresponding contract with the other party regarding the disposition. Although the concept and constituent elements of unauthorized disposition in intellectual property assignment are similar to those in the traditional civil law system, this does not mean that the relevant rules for unauthorized disposition can be directly applied to disputes involving unauthorized disposition in intellectual property assignments. The main reason for this is the diversity of different types of

[78] Li, G. (2009). 'Wuti caichan gainian dui xiandai suoyouquan guannian de yingxiang' ['The impact of the concept of incorporeal property on modern ownership concepts']. *Dangdai Faxue [Contemporary Law Review]*, 4, 46.

[79] Wang, L. (2001). 'Lun wuquan chufen' ['On unauthorized disposition'], *Zhongguo Faxue [China Legal Science]*, 3, 77.

intellectual property and the differences in the applicable rules. On the one hand, intellectual property rights encompass rights such as copyright, patent rights, and trademark rights, with each having different characteristics. For example, copyright law covers both property rights such as the right of reproduction, right of distribution, and rental right, and moral rights such as the right of publication and the right of authorship. On the other hand, due to the differences in the nature of these rights, the relevant rules for intellectual property assignment also vary under Chinese law. The assignment of patent application rights and patents takes effect upon registration, while trademark rights take effect upon publication, and copyright law only requires a contract to be concluded, without mandating compulsory registration or announcement procedures.

Different protection rules for bona fide counterparties in intellectual property assignment When facing unauthorized dispositions in intellectual property assignments, another important issue to consider is the protection of bona fide parties. In the current civil law system, unauthorized dispositions by a person without disposition rights are addressed through the establishment of a bona fide acquisition system to protect the legitimate rights of third parties, as exemplified by Article 311 of the *Civil* Code. As long as the bona fide party meets the legal requirements for bona fide acquisition, they can acquire ownership of movable or real property according to the regulations, and the original right holder loses ownership of the property. Given the differences as well as the relevant legal provisions governing intellectual property rights and property rights, there are different views in theory regarding whether bona fide acquisition applies to intellectual property. Scholars who support the positive view argue that intellectual property can be subject to similar provisions in property law concerning bona fide acquisition. They consider this question based on factors such as the similarities between intellectual property rights and property rights in terms of the form of the subject matters of rights, the value orientation of property rules, and the need to promote transaction security and enhance social welfare.[80] On the other hand, scholars who hold the negative view argue that the bona fide acquisition system should not apply to intellectual property. They base this opinion on the non-exhausted nature of intellectual property information, the external appearance of intellectual property rights, and the absence of imputable elements, concluding that the bona fide acquisition system is unsuitable for intellectual property.[81] Furthermore, there are two distinct approaches in judicial practice when dealing with this issue. For

[80] Wang, G. (2012). 'Zhishi chanquan shanyi qude de helixing fenxi-jianlun zhishi chanquan zhidu yu wuquan zhidu de jianrongxing' ['Analysis on the rationality of good faith acquisition of intellectual property—Also discussing the compatibility of intellectual property system and property rights system'], *Hainan Daxue Xuebao (Renwen Shehui Kexueban) [Journal of Hainan University (Humanities and Social Sciences Edition)]*, 4, 87.

[81] Liu, J. (2003). 'Lun zhishi chanquan yu zhanyou zhidu' ['On intellectual property and the system of possession'], *Faxue [Law Studies]*, 10, 56–63; Peng, C. (2002). 'Zhili chengguo, zhishi chanquan yu zhanyou zhidu' ['Intellectual achievements, intellectual property, and the system of possession'], *Fashang Yanjiu [Journal of Commercial and Economic Law]*, 6, 91–97; Wang, X. (2020). 'Zhuanli quanshu jiufen Zhong shanyi shourangren baohu wenti yanjiu' ['Study on the protection of good faith assignees in patent ownership disputes'], *Keji Yu Falv [Science and Law]*, 2, 24–30.

example, in cases involving the bona fide acquisition of registered trademarks, judgments supporting the application of the bona fide acquisition system include the case of *Guo Yuegong*,[82] the case of *Cao Qingzhang*,[83] and the case of *Zhang Liqiu*.[84] The courts in these cases acknowledged the public credibility of trademark registration by the National Trademark Office, and considering the need for market transaction security and stability, concluded that the bona fide acquisition system could apply to trademark rights. In contrast, in the *Li Qingsen case*[85] and the *Liu Shulan case*,[86] the courts focused on the current legal provisions for bona fide acquisition, concluding that trademark rights fall outside the scope of the bona fide acquisition system and therefore excluded its application. Thus, both the theoretical and practical fields hold different views on whether the bona fide acquisition system applies to intellectual property rights, resulting in uncertainties in the protection of bona fide parties.

Market risks in intellectual property assignments In addition to issues such as unauthorized disposition and the protection of bona fide counterparties, attention should also be paid to the market risks that may arise in intellectual property assignments. According to legal provisions, whether the assignment involves patent rights, trademark rights, or copyright, a corresponding agreement of assignment should be signed. The purpose of signing an assignment agreement is to ensure the stability and security of intellectual property transactions, which is the essential role of the law in providing protection. However, intellectual property assignment, as part of the market transaction process, inevitably carries associated market risks. Additionally, the differences in how to change the title of various types of intellectual property rights further increase the possibility of these risks. The occurrence of these risks can primarily be attributed to two factors:

First, due to the inducement of economic benefits, actors may attempt to obtain unlawful profits through the assignment of intellectual property rights,[87] specifically manifested in unauthorized dispositions and the situations of 'one right sold to multiple buyers'. Second, risks arise mainly from force majeure or changes in circumstances that result in an impossibility to perform contracts, which may hinder the assigning process of intellectual property. The occurrence of market risks undoubtedly brings significant inconvenience to both parties to the contract, and may even harm their legitimate interests. On the one hand, it can lead to a reduction in the market share of the products of the assignor. In the process of signing an contract for intellectual property assignment, if the assignor has no disposition rights over the relevant rights, and the assignee meets the conditions for bona fide acquisition,

---

[82] Xiamen Intermediate People's Court, Fujian (2016) *Min 02 Min Zhong Zi Second Instance Civil Judgment No. 3857.*

[83] Fujian High People's Court (2015) *Min Min Zhong Zi Second Instance Civil Judgment No. 188.*

[84] Hebei High People's Court (2015) *Ji Min San Zhong Zi Civil Judgment No. 114.*

[85] Shandong High People's Court (2015) *Lu Min Ti Zi Civil Judgment No. 72.*

[86] Chongqing High People's Court (2005) *Yugao Fa Min Zhong Zi Second Instance Civil Judgment No. 187.*

[87] Yang, L. & Zhu, Z. (2020). 'Jishu lei zhishi chanquan jiaoyi weiyue fengxian fangfan yanjiu' ['Research on the prevention of default risks in technology-related intellectual property transactions']. *Nandu Xuetan [Southern Metropolis Forum]*, 1, 78.

once the court determines that the assignee can acquire the ownership of intellectual property rights through the bona fide acquisition system, the transfer of ownership of intellectual property rights will result in a decrease in the product market share of the true right holder, severely damaging the market interests of the true right holder. Even if the court determines that the bona fide acquisition system shall not apply, the uncertainty of intellectual property ownership during the litigation process can still impact the market interests of the true right holder; On the other hand, the duty of the assignee to examine the defects of titles may be expanded. According to Article 612 of the *Civil Code*, the seller should bear the warranty obligation against defects in title and ensure that the delivered subject matter is free from third-party encumbrances. However, in intellectual property assignments, if an unauthorized disposition occurs and the bona fide acquisition system cannot be applied, then the legitimate rights of the assignee as the subject matter may not be protected. Therefore, to ensure transaction security, the assignee will have to spend more time and effort examining the ownership of the intellectual property being assigned, which undoubtedly expands the obligation of the assignee to inspect for defects in the title of rights.

6.3.2 *Unauthorized Disposition in Assignments of Intellectual Property Rights*

6.3.2.1 Determination of Effectiveness

Since the provision of the unauthorized disposition system in Article 51 of the original *Contract Law*, the controversy over the unauthorized disposition system has never ceased. Both in the theoretical and practical circles, intense debates kept being brought up regarding this system, and the issue of the validity of contract in unauthorized disposition cases has become a focal point in many discussions. During the era of the original *Contract Law*, scholars in the theoretical field engaged in discussions on the validity of contracts in unauthorized dispositions based on Article 51 of the original *Contract Law* and Article 3 of the Supreme Court's *Judicial Interpretation on the Contract of Sale*. This eventually led to three mainstream viewpoints: First, valid contract theory. Scholars supporting this theory, based on the distinction between juristic acts of claims and juristic acts of real rights, recognize the validity of contracts in unauthorized dispositions while considering the juristic acts of real rights involved in unauthorized dispositions to be in a state of 'pending validity'[88];

[88] Han, S. (2018). *Hetong fa zonglun (Di si ban) [General Principles of Contract Law (4th ed.)]*. Falv Chubanshe [Law Press]. 312–319; Wu, G. (2005). 'Lun wuquan chufen de shiyong fanwei' ['On the scope of application of unauthorized disposition'], *Zhongwai Faxue [Chinese and Foreign Law]*, 3, 337; Zhang, Z. (2018). 'Tongyi de wuquan chufen zhidu zhi goujian jiqi fangfa' ['The construction and methods of a unified unauthorized disposition system']. *Suzhou Daxue Xuebao(Faxue Ban) [Journal of Suzhou University (Law Edition)]*, 2, 55; Peng, C. & Li, J. (2009). 'Shanyi qude hetong xiaoli de lifa jiexi yu luoji zhengcheng' ['Legislative analysis and logical justification of the good faith acquisition of contract validity']. *Zhongguo Faxue [Chinese Law Science]*, 4, 87–91.

Second, pending validity theory. In contrast to the first view, proponents of this theory argue that the validity of a sales contract should be considered as a whole and the acts of encumbrance cannot be judged independently from the acts of disposition. If the seller does not have the right to dispose of the subject matter, the contract is considered to have pending validity due to the lack of a necessary disposition right[89]; Third, bona fide *vs.* malicious theory. Scholars advocating this theory suggest that unauthorized disposition should be analysed on a case-by-case basis, focusing on protecting the legitimate interests of bona fide counterparties. If the counterparty meets the conditions for bona fide acquisition, the contract remains valid even if the original right holder refuses to ratify the contract.[90] In response to the intense debate surrounding these views, Paragraph 1 of Article 597 of the *Civil Code* redefines the rules regarding unauthorized disposition.[91] By incorporating the provisions of Article 51 of the original *Contract Law* and Article 3 of the Supreme Court's *Interpretation on the Judicial Application of the Contract of Sale*, and combining them with specific judicial practices, Paragraph 1 of Article 597, adheres to the principle of distinguishing between juristic acts of claims and juristic acts of real rights.[92] It clearly stipulates that unauthorized disposition does not affect the validity of the sales contract, which ensures the scientific approach in lawmaking.

Applying the latest provisions of the *Civil Code* regarding unauthorized disposition actions on intellectual property assignments will give rise to the following two legal effects: First, the contract for unauthorized disposition in intellectual property assignment is valid. This means that even if the assignor does not have the right to dispose the intellectual property, the intellectual property assignment agreement signed with the counterparty remains valid. A typical example is the 'one right sold to multiple buyers' situation in copyright assignment. Even if the copyright holder has lost the ownership of the copyright in subsequent assignment agreements, it does not affect the validity of the multiple assignment agreements signed with the counterparty;Second, if the true right holder ratifies the contract, the effect on the change of intellectual property ownership may occur. According to the relevant provisions of the *Civil Code*, unauthorized disposition in intellectual property assignment follows the distinction between juristic acts of claims and juristic acts of real rights. This means that whether the intellectual property ownership changes will depend on the

[89] Liang, H. (2000). 'Ruhe lijie hetongfa di wushiyi tiao' ['How to understand Article 51 of the *Contract Law*']. Renmin Faxue Bao *[People's Court Daily]*, 8 January, p. 3; Cui, J. (2003). 'Wuquan chufen bian – Hetong fa di 51 tiao guiding de jieshi yu shiyong' ['Distinction of unauthorized disposition – Interpretation and application of Article 51 of the *Contract Law*']. *Faxue Yanjiu [Legal Studies]*, 1, 3.

[90] Wang, L. (2001). 'Lun wuquan chufen' ['On unauthorized disposition']. *Zhongguo Faxue [Chinese Law Science]*, 3, 90.

[91] See Article 597 of *Civil Code of the People's Republic of China*: "If the seller has not obtained the right to dispose of the subject matter, resulting in the inability to transfer ownership, the buyer may terminate the contract and request the seller to bear liability for breach of contract."

[92] Sun, X. (2022). 'Guanyu wuquan chufen wenti de jidian kanfa – ping minfadian caoan dui <Hetongfa> di 51 tiao de fangqi' ['A few views on the issue of unauthorized disposition – A review of the *Civil Code* draft's abandonment of Article 51 of the *Contract Law*'], *NetEase*, https://www.163.com/dy/article/F19KKAR00516C2P4.html, accessed on 22 July 2022.

ratification by the true right holder.[93] In summary, in intellectual property assignment agreements, even if the assignor does not have the intellectual property rights, it does not affect the validity of the contract, as whether the intellectual property ownership ultimately changes still depends on the ratification by the true right holder.

6.3.2.2 Specific Types

Although the *Civil Code* makes provisions on the acts of unauthorized disposition, various special circumstances continue to emerge in judicial practice. It is necessary to adopt a 'case-by-case' approach to consider the specific details of each case. This requires a detailed analysis of situations in intellectual property assignment such as 'one right sold to multiple buyers', unauthorized agency in a narrow sense, and apparent agency, so as to explore the potential challenges in applying the law and approach to their resolution.

'One right sold to multiple buyers' in intellectual property assignments Similar to the concept of 'one item sold to multiple buyers' for tangible property, 'one right sold to multiple buyers' in intellectual property assignment refers to the assignment of intellectual property by the right holder to multiple parties. However, the distinguishing feature in intellectual property is that this situation is often harder to assess due to the unique nature of intellectual property itself. Such particularities primarily stem from the fact that whether it is a patent, trademark, or a work, they are essentially information. The inherent fluidity and replicability of information mean that once it is disseminated, it can easily be copied and circulated in large quantities, and the right holder thus loses exclusive control over that information. The reason information can become property and can be exclusively controlled by intellectual property right holders is due to laws enacted by the state to meet specific public policy needs.[94] Moreover, due to the diversity in types of intellectual property, 'one right sold to multiple buyers' in different types of intellectual property assignment should be analysed according to the specific circumstances. Taking copyright as an example, due to the absence of a rights registration system and the automatic generation nature of copyright, the phenomenon of 'one right sold to multiple buyers' is quite common in the field of copyright.[95] In practice, copyright holders often assign their copyrights multiple times thus create multiple copyright assignment agreements. Unless there are justifications for invalidating the contracts, all such assignment agreements are valid. However, only one of the contracts can ultimately be performed, and for the

[93] Liu, H. (2018). 'Zhishi chanquan wuquan chufen wenti chutan' ['An initial exploration of the issue of unauthorized disposition of intellectual property']. Shidai Jingmao [*Times of Economics and Trade*], 9, 91.

[94] Wang, Q. (2021). *Zhishi chanquanfa jiaocheng(Di qi ban)* [*Intellectual Property Law Textbook (7th ed.)]*. Zhongguo Renmin Daxue Chubanshe [China Renmin University Press]. 3.

[95] Lv, B. (2017). 'banquan 'yi nv duo jia' de jiejue zhidao – Yi shanyi xiangduifang baohu wei zhongxin'['The solution to the issue of 'one copyright, multiple marriages' – Centered on the protection of good faith counterparties']. Jinan Xuebao (Zhexue Shehui Kexue Ban) [*Journal of Jinan University (Philosophy and Social Sciences Edition)*], 12, 34.

other non-performing contracts, the counterparties can assert claims for breach of contract or tort liabilities to protect their legitimate rights and interests. At the same time, considering the particularities of intellectual property, when handling 'one right sold to multiple buyers' in intellectual property assignment, judicial practice should also take into account the legislative objectives of the intellectual property law,[96] ensuring the legitimate interests of bona fide counterparties from the perspective of promoting market transactions and maintaining market security.

'Unauthorized agency in a narrow sense' in intellectual property assignment In the process of intellectual property assignment, not only can unauthorized disposition occur, but also unauthorized agency in a narrow sense. Unlike unauthorized disposition, narrow unauthorized agency refers to an agent acting in their own name to perform a civil act.[97] When applied to intellectual property assignment, this refers to an agent performing the intellectual property assignment in the name of the intellectual property right holder without having the authority to do so. In such cases, Article 171 of the *Civil Code* on unauthorized agency should be applied,[98] rather than the provisions of Article 597 regarding unauthorized disposition.[99] For the phenomenon of a 'narrow unauthorized agency' in intellectual property assignment, the principal, i.e., the intellectual property right holder, has the right to ratify the act of unauthorized agency. If it is not ratified, the principal is not bound by such an act. Additionally, the counterparty has the right to demand performance, and a bona fide counterparty has the right to rescind the contract as well as a claim against the agent, requesting the agent for specific performance of the obligations or pay compensation. However, judicial practice is not always so straightforward, and it is also possible for unauthorized disposition and unauthorized agency to overlap. In such cases, the specific circumstances of the case should be analysed, taking into account the type of intellectual property involved and the legislative objectives, in order to protect the legitimate interests of both the true right holder and the bona fide counterparty.

'Apparent agency' in intellectual property assignment In order to maintain transaction security and protect the legitimate interests of bona fide counterparties, the *Civil Code* also sets up an apparent agency system. Broadly speaking, apparent agency is a type of unauthorized agency.[100] However, unlike unauthorized agency, although the apparent agency also acts against the will of the principal in essence, the act is not necessarily invalid if the bona fide counterparty has reasonably relied on the

---

[96] Wang, H. & Hou, G. (2013). 'Wuquan chufen yu yiwu shumai de lilun he shijian wenti- 'Wuquan chufen yu yiwu shumai'zhuanti xueshu yantaohui zongshu' ['Theoretical and practical issues of unauthorized disposition and multiple sales of the same item – A summary of the 'Unauthorized Disposition and Multiple Sales of the Same Item' academic seminar']. Xinan Zhengfa Daxue Xuebao [*Journal of Southwest University of Political Science and Law*], 5, 26.

[97] Wang, L. (2001). 'Lun wuquan chufen' ['On unauthorized disposition']. *Zhongguo Faxue [Chinese Law Science]*, 3, 78.

[98] Article 171. *Civil Code of the People's Republic of China.*

[99] Cui, J. (2020). 'Wuquan chufen zaibian'['Reconsideration of unauthorized disposition']. *Zhongwai Faxue [Chinese and Foreign Law]*, 4, 868.

[100] Wang, L. et al. (2020). *Minfa xue (Di liu ban) [Civil Law (6th ed.)]*, Falv Chubanshe [Law Press]. 261.

appearance of the authority of the agent, as a result, the principal must bear the legal effects of the unauthorized agency.[101] It can be seen from Article 172 of the *Civil Code* that the constituent elements of apparent agency mainly include three aspects: First, the agent does not obtain authorization from the principal, which includes acting without agency authority, acting beyond the scope of authorization or when the agency authority has terminated; Second, the agent performs an unauthorized act; Third, the counterparty has reasonable grounds to believe that the agent has the authority to act, thus generating a reliance interest. In the process of intellectual property assignment, the phenomenon of apparent agency is often seen in cases where a legal representative of a company assigns the intellectual property of the company. In such cases, although the intellectual property belongs to the company and the legal representative has not obtained authorization from the company, if the legal representative uses their position to make the counterparty reasonably believe that they have obtained authorization from the company, and the counterparty enters into an assignment agreement with them, the contract remains valid and binds the company directly. However, recognizing apparent agency is not an easy task, and in judicial practice, disputes often arise over whether the counterparty is 'bona fide'. Therefore, the issue of apparent agency in intellectual property assignments cannot be addressed by a unique approach, rather, it should be analysed on a case-by-case basis.

Indeed, the system of unauthorized disposition involves complex and obscure issues, and the debates in academic circles concerning this system are truly remarkable. As an important part of the civil law system, intellectual property has its own unique research value and significance regarding unauthorized disposition. In addressing unauthorized disposition in the assignment of intellectual property, it is essential to consider the differences of rules regarding various types of intellectual property rights. A targeted analysis of each key point of unauthorized disposition should be conducted, in conjunction with the specific circumstances of individual cases, to ensure the protection of the interests of bona fide counterparties. Moreover, it is necessary to approach the issue from the perspective of the legislative intent behind intellectual property law and the need to maintain market transaction security, in order to promote the circulation and transfer of intellectual property and unlock its market value. From a legislative perspective, there are still coordination issues between unauthorized disposition and the civil law system. Judicial practice has yet to form a unified approach to adjudication. Therefore, how to appropriately handle unauthorized disposition in intellectual property assignments and genuinely protect the interests of both intellectual property right holders and bona fide counterparties remains a subject that worths further study.

---

[101] Shi, S. (2000). *Minfa zonglun [General Principles of Civil Law]*. Zhongguo Zhengfa Daxue Chubanshe [China University of Political Science and Law Press]. 547.

6.3.3 Protection of Bona Fide Counterparties in Intellectual Property Assignments

6.3.3.1 Existing Issues

Judgment of 'good faith' For the protection of bona fide counterparties in intellectual property assignments, Article 311 of the *Civil Code* not only provides a system of bona fide acquisition but also remedies for bona fide counterparties in cases of unauthorized agency under Article 171. However, a key issue arises when applying these provisions to intellectual property assignment cases, specifically: how to determine if the counterparty is 'bona fide'. In fact, Article 14 of the *Judicial Interpretation on the Book of Property I* issued by the Supreme Court clearly outlines the standard for determining 'good faith', which includes two main elements: first, the assignee must be unaware that the assignor lacks the right to assign the property, and second, the assignee must not have acted with gross negligence. However, applying this standard in the context of intellectual property assignment is not straightforward. Taking patent assignment as an example, if the general manager of a company assigns the patent rights of the company to a third party, and the counterparty is unaware of the general manager's lack of authority, then after signing the assignment agreement and affixing the seal of the company, can the counterparty be directly considered 'bona fide'? Does the counterparty still need to obtain the general manager's authorization or a resolution from the meeting of shareholders of the company?[102] In contrast to a patent assignment, copyright assignments do not require mandatory registration, and since copyright has strong personal attributes, issues arise when a copyright owner, after assigning the copyright, still signs assignment agreements with others under the name of the author. In such cases, determining the 'bona fide' status of the counterparty in the agreement becomes a complex issue. Therefore, while there are judicial decisions supporting the application of the bona fide acquisition system in intellectual property cases, this does not mean that the system can be universally applied to all types of intellectual property cases. Specifically, the determination of 'good faith' by the counterparty should be analyzed in light of the specific judicial practice and circumstances involved.

The public credibility of intellectual property assignment In protecting the legitimate interests of bona fide counterparties through the system of bona fide acquisition, the issue of public credibility in intellectual property assignments must also be addressed. Due to the diversity of types of intellectual property and the particularities of intellectual property rights, different applicable rules for the changes in the title of rights have been established for different types of intellectual property. In the process of bona fide acquisition of intellectual property, patent and trademark

---

[102] Xie, L. (2018). 'Zhuanliquan wuquan chufen yu shanyi xiangduifang baohu' ['Unauthorized disposition of patent rights and protection of good faith counterparties']. *Ha'er bin shifan daxue shehui kexue xuebao [Journal of Social Sciences]*, 1, 44.

rights have publication effects due to their registration and public announcement.[103] As such, actors can rely on the registration and announcement of patents and trademarks to ascertain their ownership. However, copyrights and trade secrets, due to the unique nature of their rights, cannot be disclosed in a similar manner: on the one hand, in the case of copyright, according to current legal provisions, the copyright law of China adopts an automatic generation system. Copyright automatically arises once a work is created. Furthermore, Article 12 of the *Copyright Law* specifies that registration of a work is not mandatory; copyright holders may voluntarily register their works with the relevant registry. On the other hand, the special nature of copyright and trade secrets makes it unsuitable to use registration or publication to disclose their contents. If registered or published, there is an inevitable risk of content exposure, which could harm the legitimate interests of the right holder, thus contradicting the purpose of intellectual property protection.[104] Therefore, due to the lack of clear publication procedures and the special nature of these rights, it is difficult for an actor to identify the true ownership of copyright or trade secrets, let alone to determine 'good faith'. Moreover, while the assignment of patent and trademark rights is subject to registration or publication, this does not necessarily imply that the assignment has public credibility. For registration to have public credibility, it must be supported by legal provisions and corresponding measures. The current patent and trademark registries do not meet such criteria.[105] Thus, protecting the bona fide counterparties is not a straightforward process. It requires a careful analysis of the potential issues that may arise in intellectual property assignments and the identification of the best approach to safeguarding the legitimate rights of bona fide counterparties.

Different attitudes towards protecting bona fide counterparties in practice In addressing the issue of unauthorized dispositions in intellectual property assignments, how to ensure the protection of the legitimate interests of the bona fide counterparties, as well as balance the interests between the true right holders and the bona fide counterparties, has become a focal point in legal practice. Currently, there are different approaches to protecting bona fide counterparties, mainly reflected in the lack of comprehensive regulatory standards and inconsistent judicial attitudes. First, inadequate regulatory standards. At the legislative level, there is still insufficient

---

[103] Liu, Q. (2009). 'Shangbiaoquan shanyi qude zhidu yanjiu —— Yi zhuce shangbiao zhuanyongquan de zhuanrang wei kaocha shijiao' ['Study on the system of good faith acquisition of trademark rights – From the perspective of the transfer of exclusive rights to registered trademarks']. *Zhengzhi Yu Falv [Politics and Law]*, 11, 133–141; Yuan, B. (2011). 'Zhuce shangbiao shanyi qude falv yiju' ['Legal basis for good faith acquisition of registered trademarks']. *Renmin Sifa [People's Justice]*, 22, 44–45; Cai, R. (2019). 'Shanyi qude zhidu zai zhuanlifa zhong zhuanyong de helixing fenxi' ['Analysis on the rationality of applying the system of good faith acquisition in patent law']. Zhongguo Faming Yu Zhuanli *[China Invention and Patent]*, 1, 84–87.

[104] Liu, H. (2018). 'zhishi chanquan wuquan chufen wenti chutan' ['An initial exploration of the issue of unauthorized disposition of intellectual property']. *Shidai Jingmao [Times of Economics and Trade]*, 9, 91.

[105] Bu, Y. (2010). 'Zhishi chanquan de shanyi qude' ['Good faith acquisition of intellectual property']. *Zhongde Faxue Luntan [Sino-German Law Forum]*, 8, 306.

clarity on whether the system of bona fide acquisition can be applied to intellectual property. The existing legal instruments that address the bona fide acquisition of intellectual property primarily include the *Answers to Several Issues Regarding the Trial of Trademark Civil Disputes* issued by the Beijing Higher People's Court. Article 40 of this document specifies that an assignee cannot acquire a trademark if it was assigned without authorization, clearly rejecting the application of the bona fide acquisition system to registered trademarks.[106] However, this document only pertains to registered trademarks and does not cover other types of intellectual property, such as patents or copyrights. Furthermore, due to the relatively low level of authority of this document, it does not provide clear or unified guidance for judicial practice; Second, inconsistent judicial attitudes: taking the case of bona fide acquisition of registered trademarks as an example, judicial practice has shown differing attitudes. Courts that support the application of bona fide acquisition to registered trademarks argue that although trademark rights are not classified as property rights, the registration and assignment of trademarks have been approved and recorded by the national trademark office, which in fact shows a certain degree of public credibility. From the perspective of market security and transaction facilitation, the bona fide acquisition system can be applied to the circulation of trademarks.[107] On the other hand, courts opposing this view refer to the Beijing High Court's document, arguing that unauthorized assignment of registered trademarks constitutes trademark infringement and that the assignee cannot acquire the trademark, thereby denying the application of the bona fide acquisition system.[108] In summary, whether intellectual property can be subject to bona fide acquisition in order to protect the legitimate interests of bona fide counterparties remains a matter of differing judicial attitudes, both at the legislative and judicial levels. Different regional courts have varied approaches depending on the specific case. How to effectively protect the legitimate interests of bona fide counterparties requires a more nuanced approach by returning to the specific circumstances of each case for targeted analysis.

6.3.3.2 Rules for Dealing with the Protection of Bona Fide Counterparties

Currently, the protection of bona fide counterparties in intellectual property assignments cannot be generalized. Instead, it should be based on the overall civil law system, recognizing the differences and connections between intellectual property rights and property rights. Additionally, it should take into account the legislative purposes and mechanisms for different types of intellectual property, and be grounded in the specific circumstances that arise in practice. Appropriate, targeted measures

[106] See *Beijing High People's Court Answers to Several Issues on the Trial of Trademark Civil Dispute Cases*, Jing Gao Fa Fa [2004] No. 48, released on 18 February 2004.

[107] Xiamen Intermediate People's Court, Fujian Province (2016) *Min 02 Min Zhong Second Instance Civil Judgment No. 3857.*

[108] Shandong Provincial Higher People's Court (2015) *Lu Min Ti Zi Civil Judgment No. 72.*

should be adopted to protect the legitimate interests of bona fide counterparties. Specifically, this includes the following two aspects:

Legislation should focus on the protection of bona fide counterparties In addressing illegal actions in intellectual property assignments, such as unauthorized disposition or unauthorized agency, legislation should respond promptly to practical concerns and focus on the protection of bona fide counterparties. Regarding the bona fide acquisition of intellectual property, this involves not only issues of system applicability but also considerations related to promoting intellectual property market transactions and ensuring market safety. Currently, there are gaps in the legislation on the bona fide acquisition of intellectual property, particularly regarding the changes in rights related to different types of intellectual property assignments and the applicability of bona fide acquisition. Essentially, these issues involve protecting bona fide counterparties and fulfilling the legislative purposes of intellectual property. Timely legislative attention to potential problems in intellectual property assignments will help reduce the risks that bona fide counterparties may face, ensuring market transaction safety and the maintenance of market order. It will also address the coordination and conflict between intellectual property and property rights, ensuring the improvement and smooth functioning of the overall legislative system, while providing clear guidance and norms for judicial practice.

Judicial decisions should adhere to the principle of 'one claim, one discussion' Given that there is currently no unified or clear institutional guidance at the legislative level, and considering the distinct rules for different types of intellectual property assignments as well as the particularities of the subject of intellectual property, judicial practice should still be based on the actual facts of each case. Relevant legal provisions regarding the protection of bona fide counterparties should be considered, focusing on the differences of each case. The principle of 'one claim, one discussion' should be upheld in judicial decisions, with specific issues analyzed in detail. By adhering to this principle and ensuring that judicial decisions are based on facts and law, the legitimate interests of both the true intellectual property owners and bona fide counterparties can be effectively protected, and the application difficulties in intellectual property assignments can be properly addressed.

6.4 Institutional Arrangements and Improvements for the Capitalization of Intellectual Property Rights

Intellectual property capitalization is a new concept that has evolved from the ideas of intellectual capital, knowledge capitalization, as well as the practices of intellectual property commodification and industrialization. Intellectual property capitalization refers to the process of transforming intellectual property from a product factor into an investment factor, valuing and using it as an input to the production and business process, thereby quantifying it into capital and value-added assets.[109] In the context of the rapid development of the knowledge economy, China pushes to establish an efficient comprehensive intellectual property management system, and the integration of the full chain of intellectual property creation, utilization, protection, management, and service, intellectual property capitalization can enrich the utilization of intellectual property, promote the integration of intellectual property and financial resources, expand financing channels for enterprises, and stimulate knowledge innovation. However, due to the intangible, regional, and temporal nature of intellectual property, combined with the complexity of the existing financial system, intellectual property capitalization faces many risks, especially in the current context where the operational model of intellectual property capitalization in China is still unmatured. Therefore, intellectual property capitalization requires careful consideration and systematic research to ensure its smooth operation. Thus, it is of significant practical importance to summarize the issues currently faced in intellectual property capitalization, analyse the causes of these issues and find countermeasures. This section will analyse the current forms of intellectual property capitalization operation, the difficulties and defects in its operation as well as possible solutions, in order to provide insights for the improvement of the financial capital legal system and intellectual property system of China, and to offer guidance for enterprises engaged in intellectual property capitalization practices.

6.4.1 Main Forms of Intellectual Property Capitalization

6.4.1.1 Intellectual Property Pledge

Concepts Intellectual property pledge financing is a type of financing activity where intellectual property is pledged as collateral. It refers to a situation in which a debtor or a third party pledges specific intellectual property rights to a creditor as collateral to secure the performance of a debt. If the debt is not paid on time, the creditor has the right to prioritize repayment by auctioning or selling the pledged intellectual property.[110] In the *14th Five-Year Plan* outline, the terminology of 'intellectual property pledge financing' is explained as 'a financing method where enterprises pledge the economic rights of patents, trademarks, and copyrights (after evaluation) to secure loans from banks, the goal is to help small and medium-sized technology enterprises

---

[109] Chen, J. (2015). 'Zhishi chanquan zibenhua de tiaojian yu jiazhi pinggu' ['Conditions and value assessment of intellectual property capitalization']. *Xueshujie [Academic Circle]*, 8, 91.

[110] Feng, X. (2012). 'Woguo qiye zhishi chanquan zhiya rongzi ji qi wanshan duice yanjiu' ['Research on intellectual property pledge financing of enterprises in China and its improvement strategies']. *Hebei Faxue [Hebei Law Science]*, 12, 40.

address financing difficulties caused by the lack of real estate collateral'.[111] Intellectual property pledge financing is a type of rights pledge security and is the most common model in intellectual property financing.[112] However, since the pledged asset is different in form from conventional collateral, intellectual property pledge financing carries certain unique characteristics.

Relevant legal basis Due to the relatively long development history of intellectual property pledge financing, it is currently the most common model in intellectual property capitalization. The state has issued a number of laws, regulations, and policies to regulate this sector. However, at present, intellectual property pledge financing has not yet formed a unified and flawless legal system. On one hand, the existing legislation is ranked at a lower level in the legislative hierarchy, there is a lack of high-level legislative guidance; on the other hand, there is a lack of comprehensive operational guidance and evaluation standards, which has affected the practical development of intellectual property pledge financing.[113]

Currently, the relevant laws and regulations are divided into two categories: on one hand, there are provisions related to the basic laws of intellectual property. Article 89 of the *Implementation Rules of the Patent Law* stipulates that the State Council's patent administrative department shall maintain a patent registry, which includes matters related to patent applications and patent rights, including information on patent pledges, preservation, and their cancellation. The *Measures for Pledge Registration of Patent Rights*, issued by the State Intellectual Property Office, specifically regulates the pledge of patent rights. Article 3 of the *Measures for Registration of Copyright Pledge Rights* stipulates that 'the economic rights related to copyright and associated rights provided by *Copyright Law of the People's Republic of China* can be pledged', and the National Copyright Administration is responsible for copyright pledge registration. The *Regulations on the Pledge Registration Procedure for Registered Trademark Exclusive Rights* provide specific guidelines for the pledge registration of registered trademark exclusive rights. On the other hand, there are laws related to pledge transactions. Articles 440 and 444 of the *Civil Code* stipulate the types of rights that can be pledged by the debtor or a third party, including the 'transferable exclusive rights to registered trademarks, patent rights, economic rights of copyrights, and other intellectual property rights'. It also specifies that 'the

[111] National Development and Reform Commission. (2021). "Shi si wu' guihua mingci jieshi | Zhishi chanquan zhiya rongzi' "14th Five-Year Plan' *Outline* Glossary-Intellectual Property Pledge Financing', https://www.ndrc.gov.cn/fggz/fzzlgh/gjfzgh/202112/t20211224_1309284.html, accessed on 18 July 2022.

[112] Tao, L. & Ruan, J. (2017). 'Woguo zhishi chanquan zhiya rongzi: shijian yangtai he lifa zhidu shenshi ——jiyu zhishi chanquan zhanlue he minfadian bianzuan de beijing' ['Intellectual property pledge financing in China: Practical patterns and legislative system review – Based on the background of intellectual property strategy and the compilation of the Civil Code']. *Shehui Kexue Yanjiu [Social Science Research]*, 5, 111.

[113] Guo, H. (2019). 'Woguo zhishi chanquan zhiya rongzi de xianshi zhangai yu lujing tantao' ['Practical obstacles and path exploration of intellectual property pledge financing in China']. *Jinrong Fazhan Yanjiu [Research on Financial Development]*, 8, 88.

pledge of economic rights of intellectual property such as exclusive rights to registered trademarks, patent rights, and copyright rights is established upon completion of pledge registration'. Furthermore, after the economic rights of intellectual property are pledged, the pledgor is prohibited from assigning or licensing others to use the pledged rights, along with other specific situations. In addition, some laws related to the application of intellectual property also mention intellectual property pledge financing. For example, Article 35 of the *Law on Promoting the Transformation of Scientific and Technological Achievements*[114] and Article 40 of the *Film Industry Promotion Law* stipulate that: "The state encourages financial institutions to provide financing services for film activities and improve film infrastructure, legally carrying out intellectual property pledge financing related to films and supporting the development of the film industry through credit and other methods."

At the policy level, the *Outline for Building a Strong Intellectual Property Country (2021–2035)* mentions that: "...to actively and steadily develop intellectual property finance, improve intellectual property pledge information platforms, encourage the development of various types of intellectual property mixed pledges and insurance, and standardize and explore innovations in intellectual property financing models. It also aims to improve copyright transaction and service platforms, and strengthen services such as work asset evaluation, registration and certification, and pledge financing." The *14th Five-Year Plan for National Intellectual Property Protection and Utilization* proposes: "...to optimize the intellectual property pledge financing system, improve the risk management mechanism for intellectual property pledge financing, and perfect the mechanism for the disposal of pledged assets. It also calls for the construction of an intellectual property pledge information platform. Support banks in innovating internal assessment management models, promote banking financial institutions to effectively utilize separate credit plans, and optimize regulatory policies such as non-performing loan ratio assessments, aiming to expand the scale of intellectual property pledge loans under the premise of controllable risks." The *Implementation Annual Promotion Plan for the Construction of a Strong Intellectual Property Country and the 14th Five-Year Plan* highlights the need to advance the construction of intellectual property pledge information platforms, explore new models for sharing risks in intellectual property pledge financing, and improve intellectual property pledge registration as well as the assignment and licensing filing-record systems.

In addition, relevant government departments have also launched several special initiatives. For example, in 2021, the National Intellectual Property Office, the China Banking and Insurance Regulatory Commission, and the National Development and Reform Commission jointly formulated the *Intellectual Property Pledge Financing into the Park to Benefit Enterprises Action Plan (2021–2023)*, the aim is to ensure that intellectual property pledge financing benefits high-tech parks and enterprises'.

[114] Article 35 of *Law on Promoting the Transformation of Scientific and Technological Achievements* provides: "The state encourages banking financial institutions to innovate in terms of organizational form, management mechanisms, financial products, and services, and encourages the development of intellectual property pledge loans, equity pledge loans, and other loan businesses to provide financial support for the transformation of scientific and technological achievements."

Furthermore, during the COVID-19 pandemic, to alleviate the operational difficulties faced by small and medium-sized enterprises, relevant departments conducted a series of supportive activities. These included initiatives like the '*Zhi Hui Xing*' special program, which used trademark pledges to assist key industries in overcoming financial difficulties.[115]

Intellectual property pledge financing practice In 2009, China began piloting intellectual property pledge financing, initially designating 6 pilot units, followed by approval for three more batches of 16 cities to conduct intellectual property pledge financing trials.[116] In 2016, the State Intellectual Property Office launched 40 pilot regions and units for patent pledge financing.[117] China has accumulated rich experience in intellectual property pledge financing through numerous trials, leading to the development of several distinctive financing models. Currently, these include various approaches such as 'bank + enterprise patent or trademark pledge', 'bank + government fund guarantee + patent reverse guarantee', and 'bank + technology guarantee company + patent reverse guarantee'.[118] From the perspective of leading entities, these models can be categorized into government-led, market-led, and government-guided models. In the government-led model, the government formulates relevant policies, establishes financing tools, and bears the main risks of intellectual property pledge financing. Notable examples of this model include the Shanghai model and the Chengdu model.[119] The market-led model is suitable for environments with developed intellectual property, clear ownership, and abundant market information. In this model, the government plays a supportive role, providing public services.[120] In the government-guided model, the government primarily facilitates the development of

---

115 China National Intellectual Property Administration. (2022). 'Guojia zhishi chanquanju zhongguo yinhang gufen youxian gongsi guanyu kaizhan shangbiao zhiya zhuli canyin, wenlv deng zhongdian xingye shukun 'Zhi Huixing' zhuanxiang huodong de tongzhi' 'Notice on the 'Zhi Hui Xing' Special Activity to Support Key Industries such as Catering and Culture & Tourism through Trademark Pledge, jointly with the Industrial and Commercial Bank of China', https://www.cnipa.gov.cn/art/2022/6/28/art_550_176262.html, accessed on 18 July 2022.

116 The Central People's Government. (2010). 'Zhishi chanquanju pifu disanpi zhishi chanquan zhiya rongzi shidian mingdan' ['Intellectual Property Office approves the third batch of intellectual property pledge financing pilot list'], http://www.gov.cn/gzdt/2010-07/13/content_1652676.htm, accessed on 18 July 2022.

117 The Central People's Government. (2016). 'Zhishi chanquanju qidong zhuanliquan zhiya rongzi he zhuanli baoxian shidian shifan gongzuo' 'Intellectual Property Office launches pilot demonstration work on patent pledge financing and patent insurance', http://www.gov.cn/xinwen/2016-08/26/content_5102624.htm, accessed on 18 July 2022.

118 National Development and Reform Commission. (2021). ' 'Shi si wu' guihua <gangyao> mingci jieshi | Zhishi chanquan zhiya rongzi' ['14th Five-Year Plan *Outline* Glossary- Intellectual Property Pledge Financing'], https://www.ndrc.gov.cn/fggz/fzzlgh/gjfzgh/202112/t20211224_1309284.html, accessed on 18 July 2022.

119 Song, G. & Tian, L. (2016). 'Jishuxing Zhongxiao qiye zhishi chanquan zhiya rongzi moshi de guoneiwai bijiao yanjiu' ['A comparative study of intellectual property pledge financing models for technology-based SMEs at home and abroad']. *Jinrong Fazhan Yanjiu [Research on Financial Development]*, 2, 52.

120 Cui, H., Pan, M. & Zhang, C. (2019). 'Zhishi chanquan zhiya rongzi zongxiang gaoxiao shichanghua de lujing yanjiu – Yi guangdongsheng wei li' ['Research on the path of efficient

intellectual property pledge financing by building public service platforms, investing in financial and special funds, and offering interest subsidies and financial incentives to guide banks, enterprises, and intermediaries to engage in these activities.[121]

In summary, given the differences in intellectual property development, market environments, financial levels, and local development strategies across various regions, there is no one-size-fits-all solution for intellectual property pledge financing models. The diversification and regionalization of intellectual property pledge financing are more suitable directions for the current stage of development of China.

6.4.1.2 Intellectual Property Trusts

Concepts The concept of trust is clearly defined in Article 2 of the *Trust Law*.[122] An intellectual property trust is the application of trust in the field of intellectual property. It refers to the act where the intellectual property right holder, based on trust in the trustee, entrusts their intellectual property to the trustee. The trustee, in their own name, acts in accordance with the wishes of the settlor to manage or dispose of the intellectual property for the benefit of the settlor.[123]

Relevant legal basis Currently, there are relatively few laws and regulations governing the trust sector in China, and there is no sector-specific laws or regulations that explicitly address intellectual property trusts.

The establishing requirements for intellectual property trusts are not explicitly defined in the law. However, insights can be drawn from Article 7 of the *Trust Law*,[124] which outlines the general requirements for establishing a trust from a broader perspective. While this provision does not specifically address intellectual property trusts, it does not exclude trusts of intellectual property from its application either.

It is important to note that Article 20 of the *Regulations on the Administration of Trust Investment Companies* clearly stipulates that intellectual property can be included within the scope of the business operations of a trust investment company,[125] which effectively affirms the possibility of intellectual property being part of a trust. However, although this provision sets up a legal basis for intellectual property trusts, yet the regulation has been abolished, and it also did not provide corresponding

---

marketization of intellectual property pledge financing – A case study of Guangdong Province']. *Jianghuai Luntan [Jianghuai Forum]*, 6, 84.

121 Zhang, H. (2020). 'Goujian shichang zhudaoxing zhishi chanquan zhiya rongzi moshi' ['Building a market-driven intellectual property pledge financing model'], *Renmin Luntan [People's Forum]*, 30, 118.

122 Article 2. *Trust Law of the People's Republic of China.*

123 Zhang, W. (2011). 'Jiyu zhishi chanquan jiezhi de kejixing Zhongxiao qiye zhuanlihua rongzi de jili fenxi' ['Mechanism analysis of patent industrialization financing for technology-based SMEs based on intellectual property media']. *Caikuai Tongxun [Financial and Accounting Communications]*, 30, 130.

124 Article 7. *Trust Law of the People's Republic of China.*

125 Article 20. *Measures for the Administration of Trust Investment Companies.*

specific implementation rules. As a result, the practical rules for the implementation of intellectual property trusts remain in a state of ambiguity.

At the policy level, the *2019 National Intellectual Property Strategy Implementation Plan to Accelerate the Construction of a Strong Intellectual Property Nation* explicitly mentions that: "Encourage trust companies to comprehensively utilize equity, debt, investment-loan linkage, industrial funds, intellectual property trusts, and other methods to carry out intellectual property investment and financing activities. Encourage financing guarantee companies to develop credit guarantee products suitable for intellectual property, and increase support for intellectual property financing for small and micro enterprises." This statement explicitly highlights intellectual property trusts as a form of investment and financing. However, its nature leans more towards policy advocacy, without addressing specific implementation measures.

Practice of intellectual property trusts Compared to the extensive and long-standing practices of intellectual property pledge financing, the practice of intellectual property trusts is relatively less developed. On April 30, 2011, China's first intellectual property financing trust plan, the '*Zhongguancun Independent Innovation Intellectual Property Financing Collective Trust Plan (Phase I)*' launched by COFCO Trust, was officially established.[126] In 2018, Hefei province explored a pilot for intellectual property trust transactions, establishing a new model of 'high-tech enterprises + industrial parks + guarantees + trusts', marking the first intellectual property trust pilot in China.

In 2022, Nanjing province introduced the '*Jiangbei Sci-Tech Investment-Green Guarantee Lingque Intellectual Property Asset-Backed Special Plan (Phases 1–5)*', which adopted a trust framework for intellectual property securitization. However, this primarily represents a securitization application rather than a pure trust model. These examples demonstrate that intellectual property trusts in China are still at an early stage of development, further pilot programs are necessary to accumulate specialized practical experience in this field.

6.4.1.3 Intellectual Property Securitization

Concepts Intellectual property securitization represents the application of securities as a financial tool in the field of intellectual property. Specifically, it refers to the process whereby intellectual property right holders transfer their owned intellectual property with predictable cash flows as underlying assets to a Special Purpose Vehicle (SPV). The SPV then issues tradable certificates of rights based on the cash flows

[126] State-owned Assets Supervision and Administration Commission of the State Council (2022). 'Zhongliang xintuo faqi sheli guonei shouli zizhu chuangxin zhishi chanquan rongzi xintuo jihua' ['Sinochem Trust initiates the establishment of the first domestic self-innovation intellectual property financing trust plan'], http://www.sasac.gov.cn/n2588025/n2588124/c3981306/content.html, accessed on 19 July 2022.

generated by these underlying assets.[127] Intellectual property securitization diversifies investment types in the capital market, providing enterprises with additional financing possibilities and offering a novel and viable pathway for the utilization of intellectual property.

Relevant legal basis At present, China has not promulgated specific laws designated to intellectual property securitization, and the relevant provisions on intellectual property securitization are relatively scattered. On the one hand, they involve fundamental intellectual property laws, related laws and regulations, and relevant judicial interpretations concerning intellectual property as underlying assets, such as the *Patent Law*, the *Trademark Law*, the *Copyright Law*, the *Civil Code*, and the *Interpretation on Issues Concerning the Application of Law in the Trial of Disputes over Financial Leasing Contracts*. On the other hand, trading and supervision are mainly governed by laws and regulations related to securitization business, such as the *Company Law*, the *Securities Law*, the *Administrative Provisions on the Asset Securitization Business of Subsidiaries of Securities Companies and Fund Management Companies*, the *Guidelines on Information Disclosure for Asset Securitization Business of Subsidiaries of Securities Companies and Fund Management Companies*, the *Asset Securitization Business Guidelines of the Shanghai Stock Exchange*, and the *Asset Securitization Business Guidelines of the Shenzhen Stock Exchange* etc.

In addition to laws, regulations, and judicial interpretations, some policies also address intellectual property securitization. In March 2015, the *Opinions of the Central Committee of the Communist Party of China and the State Council on Deepening the Reform of Institutional Mechanisms and Accelerating the Implementation of the Innovation-Driven Development Strategy* proposed exploring the development of intellectual property securitization. In September 2017, the *Notice of the State Council on Issuing the National Technology Transfer System Construction Plan* suggested launching pilot projects for intellectual property securitization financing. In December 2018, China's first intellectual property securitization project, the First Capital—Wenke Leasing 2017 Asset-Backed Special Plan, was successfully issued on the Shenzhen Stock Exchange, marking the realization of intellectual property securitization. Subsequently, multiple intellectual property securitization projects were issued, achieving a quantitative breakthrough. In August 2019, the *Opinions of the Central Committee of the Communist Party of China and the State Council on Supporting Shenzhen in Building a Pilot Demonstration Zone of Socialism with Chinese Characteristics* proposed exploring intellectual property securitization and building intellectual property and technology achievement property rights trading centers in a standardized and orderly manner. These initiatives provide guidance for intellectual property securitization in China to follow a standardized development path and achieve high-quality growth.

[127] Zhang, H. & Li, M. (2016). 'Zhishi chanquan zhengquanhua zhi jichu zichan tanxi' ['Analysis of underlying assets in intellectual property securitization']. *Falv Shiyong [Application of Law]*, 9, 36.

Practice of intellectual property securitization Theoretically, according to Article 3 of the *Administrative Provisions on Asset Securitization Business of Subsidiaries of Securities Companies and Fund Management Companies*, the definition and scope of underlying assets are relatively flexible, without strictly limiting the possibility of intellectual property being securitized as an underlying asset.[128] According to this provision, in theory, any intellectual property that is independent, capable of being specified, and capable of generating predictable cash flows can be securitized.

In practice, types of assets eligible for securitization in international intellectual property securitization include existing intellectual property, claims derived from existing intellectual property, future intellectual property, and future claims derived from future intellectual property.[129] Based on current practices in China, common types of securitizable intellectual property from the perspective of product types include accounts receivable securitization, pledge loan securitization, licensing fee receivable securitization, and leasing securitization. These common types of assets that can be securitized also influence corresponding intellectual property securitization transaction models. At present, the main intellectual property securitization models in China include the loan and pledge model,[130] secondary patent licensing model,[131] supply chain model,[132] leasing model,[133] and trust model.[134] Among these common models, the loan and pledge model are the most prevalent. According to the *2018–2021 China Intellectual Property Securitization Market Statistics Report*, as of the end of 2021, out of the 59 intellectual property securities issued on the Shanghai and Shenzhen stock exchanges, 37 were small loan debt securities, with an issuance scale of 8.487 billion yuan, accounting for the largest proportion. Securities of right of claims for patent licensing fee based on ranked second in terms of issuance quantity and scale, followed by accounts receivable debt, leasing debt, and intellectual property securities on right of claims for trademark licensing fee.[135]

---

[128] Article 3. *Regulations on Asset Securitization Business Management of Subsidiaries of Securities Companies and Fund Management Companies.*

[129] Kong, L. (2017). 'Zhishi chanquan zhengquanhua zhong ke zhengquanhua zichan de xuanze ji fengxian fangkong' ['Selection of securifiable assets and risk prevention in intellectual property securitization'], *Keji Yu Falv [Science and Technology and Law]*, 1, 72.

[130] For the specific transaction structure, see *Ping An Securities - Gao Xin Investment Intellectual Property No. 1 Asset-Backed Special Plan'.*

[131] For the specific transaction structure, see *Guangzhou Development Zone 'Xingye Yuanrong - Guangzhou Development Zone Patent Licensing Asset-Backed Special Plan' project.*

[132] For the specific transaction structure, see *'Qiyi Century Intellectual Property Supply Chain Finance Asset-Backed Special Plan'.*

[133] For the specific transaction structure, see *'First Entrepreneurship - Wenke Leasing Phase I Asset-Backed Special Plan'.*

[134] For the specific transaction structure, see *'Jiangbei Ke Investment - Green Guarantee Lingque Intellectual Property Asset-Backed Special Plan'.*

[135] China High-tech Industry Guide, (2022). 'Liang da jiaoyisuo faxing zhishi chanquan zhengquanlei chanpin guimo jin 150 yi yuan' ['Two stock exchanges issue intellectual property securities products with a scale of nearly 15 billion yuan'], http://paper.chinahightech.com/pc/content/202202/14/content_46013.html, accessed on 22 July 2022.

6.4.1.4 Intellectual Property Contribution

Concepts Intellectual property contribution refers to a method in which the owner of intellectual property transfers the ownership of appraised intellectual property to a company, thereby obtaining shareholder status. The contributor is granted with shareholder rights and assumes shareholder obligations based on the proportion of registered capital represented by the intellectual property contribution.[136]

Relevant legal basis At present, there are no separate or unified provisions regarding intellectual property contribution as a form of intellectual property capitalization. Relevant regulations are scattered among related laws and regulations, with the main legal basis including provisions on shareholder contributions under the company law and provisions related to contributions under the basic intellectual property legal system.

Paragraph 1 of Article 27 of the *Company Law* explicitly stipulates that intellectual property can be contributed as capital after valuation, providing a clear legal basis for intellectual property contribution.[137] Article 28 of the *Company Law* states that: "...for contributions made with non-monetary assets, the transfer of ownership of the assets must be managed in accordance with the law," the 'transfer' mentioned in this provision is thus linked to the provisions on intellectual property assignment within the fundamental intellectual property legal framework. Regarding the proportion of intellectual property contributions, the *Company Law* has been amended twice to gradually increase the allowable proportion of intellectual property contributions. The current version of the *company law* has completely removed any restrictions on the proportion, meaning that intellectual property contributions can constitute up to 100% of the registered capital. This reflects the emphasis of China on the utilization of intellectual property and creates a more flexible policy environment for intellectual property contributions.

In the foundational legal framework of intellectual property, provisions closely related to capital contributions are scattered across individual laws and regulations, such as the *Copyright Law*, *Patent Law*, and *Trademark Law*. These primarily address issues of intellectual property assignment, duration, and validity. Taking patent rights as an example, Article 10 of the *Patent Law* specifies the procedures for assigning patent rights.[138] According to this article, if patent rights are used as capital contributions, the ownership transfer procedures under Article 28 of the *Company Law* must include registration. Failure to complete this process could affect the validity of the contribution. Article 42, Paragraph 1 of the *Patent Law* provides general stipulations regarding the duration of patent rights, while Paragraphs 2 and 3 address unreasonable delays in the granting process and the compensation period for new drug approvals.

---

[136] Sun, C. & Yu, Y. (2008). 'Zhishi chanquan chuzi suoshui shi de gudong zeren' ['Shareholder liability when intellectual property capital contribution is diminished'], *Jishu Jingji Yu Guanli Yanjiu [Technology Economics and Management Research]*, 4, 44.

[137] Article 27, Paragraph 1. *Company Law of the People's Republic of China.*

[138] Article 10. *Patent Law of the People's Republic of China.*

Consequently, patent rights are subject to duration limitations. However, the equities acquired through patent rights as capital contributions—unless the equities of the patent holder are expelled or removed—are not subject to any time limitations in theory.[139] This means that patent rights contributed as capital effectively extend the value of the patent. Furthermore, patent rights are inherently unstable. Articles 45, 46, and 47 of the *Patent Law* outline the effects of procedures for invalidating patent rights and the effect of retroactive invalidity from the outset. If a patent right is declared invalid after being contributed as capital, questions regarding whether stakeholders can demand the shareholder to make up the shortfall in capital contributions may arise.[140] Such issues significantly impact the execution of intellectual property transactions.

6.4.2 Difficulties and Pain Points

In the context of the knowledge economy, intellectual property capitalization transforms intellectual property from a product factor into an investment factor. Based on value assessment, it achieves full utilization of intellectual property and quantitative enhancement of its capital value. Value assessment, as a critical pathway to achieving intellectual property capitalization, inevitably requires an objective valuation of intellectual property grounded in the market environment and on the interests of both supply and demand sides. In practice, the pricing of intellectual property products is influenced not only by consumer demand for the products but also by consumers' ability to pay for the products or services. During the process of intellectual property capitalization, the endowment effect often leads suppliers to have overly optimistic price expectations for their intellectual property products or services, aiming to exchange them at a price higher than the normal market level to maximize returns. Conversely, the demand side typically seeks to pay a lower price to avoid excessive costs that may harm their interests. This creates a price bargaining dynamic between suppliers and consumers, yet the progress of such bargaining is often hindered by the intangible nature and instability of intellectual property rights. A typical example is the use of intellectual property as a capital contribution. Although there are relevant legal provisions addressing this practice, intellectual property contributions not only face the challenge of value assessment difficulties but also difficulties in subsequent fulfilment of contribution obligations due to the instability of the rights, which further creates transaction risks. Therefore, it is essential to identify the challenges and pain

[139] Ma, B. (2015). 'Lun gongsi zhuce ziben dengji zhidu gaige dui zhuanliquan chuzi de yingxiang' ['On the impact of the reform of the company registered capital registration system on patent capital contribution']. *Faxue Zazhi [Legal Studies Journal]*, 4, 61.

[140] Qinghai Weidesheng Biotechnology Co., Ltd. v. Beijing Weidesheng Biotechnology Co., Ltd., Yin, and Zhang on *capital increase dispute*, Supreme People's Court (2019) SPC Civil Final Judgment No. 959.

points that may arise in the process of intellectual property capitalization, so as to effectively address obstacles and facilitate the successful realization of intellectual property capitalization.

6.4.2.1 Difficulties in Securing the Stability of Rights

Stability is the foundation of development. The stability of intellectual property rights signifies the consistent existence of rights within the statutory protection period, without being invalidated or revoked for any reason, which would lead to the loss of rights.[141] Specifically, this includes aspects such as the existence and validity of rights, the scope of rights, ownership of rights, as well as whether there are defects in the rights.[142] However, due to the inherent nature of intellectual property and its institutional design, intellectual property shows the inherent characteristic of instability, primarily manifested in the following aspects:

Instability as to the existence of rights Within the current framework of intellectual property law, unlike the establishment of general property rights for tangible property, the types and scope of intellectual property are determined by the state, and intellectual property is granted legal protection only after it went through formal or substantive examination by the state.[143] However, due to the surge in the number of intellectual property rights, the design of examination systems, and limited examination resources, the existing intellectual property system tolerates a certain degree of instability in rights after weighing the costs and benefits of granting rights.

This implies that even though intellectual property rights are approved by state examination, they cannot be guaranteed with absolute validity, but rather in a presumptively valid state. The existence of such rights can ultimately be determined only when litigation arises.

Instability as to the scope of rights Since intellectual property is intangible, for the law, 'how to determine the scope of this 'thing beyond statement'—the intangible form of the subjective matter of the right, is the focus of the system.'[144] The registration system cleverly replaces the traditional method of defining property boundaries by shifting from the essence of intangible property into the expression in the

---

[141] Zhang, B. (2009). 'Zhishi chanquan zhiya rongzi de fengxian fenjie yu fenbu kongzhi' ['Risk decomposition and step-by-step control of intellectual property pledge financing'], *Zhishi Chanquan [Intellectual Property]*, 2, 32.

[142] Huang, G. & Zhu, X. (2009). 'Zhishi chanquan zhengquanhua de fengxian yanjiu – jiyu zhishi chanquan texing de fenxi' ['Research on the risks of intellectual property securitization – based on the analysis of intellectual property characteristics']. *Keji Guanli Yanjiu [Science and Technology Management Research]*, 12, 510.

[143] Li, Y. & Lü, Y. (2004). 'Lun zhishi chanquan zhi gongquan xingzhi – Dui 'zhishi chanquan shuyu siquan' de buchong' ['On the public nature of intellectual property – an addition to 'intellectual property as private rights"]. *Zhejiang Daxue Xuebao (Renwen Shehui Kexue Ban) [Journal of Zhejiang University (Humanities and Social Sciences)]*, 4, 65.

[144] Li, C. (2005). *Lun zhishi chanquanfa de tixihua [On the Systematization of Intellectual Property Law]*. Beijing Daxue Chubanshe [Peking University Press]. 58.

documents. The legal emphasis thus moves toward regulating these documents and restricting the scope of the right through limitations on application documents.[145] However, the registration system does not fully resolve the issue of the stability of the boundaries of intangible property rights. Questions such as what constitutes a 'work', what qualifies as 'creativity', how to distinguish between ideas and expressions, or how to interpret patent claims remain problematic. These ambiguous concepts and principles allow the system to accommodate emerging types and scenarios but simultaneously makes it difficult to determine the boundaries of rights at the outset, thus create uncertainties as to the scope of intellectual property.

The instability as to the ownership of rights The instability of ownership in intellectual property arises partly from its divisibility. Through simple contractual arrangements, an intellectual property right can be shared among multiple parties, and such sharing is not easily perceptible to non-contractual parties, leading to an uncertainty regarding ownership to the outside world.[146] Additionally, the fragmentation of the intellectual property registration system contributes to this instability. Patents, trademarks, and copyrights are registered with different authorities. Therefore, when a right holder seeks to capitalize a bundle of various IP rights, the complexity and dispersion of registration authorities further exacerbate the instability of ownership to some extent.[147]

6.4.2.2 Difficulties in the Valuation of Intellectual Property Based on Close Substitutability

The valuation of intellectual property based on close substitutability, also known as the market comparison method, involves using the transaction prices of identical or similar intellectual property as benchmarks. By comparing and adjusting these benchmarks according to the characteristics of the subject asset, its value can thereby be determined. In addition to this method, commonly used intellectual property valuation approaches include the cost method and the income method. Some scholars have also proposed innovative evaluation methods such as the real options method, comprehensive valuation method, and machine learning techniques.[148]

The application of the market approach is explicitly provided in Article 23 of the *Asset Appraisal Practice Guidelines – Intangible Assets* issued by the China

---

[145] Sherman, B. (2012). *Xiandai zhishi chanquanfa de yanjing [The Evolution of Modern Intellectual Property Law]* (Jin, H. trans.). Beijing Daxue Chubanshe [Peking University Press]. 69.

[146] Kong, L. (2017). 'Zhishi chanquan zhengquanhua zhong ke zhengquanhua zichan de xuanze ji fengxian fangkong' ['Selection of securifiable assets and risk prevention in intellectual property securitization']. *Keji Yu Falv [Science and Technology and Law]*, 1, 74.

[147] Li, Z. & Zheng, Y. (2010). 'Zhongxiao qiye zhishi chanquan zhiya daikuan de fengxian fenxi yu moshi goujian' ['Risk analysis and model construction of intellectual property pledge loans for small and medium-sized enterprises']. *Hongguan Jingji Yanjiu [Macroeconomic Research]*, 4, 60.

[148] Zhu, R., Zhang, Y. & Ge, L. (2022). 'Zhishi chanquan jiazhi pinggu yanjiu zongshu' ['A review of research on intellectual property valuation']. *Zhongguo Zichan Pinggu [China Asset Valuation]*, 1, 66.

Appraisal Society.[149] It proposes evaluation methods such as comparative analysis of similar cases and information collection, offering directions for the implementation of the market approach. However, when placed within the current intellectual property development environment, numerous challenges remain in its application and execution.

The current intellectual property valuation assessment is hindered by factors such as its strong subjectivity, inconsistent valuation standards, and unstandardized practices among value assessment institutions. These problems can be alleviated or resolved through measures such as formulating relevant evaluation guidelines and controlling the assessment process. However, a more challenging issue lies in determining a market-recognized objective value and making subjective adjustments based on specific transaction circumstances.[150] On one hand, the value of intellectual property primarily reflects its application value, focusing on the expected returns after its utilization. The value is 'assessed' by hypothesizing market conditions, resulting in a 'hypothetical price' rather than a 'natural value'. This hypothetical price, being artificially generated, inevitably diverges from the real value of the intellectual property.[151] Additionally, due to the instability of intellectual property value, influenced by factors such as technological progress, market dynamics, and changes in the validity period of relevant rights, the gap between hypothetical prices and real values can fluctuate significantly. On the other hand, the application of the market approach depends on an open and active intellectual property trading market, where abundant reference information is available to capture the essence of comparison and analogy underlying the approach. However, the current intellectual property trading market in China is underdeveloped. Many transactions are not publicly disclosed, and some intellectual properties are not valued by transactions, for instance, certain right holders acquire trademarks or patents for defensive purposes, aiming to block competitors from entering specific markets.[152] As a result, it is difficult to apply the market approach to assess intellectual property value when the existing market and information conditions cannot provide sufficient support.

---

[149] See Article 23 of *Asset Valuation Practice Standards – Intangible Assets*.

[150] Xu, H. (2014). 'Jiazhi liuzhuan Zhong de zhishi chanquan pinggu yanjiu' ['Research on intellectual property evaluation in value circulation']. *Zhishi Chanquan [Intellectual Property]*, 6, 70.

[151] Liu, C. (2013). 'Zhishi chanquan jiazhi goucheng jiben fanchou de zhidu quanshi' ['Institutional interpretation of the basic categories of intellectual property value composition']. *Hebei Jignmao Daxue Xuebao [Journal of Hebei University of Economics and Business]*, 6, 146.

[152] Liu, Y. (2016). '*Zhuanliquan* jingji jiazhi fenxi de xiangguan yanjiu shuli ji pingxi' ['A review and critique of research on the economic value analysis of patent rights']. *Keji Guani Yanjiu [Science and Technology Management Research]*, 2, 150.

6.4.2.3 Conflicts Between the Stability of Rights Required by the Operation of Capitalization and the Demand of Circulation of Property Rights by Right Holders

Capital inherently seeks profit, yet the capitalization of intellectual property requires the stability of rights. Fundamentally, this requirement for stability ensures the anticipated capital returns from intellectual property. The conflict between the stability demanded by capitalization and the right holder's need for the circulation of property rights lies in the fact that such circulation may undermine the guarantee of expected returns. On one hand, due to the intangible nature of intellectual property, its possession is not constrained by spatial boundaries. The same intellectual property can be used simultaneously by multiple entities in the same time and space. Such uses do not violate intellectual property laws and, in some cases, is even encouraged by law to promote the flow of knowledge. However, this flow can significantly impact anticipated returns in the process of intellectual property capitalization, as the returns from exclusivity differ markedly from those derived from shared use. On the other hand, the demand for the value of intellectual property is primarily reflected in its utility value. This means that intellectual property itself does not generate returns; rather, returns must depend on a specific operational team and must be integrated with certain production conditions, such as production facilities, sales channels, and after-sales services, so as to produce a stable cash flow.[153] This indicates that if intellectual property changes hands during the capitalization process, the methods of use, operating environment, or even value orientation of the intellectual property may change. Such changes to the human and material conditions underpinning the anticipated returns introduce risks that can render returns highly uncertain, thereby significantly increasing the operational risks of capitalization.

Therefore, there exists a tension between the stability of rights required for capitalization operations and the circulation of property rights demanded by right holders. This tension is particularly pronounced in intellectual property pledges. In most other forms of capitalization, the transfer of rights weakens the right holder's control over the intellectual property. However, in intellectual property pledges, since there is no transfer of rights, the right holder retains strong control over the intellectual property, and the obstacles to further disposition after the pledge are relatively minimal. This raises the following two questions: Can intellectual property be re-pledged after an initial pledge? Can intellectual property be assigned after being pledged?

Regarding whether intellectual property can be re-pledged after an initial pledge, Article 440 of the *Civil Code* explicitly states that the economic rights within intellectual property that can be assigned and are disposable by the debtor or a third party may be pledged. However, the provision does not explicitly address whether the same right can be subject to multiple pledges. In higher-level laws, such as the *Patent Law* and the *Copyright Law*, there are no specific provisions on this issue. In

[153] Chen, Y. & Song, Y. (2012). 'Zhishi chanquan zhiya rongzi de jiazhi pinggu fengxian kongzhi' ['Risk control in the value assessment of intellectual property pledge financing']. *Quyu Jinrong Yanjiu [Regional Financial Research]*, 7, 55.

subordinate regulations, both the *Measures for the Registration of Copyright Pledges* and the *Procedures for the Pledge Registration of Exclusive Rights to Use Registered Trademarks* are silent on whether repeat pledges are permissible. However, Article 11 of the *Measures for the Registration of Patent Pledges* clearly stipulates that if a patent right has already been registered for a pledge and is under a pledge period, further registration applications will not be accepted. This effectively negates the possibility of multiple pledges for patents. In summary, the current legal framework on repeated pledging of intellectual property reveals ambiguity in higher-level laws and inconsistency in lower-level regulations.

Regarding the assignment and licensing of intellectual property after it has been pledged, Article 444 of the *Civil Code* explicitly regulates the pledging of property rights within intellectual property. However, the *Patent Law* and *Copyright Law* do not provide specific provisions on this matter. At the level of subordinate regulations, Article 18 of the *Measures for the Registration of Patent Pledges* refines the implementation of patent pledges, clarifying the rights and obligations between the pledgor and the pledgee. Similarly, Article 14 of the *Measures for the Registration of Copyright Pledges* contains comparable provisions. Overall, the higher-ranking laws and subordinate regulations are relatively consistent on the transfer and licensing of intellectual property after pledging, setting two primary conditions: first, consent of the pledgee; second, advance repayment or deposit. While the transfer or licensing must be subject to the pledgee's approval can be seen as a measure to secure the transactional information; the requirement that debt secured by the pledge must either be repaid in advance or an equivalent amount must be deposited is rather doubting. The core function of a pledge lies in controlling the exchange value of the pledged property. For transfers or licenses of the pledged intellectual property that do not impair its exchange value, there seems to be no necessity for interference. It is inappropriate to restrict the transfer or licensing of pledged intellectual property merely because a pledge exists, without considering the specific circumstance of each case.[154] If such actions neither undermine the security function of the intellectual property pledge nor diminish the value of the pledged asset, the appropriateness of the 'advance repayment' requirement is indeed open to challenge.[155]

6.4.3 Coping Measures

Contract theory and price theory serve as fundamental frameworks for explaining the functioning of intellectual property transactions. Their primary purpose is to

154 Jiang, X. (2007). 'Zhongguo zhuanliquan zhiya zhidu cunzai de wenti jiqi wanshan' ['The issues and improvements of the patent pledge system in China']. mYanjiui Yu Fazhan Guanli [*Research and Development Management*], 3, 81.

155 Chen S. (2022). 'Yi chuzhi zhishi chanquan xuke shiyong guize de guifan jieshi yu falv xuzao' ['Normative interpretation and legal reconstruction of rules for the licensing of pledged intellectual property']. *Xi'nan Minzu Daxue Xuebao (Renwen Shehui Kexueban) [Journal of Southwest University for Nationalities (Humanities and Social Sciences Edition)]*, 7, 77.

ensure the successful realization of intellectual property transactions and to provide suitable solutions to the challenges inherent in intellectual property capitalization. The difficulties surrounding intellectual property capitalization, such as the stability of intellectual property rights, valuation issues, and the definition of claims, are pivotal factors influencing the bargaining dynamics between the transacting parties. Asymmetric information increases transaction costs of the transacting parties, while the inherent difficulties in valuation introduce potential crises in the capitalization process. These crises often manifest as threats to the security and stability of intellectual property transactions. For instance, in intellectual property capitalization, valuation problems frequently arise as right holders aim to present their intellectual property as highly valuable assets in the intellectual property capitalization process, so as to maximize the utility of the relevant intellectual property. However, the multitude of factors[156] affecting valuation means that excessively high market prices may hinder, rather than facilitate, the efficient operation of intellectual property capitalization. The crux of successful capitalization lies in the reasonable determination of the value of intellectual property. From the perspectives of contract theory and price theory, the primary challenge in intellectual property capitalization is managing the imbalances caused by informational asymmetries and valuation difficulties, as well as mitigating the risk of market failures that may result from the lack of applicable systems. To address these issues, it is essential to improve mechanisms for information exchange, thereby promoting the flow of information and enhancing transaction efficiency. Additionally, it is imperative to develop robust institutional frameworks and theoretical research to effectively manage the collaborative dynamics among various stakeholders in the capitalization process. Such efforts will help mitigate individual risks and provide a stable institutional and theoretical foundation for intellectual property capitalization.

6.4.3.1 Improving the Information Exchange Mechanism

Based on the challenges and pain points discussed regarding the operation of intellectual property capitalization, it becomes evident that the underlying issues, whether related to the stability of intellectual property rights or the difficulties in applying market-based valuation methods, often trace back to insufficient, untimely, or incomplete information acquisition, as well as high information acquisition costs. While China currently lacks a specialized and unified mechanism for intellectual property capitalization information exchange, the existing registration system serves as the primary framework for information exchange. For small-scale transactions, the current registration system can sufficiently fulfils this role. However, for large-scale or full-chain intellectual property transactions, the overly fragmented registration system falls short of meeting market demands for comprehensive information. There

[156] Thomas, M. (2023). 'Heuristic price theory: A model of pluralistic price evaluations', *Consumer Psychology Review*, 6(1), 75–91.

is in need of a more integrated and efficient information exchange system. The *Decision of the State Council on Implementing Unified Registration of Movable Properties and Rights-Based Collateral* excludes intellectual property from its scope because it acknowledged the unique and complex nature of intellectual property. Instead, the task of integrating dispersed information and enhancing financing efficiency is entrusted to IP-related and financial departments. Going forward, these departments must spearhead efforts to promote information integration. Given the rapid advancements in big data, it is feasible now to create a unified registration platform by integrating and interfacing existing information systems.

In addition to integrating existing information, it is also essential to explore the collection and disclosure of more transaction-related information. Information disclosure is a fundamental principle of capital market transactions, and since intellectual property capitalization involves introducing capital into the intellectual property domain, aligning with the basic systems of the capital market is both necessary and justified. Especially given the intangible nature of intellectual property, the transactional structures in intellectual property capitalization are inherently more complex, thus exacerbating the issue of information asymmetry. Therefore, the design of an intellectual property capitalization information disclosure system must impose stricter requirements.[157]

6.4.3.2 Improving Institutional Construction

The capitalization of intellectual property transactions involves multiple stakeholders, including government agencies, banking institutions, regulatory bodies, enterprises, and intermediaries. The effective interaction and collaboration among these entities are crucial for mitigating individual risks within collective operations. To this end, institutional improvements can be made in the following ways: On the one hand, standardization management should be enhanced within the existing institutional framework. Specifically, intellectual property valuation agencies, intellectual property-related departments, and financial departments can establish guiding rules, procedural standards, and operational norms to reduce the subjectivity of intellectual property valuation and enhance its scientific and objective accuracy. On the other hand, adjustments can be made to the functional positioning and operational roles of institutions within the current framework. For example, drawing on international practices, a capitalization model led by policy banks with supplementary participation from commercial banks can be established.[158] Furthermore, considering the cross-disciplinary and highly specialized nature of intellectual property

[157] Kong, L. (2017). 'zhishi chanquan zhengquanhua Zhong ke zhengquanhua zichan de xuanze ji fengxian fangkong' ['Selection of securitizable assets and risk prevention in intellectual property securitization']. *Keji Yu Falv [Science and Law]*, 1, 76.

[158] Fan, X. (2010). 'Zhishi chanquan danbao rongzi fengxian kongzhi yanjiu' ['Research on risk control in intellectual property collateral financing']. *Zhejiang Xuekan [Zhejiang Journal]*, 3, 160.

capitalization, independent third-party regulatory agencies and risk warning institutions may be introduced. Given the functional limitations of government agencies, which hinder their ability to fully meet the cross-disciplinary knowledge requirements of intellectual property capitalization, social organizations with more diverse personnel compositions may be better positioned to address its multifaceted demands. For instance, drawing from the current experience of intellectual property protection centers, a dedicated Intellectual Property Capitalization Risk Warning Center could be established to effectively identify and provide early warnings of potential risks in the capitalization process.

6.4.3.3 Enhancing Theoretical Research

The various stages of intellectual property capitalization require robust theoretical support, such as the principles of intellectual property valuation, which must be explained by integrating labour value theory and distribution value theory.[159] However, due to the short development period of intellectual property capitalization, its theoretical foundation is relatively weak, and the integration of theory with practice remains in the exploratory phase. To address current deficiencies in theoretical research, efforts should be made in two main areas: First, consolidating research resources and refining research directions. Intellectual property subcategories, such as patent rights, copyrights, and trademark rights, each possess unique characteristics that are reflected in their practical applications and capitalization models. These distinct operational models require tailored theories to guide their implementation and manage associated risks. While the existing researches have been carried out over different types of intellectual property individually, there is a lack of integration among these studies, and valuable practical experiences are yet to be sufficiently extracted and refined. One the other hand, the breadth and depth of the existing research need to be expanded. Given the close relationship between intellectual property and social development, intellectual property is evolving along with the progress of social development. Each technological breakthrough and enrichment of cultural and artistic expressions expands the forms and scope of intellectual property. This dynamic nature and inherent instability of intellectual property requires a more solid theoretical underpinning. For instance, in the field of intellectual property valuation, when facing new industries or models, should traditional methods such as the market approach, cost approach, and income approach be maintained, or should newer methods like the real options approach or integrated analysis be adopted? Alternatively, is the creation of an entirely new methodology necessary? Furthermore, how should specific evaluation indicators and parameters for each method be determined? These questions all require deeper research and investigation. Besides, interaction between theory and practice needs to be further enhanced,

159 Wang, Z. & Li, Q. (2011). 'Shangbiaoquan zhiya rongzi jiazhi pinggunan wenti de fenxi jiqi duice' ['Analysis of difficulties in trademark pledge financing valuation and its countermeasures']. *Zhejiang Jinrong [Zhejiang Finance]*, 3, 38.

theories must withstand the test of practical application, and practice must actively inform and refine theoretical frameworks. Taking intellectual property valuation as an example, many current studies adopt the methodology of empirical research based on real-world data, however, the limited availability and flow of intellectual property capitalization data hinder the scope of research and reduce the general acceptability and application of such conclusions. Moving forward, it is crucial to strengthen the interaction between theoretical research and practical implementation. This requires improving the flow of intellectual property capitalization information, thereby enriching academic achievements in this field and enhancing the governance of research endeavours. Moreover, a stronger exchange between theory and practice will provide a richer reservoir of theoretical resources to guide and support the practical processes of intellectual property capitalization.

6.5 Summary of This Chapter

The study of market transactional behaviour is, in essence, an exploration of the equilibrium price negotiation process in intellectual property transactions. Intellectual property transactions are accompanied by numerous theoretical and practical challenges. This chapter focuses primarily on the specific types of intellectual property transactions, analysing the market attributes exhibited in transaction markets centered on intellectual property. They are not merely market manifestations of private rights but are also critical factors in promoting social innovation and influencing market competition. Intellectual property is gradually becoming a significant driver of economic growth, supported by the progressively refined intellectual property policy and legal systems of China, which form an institutional framework ensuring the regulation of intellectual property transactions. Building on an in-depth analysis of major transactional modes, such as intellectual property licensing, assignment, and capitalization, this chapter identifies the specific legal issues associated with each model, furthermore, it examines the regulatory approaches currently employed within the existing framework and proposes corresponding recommendations for addressing the challenges identified.

References

Bohannan, C., & Hovenkamp, H. (2010–2011). Concerted refusals to license intellectual property rights. *Harvard Business Law Review Online, 1*, 23

Bu, Y. (2010). 'Zhishi chanquan de shanyi qude [Good faith acquisition of intellectual property]. *Zhongde Faxue Luntan [Sino-German Law Forum], 8*, 306

Cai, R. (2019). Shanyi qude zhidu zai zhuanlifa zhong zhuanyong de helixing fenxi [Analysis on the rationality of applying the system of good faith acquisition in patent law]. *Zhongguo Faming Yu Zhuanli [China Invention and Patent], 1*, 84–87.

Cao, X. (2005). Zhishi chanquan yu minfadian lianjie moshi zhi xuanze - <zhishi chanquan fadian> de bianzuan wei shijiao [The choice of connection model between intellectual property and the Civil Code: A perspective on the compilation of the 'Intellectual Property Code']. *Fashang Yanjiu [Legal and Business Studies], 1*, 27.

Celtekligil, K. (2020). Transaction cost theory. In H. Dincer & S. Yüksel (Eds.), *Strategic priorities in competitive environments*. Springer.

Chen S. (2022). Yi chuzhi zhishi chanquan xuke shiyong guize de guifan jieshi yu falv xuzao [Normative interpretation and legal reconstruction of rules for the licensing of pledged intellectual property]. *Xi'nan Minzu Daxue Xuebao (Renwen Shehui Kexueban) [Journal of Southwest University for Nationalities (Humanities and Social Sciences Edition)], 7*, 77.

Chen, C. (2022). Lun zhuanli kaifang xuke zhidu zai woguo shishi Zhong de wenti yu jiejue fangan [On the issues and solutions in the implementation of the patent open licensing system in China]. *Dongnan Daxue Xuebao (Zhexue Shehui Kexuebao) [Journal of Southeast University (Philosophy and Social Sciences Edition)]*, Supplement, 106

Chen, J. (2015). Zhishi chanquan zibenhua de tiaojian yu jiazhi pinggu [Conditions and value assessment of intellectual property capitalization]. *Xueshujie [Academic Circle], 8*, 91.

Chen, J. (2016). Zhishi chanquan moshi xuke lilun yanjiu [Theoretical research on implied licensing of intellectual property]. *[Jinan Journal (Philosophy and Social Sciences Edition)], 10*, 84.

Chen, L., & Xu, Q. (2018). Zhishi chanquan jiaoyishichang jianshe taishi yu lujing zhaoxun [The construction trend and path search of the intellectual property transaction market]. *Gaige [Reform], 5*, 122.

Chen, Y. (2018). *Zhuanli moshi xuke yanjiu [A study on patent implied licenses]* (Ph.D. thesis). Southwest University of Political Science and Law, 54.

Chen, Y., & Song, Y. (2012). Zhishi chanquan zhiya rongzi de jiazhi pinggu fengxian kongzhi [Risk control in the value assessment of intellectual property pledge financing]. *Quyu Jinrong Yanjiu [Regional Financial Research], 7*, 55.

China High-tech Industry Guide. (2022). Liang da jiaoyisuo faxing zhishi chanquan zhengquanlei chanpin guimo jin 150 yi yuan [Two stock exchanges issue intellectual property securities products with a scale of nearly 15 billion yuan]. http://paper.chinahightech.com/pc/content/202202/14/content_46013.html. Accessed on 22 July 2022.

China National Intellectual Property Administration. (2022). *Guojia zhishi chanquanju zhongguo yinhang gufen youxian gongsi guanyu kaizhan shangbiao zhiya zhuli canyin, wenlv deng zhongdian xingye shukun 'Zhi Huixing' zhuanxiang huodong de tongzhi [Notice on the 'Zhi Hui Xing' Special Activity to Support Key Industries such as Catering and Culture & Tourism through Trademark Pledge, jointly with the Industrial and Commercial Bank of China]*. https://www.cnipa.gov.cn/art/2022/6/28/art_550_176262.html. Accessed on 18 July 2022.

China National Intellectual Property Administration. (2022). Hubeisheng zhishi chanquanju zhaokai zhuanli kaifang xuke shidian gongzuo tuijian zuotanhui [Hubei Provincial Intellectual Property Office holds a seminar to promote the patent open licensing pilot project]. https://www.cnipa.gov.cn/art/2022/7/28/art_57_176884.html. Accessed on 20 July 2022.

Cui, H., Pan, M., & Zhang, C. (2019). Zhishi chanquan zhiya rongzi zongxiang gaoxiao shichanghua de lujing yanjiu – Yi guangdongsheng wei li [Research on the path of efficient marketization of intellectual property pledge financing – A case study of Guangdong Province]. *Jianghuai Luntan [Jianghuai Forum], 6*, 84.

Cui, J. (2003). Wuquan chufen bian – Hetong fa di 51 tiao guiding de jieshi yu shiyong [Distinction of unauthorized disposition – Interpretation and application of Article 51 of the *Contract Law*]. *Faxue Yanjiu [Legal Studies], 1*, 3.

Cui, J. (2020). Wuquan chufen zaibian [Reconsideration of unauthorized disposition]. *Zhongwai Faxue [Chinese and Foreign Law], 4*, 868.

Dai, F. (2022). Zhishi chanquan lanyong guizhi de lilun jichu ji zhidu wanshan [Theoretical foundation and institutional improvement of intellectual property abuse regulation]. *Zhishi Chanquan [Intellectual Property], 3*, 112.

Dong, M. (2011). Yingmei faxi yu dalu faxi Zhong banquan bei xukeren su wenti bijiao yanjiu- Yi <Qinquan zerenfa wei chufadian> [A comparative study of the rights of copyright licensees in the common law and civil law systems: From the perspective of the tort liability law]. *Zhishi Chanquan [Intellectual Property], 8*, 90.

Dong, M. (2013). *Zhishi chanquan xuke yanjiu [Research on intellectual property licensing]*. Falv Chubanshe [Law Press].

Drexl, J. (2003). *Zhishi chanquan xuke: Shang [Intellectual Property Licensing: Volume 1]*. (Wang, C., Trans., pp. 181–183). Qinghua Daxue Chubanshe [Tsinghua University Press].

Fan, X. (2010). Zhishi chanquan danbao rongzi fengxian kongzhi yanjiu [Research on risk control in intellectual property collateral financing]. *Zhejiang Xuekan [Zhejiang Journal], 3*, 160.

Feng, X. (2012). Woguo qiye zhishi chanquan zhiya rongzi ji qi wanshan duice yanjiu [Research on intellectual property pledge financing of enterprises in China and its improvement strategies]. *Hebei Faxue [Hebei Law Science], 12*, 40.

Fu, H., & Tan, H. (2017). *Zhishi chanquan yunyin guangli falv shiwu yu zhongdian wenti quanshi [Intellectual property operation management legal practice and interpretation of key issues]*. Zhongguo Fazhi Chubanshe [China Legal Publishing House].

Gao, F. (2009). *Minfa xue [Civil law studies]*. Falv Chubanshe [Legal Publishing].

Gu, D. (2015). Zhishi chanquan susong zhong wuquanfa guifan de leitui shiyong [The analogical application of property law norms in intellectual property litigation]. In R. He (Ed.), *sifa tizhi gaige yumin shangshi falv shiyong wenti yanjiu: quanguo fayuan di 26 jie xueshu taolunhui huojiang lunwenji [Research on Judicial System Reform and the Application of Civil and Commercial Laws: Award-Winning Papers from the 26th National Court Academic Seminar]*. Renmin Faxue Chubanshe [People's Court Press].

Guo, H. (2019). Woguo zhishi chanquan zhiya rongzi de xianshi zhangai yu lujing tantao [Practical obstacles and path exploration of intellectual property pledge financing in China]. *Jinrong Fazhan Yanjiu [Research on Financial Development], 8*, 88.

Han, S. (2018). *Hetong fa zonglun (Di si ban) [General Principles of Contract Law (4th ed.)]* (pp. 312–319). Falv Chubanshe [Law Press].

Huang, G., & Zhu, X. (2009). Zhishi chanquan zhengquanhua de fengxian yanjiu – jiyu zhishi chanquan texing de fenxi [Research on the risks of intellectual property securitization – based on the analysis of intellectual property characteristics]. *Keji Guanli Yanjiu [Science and Technology Management Research], 12*, 510.

Ji, P., Sun, F., & Zhao, X. (2018). Zhishichanquan dui jingji zengzhang zuoyong de shizheng yanjiu [An empirical study on the role of intellectual property in economic growth]. *Honguan Jingji Yanjiu [Macroeconomic Research], 12*, 54.

Jiang, X. (2007). Zhongguo zhuanliquan zhiya zhidu cunzai de wenti jiqi wanshan [The issues and improvements of the patent pledge system in China]. *mYanjiui Yu Fazhan Guanli [Research and Development Management], 3*, 81.

Kong, L. (2017). Zhishi chanquan zhengquanhua zhong ke zhengquanhua zichan de xuanze ji fengxian fangkong [Selection of securifiable assets and risk prevention in intellectual property securitization]. *Keji Yu Falv [Science and Technology and Law], 1*, 72.

Kong, L. (2017). Zhishi chanquan zhengquanhua zhong ke zhengquanhua zichan de xuanze ji fengxian fangkong [Selection of securifiable assets and risk prevention in intellectual property securitization]. *Keji Yu Falv [Science and Technology and Law], 1*, 74.

Kong, L. (2017). Zhishi chanquan zhengquanhua Zhong ke zhengquanhua zichan de xuanze ji fengxian fangkong [Selection of securitizable assets and risk prevention in intellectual property securitization]. *Keji Yu Falv [Science and Law], 1*, 76.

Larenz, K. (2003). *Deguo minfa tonglun [General Theory of Civil Law]* (Wang, X., et al., Trans.). Falv Chubanshe [Legal Publishing].

Li, C. (2005). *Lun zhishi chanquanfa de tixihua [On the Systematization of Intellectual Property Law]*. Beijing Daxue Chubanshe [Peking University Press].

Li, G. (2009). Wuti caichan gainian dui xiandai suoyouquan guannian de yingxiang [The impact of the concept of incorporeal property on modern ownership concepts]. *Dangdai Faxue [Contemporary Law Review], 4*, 46.

Li, Y., & Lü, Y. (2004). Lun zhishi chanquan zhi gongquan xingzhi – Dui 'zhishi chanquan shuyu siquan' de buchong [On the public nature of intellectual property – an addition to 'intellectual property as private rights]. *Zhejiang Daxue Xuebao (Renwen Shehui Kexue Ban) [Journal of Zhejiang University (Humanities and Social Sciences)], 4*, 65.

Li, Z. (2021). Lun gonggong jiankang xuqiu xia de yaopin zhuanli qiangzhi xuke [On the compulsory licensing of pharmaceutical patents under public health needs]. *Zhongguo Faming Yu Zhuanli [China Invention and Patent], 8*, 71.

Li, Z., & Zheng, Y. (2010). Zhongxiao qiye zhishi chanquan zhiya daikuan de fengxian fenxi yu moshi goujian [Risk analysis and model construction of intellectual property pledge loans for small and medium-sized enterprises]. *Hongguan Jingji Yanjiu [Macroeconomic Research], 4*, 60.

Liang, H. (2000). Ruhe lijie hetongfa di wushiyi tiao [How to understand Article 51 of the *Contract Law*]. Renmin Faxue Bao *[People's Court Daily]*, 8 January.

Liang, Z., Luo, Y., & Deng, X. (2016). Jiyu jiazhilian shijiao de zhishi chanquan qiangguo jianshe lujing yanjiu [Research on the path of building a strong intellectual property country from the perspective of the value chain]. *Zhongguo kexueyuan yuankan [Bulletin of the Chinese Academy of Sciences], 9*, 1011.

Lin, W. (2022). Lun minfadian shidai <Zhishi chanquan fa tongze> de zhiding [On the formulation of the General Principles of Intellectual Property Law in the era of the Civil Code]. *Chongqing guangbo dianshi daxue xuebao [Journal of Chongqing Radio and Television University], 1*, 45.

Liu, C. (2013). Zhishi chanquan jiazhi goucheng jiben fanchou de zhidu quanshi [Institutional interpretation of the basic categories of intellectual property value composition]. *Hebei Jignmao Daxue Xuebao [Journal of Hebei University of Economics and Business], 6*, 146.

Liu, C. (2014). *Zhishi Chanquanfa [Intellectual property law]*. Renmin Daxue Chubanshe [Renmin University Press]

Liu, H. (2018). Zhishi chanquan wuquan chufen wenti chutan [An initial exploration of the issue of unauthorized disposition of intellectual property]. *Shidai Jingmao [Times of Economics and Trade], 9*, 91.

Liu, H., & Meng, Q. (2009). Zhishi chanquan gonggong zhengce de moshi xuanze yu tixi goujian [Model selection and system construction of intellectual property public policy]. *Zhongguo Ruankexue [China Soft Science], 7*, 11.

Liu, J. (2003). Lun zhishi chanquan yu zhanyou zhidu [On intellectual property and the system of possession]. *Faxue [Law Studies], 10*, 56–63.

Liu, J. (2016). *Zhishi chanquan xuk xianzhixing tiaokuan fanlongduan guizhi yanjiu [Research on the antitrust regulation of restrictive clauses in intellectual property licenses]*. Zhishi chanquan chubanshe [Intellectual Property Publishing House].

Liu, Q. (2009). Shangbiaoquan shanyi qude zhidu yanjiu —— Yi zhuce shangbiao zhuanyongquan de zhuanrang wei kaocha shijiao [Study on the system of good faith acquisition of trademark rights – From the perspective of the transfer of exclusive rights to registered trademarks]. *Zhengzhi Yu Falv [Politics and Law], 11*, 133–141.

Liu, Q., & Sun, Q. (2020). <Minfadian> Zhishi chanquan tiaokuan lifa yanjiu – jianlun 'minshang zhiheyi' lifa tili de goujian' [Legislative study on intellectual property provisions in the Civil Code: A discussion on the construction of the 'unified civil and commercial law' legislative system]. *Zhongnan Daxue Xuebao (Shehui Kexue Bao) [Journal of Central South University (Social Science Edition)], 6*, 62.

Liu, Y. (2016). *Zhuanliquan* jingji jiazhi fenxi de xiangguan yanjiu shuli ji pingxi [A review and critique of research on the economic value analysis of patent rights]. *Keji Guani Yanjiu [Science and Technology Management Research], 2*, 150.

Lü, B. (2009). Wangluo shidai de banquan moshi xuke zhidu: Liangqi Google an de fenxi [The implied copyright licensing system in the internet age: Analysis of two Google cases]. *Dianzi zhishi chanquan [Electronic Intellectual Property], 4*, 74.

Lv, B. (2017). Banquan 'yi nv duo jia' de jiejue zhidao – Yi shanyi xiangduifang baohu wei zhongxin [The solution to the issue of 'one copyright, multiple marriages' – Centered on the protection of good faith counterparties]. Jinan Xuebao (Zhexue Shehui Kexue Ban) *[Journal of Jinan University (Philosophy and Social Sciences Edition)], 12*, 34

Ma, B. (2015). Lun gongsi zhuce ziben dengji zhidu gaige dui zhuanliquan chuzi de yingxiang [On the impact of the reform of the company registered capital registration system on patent capital contribution]. *Faxue Zazhi [Legal Studies Journal], 4*, 61.

National Development and Reform Commission. (2021). 'Shi si wu' guihua <gangyao> mingci jieshi I Zhishi chanquan zhiya rongzi [14th Five-Year Plan *Outline* Glossary- Intellectual Property Pledge Financing]. https://www.ndrc.gov.cn/fggz/fzzlgh/gjfzgh/202112/t20211224_1309284.html. Accessed on 18 July 2022.

National Development and Reform Commission. (2021). 'Shi si wu' guihua mingci jieshi I Zhishi chanquan zhiya rongzi' '14th Five-Year Plan' *Outline* Glossary-Intellectual Property Pledge Financing'. https://www.ndrc.gov.cn/fggz/fzzlgh/gjfzgh/202112/t20211224_1309284.html. Accessed on 18 July 2022.

Peng, C. (2002). Zhili chengguo, zhishi chanquan yu zhanyou zhidu [Intellectual achievements, intellectual property, and the system of possession]. *Fashang Yanjiu [Journal of Commercial and Economic Law], 6*, 91–97.

Peng, C., & Li, J. (2009). Shanyi qude hetong xiaoli de lifa jiexi yu luoji zhengcheng [Legislative analysis and logical justification of the good faith acquisition of contract validity]. *Zhongguo Faxue [Chinese Law Science], 4*, 87–91.

Sherman, B. (2012). *Xiandai zhishi chanquanfa de yanjing [The Evolution of Modern Intellectual Property Law]* (Jin, H., Trans.). Beijing Daxue Chubanshe [Peking University Press].

Shi, S. (2000). *Minfa zonglun [General Principles of Civil Law]*. Zhongguo Zhengfa Daxue Chubanshe [China University of Political Science and Law Press].

Shi, S. (2000). *Wuquanfa lun [The theory of property law]*. Zhongguo Zhengfa Daxue Chubanshe [China University of Political Science and Law Press]

Sichuan Provincial Intellectual Property Service and Promotion Center. (2022). 'Sichuansheng zhuanli kaifang xuke shidian gongzuo jinru quanmian tuijin jieduan [Sichuan's patent open licensing enters full promotion phase], *Sichuan Provincial Intellectual Property Service and Promotion Center*. http://scipspc.sc.gov.cn/ztzl/cycj/202207/t20220705_30705.html. Accessed on 20 July 2022.

Song, G., & Tian, L. (2016). Jishuxing Zhongxiao qiye zhishi chanquan zhiya rongzi moshi de guoneiwai bijiao yanjiu [A comparative study of intellectual property pledge financing models for technology-based SMEs at home and abroad]. *Jinrong Fazhan Yanjiu [Research on Financial Development], 2*, 52.

State-owned Assets Supervision and Administration Commission of the State Council, (2022). *Zhongliang xintuo faqi sheli guonei shouli zizhu chuangxin zhishi chanquan rongzi xintuo jihua [Sinochem Trust initiates the establishment of the first domestic self-innovation intellectual property financing trust plan]*. http://www.sasac.gov.cn/n2588025/n2588124/c3981306/content.html. Accessed on 19 July 2022.

Sun, C., & Yu, Y. (2008). Zhishi chanquan chuzi suoshui shi de gudong zeren [Shareholder liability when intellectual property capital contribution is diminished]. *Jishu Jingji Yu Guanli Yanjiu [Technology Economics and Management Research], 4*, 44.

Sun, X. (2009). Zhongguo wuquanfa zonglun (Di 2 ban) *[General Theory of Chinese Property Law (2nd ed.)]. Falv Chubanshe* [Legal Publishing House].

Sun, X. (2022). Guanyu wuquan chufen wenti de jidian kanfa – ping minfadian caoan dui <Hetongfa> di 51 tiao de fangqi [A few views on the issue of unauthorized disposition – A review of the *Civil Code* draft's abandonment of Article 51 of the *Contract Law*], *NetEase*, https://www.163.com/dy/article/F19KKAR00516C2P4.html. Accessed on 22 July 2022.

Tao, L., & Ruan, J. (2017). Woguo zhishi chanquan zhiya rongzi: Shijian yangtai he lifa zhidu shenshi —— jiyu zhishi chanquan zhanlue he minfadian bianzuan de beijing [Intellectual property pledge financing in China: Practical patterns and legislative system review – Based on the background of intellectual property strategy and the compilation of the Civil Code]. *Shehui Kexue Yanjiu [Social Science Research], 5*, 111.

The Central People's Government. (2010). *Zhishi chanquanju pifu disanpi zhishi chanquan zhiya rongzi shidian mingdan [Intellectual Property Office approves the third batch of intellectual property pledge financing pilot list].* http://www.gov.cn/gzdt/2010-07/13/content_1652676.htm. Accessed on 18 July 2022.

The Central People's Government. (2016). *Zhishi chanquanju qidong zhuanliquan zhiya rongzi he zhuanli baoxian shidian shifan gongzuo [Intellectual Property Office launches pilot demonstration work on patent pledge financing and patent insurance].* http://www.gov.cn/xinwen/2016-08/26/content_5102624.htm. Accessed on 18 July 2022.

Thomas, M. (2023). Heuristic price theory: A model of pluralistic price evaluations. *Consumer Psychology Review, 6*(1), 75–91.

Tosato, A. (2018). Intellectual property license contracts: Reflections on a prospective UNCITRAL project. *University of Cincinnati Law Review, 86*, 1251.

Wang, D. (2015). *Xingwei jingjixue yaoyi [The essentials of behavioural economics].* Shanghai Renmin Chubanshe [Shanghai People's Publishing House].

Wang, G. (2012). Zhishi chanquan shanyi qude de helixing fenxi- Jianlun zhishi chanquan zhidu yu wuquan zhidu de jianrongxing [Analysis on the rationality of good faith acquisition of intellectual property—Also discussing the compatibility of intellectual property system and property rights system], *Hainan Daxue Xuebao (Renwen Shehui Kexueban) [Journal of Hainan University (Humanities and Social Sciences Edition)]*, 4, 88.

Wang, G. (2012). Zhishi chanquan shanyi qude de helixing fenxi-jianlun zhishi chanquan zhidu yu wuquan zhidu de jianrongxing [Analysis on the rationality of good faith acquisition of intellectual property—Also discussing the compatibility of intellectual property system and property rights system]. *Hainan Daxue Xuebao (Renwen Shehui Kexueban) [Journal of Hainan University (Humanities and Social Sciences Edition)]*, 4, 87.

Wang, H., & Hou, G. (2013). Wuquan chufen yu yiwu shumai de lilun he shijian wenti- 'Wuquan chufen yu yiwu shumai'zhuanti xueshu yantaohui zongshu [Theoretical and practical issues of unauthorized disposition and multiple sales of the same item—A summary of the 'Unauthorized Disposition and Multiple Sales of the Same Item' academic seminar]. *Xinan Zhengfa Daxue Xuebao [Journal of Southwest University of Political Science and Law], 5*, 26.

Wang, L. (2001). Lun wuquan chufen [On unauthorized disposition]. *Zhongguo Faxue [China Legal Science], 3*, 77.

Wang, L., et al. (2020). *Minfa Xue (Di Liu Ban) [Civil Law Studies (6th ed.)].* Falu Chubanshe [Law Press China].

Wang, Q. (2021). *Zhishi chanquan fa jiaocheng (Di qi ban) [Intellectual property law textbook (7th Edition)].* Zhongguo Renmin Daxue Chubanshe [China Renmin University Press].

Wang, X. (2020). Zhuanli quanshu jiufen Zhong shanyi shourangren baohu wenti yanjiu [Study on the protection of good faith assignees in patent ownership disputes]. *Keji Yu Falv [Science and Law], 2*, 24–30.

Wang, Z., & Li, Q. (2011). Shangbiaoquan zhiya rongzi jiazhi pinggunan wenti de fenxi jiqi duice [Analysis of difficulties in trademark pledge financing valuation and its countermeasures]. *Zhejiang Jinrong [Zhejiang Finance], 3*, 38.

Weber, L., & Mayer, K. (2014). Transaction cost economics and the cognitive perspective: Investigating the sources and governance of interpretive uncertainty. *AMR, 39*, 344–363.

Wu, G. (2005). Lun wuquan chufen de shiyong fanwei [On the scope of application of unauthorized disposition]. *Zhongwai Faxue [Chinese and Foreign Law], 3*, 337.

Wu, H. (2003). Zhishi chanquan lifa tili yu minfadian bianzuan [The legislative framework of intellectual property and the compilation of the Civil Code]. *Zhongguo Faxue [Chinese Law Review], 1*, 50.

Wu, H. (2009). Guoji biange dashi yu zhongguo fazhan daju zhong de zhishi chanquan zhidu [Intellectual property system in the context of international changes and China's development]. *Faxue Yanjiu [Legal Studies], 2*, 16.

Wu, H. (2009). *Zhishi chanquan zhidu jichu lilun yanjiu [Research on the Basic Theories of Intellectual Property System]*. Zhishi Chanquan Chubanshe [Intellectual Property Publishing House]

Wu, H. (2018). Zhongguo zhishi chanquan falv bianqian de jiben mianxiang [The basic aspects of the evolution of China's intellectual property law]. *Zhongguo shehui kexue [Social Sciences in China], 8*, 112.

Wu, L. (2005). *Lun zhishi chanquan de kuozhang yu xianzhi [On the expansion and limitation of intellectual property*] (Master's thesis). Shanxi University, 17.

Xie, L. (2018). Zhuanliquan wuquan chufen yu shanyi xiangduifang baohu [Unauthorized disposition of patent rights and protection of good faith counterparties]. *Ha'er bin shifan daxue shehui kexue xuebao [Journal of Social Sciences], 1*, 44.

Xu, H. (2014). Jiazhi liuzhuan Zhong de zhishi chanquan pinggu yanjiu [Research on intellectual property evaluation in value circulation]. *Zhishi Chanquan [Intellectual Property], 6*, 70.

Xue, X., & Peng, C. (2019). Zhishi chanquan jiaoyi shichang de jianquan yu wanshan *[The improvement and perfection of the intellectual property transaction market*]. *Renmin Luntan [People's Forum], 7*, 85.

Yang, L., & Zhu, Z. (2020). Jishu lei zhishi chanquan jiaoyi weiyue fengxian fangfan yanjiu [Research on the prevention of default risks in technology-related intellectual property transactions]. *Nandu Xuetan [Southern Metropolis Forum], 1*, 78.

Yi, J. (2017). Zhishi chanquan fading zhuyi jiqi huanhe——Jian dui <Minfa Zongze> Di 123 tiao tiaowen de fenxi [Intellectual property legalism and its moderation: An analysis of Article 123 of the General Principles of Civil Law]. *Zhishi Chanquan [Intellectual Property], 5*, 9.

Yi, J. (2017). Zhuanlifa de zhuanxing: cong eryuan jiegou dao sanyuan jiegou [The transformation of patent law: From a dual structure to a triadic structure]. *Faxue Zazhi [Legal Studies Journal], 7*, 46.

Yuan, B. (2011). Zhuce shangbiao shanyi qude falv yiju [Legal basis for good faith acquisition of registered trademarks]. *Renmin Sifa [People's Justice], 22*, 44–45.

Zhang, B. (2009). Zhishi chanquan zhiya rongzi de fengxian fenjie yu fenbu kongzhi [Risk decomposition and step-by-step control of intellectual property pledge financing]. *Zhishi Chanquan [Intellectual Property], 2*, 32.

Zhang, H. (2020). Goujian shichang zhudaoxing zhishi chanquan zhiya rongzi moshi [Building a market-driven intellectual property pledge financing model], *Renmin Luntan [People's Forum], 30*, 118.

Zhang, H., & Li, M. (2016). Zhishi chanquan zhengquanhua zhi jichu zichan tanxi [Analysis of underlying assets in intellectual property securitization]. *Falv Shiyong [Application of Law], 9*, 36.

Zhang, P. (2014). Zhishi chanquan gongong zhengce tixi de lilun kuangjia, goucheg yaosu he jianshe fangxiang yanjiu [Research on the theoretical framework, components, and construction directions of the public policy system for intellectual property]. *Zhishi chanquan [Intellectual Property], 12*, 70.

Zhang, S., & Liang, Z. (2010). Lun shangye texu jingyingquan Zhong de zhishi chanquan falv baohu [On intellectual property legal protection in commercial franchising]. *Jingji Yu Fazhi [Economics and Law], 6*, 234.

Zhang, W. (2003). *Falixue* (Di er ban) [*Jurisprudence* (2nd ed.)]. Gaodeng jiaoyu chubanshe [Higher Education Press].

Zhang, W. (2011). Jiyu zhishi chanquan jiezhi de kejixing Zhongxiao qiye zhuanlihua rongzi de jili fenxi [Mechanism analysis of patent industrialization financing for technology-based SMEs based on intellectual property media]. *Caikuai Tongxun [Financial and Accounting Communications], 30*, 130.

Zhang, X. *From the State Council institutional reform to the market-oriented operation of enterprise intellectual property, IPRdaily Chinese Network.* http://www.iprdaily.cn/article_18536.html. Accessed on 23 July 2022.

Zhang, Y. (2019). Zeren guize shijiao xia de zhuanli kaifang xuke zhidu [Patent open licensing system from the perspective of liability rules]. *Qinghua Faxue [Tsinghua Law Review], 5*, 187.

Zhang, Z. (2018). Tongyi de wuquan chufen zhidu zhi goujian jiqi fangfa[The construction and methods of a unified unauthorized disposition system]. *Suzhou Daxue Xuebao(Faxue Ban) [Journal of Suzhou University (Law Edition)], 2*, 55.

Zhao, R. (2021). *Hulianwang huanjing xia banquan xuke zhidu yanjiu [Research on copyright licensing system in the internet environment]* (p. 107). Zhishi chanquan chubanshe [Intellectual Property Publishing House].

Zhao, R. (2021). *Hulianwang huanjing xia banquan xuke zhidu yanjiu [Research on copyright licensing system in the internet environment]* (p. 108). Zhishi chanquan chubanshe [Intellectual Property Press].

Zhejiang Provincial Government. (2022). Zhejiang tuijin 'zhuanli kaifang xuke'zhidu [Zhejiang promotes the 'patent open licensing' system]. *Democracy and Law Net*. http://www.mzyfz.com/html/1993/2022-04-26/content-1561214.html. Accessed on 20 July 2022.

Zheng, Y. (1997). *Minfa xue [Civil Law Studies]*, Zhongguo Zhengfa Daxue Chubanshe [China University of Political Science and Law Press].

Zhou, J., & Shen, Y. (2008). Hetongfa zai zhishi chanquan qinquan anjian zhong de shiyong moshi chutan —— yi fali shengsi ji shili kaocha wei yanjiu yituo [An initial exploration of the application model of contract law in intellectual property infringement cases—based on legal reflections and case studies]. In P. Gong (Ed.), *Sikao Yu Tansuo [Thinking and Exploration, The Path We Have Taken]*. Zhongguo Fazhi Chubanshe [China Legal Publishing House].

Zhu, R., Zhang, Y., & Ge, L. (2022). Zhishi chanquan jiazhi pinggu yanjiu zongshu [A review of research on intellectual property valuation]. *Zhongguo Zichan Pinggu [China Asset Valuation], 1*, 66.

Zhu, Y. (2020). Lun zhishi chanquan fading zhuyi cunzai de quexian jiqi kefu [On the defects of the legalism of intellectual property law and its remedies]. *Sifa [Private Law], 2*, 279.

Chapter 7
Antitrust Issues in Intellectual Property Transactions

7.1 Competition and Monopoly in Intellectual Property Transactions

The smooth operation of market transactions should inherently be free, with regulatory intervention applied only in cases of market failure. Antitrust measures, as a critical regulatory tool, serve dual functions: reducing transactional failures to ensure the continuity of transactions while safeguarding and restructuring the competitive order of the market. As a right inherently intertwined with monopoly from its inception, intellectual property frequently raises concerns over abuse, therefore, this chapter focuses on analysing monopolistic behaviour and its competitive effects arising from intellectual property transactions. Following the classification of intellectual property transactions in preceding chapters, it begins by elaborating the competition and monopoly issues that arise from such transactions. On the foundational premise that intellectual property is a right with monopolistic attributes, this chapter analyses specific competitive issues and behaviours stemming from these transactions by applying the fundamental principles of antitrust regulation, seeking to delineate the boundaries between free competition and monopolistic practices in the intellectual property transaction domain. Particular attention is given to antitrust regulatory issues triggered by restrictive practices in intellectual property licensing, assignment, and collaborative restrains through transactions.

With the deepening of the new wave of technological revolution and industrial transformation, economic development has shifted from high-speed growth to high-quality growth. The innovation-driven development strategy explicitly emphasizes that technological innovation is the core pillar of national strength, critical to the destiny of the nation. Against this backdrop, intellectual property, as a strategic resource for national development and a core element of international competitiveness, plays an increasingly significant role.[1] However, the intellectual property

[1] The Central Committee of the Communist Party of China and the State Council, 'Zhishi chanquan qiangguo jianshe gangyao(2021–2035) ['*Outline for Building a Strong Intellectual Property Nation*

© Intellectual Property Publishing House Co., Ltd. 2025

M. Yang, *Basic Theories of Intellectual Property Transaction*,
https://doi.org/10.1007/978-981-96-7039-0_7

market continues to face numerous challenges and shortcomings.[2] This section aims to review and summarize the issues related to competition and antitrust concerns arising from intellectual property transactions. From the perspective of competition, it seeks to analyse and study the problems associated with the abuse of intellectual property rights to exclude or restrict competition.

7.1.1 Basic Understanding of Antitrust Issues Arising from Intellectual Property Transactions

Since the issuance of the *Guiding Opinions on Establishing and Improving the Intellectual Property Transaction Market* jointly released by multiple ministries of the State Council in 2007, efforts have been directed toward promoting the standardized development of the intellectual property market and building a multi-layered intellectual property transaction market system. In recent years, a series of laws and regulations concerning intellectual property protection, transfer, licensing, and pledging have been introduced, providing strong support for the establishment of the intellectual property transaction market. On the supply side, according to the *Intellectual Property Statistical Briefing* issued by the National Intellectual Property Administration, the number of patent and trademark applications in China reached a new high record in 2020. On the platform side, the number of registered intellectual property transaction institutions in China has exceeded 1000, with the continuous improvement and development of comprehensive transaction markets.[3] Together, these developments have laid a solid foundation for the construction of the intellectual property market. However, the development of related industries faces a series of challenges. According to surveys, 71.1% of intellectual property service institutions identify malicious market competition as a primary issue in their development. The China Antitrust Enforcement Annual Report 2021 highlighted a case where Tencent Music, by acquiring equity in China Music Group without filing prior notification, secure a monopolistic position in the online music market through exclusive music copyrights. Similarly, in the semiconductor industry, incumbent undertakings like Samsung, SK Hynix, and Micron have established high technological barriers, hindering new entrants from exerting competitive constraints.[4]

(2021–2035)'], available at the official website of the Chinese government: http://www.gov.cn/zhengce/2021-09/22/content_5638714.htm, accessed on July 20, 2022.

[2] State Council, 2021. '"Shi Si Wu" guo jia zhi shi chan quan bao hu he yun yong gui hua' ['14th Five-Year Plan for National Intellectual Property Protection and Utilization'], available at: http://www.gov.cn/xinwen/2021-10/28/content_5647335.htm, accessed on 14 July 2022.

[3] Tong, X. (2022). 'Dali fazhan zhishi chanquan jinrong zhuli keji chengguo zhuanyi zhuanhua' ['Vigorously develop intellectual property finance to promote the transfer and transformation of scientific and technological achievements']. *Chanquan Daohang* [*Property Navigation*], 1, 32.

[4] State Administration for Market Regulation, 2021. 'Zhong guo fan long duan zhi fa nian du bao gao (2021)' ['China Antitrust Enforcement Annual Report (2021)'], available at: https://www.samr.gov.cn/xw/zj/202206/t20220608_347582.html, accessed on 11 August 2022. 40.

These instances illustrate that intellectual property has become a critical tool for undertakings to gain competitive advantages or even monopolistic positions in the market. Furthermore, based on enforcement reports and high-profile IP-related antitrust cases, the abuse of intellectual property rights to exclude or restrict competition frequently occurs across various intellectual property fields. The most common practices suspected of violating the Anti-Monopoly Law of China include the abuse of a dominant position and concentrations of undertakings.

In fact, both intellectual property protection and antitrust law share the same legislative purpose of stimulating competitive behaviour among market participants to enhance the efficiency of market resource allocation. However, their approaches to promoting competition are fundamentally different. The legislative purpose of antitrust law is to eliminate and prevent monopolistic behaviours in the market, primarily by establishing prohibitive rules to maintain market order and promote fair competition.[5] In contrast, intellectual property operates by granting and protecting exclusive rights (through permissive norms), thereby lawfully restricting competition to guide market participants in competing within the economic domain of intellectual property.

Conversely, the exercise of intellectual property rights and monopolistic behaviour both carry risks of restricting or obstructing market competition. The 2022 revision of the Anti-Monopoly Law (hereinafter referred to as *Anti-Monopoly Law* (2022)) introduces 'encouraging innovation' as a legislative purpose, further affirming the intrinsic connection between innovation in the field of intellectual property and the maintenance of a fair competitive order.

On the one hand, intellectual property rights promote competition. The essence of intellectual property lies in safeguarding innovation by legally monopolizing the free dissemination of information. However, from a macro and dynamic perspective, it still functions as a mechanism to promote competition.[6] This complex relationship underscores the unique status of intellectual property within competition law. The fundamental and primary goal of the intellectual property system is to incentivize innovation. If the intellectual creations and interests of creators cannot be protected, others may freely and gratuitously use these innovations. In the long term, this would dampen the incentive for intellectual creation, ultimately hindering technological progress and impeding socio-economic development. Therefore, granting creators of intellectual assets lawful monopoly rights is necessary to achieve the core objectives of the intellectual property system. It can be viewed as the legal framework of the state for addressing the externalities of intellectual products, thereby preventing 'free-riding' behaviours such as replication and counterfeiting that exploit the intellectual achievements of others without compensation, i.e. encouraging competitors to

[5] Wang, X. (2004). 'Zhishi chanquan lanyong xingwei de fanlongduanfa guizhi' ['Antitrust regulation of intellectual property abuse']. *Fa Xue* [*Jurisprudence*], 3, 100–106.

[6] Wang, X. (2009). 'Jingzhengfa shiye de zhishi chanquan wenti lungang' ['An outline of intellectual property issues from the perspective of competition law']. *Zhonguo Faxue* [*Chinese Law Journal*], 4, 5–15.

legitimately enjoy monopolistic benefits through innovation in market competition, which ultimately promotes economic growth and social progress.

On the other hand, the abuse of intellectual property rights can impose certain restrictions on competition. Some scholars argue that exercising intellectual property rights in violation of antitrust laws constitutes a form of abuse of intellectual property rights.[7] They define abuse of intellectual property rights as 'circumstances where the exercise of rights exceeds statutory boundaries, thereby losing legitimacy and harming the interests of others and public welfare.'[8] Others differentiate between legitimate and illegitimate monopolies inherent in intellectual property, asserting that only the latter constitutes abuse of intellectual property rights.[9] According to these views, restricting or excluding competition does not align with the legislative intent and fundamental principles of intellectual property law and thus constitutes a prerequisite for defining intellectual property rights abuse. Article 68[10] of the *Anti-Monopoly Law* (2022) of China bridges the gap between antitrust law and intellectual property law, forming the core of an external framework for harmonizing conflicts between the two laws and providing a legal foundation for regulating the abuse of intellectual property rights in China.[11]

However, since this article lacks specific constituent elements of violation, it should not be directly applied in resolving substantive issues in individual cases. Instead, the determination of whether an act constitutes a monopoly agreement, abuse of a dominant position, or a concentration of undertakings that excludes or restricts competition should be analysed under Chapters 2, 3, and 4 of the *Anti-Monopoly Law* (2022).[12] The application of these provisions reflects the principle that intellectual property rights, as private rights, should be regulated to prevent abuse in a market economy. Clarifying the boundary between the applicability of antitrust

[7] Zhang, S. (2020). 'Lanyong zhishi chanquan yu lanyong shichang zhipei diwei zhibian' ['Abuse of *Intellectual Property and Abuse of Market Dominance*']. *Renda Falv Pinglun* [*Renmin University Law Review*], 2, 87–134.

[8] Qiao, S. and Tao, X. (2005). 'Woguo xianzhi zhishi chanquan lanyong de falv sikao' ['Legal thoughts on restricting the abuse of intellectual property in china']. *Xiandai Faxue* [*Modern Law Science*], 1, 112.

[9] Fei, A. (2008). 'Lun fang zhi zhi shi chan quan lan yong de zhi du li nian' ['On the institutional concept of preventing the abuse of intellectual property']. *Zhishi Chanquan* [*Intellectual Property*], 3, 5.

[10] Article 68 of *Anti-Monopoly Law* provides: "The exercise of intellectual property rights by undertakings in accordance with relevant laws and administrative regulations is not subject to this Law; however, the abuse of intellectual property rights by undertakings to exclude or restrict competition is subject to this Law.".

[11] Dong, D. (2012). 'Zhong guo < Fan Long Duan Fa > di 55 tiao de jie shi yu shi yong' ['Interpretation and application of Article 55 of China's Anti-Monopoly Law']. *Chongqing Ligong Daxue Xuebao (Shehui Kexue Ban)* [*Journal of Chongqing University of Technology (Social Science Edition)*], 5, 54–58.

[12] Wang, X. (2013). 'Woguo fa longduanfa shiyong yu zhishi chanquan lingyu de zai sikao' ['Reconsideration of the application of China's Anti-Monopoly Law to the field of intellectual property']. *Nanjing Daxue Xuebao(Zhexue, Renwen Kexue, Shehui Kexue Ban)* [*Journal of Nanjing University (Philosophy, Humanities, and Social Sciences Edition)*], 1, 34–43.

law and intellectual property law remains a key research focus. The root cause of this issue lies on the blurred boundary between competition and monopoly in the intellectual property market.

Moreover, observing antitrust phenomena arising from intellectual property transactions through the lens of price theory fundamentally involves confirming the pricing process associated with monopolistic behaviours in such transactions. Transforming antitrust enforcement issues into pricing issues has increasingly drawn scholarly attention.[13] The objective is to use price theory to determine prices in intellectual property transactions, allowing for an objective and fair assessment of monopolistic behaviours that may arise during these transactions. The primary manifestations of monopolistic behaviour in intellectual property transactions are the establishment of monopolistic pricing and the formation of price discrimination. Monopolistic pricing typically reflects unreasonably high monopoly prices, where right holders, seeking to maximize the benefits of intellectual property transactions, license their rights at excessive prices in the market. From a distributive perspective, the imposition of monopolistic high prices can result in unequal distribution and a decline in overall social welfare. Additionally, monopolistic phenomena arising from price discrimination aim to enable the right holder to extract the entire surplus from various implementers by formulating differentiated pricing strategies to maximize utility. The preconditions for implementing price discrimination include the right holder achieving market dominance based on their intellectual property and gathering sufficient informational resources about the implementers to devise tailored pricing strategies. Furthermore, if the right holder's intellectual property is substitutable, the prevalence of price discrimination becomes even more pronounced. In fact, competition, characterized by bargaining between transacting parties, emphasizes the redefinition of supply–demand relationships and the interpretation of market information.[14] Monopolistic behaviours disrupt normal supply–demand dynamics and hinder the orderly development of competition. As monopolistic behaviour represents a normal phenomenon in the evolution of market competition, legislative attention extends beyond regulating fairness issues arising from such behaviour to addressing efficiency concerns in fostering orderly market competition. Correctly addressing monopolistic phenomena in intellectual property transactions has become a significant challenge in the exploitation and protection of intellectual property rights.

In conclusion, since intellectual property protection ultimately aims to enter into the market and foster market competition through innovation, therefore, encouraging the development of intellectual property should consistently remain a fundamental legal objective. However, there exist boundaries for the exercise of any rights,

---

[13] Ordover, J.A. and Willig, R.D. (1981). 'An economic definition of predation: pricing and product innovation'. *Yale Law Journal*, 91(1), 8–53; Baumol, W.J. and Sidak, J.G. (1994). 'The pricing of inputs sold to competitors'. *Yale Journal on Regulation*, 11(1), 171–202; Albon, R. (1994). 'Interconnection pricing: An analysis of the efficient component pricing rule'. *Telecommunications Policy*, 18(5), 414–420.

[14] Inoua, S.M. and Smith, V.L., (2022). 'Price Formation: Overview of the theory'. In Inoua, S.M. and Smith, V.L.(Eds.), *Economics of markets* (pp39-92). Palgrave Macmillan.

and abusive practices involving intellectual property also need to be regulated. As the core mechanism of fair competition policy, antitrust law plays a crucial role in addressing the misuse of intellectual property rights. The intersection of intellectual property protection and antitrust regulation primarily lies in how to govern conduct that abuses intellectual property to exclude or restrict competition within the antitrust legal framework.

7.1.2 Basic Analytical Framework for Intellectual Property Antitrust

Monopoly, as an economic phenomenon, arises in capitalist societies. It is both an antithesis of competition and an inevitable result of the development of competition. The monopolies regulated under the antitrust view refer to the behaviours that abuse monopoly status to exclude or restrict competition. The legislative purpose of China's *Anti-Monopoly Law* reflects the value considerations of the antitrust system of China, which include competition value, fairness value, innovation value, and so forth, and is not entirely consistent with the U.S. pursuit of efficiency value and the EU's primary focus on competition value. Although antitrust law and intellectual property law share a common goal of promoting competition and innovation while safeguarding overall consumer interests, certain situations inevitably arise during the protection of intellectual property that negatively impact market competition, thus falling within the scope of antitrust regulation. Certainly, antitrust law will fully consider the uniqueness of intellectual property in regulating its exploitation. The challenge lies in how to find, establish, and maintain a reasonable boundary when regulating the exercise of intellectual property rights by antitrust law.

Contemporary western academic schools have gradually formed an independent system of thought regarding antitrust regulation, with major representatives including the Harvard School, the Chicago School, and the Post-Chicago School.[15] These

[15] The main theoretical viewpoints of the Harvard School can be summarized using the SCP paradigm (structure-conduct-performance). According to this paradigm, market structure determines market behavior, and within a given market structure, market behavior in turn determines market performance. In this paradigm, market structure is at the source of the causal chain and is considered an exogenous factor, playing a decisive role in the effective functioning of the market. The focus of industrial organization theory is on the relationship between market power and market competition, particularly the relationship between market structure, market behavior, and market outcomes, and it proposes three criteria to evaluate effective competition in the market: market structure, market behavior, and market outcomes. Among these three criteria, the focus of industrial organization theory is market structure, see Howard, M.C. (1983). *Antitrust and trade regulation: Selected issues and case studies*. Prentice-Hall.12. The main theoretical viewpoints of the Chicago School argue that the ultimate goal of antitrust policy is to maximize the satisfaction of consumer demand. Specifically, Bork proposed that when evaluating a case, antitrust authorities should focus on two aspects of efficiency: first, allocative efficiency, which refers to whether social resources have been optimally allocated; and second, productive efficiency, which concerns whether a firm's resources have been effectively utilized, whether economies of scale have been achieved,

schools have long influenced the specific approaches to evaluating antitrust regulation from the perspectives of structuralism, behaviouralist, and strategicism, respectively.

The U.S. antitrust law has developed two very important principles in regulating monopoly agreements: the per se illegality principle and the rule of reason. Although these principles were initially applied to regulate monopoly agreements, they have since been widely used to address all forms of anti-competitive conduct. The per se illegality principle originated from the case of Dr. Miles[16] in 1911, in which the first-instance ruling determined that vertical price-fixing agreements severely restrict competition among distributors, resulting in effects akin to a price-fixing cartel, and thus should be prohibited. The U.S. Supreme Court reiterated the application of the per se illegality principle to vertical price-fixing agreements in the case of *California Retail Liquor Dealers* in 1980.[17] However, in 2007, the U.S. Supreme Court overturned the per se illegality application established in the *Dr. Miles* Case regarding minimum resale price maintenance agreements with a 5–4 ruling in the case of *Leegin Creative Leather Products*.

The rule of reason refers to the principle that certain ambiguous restrictions on competition must be evaluated carefully, considering the purpose of the conduct, the manner in which it was carried out, and its consequences, before determining their legality. While this principle is more justified and reasonable in assessing the legality of anti-competitive conduct, it also grants antitrust enforcement agencies considerable discretion, which may lead to increased enforcement costs, hinder antitrust enforcement efficiency, and reduce the predictability of illegal conduct. Therefore, in applying the rule of reason, there are also corresponding normative documents that categorize common scenarios to enhance enforcement efficiency and predictability for businesses.

The rule of reason can also be applied to determining whether there is an abuse of intellectual property rights to exclude or restrict competition. For example, in the U.S., antitrust enforcement agencies applied the rule of reason to evaluate the overall effects of patent pooling arrangements. The U.S. *Antitrust Guidelines for Intellectual Property Licenses* and related case law show that when a patent pool collectively possesses market dominance in the relevant market, the parties involved have an

---

or whether transaction costs have been reduced, see Bork, R.H. (1978). *The antitrust paradox: A policy at war with itself*. Free Press. The post-Chicago School believes that the economic theories of the Chicago School are too simplistic, while the realities of economic life are much more complex than the Chicago School imagined. The competition theory in the post-Chicago School reconciles the viewpoints of the Chicago and Harvard Schools, and this competition theory is also known as the new industrial organization theory. It argues that firms do not passively respond to given external conditions, but rather attempt to alter the market environment through strategic behavior (such as entry barriers, the number of actual and potential competitors in the market, the production technologies in the industry, the costs and speed of competitors entering the industry, and market demand preferences) in order to influence competitors' expectations, see Hovenkamp, H. (2005). *The antitrust enterprise: Principle and execution*. Harvard University Press.

[16] Dr. Miles Medical Co. v. John D. Park & Sons Co., (1911). 220 U.S. 373.

[17] California Retail Liquor Dealers' Ass'n v. Midcal Aluminum, Inc., (1980). 455 U.S. 91.

obligation to grant licenses for the patents.[18] Although China has not explicitly established the rule of reason and the per se illegality principle, the language of the *Anti-Monopoly Law* (2022) and the detailed provisions in the *Draft for Public Comment* still reflect the presence of the rule of reason.

7.1.3 Specific Rules on Intellectual Property Antitrust

7.1.3.1 Laws, Regulations and Policies

Article 8(2) of the *Agreement on Trade-Related Aspects of Intellectual Property Rights* (hereinafter referred to as the TRIPS Agreement) provides: "Appropriate measures, provided that they are consistent with the provisions of this Agreement, may be needed to prevent the abuse of intellectual property rights by right holders or the resort to practices which unreasonably restrain trade or adversely affect the international transfer of technology." Sect. 8 of Part II specifically addresses the control of anti-competitive practices in licensing agreements, as stipulated in Article 40(2): "Nothing in this Agreement shall prevent Members from specifying in their legislation licensing practices or conditions that may in particular cases constitute an abuse of intellectual property rights having an adverse effect on competition in the relevant market." This demonstrates that, even though the TRIPS Agreement was formulated under the influence of the U.S. and other Western countries, it nevertheless establishes restrictions and regulations on the abuse of intellectual property rights. As a member of the World Trade Organization, China is bound to amend its legal framework in accordance with the relevant provisions of the TRIPS Agreement.

China's regulation on the abuse of intellectual property rights originated in legal norms addressing technological monopolies. The first law to make explicit expression of the 'abuse of intellectual property rights' was Article 55 of the *Anti-Monopoly Law* enacted in 2008. Subsequently, on April 7, 2015, the State Administration for Industry and Commerce officially issued the *Provisions on Prohibiting the Abuse of Intellectual Property Rights to Exclude or Restrict Competition*, which took effect on August 1, 2015. These provisions were later revised by the State Administration for Market Regulation on October 30, 2020. Both the original and revised versions explicitly stated in Article 1 that their purpose is to 'protect fair market competition and encourage innovation', a principle that is adopted in the latest Anti-Monopoly Law.

The *Anti-Monopoly Law* 2022, effective as of August 1, 2022, incorporates 'encouraging innovation' into its legislative purpose under Article 1 of the General Provisions. Compared to the earlier version, the revised law introduces five additional references to 'innovation' throughout the text. This highlights the significance

[18] Wang, X. (2008). 'Zhishi chanquan yu fanlongduanfa: zhishi chanquan lanyong de fanlongduanfa wenti yanjiu (xiu ding ban)' [*Intellectual property and antitrust law: A study of antitrust issues in intellectual property abuse (Revised Edition)*]. Legal Publishing House. 291.

of studying the abuse of intellectual property rights from an antitrust perspective on regulating such abuses and promoting innovation. Furthermore, understanding how market competition and innovation jointly drive economic development requires some reflections.

Moreover, the *Anti-Monopoly Law* 2022 and the and *Provisions on Prohibiting the Abuse of Intellectual Property Rights to Exclude or Restrict Competition (Draft for Public Comment)*, issued by the State Administration for Market Regulation, further refine the antitrust legal framework in the field of intellectual property by placing particular emphasis on addressing typical sectors and behaviours commonly associated with intellectual property monopoly cases.

7.1.3.2 Types of Intellectual Property Transactions Subject to Antitrust Regulation

Although the governance of the abuse of intellectual property rights that exclude or restrict competition under the Anti-Monopoly Law has its particularities, such behaviour does not constitute an independent form separate from monopoly agreements, abuse of a dominant position, or anti-competitive concentrations of undertakings. As previously mentioned, Article 68 of the *Anti-Monopoly Law* (2022) provides only a general provision and cannot be directly applied in specific cases.

The abuse of intellectual property rights by undertakings to exclude or restrict competition, depending on the nature or manifestation of the conduct, may separately or simultaneously constitute monopoly agreements, abuse of a dominant position, or anti-competitive concentrations of undertakings as stipulated respectively in the *Anti-Monopoly Law* (2022). This is corroborated by Article 3 of the *Provisions on Prohibiting the Abuse of Intellectual Property Rights to Exclude or Restrict Competition (Draft for Public Comment)*. The following sections will provide a detailed analysis and explanation of the provisions related to the abuse of intellectual property rights in the *Anti-Monopoly Law* (2022) and the *Draft for Public Comment* (hereinafter referred to as the '*Draft for Public Comment*').

First, the *Anti-Monopoly Law* (2022) did not amend the content of Article 55 of the original *Anti-Monopoly Law* nor adjust its placement within the statutory framework. However, the *Draft for Public Comment* introduces significant changes. In addition to incorporating 'encouraging innovation' into the legislative purpose of the *Anti-Monopoly Law* (2022) and adding innovation (R&D) markets to the definition of relevant markets in the *Draft for Public Comment*, other aspects based on the unique characteristics of intellectual property, such as the regulation of pooling arrangements, standard-essential patents (SEPs), and collective management organizations, call for further in-depth study.

Patent pooling Also known as joint licensing, refers to arrangements where undertakings holding patents or other technologies mutually allow each other or jointly allow third parties to use their patents or technologies.[19] Such pooling behaviours take

[19] Wang, X. (2011). *Fanlongduan fa* [*Anti-Monopoly Law*], Falv Chubanshe [Law Press]. 179.

various forms, including establishing joint ventures for this purpose or entrusting one member of the pool or an independent third-party entity to organize joint licensing. Patent pooling has positive effects, such as promoting the integration of complementary technologies, reducing transaction costs, and eliminating blocking patents. However, in certain circumstances, patent pooling may adversely affect competing technologies not included in the pool, potentially excluding or restricting competition. This necessitates appropriate regulation under antitrust law.[20] The regulatory trends concerning patent pooling reflected in the *Draft for Public Comment* are mainly embodied in Article 14, which adds provisions against 'licensing pooled patents at unfairly high prices' and includes the phrase 'without justifiable reasons' in exclusivity clauses and non-compete clauses. On one hand, these changes substantively address the exclusionary and restrictive effects on competition, as unfairly high pricing essentially constitutes a form of refusal. On the other hand, the introduction of the rule of reason emphasizes the need for an analytical assessment of the competitive impact of such behaviours.

The establishment and implementation of standards facilitate compatibility and interoperability among different products and services, the unification of technical specifications ensures product quality and protects consumer interests. However, if a standard incorporates patented technology and becomes widely adopted, it will inevitably increase the costs for alternative technologies to enter the standard, thereby creating a patent hold-up effect. Consequently, when the exercise of patent rights by patent holders during the formulation and implementation of standards results in, or is likely to result in, the exclusion or restriction of competition, such conduct should be governed by the *Anti-Monopoly Law*.

The existing regulations on the issue of standard-essential patents are primarily reflected in patent law. However, Articles 15 and 16 of the latest *Draft for Public Comments* expand and refine the provisions concerning the use of standard-essential patents to exclude or restrict competition, based on the original framework. Specifically, the amendments include: (1) In the context of monopoly agreements, specific scenarios of anti-competitive conduct arising from the use of standard formulation and implementation are enumerated. (2) In cases involving the abuse of a dominant position in the standard-essential patent field, the provisions are expanded to include unfair high pricing and differential treatment practices. These modifications and refinements further strengthen the regulation of conduct involving the exercise of patent rights during the formulation and implementation of standards that results in, or is likely to result in, exclusion or restriction of competition.

Monopoly of collective management organizations Copyright collective management organizations are specific institutions established by law for the benefit of copyright holders, authorized to uniformly manage copyrights and their ancillary rights based on the permission of the copyright holders. Compared to the exercise

---

[20] Wang, X. (2019). 'Lun woguo fanlongduanfa zai zhishi chanquan lingyu de shishi' ['On the implementation of China's Anti-Monopoly Law in the field of intellectual property']. *Shanghai Jiaotong Daxue Xuebao(Zhexue Shehui Kexue Ban)* [*Journal of Shanghai Jiao Tong University (Philosophy and Social Science Edition)*], 6, 19.

of copyrights by individual right holders, collective management organizations offer three distinct advantages: First, reduction of transaction costs. By obtaining extensive copyright authorizations, these organizations achieve economies of scale, enabling both parties of a transaction to identify each other sufficiently, thereby avoiding inefficiencies associated with individual authorizations and reducing information gathering and transaction costs. Second, reduction of supervision costs. External regulatory bodies can conduct comprehensive examinations on collective management organizations, thus preventing the waste of resource associated with decentralized regulation. Third, balancing negotiation power. By organizing through collective management entities, rights of copyright holders are better safeguarded, reversing their historically weak position in enforcing their rights and ensuring stronger protection. However, due to the inherent unequal legal status between right holders and collective management organizations, particularly given that collective management organizations in China acquire exclusive authorization from copyright holders, which eliminate competition with other collective management entities, thus left rooms for antitrust intervention. According to antitrust enforcement practices, copyright management organizations in China have shown several monopolistic issues, such as entering into blanket licensing agreements, charging excessive management fees, and refusing to engage in transactions etc. By way of leveraging their dominant positions, these monopolistic practices of collective management organizations severely restrict competition and hinder the development of related industries.

To effectively achieve full market competition, the regulatory changes reflected in Article 17 of the *Draft for Public Comments* primarily focus on adding provisions to address anti-competitive behaviours of copyright collective management organizations. Specifically, it 'prohibits collective management organizations from exchanging sensitive competitive information, unreasonably imposing restrictions related to membership qualifications or geographical scope, or group boycotting specific right holders or users in agreements with right holders, users, or other copyright collective management organizations.' Furthermore, the provision outlines five types of abuse of a dominant position, providing clearer guidance for antitrust enforcement authorities when handling related cases. This marks that specific anti-competitive behaviours of copyright collective management organizations have been explicitly delineated at the regulatory level for the first time. It represents a summary of monopolistic behaviours observed in recent years during enforcement practices by antitrust authorities.

7.2 Antitrust Regulation Related to Intellectual Property Licensing

7.2.1 Specific Manifestations of Antitrust Regulation Triggered by Intellectual Property Licensing

Intellectual property, as an exclusive right explicitly stipulated by law, is characterized by its exclusivity, allowing right holders to permit others to use their intellectual achievements by contracts or other written forms.[21] In principle, the right holder's decisions regarding whether and how to grant licenses fall under the realm of contractual freedom. However, since intellectual property right holders inherently enjoy a competitive advantage in the market, their licensing behaviour poses significant risks of restricting or eliminating competition, potentially leading to monopolistic concerns. In light of the provisions in the *Anti-Monopoly Law* (2022) and the *Anti-Monopoly Guidelines on the Field of Intellectual Property Rights* issued by the State Council Anti-Monopoly Commission (hereinafter referred to as the '*Guidelines*'), and drawing from regulatory practices in the U.S. and the EU, intellectual property licensing behaviours subject to antitrust regulation can be categorized as the following.

7.2.1.1 Refusal to License

Refusal to license intellectual property corresponds to the refusal-to-deal behaviour without justified reasons under the chapter on abuse of a dominant position in the *Anti-Monopoly Law*. This refers to the conduct of an intellectual property right holder who, aiming to consolidate and strengthen their dominant position, refuses to grant or license their intellectual property to competitors, thereby excluding or restricting competition of others.[22] Although the *Anti-Monopoly Law* does not explicitly define the concept of refusal to license intellectual property, incorporating such conduct—where the licensor uses its dominant position to monopolize the market by refusing to license, thereby creating market barriers and excluding competitors—into the regulatory scope of refusal to deal has precedents in comparative law. For instance, the EU's antitrust regulation of refusal to license intellectual property essentially extends the scope of refusal-to-deal conduct and the obligation to supply products

[21] According to Article 26 of *the Copyright Law*, "The use of another's work must be carried out through a licensing agreement with the copyright holder, unless otherwise stipulated by the Copyright Law." According to Article 12 of the *Patent Law*, "The licensor and the licensee must enter into a patent licensing agreement." According to Article 43 of the Trademark Law, "The use of a registered trademark by others must be licensed through a trademark licensing agreement.".

[22] Wang, X. (2020). *Zhishi chanquan yu fanlongduanfa——Zhishi chanquan lanyong de fanlongduan wenti yanjiu (di san ban)*[*Intellectual Property and Antitrust Law—A Study of Antitrust Issues in Intellectual Property Abuse (Third Edition)*]. Falv Chubanshe [Law Press], 300.

stipulated in Article 82 of the *Treaty Establishing the European Community* (now Article 102 TFEU) to the realm of intellectual property.[23]

As for what constitutes 'justified reasons', Article 16 of the *Interim Provisions on Prohibition of Abuse of Dominant Market Position*[24] issued by the State Administration for Market Regulation adopts a 'enumeration + catch-all' legislative approach, providing a comprehensive expression of its connotation. It is evident that determining whether a refusal to license intellectual property constitutes monopolistic behaviour requires a cautious approach and should adhere to the principle of reasonableness, only by analysing the purpose and consequences of a specific act can its legality be confirmed. Although private lawsuits against refusal-to-deal behaviour have continued to appear in the U.S. over the past decades, the U.S. government has rarely initiated such lawsuits,and moreover, related case law in the U.S. often refer to the intent of the actor as a standard for determining the illegality of such conduct.[25]

Using the content of the license as criteria, refusals to license can be categorized into refusals concerning trademark rights, patent rights, and copyright. Among these, refusals related to patent rights are the main type due to the extensive use of patented technologies in production processes as well as their potential to create technical barriers for competitors entering specific competitive fields.[26] With the advancement of internet technologies and the platform economy, the digitization of copyrights and the patenting of software copyrights have become imperative. Based on the scope of refusals to license, it can also be classified into narrow and broad refusals.[27] Broad refusals to license, also known as conditional refusals to license, encompass not only pure refusals without additional conditions or requirements, but also situations where a refusal to license is used as leverage to compel the licensee to accept unreasonable

[23] Liu, Y. (2006). 'Zhishi chanquan jujue xuke de fanlongduanfa yanjiu——Yi zhuanliquan de jujue xuke wei zhongxin' ['Antitrust law research on the refusal to license intellectual property—Focusing on patent refusal to license']. Master's Thesis, East China University of Political Science and Law, pp. 4–15. (Note: The institution changed its name to "East China University of Political Science and Law" after 2007).

[24] Article 16 of the *Interim Provisions on Prohibiting the Abuse of Market Dominance* lists justifiable reasons as follows: 1. The transaction cannot be carried out due to objective reasons such as force majeure; 2. The trading counterparty has a poor credit record or has encountered deteriorating business conditions, affecting the security of the transaction; 3. Conducting transactions with the counterparty would lead to improper losses of the operator's interests; 4. Other reasons that can demonstrate the legitimacy of the conduct.

[25] Kong, X. (2001). *Fanlongduanfa yuanli* [*Principles of Antitrust Law*]. Zhongguo Fazhi Chubanshe [China Legal Publishing House], 575; Wang, X. (2020). *Zhishi chanquan yu fanlongduanfa——zhishi chanquan lanyong de fanlongduan wenti yanjiu (di san ban)*[*Intellectual Property and Antitrust Law—A Study of antitrust issues in intellectual property abuse (Third Edition)*]. Falv Chubanshe [Law Press].301.

[26] Yuan, X. (2008). 'Zhishi chanquan jujue xuke de fanlongduanfa guizhi' ['Antitrust regulation of refusal to license intellectual property']. Master's Thesis, East China University of Political Science and Law, p. 4.

[27] Ibid., 3.

conditions, such as price discrimination.[28] Refusals to license in this chapter refers specifically to narrow refusals to license. In addition to this classification, refusals may also be divided into horizontal and vertical refusals, unilateral and collective refusals, and refuse to license from the outset as well as termination of ongoing licensing agreements etc.

7.2.1.2 Licensing at Unreasonably High Prices

According to Article 22(1) of the *Anti-Monopoly Law* (2022), monopolistic pricing by undertakings with a dominant market position constitutes an abuse of a dominant position. Monopolistic pricing includes both the sale of goods at unfairly high prices and the purchase of goods at unfairly low prices. In the context of intellectual property licensing, the licensor as the holder of rights can charge license fees from the licensee for the use of intellectual property, thereby only involving the former behaviour. Unfairly high pricing, also known as excessive pricing or unreasonably high pricing, refers to prices far exceeding fair standards, which the undertakings would not have been able to achieve under normal competitive conditions but for their market dominance.[29] Determining whether pricing is reasonable or fair cannot be concluded solely based on the absolute value of the price. Market participants naturally aim to maximize their own profits, and setting high prices is an essence of market economies on the one hand, and on the other hand, it serves to incentivize undertakings to increase R&D and investment efforts.[30] For this reason, unfairly high pricing remains unregulated either in theory or under antitrust law. In contrast, although the EU has established a framework to govern unfairly high prices, determining whether prices are excessive still requires an assessment on whether there is a reasonable relationship between the price and its economic value of a product.[31]

The issue becomes more complex when it arises in the context of intellectual property licensing, as considering the difficulty and high cost of innovation in intellectual property, it seems justifiable for the right holder to set a higher licensing fee. Therefore, in analysing and regulating the pricing of intellectual property licenses, it is necessary to coordinate intellectual property with antitrust considerations while focusing on the fundamental legislative purpose of antitrust law, which is to determine whether the behaviour in question disrupts or impedes a sufficient and effective competition in the market. Article 15 of the *Guidelines* sets out the situations of intellectual property licensing at an unfairly high price and provides five factors to

[28] Wang, X. (2020). *Zhishi chanquan yu fanlongduanfa——Zhishi chanquan lanyong de fanlongduan wenti yanjiu (di san ban)*[*Intellectual Property and Antitrust Law—A study of antitrust issues in intellectual property abuse (Third Edition)*]. Falv Chubanshe [Law Press]. 301.

[29] Ibid., 339.

[30] The U.S. Supreme Court Justice Scalia stated in the 2004 Trinko case: “Merely possessing monopoly power and charging monopoly prices is not in itself unlawful.” *Verizon Communications v. Law Office of Curtis V. Trinko*, (2004). 540 U.S. 398.

[31] United Brands Company and United Brands Continentaal BV v Commission of the European Communities, Case 27/76, [1978] ECR 207.

consider in determining whether the licensing fee constitutes an unfairly high price.[32] In addition, for licenses involving standard-essential patents, it may also be relevant to consider the overall licensing fees borne by products compliant with the relevant standards and their impact on the normal development of the related industry. Some scholars argue that determining the fairness and reasonableness of licensing fees for standard-essential patents requires a comparison on the differences of licensing prices before and after the specific patent technology was incorporated into the standard, as well as price differences for the same standard-essential patent when licensed to different implementing entities, among other factors.[33]

7.2.1.3 Bundling and Tying Licensing Modes

Tying refers to the behaviour of an undertaking, in the process of offering goods or services, uses its market dominance to force the buyer, to purchase or accept another service that the buyer does not need against their will. Tying is not uncommon in the transactional market. As a sales strategy, it can, in certain circumstances, reduce transaction costs, boost sales volume, and thereby enhance efficiency. However, for undertakings with market dominance, tying can also serve as a means to extend their competitive advantage into the market for the tied products. In judicial practice, the elements constituting illegal tying have gradually been clarified and repeatedly adopted.[34] The concept of bundling is closely related to tying, but both the EU and the U.S. have distinguished between their underlying meanings: In the report of *Antitrust Enforcement and Intellectual Property Rights: Promoting Innovation and Competition 2007* of the U.S., tying is understood as a practice in which the seller or lessor imposes a condition on the buyer or lessee requiring them to simultaneously

[32] Article 15 of the Anti-Monopoly Guidelines for the Intellectual Property Sector issued by the State Council Anti-Monopoly Committee states: "An undertaking with a dominant market position may abuse its market dominance by licensing intellectual property at unfairly high prices, thereby eliminating or restricting competition. In determining whether this constitutes an abuse of market dominance, the following factors may be considered: (1) the method of calculating the royalty and the contribution of the intellectual property to the value of the relevant goods; (2) the commitments made by the undertaking regarding intellectual property licensing; (3) the historical licensing of the intellectual property or comparable royalty standards; (4) the licensing conditions that lead to unfairly high prices, including the charging of royalties for territories or product ranges beyond the scope of the intellectual property; (5) whether royalties are charged for expired or invalid intellectual property in a package license.".

[33] Zhou, M. (2021). 'Fanlongduanfa guizhi lanyong biaozhun biyao zhuanli xingwei zhi bianjie tanjiu' ['Exploring the boundaries of antitrust regulation of the abuse of Standard-Essential Patent']. Master's Thesis, Beijing Foreign Studies University, p. 4.

[34] The elements of the offense include: (1) the bundled products and the products being bundled are independent products; (2) the bundler holds a dominant position in the market for the bundled product; (3) the bundler imposes some form of coercion on the buyer, forcing them to accept the bundled product; (4) the bundling is not legitimate, does not conform to trade practices, consumer habits, or ignores the functionality of the products; (5) the bundling has a negative effect on competition. A specific discussion can be found in the judgment (2015) Xizhongmin Si Chu Zi No. 00261.

purchase or lease additional products or services, while bundling is understood as a sales method involving a fixed combination of products. *The EU's Guidelines on The Application of Article 81 of the EC Treaty to Technology Transfer Agreements 2004* provides a similar understanding with respect to tying and bundling in the context of technology licensing.[35]

As mentioned above, in situations where the seller is capable to engage in tying, the tied product must necessarily show a certain level of market power, making it difficult for the buyer to switch their demand and refrain from purchasing. The inclusion of intellectual property in the product is typically the key factor that creates the market power of the seller.[36] In intellectual property tying transactions, if the licensee refuses to accept the tied product, they will lose the right to use or implement the intellectual property.[37] The U.S. *Antitrust Guidelines for the Licensing of Intellectual Property* provides a definition for tying agreements, clearly stating that in a licensing agreement, the conditions under which the licensee obtains the intellectual property license usually include the acceptance of other intellectual property, goods, or services that are not needed. Moreover, it emphasizes the need to consider both the anti-competitive effects of the tying arrangement and the pro-competitive factors that may promote competition. This suggests a gradual shift away from the strict application of the per se rule, with the application of the rule of reason emerging as the prevailing trend.

7.2.1.4 Other Unreasonable Licensing Conditions

The situations in which intellectual property licensing constitutes a monopoly, in addition to the aforementioned abuse of a dominant position, also include anti-competitive behaviour through the conclusion of monopoly agreements, that is, when the licensor imposes unreasonable restrictive terms such as cross-licensing, grant-back, fixed prices, etc., in the licensing agreement.

Cross-licensing refers to an arrangement in which both parties to the license agreement grant each other the right to use their respective technologies.[38] This type of licensing is typically found between intellectual property rights that are interdependent, such as between a primary patent and a subsidiary patent. Article 8 of the *Guidelines* states that cross-licensing can reduce the cost of intellectual property licensing and promote the implementation and utilization of intellectual

---

[35] Ning, L. (2010). 'Zhuanli dashou xuke de fanlongduanfa fenxi' ['Antitrust analysis of patent tying licenses']. *Shanghai Jiaotong Daxue Xuebao(Zhexue Shehui Kexue Ban)* [*Journal of Shanghai Jiao Tong University (Philosophy and Social Sciences Edition)*], 4, 5–6.

[36] Wang, X. (2020). *Zhishi chanquan yu fanlongduanfa——Zhishi chanquan lanyong de fanlongduan wenti yanjiu (di san ban)*[*Intellectual Property and Antitrust Law—A study of antitrust issues in intellectual property abuse (Third Edition)*]. Falv Chubanshe [Law Press]. 320.

[37] Zheng, Y. (2007). 'Zhishi chanquan dashou xueke de fanlongduan fenxi' ['Antitrust analysis of patent tying licenses']. *Zhongshan Daxue Xuebao Luncong* [*Journal of Sun Yat-sen University (Philosophy and Social Sciences Edition)*], 4, 171.

[38] Wang, X. (2011). *Fanlongduan Fa* [*Antitrust law*], Falv Chubanshe [Law Press]. 179.

property, but in certain circumstances, it may also have an exclusionary or restrictive effect on market competition. When analysing cross-licensing, the following factors may be considered: (1) whether the license is exclusive; (2) whether it creates barriers for third parties to enter the market; (3) whether it results in exclusionary or anti-competitive effects in the downstream market; (4) whether it increases the cost of related goods.

A grant-back clause, also known as reverse licensing or reverse authorization, refers to an arrangement where, in the course of licensing, the licensee is required to grant the licensor a right to use improved technology.[39] Based on the content of the clause, it can be classified as exclusive or non-exclusive, for considerations or free of charge, and unilateral or mutual grant-backs. This clause falls under non-price restriants in vertical monopoly agreements, and is generally subject to the rule of reason or may be exempted. Its competitive effects—both positive and negative—should be analysed comprehensively. On one hand, the grant-back clause helps promote cooperation between different intellectual property holders in competition, sharing risks and costs, and the exchange of improved technologies facilitates product updates, ultimately benefiting consumer welfare. But on the other hand, the purpose of the licensor in including a grant-back clause is to maintain a technological lead, which may result in the licensor having effective control over a particular market, while a requirement for unpaid grant-back may reduce the licensee's incentive to innovate. Article 9[40] of the *Guidelines* stipulates that exclusive and sole grant-backs[41] should adhere to the rule of reason, recognizing their role in promoting investment and utilization of new achievements, while clarifying the factors to be considered when determining their exclusionary or restrictive effects on competition.

Price fixing, as a form of price restraint in vertical relationships, is addressed under Article 18 of the *Anti-Monopoly Law* of China, which confirms the necessity of regulating vertical monopoly agreements involving the maintenance of resale prices, including fixing the resale price of goods to third parties and setting minimum resale prices. The negative externalities of vertical price restraints primarily manifest in: (1) weakening price competition within the brand; (2) harming consumer welfare; and

---

[39] Wang, X. (2020). *Zhishi chanquan yu fanlongduanfa——Zhishi chanquan lanyong de fanlongduan wenti yanjiu (di san ban)*[*Intellectual Property and Antitrust Law—A study of antitrust issues in intellectual property abuse (Third Edition)*]. Falv Chubanshe [Law Press]. 254.

[40] Article 9 of *The Guidelines on Antitrust in the Field of Intellectual Property by the State Council Antitrust Committee* provides: "When analyzing the exclusionary and exclusive rebates' effects on market competition, the following factors can be considered: (1) whether the licensor provides substantial consideration for the rebate; (2) whether the licensor and licensee mutually demand exclusive or exclusionary rebates in cross-licensing; (3) whether the rebate leads to the concentration of improvements or new results to a single operator, thereby granting or enhancing market control; (4) whether the rebate affects the licensee's incentive for improvements.".

[41] Some scholars believe that exclusive rebate clauses (also known as exclusive return clauses) have the following characteristics: unconditional, gratuitous, and non-reciprocal, see Wang, M.Q. (2007). 'Woguo zhuanliquan lanyong falv tiaozheng de guidingxing' ['The normative nature of legal regulation on the abuse of patent rights in China']. In *State Intellectual Property Office: Zhuanlifa Yanjiu* [*Research on Patent Law (2006)*], Zhishi Chanquan Chubanshe [Intellectual Property Publishing House]. 394.

(3) depriving downstream operators of the freedom of pricing. Additionally, vertical price restraints may have horizontal effects and reduce competition between brands.[42] In the field of intellectual property, a typical example of price fixing occurs when an intellectual property holder, after selling a product containing intellectual property, continues to impose restrictions on the buyer's resale price of the product. This behaviour essentially constitutes 'a restraint on the conditions (price) in subsequent transactions imposed by one party to another in a vertical transaction relationship (contract)'.[43]

7.2.2 *Application of the Traditional Analytical Framework*

From the previous section, it is evident that the main antitrust issues related to intellectual property licensing primarily involve the abuse of a dominant position by the right holder in the course of licensing (since intellectual property, as an exclusive right, inherently provides the undertaking with a dominant market position, especially when the licensed subject matter involves standard-essential patents, where the licensee often has no alternative choices), and the possibility that a licensing agreement may constitute a monopoly agreement due to unreasonable licensing conditions. However, the establishment of a monopoly agreement in the form of licensing is only one scenario involving monopoly agreements in the intellectual property field, which will be discussed in detail in the second section. The analytical approach to determining whether an undertaking is abusing a dominant position follows this logic: (1) defining the relevant market; (2) determining whether the undertaking holds a dominant position; (3) assessing whether the conduct constitutes an abuse of a dominant position.

7.2.2.1 Definition of Relevant Market

The relevant market refers to the scope of the market in which undertakings compete for specific goods or services during a particular period, including both the product scope and the geographic scope.[44] When the market scope in which undertakings compete is difficult to define, the relevant market can be determined using the 'Hypothetical Monopolist Test' approach. In practice, the smallest service and the smallest geographic area related to the case are typically used as the target service and target

---

[42] Xu, G. (2017). 'Zongxiang jiage xianzhi de fanlongduan fa lilun yu anli kaocha' ['Antitrust law theory and case study on vertical price restrictions'], *Zhengfa Luncong* [*Political and Legal Studies Journal*], 1, 3–13.

[43] Wang, X. (2020). *Zhishi chanquan yu fanlongduanfa——Zhishi chanquan lanyong de fanlongduan wenti yanjiu (di san ban)*[*Intellectual Property and Antitrust Law—A study of antitrust issues in intellectual property abuse (Third Edition)*]. Falv Chubanshe [Law Press]. 244.

[44] Meng, Y. (2017). *Fanlongduan Fa* [*Antitrust Law*], Beijing Daxue Chubanshe [Peking University Press]. 68.

geographic area, and then analysed from the perspectives of both demand substitution and supply substitution to determine whether there are other services or areas that are close substitutes to the target service or target geographic area. If the market scope is defined too broadly, the density of competitors is artificially increased, which may lower the market share of the competitors that already holding market dominance, potentially allowing them to evade from antitrust regulation. On the other hand, if the market scope is defined too narrowly, it may exaggerate the assessment of market share and market power, potentially leading to the wrongful identification of more undertakings as engaging in illegal conduct.

The core factors in defining the relevant market are the product and geographic scope, but in practice, especially in the intellectual property field, courts should also take into account the specific circumstances of each case when determining the relevant factors. Article 4 of the *Guidelines* stipulates that the definition of the relevant market should generally follow the *Guidelines on the Definition of Relevant Markets*. However, if defining the relevant product market alone cannot provide necessary factors for a comprehensive assessment of the competitive effects, the relevant technology market may also be defined. Furthermore, the duration of the exclusive rights, which is particularly important and cannot be overlooked in the field of intellectual property, determines that the timing factor should also be considered when defining the relevant market. Thus, in the antitrust regulation of intellectual property, it is necessary not only to define the relevant product market and the relevant geographic market but also to define the relevant technology market, while considering factors such as time, which are closely related to the characteristics of intellectual property.

7.2.2.2 Determination of Dominant Position

Dominant position can be understood as the degree of power or control that an undertaking holds in a particular market.[45] Although intellectual property constitutes an exclusive right, it does not necessarily result in market dominance, as reiterated in Articles 2 and 14 of the *Guidelines*. Therefore, in analysing whether an undertaking holds dominant position in the relevant market, reference should be made to the factors outlined in Articles 23 and 24 of the *Anti-Monopoly Law* (2022). A comprehensive assessment should be made by combining both qualitative and quantitative methods to determine whether the undertaking holds a dominant position within the relevant market. Market share typically refers to the proportion of an undertaking's specific product sales, sales volume, or other indicators within the relevant market over a certain period. In the U.S. and the EU, antitrust agencies and courts usually begin their evaluation of market dominance by analysing the undertaking's market share. While undertakings with market dominance often occupy a significant market share, a high market share alone is insufficient to establish a dominant position. Therefore, the actual competitive circumstances and other factors must also be considered.

[45] Ibid., 146.

The level of difficulties for competitors to enter the market is another important factor. Generally speaking, the entry of other undertakings into the relevant market depends primarily on factors such as capital, technology, and regulation.[46] The lower the 'barrier to entry', the easier it is for competitors to enter the market, indicating that a particular undertaking does not hold a dominant position in that specific relevant market. The degree of reliance other undertakings place on a particular undertaking can also be used to demonstrate whether the defendant holds a dominant position. However, it should be noted that in a transactional relationship, it is not uncommon that one party may depend on the other party or one party may hold an advantageous position against the other party. If the relevant market is determined solely by the existing transaction scope between the two parties in a dependent transaction relationship, it would be easy to conclude that the party being relied upon holds a dominant position in that relevant market. This approach conflicts with the definition of the dominant position under China's *Anti-Monopoly Law* and could lead to many disputes, which should fall under contract law or other civil legal frameworks, being categorized under antitrust law. This would also contradict the legislative purpose of antitrust law, which is to protect competitive order, safeguard consumer rights, and promote the public interest. Generally, when determining the degree of reliance other undertakings place on a particular undertaking in a transaction, factors such as the volume of transactions between the parties, the duration of the transaction relationship, and the ease with which other undertakings can shift to alternative trading partners shall be taken into considerations.

7.2.2.3 Analysis on Competitive Effects

To determine whether a particular intellectual property licensing constitutes an abuse of a dominant position (or whether it triggers regulation under antitrust law), an analysis on the competitive effects must be conducted within the relevant market. This involves analysing and comparing the positive and negative effects of the conduct on market competition, and assessing whether the behaviour leads to exclusionary or restrictive effects on competition, taking into account the characteristics of intellectual property in fostering innovation. Factors such as the impact on the dissemination and utilization of technology, as well as its effects on the efficiency of resource utilization, must be considered when determining whether the conduct excludes or restricts competition.

Taking the grant-back clause as an example for competitive effects analysis, its pro-competitive and efficiency-enhancing effects are primarily reflected in its ability to facilitate the most effective and comprehensive application of technology. The grant-back clause allows the licensor to gain timely access to updated and improved technologies, reducing the likelihood of the licensor being excluded from the market.

[46] Ibid., 156.

As a result, the licensor is more inclined to grant others the right to use their intellectual properties. After the licensee has acquired comprehensive and effective technological information, he will further stimulate the market to improve product quality, thereby benefiting consumers. The exclusionary and restrictive effects on competition are mainly that unilateral grant-backs further strengthen the licensor's market position and diminish the licensee's innovation incentives. Even seemingly fair mutual or bilateral grant-backs can lead to a possible situation where both parties lose their incentive to innovate if they are in horizontal competition. The U.S. Department of Justice and Federal Trade Commission primarily measures the monopolistic effects of grant-back clauses in two ways.[47] One the one hand, it will examine whether the licensor holds dominant position—the stronger the licensor's market control, the greater the exclusionary or restrictive effect of the grant-back clause. One the other hand, it will evaluate the extent to which the grant-back promotes market competition and the effectiveness of such promotion.

7.2.3 *Difficulties in the Traditional Analytical Framework and Breakthroughs*

7.2.3.1 Dilemma in Existing Analytical Approaches

The digital economy, as the primary economic form following the agricultural and industrial economies, is an emerging economic model based on three key elements: big data, intelligent algorithms, and computing power platforms.[48] The *14th Five-Year Plan for the Development of the Digital Economy* issued by the State Council points out that "...by 2025, the digital economy will enter a phase of comprehensive expansion, with the increased value of the core digital economy industries accounting for 10% of GDP, and the deep integration of digital technology with the real economy being the main focus." This indicates that China has fully entered the digital economy era, and the role of the digital economy in driving China's continuous economic development is becoming increasingly significant with strategic importance. As an essential component driving the development of the digital economy, regulating platform economy monopolies is crucial to promote high-quality economic growth. However, the unique nature of the platform economy means that traditional competition theories, based on unilateral market models, cannot simply be applied to explain the competitive behaviour of platforms.[49] First, in the platform economy, businesses

47 Hui, C. (2006). 'Zhishi chanquan xuk zhong de jignzhengfa wenti yanjiu' ['A study on competition law issues in intellectual property licensing'], Duiwai Jingji Maoyi Daxue [University of International Business and Economics], PhD dissertation, pp. 48–50.

48 Tencent, (2022). 'Shuzi shidai: renshi shuzi jingji chanye xianzhuang' ['Digital Age: Understanding the current state of the digital economy industry'], available at: https://new.qq.com/omn/20220419/20220419A01PBL00.html, accessed on 23 July 2022.

49 Zhang, P. (2021). *Quanqiu hulianwang falv guancha(2020–2021)* [*Global Internet Law Review (2020–2021)*], Zhongguo Fazhi Chubanshe [China Legal Publishing House]. 106.

providing products and services exhibit characteristics of a two-sided or even multi-sided market. The most notable feature of a two-sided market is that businesses target two or more interconnected consumer groups, and the continuous advancements in the internet undoubtedly make online platforms the ideal intermediaries, offering favourable external conditions for the development of two-sided markets and the flourishing of the platform economy. Moreover, in a two-sided market, the basic products or services are often offered at low prices or even completely free of charge. Second, within the internet industry, innovation competition surpasses price competition.[50] This characteristic is especially prominent in intellectual property-related business competition, where undertakings that are first to launch new products or possess leading technologies are more likely to hold dominant positions. Lastly, the profitability model of the platform economy, with its network effects and user lock-in effects, makes it easier for firms that hold dominant positions to extend their monopoly power to other markets. These unique features dictate that the methods used for defining relevant markets in the platform economy should not merely replicate the demand substitution and supply substitution methods used in traditional industries, since these substitution analysis are based on price analysis and overlook the impact of innovation on demand cross-elasticity.

Similarly, the 'Hypothetical Monopolist Test', which is usually applied to traditional industries, has shown limited effects in the platform economy. In March 2013, the Guangdong High People's Court issued a first-instance ruling in the case of *Qihoo vs. Tencent*, a landmark judgment in which the court innovatively applied the SSNIP (Small but Significant Non-transitory Increase in Price) method used in traditional industries to the internet sector, and defined the instant messaging product market as a relevant product market and the global market as the relevant geographic market.[51] Firstly, whether it is QQ, Weibo, or other software or websites included by the Guangdong High People's Court as instant messaging products, all provide basic services to users free of charge. Free internet products cannot capture the extent of a price increase; even a minimal charge would represent a significant increase for a product that was previously free.[52] Therefore, when applying the SSNIP method,

---

[50] Meng, Y. (2013). 'Hulianwang hangye xiangguan shichang jieding de tiaozhan——Yi qihu su teng xun fanlongduan an panjue wei lizheng' ['Challenges in defining relevant markets in the internet industry—A case study of Qihoo v. Tencent Antitrust Ruling']. *Dianzi Zhishi Chanquan* [*Electronic Intellectual Property*], 4, 42–45.

[51] See Guiding Case No. 78 of the Supreme Court. When defining the relevant product market, the Guangdong High Court considered both whether the hypothetical monopolist could obtain profits by reducing product quality or slightly raising implied prices (such as advertising time) for a non-temporary period, and whether, if the hypothetical monopolist began charging slightly for a sustained period, significant demand substitution would occur. At the same time, based on the openness and interoperability of the internet, the Guangdong High Court held that both operators and users have no national boundaries, so the relevant geographic market should be defined as a global market.

[52] Chen, S. (2013). 'Hulianwang chanye zhong xiangguan shangpin shichang jieding——yi qihu 360 su tengxun lanyong shichang zhipei diwei an weili' ['Defining the Relevant Product Market in the Internet Industry: A Case Study of Qihoo 360 v. Tencent on Abuse of Market Dominance']. *Yichun Xueyaun Xuebao* [*Journal of Yichun University*], 11, 31.

even a very small price increase (including implicit prices) can have a substantial impact on consumer demand. It thus becomes apparent that QQ and Weibo are considered substitutable by the Guangdong High People's Court. However, due to the user lock-in effect and network effects in the internet industry, consumers' price sensitivity has significantly decreased, rendering the SSNIP method ineffective in the platform economy. Looking together with the definition of instant messaging,[53] it can be seen that instant messaging software can be subdivided according to its functionalities, which correspond to different consumer needs. Thus, the primary factor in determining whether products are demand-substitutable is their functionality. The main function of software like Weibo or email is not its embedded instant messaging feature (and the instant messaging feature is relatively limited). Therefore, when intellectual property monopolies occur in the platform economy, defining the relevant market becomes the foremost challenge.

Secondly, the emergence and rise of networked and digital intellectual property products is an inevitable result of the digital economy era. According to the World Intellectual Property Report published by the World Intellectual Property Organization (WIPO) in April 2022, digital innovation has doubled in the past two decades, with an average annual growth rate of 13%.[54] Typical examples include electronic journals, game live streaming, and digital music. Currently, the primary licensing model for digital music in China is the 'exclusive copyright + sub-licensing' commercial model. The so-called digital music exclusive copyright are the exclusive rights to use and distribute specific music resources of downstream network music service providers acquired through an exclusive licensing agreement with upstream music record labels.[55] However, in practice, even if music service providers have signed 'exclusive agreements', these agreements often include sub-licensing clauses, preventing them from truly having exclusive use of the digital music copyrights. Therefore, it is more appropriate to understand this as an 'exclusive agency for the right of dissemination on the information network'.[56] However, there are diverging views in the academic field regarding the interpretation of exclusive copyrights, and further give rise to various theories, which in turn complicates the application of antitrust regulation to digital music exclusive copyrights. Thus, how to regulate

---

[53] The China Internet Network Information Center defines instant messaging as follows: "Instant messaging refers to system services used for real-time communication on the internet, allowing multiple users to transmit text messages, documents, voice, and video information streams in real-time using instant messaging software.".

[54] Gold, Y. (2022). 'Shijie zhishi chanquan zuzhi: Shuzihua chuangxin zai 20 niannei fanle liangfan' ['World Intellectual Property Organization: Digital Innovation Quadrupled in 20 Years']. *Diyi Caijing Ribao* [*First Financial Daily*], 13 May, p. A06.

[55] Jiang, Y. (2019). 'Shuzi yinyue zhuzuoquan xuke moshi tanjiu——jianyi fading xuke de biyaoxing ji qi zhidu goujian' ['A study on the licensing model of digital music copyright—With a discussion on the necessity of statutory licensing and its system construction']. Dongfang Faxue [*Eastern Law Review*], 1, 147–160.

[56] Gu, L. (2020). 'Shuzi yinyue dujia baiquan moshi fanlongduan fa wenti yanjiu' ['A study on the antitrust issues of exclusive digital music copyright models']. Master's thesis, Beijing Foreign Studies University, 3–6.

intellectual property products that are integrated with the internet, such as digital music, presents another dilemma under the current analytical frameworks.

Thirdly, the forms of intellectual property licensing have gradually diversified with the development of the socio-economic landscape, including cross-licensing and patent pool licensing. Patent pool licensing, also known as package licensing, can be further categorized into closed patent pools and open patent pools, depending on whether the patent holders allow third parties to use the patents within the pool.[57] A patent pool, also known as a patent alliance, is an organization that jointly exercises patents. Due to the unified 'package' licensing model, the difficulty and cost of patent usage are significantly reduced. However, because the patent pool itself involves a union of patents, it inherently has the potential to restrict competition. Thus, when patent holders collectively control the market, they can exclude other competitors. In terms of form, it is difficult to directly identify a monopoly agreement between undertakings, as a single undertaking may not have sufficient market power to be considered dominant, which brings challenges in practice. Overall, how to regulate the constantly evolving licensing models for intellectual property remains another dilemma under current analytical approaches.

7.2.3.2 Development of the Contemporary Theories and Improvement Strategies

Regarding the first dilemma, since competition involving intellectual property primarily centers on technological and product innovation in the platform economy, every time an innovation emerged it will affect the clear delineation of the boundaries of relevant product markets. Some scholars argue that the boundaries of the relevant market can be somewhat blurred so as to allow for flexibility in accommodating new products that innovations are likely to bring. Moreover, when defining the relevant geographic market, it is important to recognize that the internet itself is not a geographical location, and the interconnectivity of the internet does not eliminate competitive constraints imposed by factors such as language preferences and usage habits.[58] From the perspective of the competitive structure in the platform economy, Yang Ming argues that it is necessary to construct a dual analytical framework of 'price analysis + effective competition measurement' to achieve a balance between competition and innovation, specifically, it is important to "...emphasize the analysis of dynamic efficiency and examine whether specific business

[57] Zhang, L. (2003). 'Lun zhuanliquan jiaocha xuke ji zhuanlichi xuke moshi de fanlongduan guizhi——Meiguo de lilun yu shijian' ['On the Antitrust regulation of patent cross-licensing and patent pool licensing models: Theory and practice in the United States']. Master's thesis, University of International Business and Economics. 8–9.

[58] Meng, Y. (2013). 'Hulianwang hangye xiangguan shichang jieding de tiaozhan——Yi qihu su tengxun fanlongduan an panjue wei lizheng' ['Challenges in defining relevant markets in the internet industry: A case study of Qihoo vs. Tencent Antitrust Case']. *Dianzi Zhishi Chanquan* [*Electronic Intellectual Property*], 4, 42–45.

strategies adopted by platforms create a possible Nash equilibrium among competitors. If a strategy combination that is expected to bring optimal responses from each competitor cannot be formed, it may be necessary to consider whether the business strategy in question is harmful to effective competition."[59] Yang Dong, on the other hand, believes that the core of competition in the platform economy may not lie in a specific traditional market, but rather in the competition for resources and markets across multiple dimensions such as platforms, data, algorithms, and time.[60] He advocates for the construction of a dual regulatory system based on market dominance and relative competitive advantage. Foreign scholars also offer extensive discussions in this respect. Kingsbury, from the perspective of analytical approaches, affirms the benefits of applying the analytical framework of monopoly in the intellectual property field for the protection of copyright, trademark, and patent.[61] He believes that the narrow interpretation of competitive markets in the field of intellectual property by courts in the past has led to trade protectionism. Therefore, he suggests applying the market definition under antitrust law to provide a theoretical basis for reducing such protection, thereby safeguarding the welfare of consumers and the public, as well as fostering future innovation. Kaplow, taking a more unconventional stance, argues currently there is no and will never be an effective formula to calculate an undertaking's market share in the relevant market, under this premise, we cannot assess market power and consequently, it is impossible to properly define the relevant markets.[62]

Therefore, the current prevailing views do not completely abandon the traditional analytical framework. Instead, it seeks to optimize these methods by incorporating factors beyond price (such as product functionality, innovation levels, and even privacy terms regarding the protection of personal information). As a result, there is no need to rigidly adhere to the traditional approach of defining a clearly delineated relevant market, or place additional emphasis on effective competition apart from competition structure, because they are all in fact analysis that align with the underlying legislative purpose of antitrust law. Regarding the application of the essential facilities doctrine in the digital economy, the U.S. has maintained a relatively cautious attitude, while the EU has not denied its practicality. China, on the other hand, has shown an open attitude, adhering to the principle of focusing on the essence of competition and case-by-case analysis.

[59] Yang, M. (2022). 'Pingtai jingji fanlongduan de eryuan fenxi kuangjia' ['A dual analysis framework for antitrust in the platform economy']. *Zhongwai Faxue* [*Chinese and Foreign Legal Studies*], 2, 381–383.

[60] Yang, D. (2020). 'Lun fanlongduanfa de chonggou: yingdui shuzi jingji de tiaozhan' ['On the reconstruction of Antitrust Law: Addressing the challenges of the digital economy']. *Zhongguo Faxue* [*China Legal Science*], 3, 214–215.

[61] Kingsbury, A. F. (2004). 'Market definition in intellectual property law: Should intellectual property courts use an antitrust approach to market definition?'. *Marquette Intellectual Property Law Review*, 9(1), 64–92.

[62] Kaplow, L. (2013). 'Market definition: Impossible and counterproductive'. *Antitrust Law Journal*, 79(1), 361–379.

Regarding the second dilemma, China's regulatory authorities have long recognized that the exclusive copyright model can significantly hinder competition and have taken multiple measures to address this issue. In 2017 and 2018, the authorities held discussions with major music platforms regarding digital music copyright issues. In 2021, the State Administration for Market Regulation (SAMR) determined that Tencent's acquisition of shares in CMC constituted an illegal concentration of undertakings. In its penalty decision, the SAMR ordered Tencent to terminate its exclusive copyright agreements for online music and refrain from the ongoing payment methods such as excessive advance payments.[63]

The concentration of copyrights of Tencent is in fact a reflection of a vertical integration business strategy adopted by current content platforms. Vertical integration refers to the expansion of a business along its existing supply chain, either upstream or downstream, resulting in the integration of supply, production, and sales. As a result, it tends to have a strong exclusionary effect. In the case of *Huaduo v. NetEase* concerning the abuse of a dominant position and unfair competition, the Guangdong High People's Court concluded that the relevant product market should be the online gaming service market, rather than the *Fantasy Westward Journey 2* service market, and ultimately ruled that NetEase did not hold a dominant position in that market.[64] *NetEase* is a typical example of an undertaking employing a vertical integration strategy, and the main economic issue discussed in this case is 'how to understand the power of market control created by online game copyrights'.[65] The Judgement of Guangdong High People's Court's reflects the inertia of an static analysis and fails to reveal the trend of market competition which is evolving from ownership control to platform control.

Similarly, when applying antitrust analysis to digital music copyright protection, it is essential to focus on the essence of platform vertical integration. If regulation through antitrust law is not feasible, seeking remedies within the realm of copyright protection is a practical solution.[66] In other words, regulation should be carried out from the source of digital music copyright authorization. Therefore, to avoid exclusive licensing and promote widespread licensing of digital music copyrights, the concept of developing a centralized licensing model for digital music has gradually emerged. However, this view essentially overlooks the long-standing absence of collective management organizations for music copyrights in China. In China, the collective management organizations for music copyrights and neighboring rights,

---

[63] State Administration for Market Regulation (2021). 'Tencent Holdings Limited's Illegal Acquisition of Equity in China Music Group: Administrative Penalty Decision on the Concentration of Business Operators', Guo Shijian Chu [2021] No. 67, published on July 24, 2021.

[64] See (2018) Yue Min Zhong No. 552 Judgment.

[65] Yang, M. (2022) 'Ruhe kandai pingtai de zongxiang yitihua celue?' ['How to View the Vertical Integration Strategy of Platforms?']. Hexun, available at: http://tech.hexun.com/2022-07-19/206392841.html, accessed on 25 July 2022.

[66] Gu, L. (2020) 'Shuzi yinyue dujia baiquan moshi fanlongduan fa wenti yanjiu' ['Study on antitrust issues in the exclusive copyright model of digital music']. Master's thesis, Beijing Foreign Studies University. 59.

such as the China Music Copyright Association and the China Audio-Visual Copyright Association, are both government-led and generally adopt a comprehensive blanket licensing model, which has led to concerns about the monopolistic nature of China's music copyright collective management organizations. Consequently, some scholars have proposed introducing a statutory licensing model in the field of music copyright.[67]

Regarding the third dilemma, China's *Guidelines on Defining Relevant Markets* were formulated after considering the experiences of the EU and the U.S., specifically addressing the relevant market definition methods used in traditional product economies. Therefore, even if a competitive conduct involves intellectual property, as long as it fits within the traditional framework, the existing analytical framework can still be applied to address any antitrust disputes arising therefrom. For example, in the case of the *China Rare Earth Permanent Magnet Industry Technology Innovation Strategic Alliance* (hereinafter *the Alliance*) vs. *Hitachi Metals Ltd.* (hereinafter Hitachi Metals) for the abuse of dominant position and blocking the export of Chinese neodymium-iron-boron to Europe and the U.S., Hitachi Metals refused to grant patent licenses to Chinese undertakings, preventing many of these companies' products from being exported to Europe and the United States.

This is a typical case of abuse of intellectual property rights leading to a monopoly dispute under the traditional framework. The Ningbo Intermediate People's Court, in defining the relevant market, combined the requirements for patent protection and determined the time span of the relevant market from July 2013 to the concluding date of the first-instance trial. The downstream market was defined as the sintered neodymium-iron-boron market, while the upstream market was defined as the patent license market for sintered neodymium-iron-boron patents owned by the defendant, and the relevant geographic market was defined as the global market. The court applied the 'essential facilities doctrine' and ruled that Hitachi Metals's refusal to license constituted a refusal to deal under China's antitrust law. This case illustrates that there is a consensus between the theoretical field and judicial practice in China regarding the application of the essential facilities doctrine in cases concerning intellectual properties. Moreover, antitrust regulation triggered by intellectual property licensing can still be analysed within the traditional framework. In the case of the *Federal Trade Commission (FTC) v. Qualcomm* for the abuse of standard-essential patents (SEPs), the FTC argued that Qualcomm's refusal to license its SEPs to competing chip manufacturers violated antitrust law. Under the *Sherman Act*, unilateral refusals to license are generally permitted because firms are not obliged to assist competitors. However, refusals are typically considered illegal in 'concerted refusals to license' cases. In this case, because Qualcomm had a dominant position in the SEP supply market and could charge downstream firms monopoly prices, meanwhile, Qualcomm's refusal to license directly eliminated competition in the supply

[67] Jiang, Y. (2019). 'Shuzi yinyue zhuzuoquan xuke moshi tanjiu——jian yi fading xuke de biyaoxing ji qi zhidu goujian' ['Study on the Copyright Licensing Model of Digital Music—On the Necessity of Statutory License and Its System Construction']. *Dongfang Faxue* [*Eastern Law Studies*], 1, 147–160.

markets of the SEPs, leaving downstream firms with no alternative source for the SEPs but to accept Qualcomm's high prices. Thus, Qualcomm's unilateral refusal to license should be subject to antitrust regulation.[68]

Patent pool licensing is common in the active pharmaceutical ingredient (API) sector. Recently, the Geneva Medicines Patent Pool signed an agreement with 35 pharmaceutical companies, allowing them to produce the active ingredient nirmatrelvir (a component of Pfizer's COVID-19 oral drug Paxlovid).[69] In fact, China also applies the traditional analytical framework to specific cases rather than directly classifying patent pool licensing as a particular form of monopoly. For example, in the case of *Yangtze River Pharmaceutical Group*, Yangtze River Pharmaceutical Group licensed downstream pharmaceutical wholesalers and retail pharmacies to sell drugs, but simultaneously engaged in activities such as signing cooperation agreements, issuing price adjustment notices, and verbally notifying parties about fixed resale prices and minimum resale price agreements, this behaviour violated Article 18 of the *Anti-Monopoly Law (2022)*, resulting in a fine imposed by the State Administration for Market Regulation.

7.3 Antitrust Regulations Related to Intellectual Property Assignments

Antitrust regulation related to the assignment of intellectual property rights primarily focuses on the area of concentrations of undertakings, where the nature of the relationship between undertakings needs be considered in the light of the characteristics of the behaviours in exercising intellectual property rights. In specific cases, the types of anticompetitive behaviours resulting from the abuse of intellectual property rights must be examined based on different constituent elements of each type of violation. This section will focus on analysing the situations where the abuse of intellectual property rights violates the filing requirements for the concentrations of undertakings.

[68] Shi, W. & Ren, T. (2020). 'Chuangxin xiaolu shijiao xia SEP jujue xuke xingwei de fanlongduan fa zeren fenxi——Yi FTC su gaotong an wei qieru' ['Analysis of Antitrust liability for SEP refusal to license from the perspective of innovation efficiency—A case study of FTC v. Qualcomm']. *Keji Guanli Yanjiu* [*Science and Technology Management Research*], 17, 133–141.

[69] See 'Yaopin zhuanlichi shouquan fangzhi Huirui xinguan ko fuyao chengfen, 5 jia zhongguo yaoqi huo xuke' ['Drug Patent Pool Authorizes Generic Manufacture of Pfizer's COVID-19 Oral Drug Ingredients, 5 Chinese Pharmaceutical Companies Granted Licenses']. Sina Finance, available at: https://finance.sina.com.cn/chanjing/cyxw/2022-03-17/doc-imcwipih9019709.shtml, accessed on 25 July 2022.

7.3.1 *Specific Manifestations of Antitrust Regulation Triggered by Intellectual Property Assignments*

The acquisition of intellectual property by undertakings is a form of free transaction of intellectual property. The free transaction of intellectual property, in general, facilitates the spread of technology and promotes competition and innovation. However, in certain circumstances, concentrations of undertakings may have an adverse impact on technological progress or innovation activities. Common situations where intellectual property transactions may constitute concentrations of undertakings include the following:

A. The concentration of undertakings with technological leading positions in specific high-tech industries may reduce the speed of technological progress and innovation in that industry.
B. The acquisition of technology innovators by undertakings already holding a dominant market position in a specific industry may have an adverse impact on technological progress or innovation activities within that industry.
C. Acquiring key intellectual property from other undertakings through intellectual property assignments or exclusive licensing agreements, and thereby gaining control over or the ability to exert decisive influence on other undertakings. In such cases, undertakings should file a notification to the antitrust enforcement authorities when the transaction meets the thresholds for the filing for concentration of undertakings under antitrust law.

The regulation of anticompetitive behaviours resulting from the abuse of intellectual property must be framed within the three specific types of monopoly behaviour. When transactions or commercial activities involving intellectual property fall within the scope of regulations for concentration of undertakings, undertakings are still required to file notifications in accordance with the such regulations. Although antitrust authorities must take into account the specific characteristics of intellectual property when reviewing cases involving intellectual property-related concentrations, they must nonetheless follow the established examination procedures for monopolistic behaviors regarding general concentrations of undertakings.

In practical terms, this is manifested by the direct assignment or licensing of intellectual property, or the indirect acquisition, restriction, or use of intellectual property through controlling the undertakings. When intellectual property becomes the main purpose of a commercial transaction or has a substantial impact on the transaction, potentially leading to the exclusion or restriction of technological R&D, product innovation, or even future technological innovation competition, it may come under the scrutiny of antitrust regulations.

7.3.2 *Application of the Traditional Analytical Framework*

According to Article 33 of *Anti-Monopoly Law* (2022) of China,[70] the review of concentrations of undertakings is essentially a forecast of future competition, and therefore requires fixed review procedures and defined considerations. Overall, the analysis of intellectual property transactions involving concentrations of undertakings mainly consists of two parts: whether it constitutes a concentration of intellectual property transactions, and how to set additional conditions in cases where restrictive conditions are allowed.

7.3.2.1 Intellectual Property Transactions that Constitute Concentrations

When filing or reviewing for concentrations of undertakings, the first step is to determine whether the transaction constitutes a concentration of undertakings as defined in Article 25 of the *Anti-Monopoly Law* (2022). Secondly, when reviewing concentrations of undertakings regulated by the *Anti-Monopoly Law* (2022), antitrust enforcement authorities must make an objective assessment of the potential competitive impact of the concentration. Article 33 of the *Anti-Monopoly Law* (2022) lists several factors to be considered from multiple dimensions, however, due to the unique nature of intellectual property itself, special considerations is needed when defining the relevant market, assessing the control exerted by undertakings in the relevant market, and evaluating the impact of the concentration on market entry or technological progress. Article 12 of the newly released *Draft for Public Comment* yet to clarify these points, neither is this issue addressed in the *Draft Provisions on the Filing Standards* of *Concentrations of Undertakings (Draft for Public Comment)* by the State Council.

The factors listed in the *Antitrust Guidelines on Intellectual Property by the Antitrust Committee of the State Council* remain relevant for reference. These factors include: (1) Whether the intellectual property constitutes an independent business; (2)Whether the intellectual property generated independent and measurable revenue in the previous fiscal year; (3) The method and duration of the intellectual property licensing.[71]

---

[70] Article 33 of the *Anti-Monopoly Law* provides: "When reviewing business concentration, the following factors shall be considered: (1) the market share and market control of the participating undertakings in the relevant market; (2) the market concentration in the relevant market; (3) the impact of business concentration on market entry and technological progress; (4) the impact of business concentration on consumers and other relevant undertakings; (5) the impact of business concentration on national economic development; (6) other factors that the anti-monopoly enforcement agency of the State Council considers should be taken into account regarding the impact on market competition.".

[71] Anti-Monopoly Bureau, *Anti-Monopoly Guidelines for the Intellectual Property Field of the State Council Anti-Monopoly Committee*, Guo Fanlong Fa [2019] No. 2, issued on September 18, 2020.

According to the *Antitrust Guidelines on Intellectual Property by the Antitrust Committee* of the *State Council*, the assignment of intellectual property that constitutes an independent business may lead to concentrations of undertakings. If the revenue generated by such intellectual property exceeds the filing threshold, the transaction may need to be filed to relevant authorities as concentrations of undertakings.

7.3.2.2 Additional Restrictive Conditions

After antitrust enforcement authorities conduct a comprehensive assessment and determine that the intellectual property transaction constitutes a concentration of undertakings, the issues faced by the authorities become whether restrictive conditions should be attached to approve the concentration, and how to set such conditions. Conditional approvals mainly encompass structural conditions and behavioural conditions. Structural conditions refer to the divestment of the business involves the intellectual property. In previous cases on concentrations of undertakings, the Ministry of Commerce/Antitrust Bureau has attached divestment conditions related to R&D projects/products.[72] Behavioural conditions refer to measures such as compulsory licensing of intellectual property, maintaining the independent operation of intellectual property-related businesses, imposing constraints on intellectual property licensing conditions, and charging reasonable licensing fees. In some mergers and acquisition cases in the electronics industry, the Ministry of Commerce has also attached behavioural remedies related to the licensing of relevant patents.[73]

The recently released *Draft for Public Comment* introduces Article 13 which specifically addresses the issue of conditional approval. It outlines the restrictive conditions that may be imposed when approving concentrations of undertakings involving intellectual property. These conditions include both structural and behavioural remedies, specifically: (1) divesting intellectual property or the business related to intellectual property; (2) maintaining the independent operation of the intellectual property-related business; (3) licensing intellectual property under reasonable conditions; (4) other restrictive conditions.

According to the earlier *Antitrust Guidelines on Intellectual Property by the Antitrust Committee of the State Council*, other restrictive conditions may include

---

[72] Ministry of Commerce, 'Guanyu fujia xianzhixing tiaojian pizhun beikedun—Dijinsen gongsi yu meiguo bade gongsi hebing an jingyingzhe jizhong fanlongduan shencha jueding de gonggao' ['Announcement on the Antitrust review decision regarding the approval of the merger between Becton Dickinson and Bard with additive restrictive conditions'], Announcement No. 92 of 2017, original decision available at: http://fldj.mofcom.gov.cn/article/ztxx/201712/20171202691390.shtml.

[73] Ministry of Commerce, 'guanyu fujia xianzhixing tiaojian pizhun weiruan shougou nuojiya shebei he fuwu yewu an jingyingzhe jizhong fanlongduan shencha jueding de gonggao'[Announcement on the Antitrust Review Decision Regarding the Approval of Microsoft's Acquisition of Nokia's Devices and Services Business with Additive Restrictive Conditions], Ministry of Commerce Announcement No. 24 of 2014, original decision available at: http://www.mofcom.gov.cn/article/b/e/201404/20140400542508.shtml.

compulsory licensing of intellectual property and the requirement to charge reasonable licensing fees. Additionally, based on recent cases on concentrations of undertakings with conditional approval, the aforementioned restrictive conditions have generally been reflected in the relevant review decisions.

7.3.3 *Difficulties in the Traditional Analytical Framework and Breakthroughs*

7.3.3.1 Difficulties in Defining Relevant Markets

When intellectual property transactions involve concentrations of undertakings under antitrust law, the relevant market must first be defined in order to further determine whether the transaction falls within the scope of prohibited concentrations of undertakings under antitrust regulations. However, when cases of concentrations of undertakings involve intellectual property, due to the unique nature of intellectual property itself, difficulties often arise at the first step of defining the relevant market. In this regard, besides defining the general relevant product market and relevant geographic market, it may also be necessary to define the relevant technology market. In certain cases, it may even be necessary to define the relevant innovation market or to separately consider the impact of innovation factors on the definition of the relevant market.[74]

The relevant goods (including services) involving intellectual property often present in different forms. Some are manifested as products manufactured or services provided using intellectual property; some involve the separate licensing or assignment of intellectual property (such as related technologies); and yet others involve innovation activities like research and development of new technologies or products. Based on this, when defining the relevant market in the field of intellectual property, it is necessary to follow the general principles of market definition while also taking into account issues specific to intellectual property. Thus, on the one hand, the relevant product market and relevant geographic market must be defined from two basic dimensions as similar in other sectors; on the other hand, special issues involved in the intellectual property field must be analysed respectively.

The *Provisions on Prohibiting the Abuse of Intellectual Property to Exclude or Restrict Competition (Draft for Public Comment)* introduces two new types of markets: the relevant technology market and the relevant innovation market, and provides definitions for each. However, from the perspective of law enforcement practice, it is insufficient to simply provide the concepts without clear methods for defining these markets.

[74] Wang, X. (2016). 'Zhishi chanquan lingyu fanlongduan zhong xiangguan shichang jieding de teshu wenti'['The special issues of relevant market definition in Antitrust Law in the field of intellectual property']. *Jiage Lilun Yu Shijian* [*Price Theory and Practice*], 2, 49–53.

Major theoretical controversies of the concept of the innovation (R&D) relevant market The concept of the innovation market originated from the research and development (R&D) market concept in the *National Cooperative Research Act 1984* of the U.S. This act was the first to link market definition in antitrust enforcement with corporate R&D activities, requiring the evaluation of the competitive effects of cooperative research within properly defined relevant markets. It also suggested that the scope of the relevant market should include research and development, products, production processes, and services markets. The R&D market concept re-emerged in the *Antitrust Enforcement Guidelines for International Operations 1988*, it sets out provisions for R&D joint ventures and requires that an antitrust analysis should not only include the technologies and downstream products of the technology involved, but also the competitive effects of the joint ventures on the R&D market. While these laws link together corporate R&D activities, innovation, and antitrust analysis, nonetheless, they did not define the R&D market in a strict sense nor provide specific operational guidelines.

The formal concept of the innovation market originated from the *Antitrust Guidelines for the Licensing of Intellectual Property* jointly issued by the U.S. Department of Justice and the Federal Trade Commission in 1995. It specifically refers to the market formed by competition among undertakings in the research and development of future technologies or new products within a particular field.

The definition of the innovation market represents a new approach to antitrust issues from a dynamic perspective. It requires enforcers to recognize the role of innovation as a non-price competitive tool in promoting social welfare, and thus prevent the negative impact of monopolies on innovation. As a new concept, the innovation market has distinct characteristics compared to traditional product markets. These include: (1) no transactional behaviour; (2) maximizing inputs rather than outputs; (3) not focused on market share; (4) unilateral effects; (5) difficult to determine the optimal innovation market structure; (6) knowledge spillover.

The focus of analysing relevant innovation markets lies in research and development activities for products that have not yet been produced. It emphasizes the maximization of research inputs, making it difficult to determine market share. This is because undertakings, due to confidentiality requirements in their R&D activities, are typically reluctant to disclose their R&D inputs. Even if disclosed, there lacks a fair valuation criterion thus raising doubts as to the accuracy and reliability of such inputs. Therefore, whether and how to define the relevant innovation market is the primary issue that needs to be addressed when applying this concept.

The dilemma of innovation (R&D) related market in enforcement practice According to the *Provisions on Prohibiting the Abuse of Intellectual Property to Exclude or Restrict Competition (Draft for Public Comments)*, the relevant innovation market refers to a market formed by the competition among undertakings in the R&D of future new technologies or new products. Based on foreign practices and the enforcement practices of the antitrust authorities of China, the definition of relevant innovation markets should consider a range of factors related to intellectual property R&D investment. These factors include R&D costs, key R&D facilities, related assets, as well as the number of core technology R&D personnel with both R&D capabilities and motivations, and the evaluation of buyers and market participants.

However, when defining the relevant market in practice, considering innovation factors and introducing the concept of the relevant innovation market are two different things. The former refers to innovation as one of the comprehensive factors to be considered, while the latter, as a concept parallel to relevant product markets and relevant geographic markets, which requires a clearer method for definition. Although innovation factors have been considered in practice, there was no universal practical method established which can be consistently applied. In this circumstances, antitrust enforcement agencies may have an excessive discretionary power due to the lack of clear definition standards. And for undertakings, the enforcement actions of relevant authorities seem lack predictability and stability.

Development of the contemporary theory and improvement strategies Article 26 of the *Anti-Monopoly Law* (2022), Article 12 of the *Provisions on Prohibiting the Abuse of Intellectual Property to Exclude or Restrict Competition (Draft for Comments)*, and Article 5 of the *Regulations on the Standards for the Notification of Concentrations of undertakings (Draft for Comments)* together form the current normative foundation for concentrations of undertakings reviews. They primarily regulate behaviours in which intellectual property transactions lead to control or influence over the parties involved in the transaction. At the same time, these provisions require concentrations of undertakings to be notified for review, conducting substantial investigations into potential behaviours that may exclude or restrict competition, and impose a burden on undertakings to provide evidence to prove their behaviours do not or will not create anti-competitive effects.

Based on the above laws and draft regulations, it is evident that the main legal risks faced by intellectual property transactions under the category of concentrations of undertakings, which is a form of monopoly behaviour, are the standards for determining whether control has been acquired or whether a decisive influence can be exerted, and how to define the exclusionary or restrictive competition effects in situations that meet the aforementioned criteria. These two points are also the key challenges for antitrust enforcement agencies during the review of concentrations of undertaking.

The review of concentrations of undertakings is essentially a forecast of competitive issues. According to Article 4 of the *Review Regulations on Concentrations of Undertakings (Draft for Comments)*, which lists eight factors for determining whether a concentration of undertakings results in the acquisition of control over or decisive influence on other undertakings,[75] the assessment of 'whether control over

[75] See *Regulations on the Review of Business Concentration (Draft for Public Comments)*, Article 4: (1) The purpose and future plans of the transaction; (2) The shareholding structure of other undertakings before and after the transaction and the changes thereof; (3) The voting matters and voting mechanism of the shareholders' meeting or other governing bodies of other undertakings, as well as their historical attendance rates and voting situations; (4) The composition and voting mechanism of the board of directors or other decision-making or executive bodies of other undertakings; (5) The appointment and dismissal of senior management of other undertakings; (6) The relationships between shareholders and directors of other undertakings, including whether there is proxy voting

other undertakings or the ability to exert decisive influence through the transaction' can be summarized into three main aspects: (1) motives and objectives of the transaction; (2) the transaction method; (3) the specific issues related to the intellectual property itself.

The examination of the motives and objectives primarily aims to determine whether the intellectual property constitutes a substantial part of the concentrations of undertakings. When intellectual property is considered a substantial part of the concentrations of undertakings, its unique characteristics must be taken into account during the review process. Regarding the transaction method, different approaches such as mergers, joint ventures, and equity acquisitions involve different intellectual property issues, which need to be considered based on specific circumstances of each case.

7.4 Antitrust Regulation of Anti-Competitive Coordinated Behaviour in Intellectual Property Transactions

This section corresponds to the monopoly agreements regulated under antitrust law. The distinction between the monopoly agreements involving collusion in this section and those in Sect. 6.2 lies in the subject matter. Section 6.2 mainly concerns licensing behaviour, which involves both monopoly agreements and the abuse of a dominant position. In contrast, this section does not address licensing but primarily focuses on the collusion in the context of intellectual property transactions.

7.4.1 Specific Manifestations of Collusion in Intellectual Property Transactions that Trigger Antitrust Regulation

Collusion refers to actions in which two or more undertakings, by way of agreements or other forms, collectively agree to restrict competition in a specific market.[76] Therefore, it is manifested as the conduct of undertakings reaching and implementing monopoly agreements. Article 16 of the *Anti-Monopoly Law* of China defines monopoly agreements as agreements, decisions, or other coordinated actions that exclude or restrict competition. This behaviour can be categorized into horizontal collusion, vertical collusion, and mixed collusion based on the relationship between the participating undertakings. A horizontal relationship refers to a direct competitive relationship between undertakings, while a vertical relationship refers to the buyer–seller relationship between two or more undertakings at different phases

or concerted actions; (7) Whether the undertakings have significant commercial relationships or cooperation agreements with other undertakings; (8) Other factors that should be considered.

[76] Cao, S. (1996). *Fanlongduanfa yanjiu* [*Anti-Monopoly Law Research*]. Falv Chubanshe [Legal Publishing House]. 206.

within the same industry.[77] Based on the specific form of conduct, it can be further classified as: agreement-based collusion, resolution-based collusion, and other coordinated actions. Since the previous section has already summarized vertical collusion within the field of intellectual property, this section, in conjunction with the rules on horizontal monopoly agreements in Article 17 of the *Antitrust Law*, summarizes the types of horizontal collusion in the intellectual property field that warrant attention.

7.4.1.1 Restrictions on Production or Sales

Article 17 of the *Anti-Monopoly Law* of China provides that horizontal monopoly agreements include agreements that restrict the quantity of goods for production and sale. This behaviour, known as a quantity cartel, refers to a monopoly agreement between competitors to limit the quantities of goods they produce or sell, thereby indirectly controlling prices.[78] When undertakings restrict production or sales, they disrupt the normal supply and demand dynamics of the market, leading to price increases and enabling the long-term implementation of price-fixing. This not only reduces consumer choices but may also result in the 'bad money driving out the good', with high-quality firms being squeezed out by inferior firms involved in the quantity cartel. In the field of intellectual property, monopoly agreements involving quantity restrictions are analysed in accordance with antitrust law. Although in intellectual property licensing, the parties are typically in a vertical relationship, such agreements often involve horizontal relationships at the same time.[79] Therefore, restrictions on the quantities of production or sales are a common feature in intellectual property licensing agreements. What needs to be noted in intellectual property licensing agreements is the limitation of maximum production or sales quantities. The harm of quantity cartels lies in artificially creating market tension and distorting price functions, while limiting a maximum quantity is highly likely to reduce the market supply of intellectual property products.[80]

7.4.1.2 Division of the Intellectual Property Sales Market

Article 17 of *Anti-Monopoly Law* of China stipulates that the content of horizontal monopoly agreements includes the restriction of dividing the sales market or raw

---

[77] Li, X. & Su, H. (2007). 'Fanlongduan fa zhong lianhe xianzhi jingzheng xingwei de bijiao yanjiu'. ['A comparative study of joint restrictive competition behaviors in Anti-Monopoly Law']. *Faxue Luntan* [*Legal Forum*], 5, 62.

[78] Meng, Y. (2017). *Fanlongduan fa* [*Anti-Monopoly Law*]. Beijing Daxue Chubanshe [Beijing University Press]. 108.

[79] Wang, X. (2020). *Zhishi chanquan yu fanlongduan fa——zhishi chanquan lanyong de fanlongduan wenti yanjiu (di san ban)* [*Intellectual property and antitrust law: a study on the antitrust issues of intellectual property abuse (3rd edition)*], Falv Chubanshe [Legal Publishing House]. 224.

[80] Shi, Y. (2013). 'Zhishi chanquan lingyu fanlongduan wenti yanjiu' ['Research on Antitrust issues in the field of intellectual property']. Master's thesis, Shandong University. 10.

material procurement market. Market division refers to the act of competitors jointly defining or dividing regional markets, customer markets, or product markets.[81] In the field of intellectual property, it generally refers to the division of sales markets. Unlike restrictions on production or sales and fixed pricing, market division is an indirect control over prices, as undertakings agree on their respective sales areas to avoid competition. At the same time, the EU adheres to the principle of prohibiting licensing conditions that create absolute territorial protection when regulating market division involving intellectual property, as this would isolate a market from competition, in violation of Article 81 of the *Treaty establishing the European Community*.

7.4.1.3 Group Boycotts the Deal

Article 17 of *Anti-Monopoly Law* of China stipulates that the content of horizontal monopoly agreements includes group boycotts the deal. This behaviour, also known as concerted refusals to deal, refers to the act of competitors joining together to collectively refuse to engage in transactions with other competitors, suppliers, or customers.[82] Group boycotts deprive other undertakings of the choice to participate in competition, thereby undermining market competition rules. Taking licensing behaviour as an example, the refusal by a single intellectual property right holder may have a negligible negative impact on market competition, but the concerted refusals by multiple intellectual property right holders clearly restricts competition and has almost no positive effect in promoting competition.

7.4.2 Application of the Traditional Analytical Framework

The principles of per se illegality and the rule of reason originated from the British system of regulation on restrictive trade agreements. They were formally established through the application of the first and second provisions of the *Sherman Act* by the U.S. Supreme Court in its adjudication of the *Standard Oil* and *American Tobacco* cases.[83] These two principles were initially used to regulate monopoly agreements but were later widely applied to all anti-competitive conducts with the distinction being gradually blurred. Instead, they can be viewed as two parts of a holistic analysis.[84]

---

[81] Meng, Y. (2017). *Fanlongduan fa* [*Anti-Monopoly Law*]. Beijing Daxue Chubanshe [Beijing University Press].109.

[82] Ibid., 112.

[83] Ibid., 134.

[84] Wang, X. (2009). *Jingzheng faxue* [*Competition Law*]. Zhongguo Renmin Daxue Chubanshe [China Renmin University Press]. 246–247.

7.4.2.1 Determination Based on Per Se Illegality

The principle of per se illegality refers to certain exclusionary or restrictive competitive behaviours in the market that can be directly deemed to harm competition and should be prohibited, without further need to consider the specific circumstances and consequences of the behaviour.[85] This is essentially a principle of determination based on experience. Since these anti-competitive behaviours (such as price cartels and quantity cartels) have a severe negative impact on market competition, and their destructive effects are clear and stable which cannot be changed substantially by external factors. As such, these anti-competitive behaviours can be directly deemed illegal without the need for a competitive effects analysis. This principle means 'illegal by existence'. Thus, the focus of the per se illegality principle lies in the positioning of the facts.[86]

The advantages of the principle of per se illegality are mainly as follows: (1) It categorizes monopoly behaviours in advance, making its application simple and significantly saving enforcement and judicial resources. At the same time, by simplifying the procedures of investigation and evidence collection by enforcement agencies and courts, it reduces the time and financial investment required from the parties involved, avoiding the lengthy and burdensome litigation process that is time-consuming and labour-intensive. Additionally, the prompt decisions made by the relevant authorities can shorten the time during which the market is disrupted, helping to quickly restore order and bringing market competition back on track. (2) It reflects the value of legal certainty. Under the guidance of clear and definite behavioural guidelines, undertakings can foresee the consequences of their actions. On one hand, when an undertaking's behaviour is subject to the per se illegality principle, the undertaking can reasonably expect the responsibility it will bear (such as the amount of fines), which helps avoid other disputes and conflicts. On the other hand, the undertaking can attempt and develop other competitive methods outside the scope of the per se illegal behaviours, which stimulates market dynamism and promotes technological progress, among other things. (3) It has a preventive effect. Because under this principle, once a behaviour that falls under per se illegality is proven, the undertaking will inevitably bear legal liability, thereby pressuring undertakings to standardize their operations and avoid engaging in such behaviour.

The main flaw of the principle of per se illegality is that it may harm fairness and justice, while sacrificing economic efficiency. Based on experience, the principle regulates behaviours that significantly harm market competition, but as with any experience-based approach, there are exceptions. The simplified standard used in the per se illegality principle may lead to certain behaviours being deemed illegal without sufficient proof, as it skips the analysis of competitive effects, thus not being conducive to maintaining fairness and justice. Moreover, this oversight of the

[85] Wang, B. (1999). *Jingjifa yuanli* [*Principles of Economic Law*]. Shehui Kexue Wenxian Chubanshe [Social Sciences Academic Press]. 230–231.

[86] Chen, C. (2012). 'Zhishi chanquan lanyong de fanlongduan guizhi yanjiu' ['Research on the Antitrust regulation of intellectual property abuse']. Fudan University. 16.

complexity of economic behaviour can lead to errors that are detrimental to the improvement of economic efficiency.

Based on the above analysis, various countries have made adjustments to the application of the principle of per se illegality. For instance, in recent years, U.S. courts have developed two distinct forms of the principle of per se illegality: the pure per se illegality principle and the modified per se illegality principle. Additionally, monopoly agreements involving small market shares are no longer automatically subject to the per se illegality principle but are instead subject to the rule of reason.[87] In contrast, China has adopted a 'prohibition + exemption' legislative model in its *Anti-Monopoly Law*. In intellectual property licensing agreements, if they include restrictive clauses that clearly exceed the scope of the intellectual property, such as the typical horizontal restrictions mentioned in Part (1) of this section—such as output limitations, market division, and group boycotts the deal—they constitute typical collusive monopoly behaviours. Furthermore, price restriction behaviours in vertical monopoly agreements can generally be subject to the per se illegality principle for determination.

7.4.2.2 Determination Based on the Rule of Reason

The rule of reason, also known as the 'harm prohibition' principle, refers to the situation where the restriction caused by certain competitive behaviours or conditions is relatively unclear, making it impossible to determine that they are inherently illegal. Therefore, a judgment must be made after considering factors such as the subjective purpose of the undertaking, method of conduct, and the consequences of the behaviour. Subjectively, it requires the presence of an intention to monopolize; objectively, the behaviour must not be based on 'legitimate means' and must result in a substantial restriction on competition for it to be deemed illegal.[88] Whether the intent of the undertaking is legitimate and whether the means to achieve that intent are reasonable depend on the discretion of the judge. When applying the rule of reason, EU courts generally consider factors such as the market share, market position, financial resources, product range, trade volume, entry barriers, and the scope of the impact of the behaviour of the undertaking.

The advantages of the rule of reason are mainly as follows: (1) It compensates for the flaw of the per se illegality principle, which is based on experience but lacks sufficient reasoning, making the determination of illegality more justified. (2) The rule of reason grants enforcement agencies and courts discretionary power, enabling them to consider the actual situation comprehensively when regulating competitive behaviours, thereby promoting the overall social benefit and ensuring economic efficiency.

---

[87] Meng, Y. (2017). *Fanlongduan fa* [*Antitrust Law*]. Beijing Daxue Chubanshe [Peking University Press]. 137.

[88] Meng, Y. (2017). *Fanlongduan fa* [*Antitrust Law*]. Beijing Daxue Chubanshe [Peking University Press]. 138.

On the other hand, the flaws of the rule of reason are mainly as follows: (1) It increases the cost of enforcement and judicial proceedings, and the review process may take longer. (2) The expansion of discretionary power raises concerns as to the fairness of public policies. Due to the limitations of human knowledge and the ambiguity of textual interpretation, public decision-makers inevitably face the possibility of erroneous or abusive exercise of discretion. (3) The application of the rule of reason increases the uncertainty of corporate behaviour. In intellectual property licensing agreements, certain restrictive clauses or unreasonable conditions may contain some reasonable factors while could also be abused, therefore, the rule of reason can be applied in its determination.

7.4.3 Difficulties in the Traditional Analytical Framework and Breakthroughs

7.4.3.1 Dilemma in the Existing Analytical Approach

Drawing on the experiences of the U.S. and the EU, China has currently established the application of the per se illegality principle to horizontal agreements such as price-fixing, output restriction, market division, group boycotts, and vertical resale price maintenance agreements. However, not all agreements that impact prices are deemed per se illegal. Article 20 of the *Anti-Monopoly Law* (2022) clearly stipulates that some cooperative behaviours conducted by groups and organizations aimed at achieving beneficial objectives may be exempt from antitrust regulation. The rule of reason must be applied to make a judgment as for which agreements meet the statutory conditions. In summary, the transition from the per se illegality principle to the rule of reason has become a general trend. It must be acknowledged that the superiority of the rule of reason is particularly evident today, where anti-competitive behaviours are becoming increasingly diverse and concealed, and their anti-competitive effects are becoming stronger and long lasting. This is especially true in antitrust issues related to intellectual property, where the application of the rule of reason is justified. The realization of intellectual property manifests dynamic efficiency because, even if the intellectual property holder currently holds dominant power in the relevant market, they will inevitably be replaced by new innovative products at some point in the future, that why Schumpeter described it as dynamic competition,[89] therefore dynamic analysis and value judgment are needed, whereas the per se illegality principle is a direct result-based approach,[90] focusing on factual issues that do not require value judgment.

---

[89] Schumpeter, J. (1976). *Capitalism, socialism, and democracy*. Routledge. 84.

[90] Zhang, S. (2020). 'Jieguolun yu mudilun: longduan xieyi rending de falv yuanli' ['Outcome and purpose: Legal principles in the identification of Antitrust agreements']. *Zhongwai Faxue* [*Political and Legal Review*], 3, 5.

However, the application of the rule of reason also presents some difficulties and has given rise to new issues. For example, the rule of reason increases institutional costs in areas such as compliance and rent-seeking prevention.[91] First, it is extremely difficult to fulfil the burden of proof in private litigations. In the case of *Qihoo vs. Tencent* in 2013 concerning abuse of dominant position, the court dismissed the case due to unclear market definition or erroneous determination on dominant position. This type of evidentiary work is overly stringent for the plaintiff, leading to almost no success for plaintiffs in antitrust law cases within the five years since its implementation. This 'zero breakthrough' was only achieved on August 1, 2013, when the Beijing Rui BangYong He Ltd. won the case against Johnson & Johnson (Shanghai) and Johnson & Johnson (China) for reaching a minimum resale price maintenance agreement. Second, although antitrust law enforcement agencies have stronger investigative and evidentiary abilities in public enforcement, there is an excessively high requirement on the analytical skills of enforcement staffs, especially their ability to predict the potential harm that relevant behaviours may cause to competition.[92] Finally, the rule of reason is considered one of the most ambiguous and open rules in the field of antitrust law,[93] whereas the universal applicability of law requires a certain level of abstraction, certainty, and predictability. As such, the rule of reason may conflict with the normative nature of the law. On one hand, this conflict weakens the deterrent effect of antitrust law, potentially leading undertakings to engage in speculative behaviour driven by profit motives. On the other hand, it could result in a deviation in the cost/benefit analysis of legal regulation. Therefore, the various issues surrounding the application of the rule of reason are gradually giving rise to further thinkings.

7.4.3.2 The Development of the Contemporary Theories and Its Improvement Strategies

In response to the aforementioned issues, Judge Easterbrook proposed the error-cost analysis theory, which classifies anti-competitive behaviours into two types of errors: the cost of false negatives (classifying anti-competitive behaviours as legal) and the cost of false positives (classifying benign behaviours as illegal). Due to practical constraints, these error costs cannot be fully eliminated. However, the cost of false negatives is generally acceptable because most market behaviours are beneficial, and

---

[91] Li, J. (2019). 'Zhidu chengben yu guifanhua de fanlongduan fa——Dangran weifa yuanze de huigui' ['Institutional costs and the normalization of Antitrust Law: The return of the per se illegality rule']. *Zhongwai Faxue* [*Chinese and Foreign Law Review*], 4, 1012.

[92] Yang, Y. (2017). 'Heli yuanze zai yu zhishi chanquan xiangguan de fanlongduan wenti zhong de shiyong——Lilun shang de helixing ji zhixingzhong de kunnan' ['Application of the reasonableness principle in Antitrust issues related to intellectual property: Theoretical rationality and practical difficulties']. *Tianfu Xinlun* [*Tianfu New Discussion*], 1, 136.

[93] Robertson, E. L. (2009). 'Does antitrust regulation violate the rule of law?'. *Loyola Consumer Law Review*, 22(1), 109.

correcting monopolistic behaviours is easier for the economic system than correcting judicial errors.[94] This theory aligns with the expansion of the rule of reason.

However, there are alternative views within academia. Li Jian argues that the premise for the universal applicability of legal regulation is to abstract the regulatory object so as to identify its most core attributes. When facing with real-world diversity, the task on typology should be gradually improved, and the repeated application of rules can reduce institutional costs. The current insufficient application of the per se illegality principle is because the typological analysis is not deep and detailed enough.[95] Lan Lei acknowledges the importance of typology but believes that current theoretical and practical understanding of the rule of reason remains at a rough stage that has persisted for the past century. As a result, there is a fear of difficulty, not because of the ambiguity of legal norms in antitrust law, but because regulating monopoly behaviours inevitably requires high costs.[96] Furthermore, the ambiguity of legal norms is not unique to antitrust law.

The analysis of the legality of monopolistic behaviour has always been the most challenging issue in antitrust law. The debate among scholars regarding the per se illegality principle and the rule of reason ultimately revolves around the core idea of focusing on the essence of competitive behaviour in the analysis. This perspective emphasizes that monopolistic behaviour, in certain circumstances, may have positive effects and should not be deemed illegal simply because it has negative effects. Instead, a further analysis is required to determine whether the monopolistic behaviour should be exempted.

Currently, there exists a compromised approach between empirical judgment and economic efficiency analysis, namely the fast-track review principle. This is not an independent concept but rather a phased interpretation of the burden of proof in the absence of relevant judicial experience, which can alleviate the difficulties faced by plaintiffs in proving their case to a certain extent.

7.5 Summary of This Chapter

This chapter discusses the regulation of monopolistic behaviours arising from intellectual property transactions. Based on the fundamental premise that monopolistic conducts caused by intellectual property transactions should be corrected, and because intellectual property protection will ultimately enter and foster market competition through innovation, it is necessary to encourage the development of

[94] Easterbrook, F. H. (1984). 'The limits of antitrust'. *Texas Law Review*, 63, 1.

[95] Li, J. (2019). 'Zhidu chengben yu guifanhua de fanlongduan fa——dangran weifa yuanze de huigui' ['Institutional costs and the normalization of Antitrust Law: The return of the per se illegality rule']. *Zhongwai Faxue* [*Chinese and Foreign Law Review*], 4, 1012.1018–1019.

[96] Lan, L. (2020). 'Chonggu de heli yuanze de zhidu chengben——Jianping < zhidu chengben yu guifanhua de fanlongduan fa > ' ['Reevaluating the institutional costs of the reasonable principle: A review of institutional costs and the standardization of Antitrust Law']. Jingmao Falv Pinglun [*Economic and Trade Law Review*], 3, 102–126.

intellectual property within the legal scope of protection. However, there are boundaries for the exercise of any rights, thus abuses of intellectual property rights should also be regulated. As the core system of fair competition policy, antitrust law plays an important role in regulating the abuse of intellectual property rights. Therefore, the intersection of intellectual property protection and antitrust law primarily lies in how to regulate behaviours that abuse intellectual property to exclude or restrict competition within the antitrust legal framework.

At the same time, based on the typological analysis of intellectual property transaction behaviours, this book also conducts a detailed study of monopolistic issues. It addresses the potential monopolistic phenomena that may arise, the application of existing antitrust legal rules, and the challenges in determining the nature of the behaviours and defining the regulatory content within the current analytical frameworks. Additionally, it provides suggestions on how to overcome these difficulties. There exist ambiguities in applying the anti-trust rules to intellectual property licensing, assignment, and collusive anti-competitive behaviours in the current antitrust regulatory framework, meanwhile, the existing framework is impacted by the network effects from the internet. Nevertheless, given the responsive capacity of the existing legal framework, alongside the development of new theoretical approaches, a clearer path for identifying and regulating new forms of monopolistic behaviour is emerging.

References

Albon, R. (1994). Interconnection pricing: An analysis of the efficient component pricing rule. *Telecommunications Policy, 18*(5), 414–420.

Baumol, W. J., & Sidak, J. G. (1994). The pricing of inputs sold to competitors. *Yale Journal on Regulation, 11*(1), 171–202.

Bork, R. H. (1978). *The antitrust paradox: A policy at war with itself*. Free Press.

Cao, S. (1996). *Fanlongduanfa yanjiu* [*Anti-Monopoly Law Research*]. Falv Chubanshe [Legal Publishing House].

Chen, C. (2012). *Zhishi chanquan lanyong de fanlongduan guizhi yanjiu [Research on the Antitrust regulation of intellectual property abuse]*. Fudan University.

Chen, S. (2013). Hulianwang chanye zhong xiangguan shangpin shichang jieding——yi qihu 360 su tengxun lanyong shichang zhipei diwei an weili [Defining the Relevant Product Market in the Internet Industry: A Case Study of Qihoo 360 v. Tencent on Abuse of Market Dominance]. *Yichun Xueyaun Xuebao [Journal of Yichun University], 11*, 31.

Dong, D. (2012). Zhong guo <Fan Long Duan Fa> di 55 tiao de jie shi yu shi yong [Interpretation and application of Article 55 of China's Anti-Monopoly Law]. *Chongqing Ligong Daxue Xuebao (Shehui Kexue Ban) [Journal of Chongqing University of Technology (Social Science Edition)], 5*, 54–58.

Easterbrook, F. H. (1984). The limits of antitrust. *Texas Law Review, 63*, 1.

Fei, A. (2008). Lun fang zhi zhi shi chan quan lan yong de zhi du li nian ['On the institutional concept of preventing the abuse of intellectual property]. *Zhishi Chanquan [Intellectual Property], 3*, 5.

Gold, Y. (2022, May 13). Shijie zhishi chanquan zuzhi: Shuzihua chuangxin zai 20 niannei fanle liangfan [World Intellectual Property Organization: Digital Innovation Quadrupled in 20 Years]. *Diyi Caijing Ribao [First Financial Daily]*, p. A06

Gu, L. (2020) Shuzi yinyue dujia baiquan moshi fanlongduan fa wenti yanjiu [Study on antitrust issues in the exclusive copyright model of digital music]. Master's thesis, Beijing Foreign Studies University.

Hovenkamp, H. (2005). *The antitrust enterprise: Principle and execution*. Harvard University Press.

Howard, M. C. (1983). *Antitrust and trade regulation: Selected issues and case studies*. Prentice-Hall.

Hui, C. (2006). Zhishi chanquan xuk zhong de jignzhengfa wenti yanjiu [A study on competition law issues in intellectual property licensing]. Duiwai Jingji Maoyi Daxue [University of International Business and Economics], PhD dissertation.

Inoua, S. M., & Smith, V. L. (2022). Price formation: Overview of the theory. In S. M. Inoua & V. L. Smith (Eds.), *Economics of markets* (pp. 39–92). Palgrave Macmillan.

Jiang, Y. (2019). Shuzi yinyue zhuzuoquan xuke moshi tanjiu——jianyi fading xuke de biyaoxing ji qi zhidu goujian [A study on the licensing model of digital music copyright—With a discussion on the necessity of statutory licensing and its system construction]. *Dongfang Faxue [Eastern Law Review], 1*, 147–160.

Kaplow, L. (2013). Market definition: Impossible and counterproductive. *Antitrust Law Journal, 79*(1), 361–379.

Kingsbury, A. F. (2004). Market definition in intellectual property law: Should intellectual property courts use an antitrust approach to market definition? *Marquette Intellectual Property Law Review, 9*(1), 64–92.

Kong, X. (2001). *Fanlongduanfa yuanli* [*Principles of Antitrust Law*]. Zhongguo Fazhi Chubanshe [China Legal Publishing House].

Lan, L. (2020). Chonggu de heli yuanze de zhidu chengben——Jianping <zhidu chengben yu guifanhua de fanlongduan fa> ['Reevaluating the institutional costs of the reasonable principle: A review of institutional costs and the standardization of Antitrust Law]. *Jingmao Falv Pinglun [Economic and Trade Law Review], 3*, 102–126.

Li, J. (2019). Zhidu chengben yu guifanhua de fanlongduan fa——Dangran weifa yuanze de huigui [Institutional costs and the normalization of Antitrust Law: The return of the per se illegality rule]. *Zhongwai Faxue [Chinese and Foreign Law Review], 4*, 1012.

Li, X., & Su, H. (2007). Fanlongduan fa zhong lianhe xianzhi jingzheng xingwei de bijiao yanjiu [A comparative study of joint restrictive competition behaviors in Anti-Monopoly Law]. *Faxue Luntan [Legal Forum], 5*, 62.

Liu, Y. (2006). Zhishi chanquan jujue xuke de fanlongduanfa yanjiu——Yi zhuanliquan de jujue xuke wei zhongxin [Antitrust law research on the refusal to license intellectual property—Focusing on patent refusal to license]. Master's Thesis, East China University of Political Science and Law.

Meng, Y. (2013). Hulianwang hangye xiangguan shichang jieding de tiaozhan——Yi qihu su teng xun fanlongduan an panjue wei lizheng [Challenges in defining relevant markets in the internet industry—A case study of Qihoo v. Tencent Antitrust Ruling]. *Dianzi Zhishi Chanquan [Electronic Intellectual Property], 4*, 42–45.

Meng, Y. (2017). *Fanlongduan fa* [*Anti-Monopoly Law*]. Beijing Daxue Chubanshe [Beijing University Press].

Ministry of Commerce, Guanyu fujia xianzhixing tiaojian pizhun beikedun—Dijinsen gongsi yu meiguo bade gongsi hebing an jingyingzhe jizhong fanlongduan shencha jueding de gonggao [Announcement on the Antitrust review decision regarding the approval of the merger between Becton Dickinson and Bard with additive restrictive conditions], Announcement No. 92 of 2017, original decision. http://fldj.mofcom.gov.cn/article/ztxx/201712/20171202691390.shtml.

Ministry of Commerce, Guanyu fujia xianzhixing tiaojian pizhun weiruan shougou nuojiya shebei he fuwu yewu an jingyingzhe jizhong fanlongduan shencha jueding de gonggao [Announcement on the Antitrust Review Decision Regarding the Approval of Microsoft's Acquisition of Nokia's Devices and Services Business with Additive Restrictive Conditions], Ministry of Commerce Announcement No. 24 of 2014, original decision. http://www.mofcom.gov.cn/article/b/e/201404/20140400542508.shtml.

Ning, L. (2010). Zhuanli dashou xuke de fanlongduanfa fenxi [Antitrust analysis of patent tying licenses]. *Shanghai Jiaotong Daxue Xuebao(Zhexue Shehui Kexue Ban) [Journal of Shanghai Jiao Tong University (Philosophy and Social Sciences Edition)], 4*, 5–6.

Ordover, J. A., & Willig, R. D. (1981). An economic definition of predation: Pricing and product innovation. *Yale Law Journal, 91*(1), 8–53.

Qiao, S., & Tao, X. (2005). Woguo xianzhi zhishi chanquan lanyong de falv sikao [Legal thoughts on restricting the abuse of intellectual property in china]. *Xiandai Faxue [Modern Law Science], 1*, 112.

Robertson, E. L. (2009). Does antitrust regulation violate the rule of law? *Loyola Consumer Law Review, 22*(1), 109.

Schumpeter, J. (1976). *Capitalism, socialism, and democracy*. Routledge.

Shi, W., & Ren, T. (2020). Chuangxin xiaolu shijiao xia SEP jujue xuke xingwei de fanlongduan fa zeren fenxi——Yi FTC su gaotong an wei qieru [Analysis of Antitrust liability for SEP refusal to license from the perspective of innovation efficiency—A case study of FTC v. Qualcomm]. *Keji Guanli Yanjiu [Science and Technology Management Research], 17*, 133–141.

Shi, Y. (2013). Zhishi chanquan lingyu fanlongduan wenti yanjiu [Research on Antitrust issues in the field of intellectual property]. Master's thesis, Shandong University.

State Administration for Market Regulation, 2021. Zhong guo fan long duan zhi fa nian du bao gao (2021) [China Antitrust Enforcement Annual Report (2021)]. https://www.samr.gov.cn/xw/zj/202206/t20220608_347582.html. Accessed on 11 August 2022.

State Council, 2021. "Shi Si Wu" guo jia zhi shi chan quan bao hu he yun yong gui hua [14th Five-Year Plan for National Intellectual Property Protection and Utilization]. http://www.gov.cn/xinwen/2021-10/28/content_5647335.htm. Accessed on 14 July 2022.

Tencent. (2022). Shuzi shidai: renshi shuzi jingji chanye xianzhuang [Digital Age: Understanding the current state of the digital economy industry]. https://new.qq.com/omn/20220419/20220419A01PBL00.html. Accessed on 23 July 2022.

The Central Committee of the Communist Party of China and the State Council, Zhishi chanquan qiangguo jianshe gangyao(2021–2035) [*Outline for Building a Strong Intellectual Property Nation (2021–2035)*]. Available at the official website of the Chinese government: http://www.gov.cn/zhengce/2021-09/22/content_5638714.htm. Accessed on July 20, 2022.

Tong, X. (2022). Dali fazhan zhishi chanquan jinrong zhuli keji chengguo zhuanyi zhuanhua [Vigorously develop intellectual property finance to promote the transfer and transformation of scientific and technological achievements]. *Chanquan Daohang [Property Navigation], 1*, 32.

Wang, B. (1999). *Jingjifa yuanli [Principles of Economic Law]* (pp. 230–231). Shehui Kexue Wenxian Chubanshe [Social Sciences Academic Press].

Wang, M. Q. (2007). Woguo zhuanliquan lanyong falv tiaozheng de guidingxing [The normative nature of legal regulation on the abuse of patent rights in China]. In *State Intellectual Property Office*: *Zhuanlifa Yanjiu [Research on Patent Law (2006)]*. Zhishi Chanquan Chubanshe [Intellectual Property Publishing House].

Wang, X. (2004). Zhishi chanquan lanyong xingwei de fanlongduanfa guizhi [Antitrust regulation of intellectual property abuse]. *Fa Xue [Jurisprudence], 3*, 100–106.

Wang, X. (2008). Zhishi chanquan yu fanlongduanfa: zhishi chanquan lanyong de fanlongduanfa wenti yanjiu (xiu ding ban) [*Intellectual property and antitrust law: A study of antitrust issues in intellectual property abuse (Revised Edition)*]. Legal Publishing House.

Wang, X. (2009). Jingzhengfa shiye de zhishi chanquan wenti lungang [An outline of intellectual property issues from the perspective of competition law]. *Zhonguo Faxue [Chinese Law Journal], 4*, 5–15.

Wang, X. (2009). *Jingzheng faxue [Competition Law]* (pp. 246–247). Zhongguo Renmin Daxue Chubanshe [China Renmin University Press].

Wang, X. (2011). *Fanlongduan fa [Anti-Monopoly Law]*. Falv Chubanshe [Law Press].

Wang, X. (2013). Woguo fa longduanfa shiyong yu zhishi chanquan lingyu de zai sikao [Reconsideration of the application of China's Anti-Monopoly Law to the field of intellectual property]. *Nanjing Daxue Xuebao(Zhexue, Renwen Kexue, Shehui Kexue Ban) [Journal of Nanjing University (Philosophy, Humanities, and Social Sciences Edition)], 1*, 34–43.

Wang, X. (2016). Zhishi chanquan lingyu fanlongduan zhong xiangguan shichang jieding de teshu wenti [The special issues of relevant market definition in Antitrust Law in the field of intellectual property]. *Jiage Lilun Yu Shijian [Price Theory and Practice], 2*, 49–53.

Wang, X. (2019). Lun woguo fanlongduanfa zai zhishi chanquan lingyu de shishi [On the implementation of China's Anti-Monopoly Law in the field of intellectual property]. *Shanghai Jiaotong Daxue Xuebao(Zhexue Shehui Kexue Ban) [Journal of Shanghai Jiao Tong University (Philosophy and Social Science Edition)], 6*, 19.

Wang, X. (2020). *Zhishi chanquan yu fanlongduan fa——zhishi chanquan lanyong de fanlongduan wenti yanjiu (di san ban) [Intellectual property and antitrust law: a study on the antitrust issues of intellectual property abuse (3rd edition)].* Falv Chubanshe [Legal Publishing House].

Xu, G. (2017). Zongxiang jiage xianzhi de fanlongduan fa lilun yu anli kaocha [Antitrust law theory and case study on vertical price restrictions]. *Zhengfa Luncong [Political and Legal Studies Journal], 1*, 3–13.

Yang, D. (2020). Lun fanlongduanfa de chonggou: Yingdui shuzi jingji de tiaozhan [On the reconstruction of Antitrust Law: Addressing the challenges of the digital economy]. *Zhongguo Faxue [China Legal Science], 3*, 214–215.

Yang, M. (2022) Ruhe kandai pingtai de zongxiang yitihua celue? [How to View the Vertical Integration Strategy of Platforms?]. Hexun. http://tech.hexun.com/2022-07-19/206392841.html. Accessed on 25 July 2022.

Yang, M. (2022). Pingtai jingji fanlongduan de eryuan fenxi kuangjia [A dual analysis framework for antitrust in the platform economy]. *Zhongwai Faxue [Chinese and Foreign Legal Studies], 2*, 381–383.

Yang, Y. (2017). Heli yuanze zai yu zhishi chanquan xiangguan de fanlongduan wenti zhong de shiyong——lilun shang de helixing ji zhixingzhong de kunnan [Application of the reasonableness principle in Antitrust issues related to intellectual property: Theoretical rationality and practical difficulties]. *Tianfu Xinlun [Tianfu New Discussion], 1*, 136.

Yaopin zhuanlichi shouquan fangzhi Huirui xinguan ko fuyao chengfen, 5 jia zhongguo yaoqi huo xuke [Drug Patent Pool Authorizes Generic Manufacture of Pfizer's COVID-19 Oral Drug Ingredients, 5 Chinese Pharmaceutical Companies Granted Licenses]. Sina Finance. https://finance.sina.com.cn/chanjing/cyxw/2022-03-17/doc-imcwipih9019709.shtml. Accessed on 25 July 2022.

Yuan, X. (2008). *Zhishi chanquan jujue xuke de fanlongduanfa guizhi [Antitrust regulation of refusal to license intellectual property].* Master's Thesis, East China University of Political Science and Law.

Zhang, L. (2003). *Lun zhuanliquan jiaocha xuke ji zhuanlichi xuke moshi de fanlongduan guizhi——Meiguo de lilun yu shijian [On the Antitrust regulation of patent cross-licensing and patent pool licensing models: Theory and practice in the United States].* Master's thesis, University of International Business and Economics.

Zhang, P. (2021). *Quanqiu hulianwang falv guancha (2020–2021)* [*Global Internet Law Review (2020–2021)*], Zhongguo Fazhi Chubanshe [China Legal Publishing House].

Zhang, S. (2020). Jieguolun yu mudilun: Longduan xieyi rending de falv yuanli [Outcome and purpose: Legal principles in the identification of Antitrust agreements]. *Zhongwai Faxue [Political and Legal Review], 3*, 5.

Zhang, S. (2020). Lanyong zhishi chanquan yu lanyong shichang zhipei diwei zhibian [Abuse of *Intellectual Property and Abuse of Market Dominance*]. *Renda Falv Pinglun [Renmin University Law Review], 2*, 87–134.

Zheng, Y. (2007). Zhishi chanquan dashou xueke de fanlongduan fenxi [Antitrust analysis of patent tying licenses]. *Zhongshan Daxue Xuebao Luncong [Journal of Sun Yat-sen University (Philosophy and Social Sciences Edition)], 4*, 171.

Zhou, M. (2021). *Fanlongduanfa guizhi lanyong biaozhun biyao zhuanli xingwei zhi bianjie tanjiu [Exploring the boundaries of antitrust regulation of the abuse of Standard-Essential Patent].* Master's Thesis, Beijing Foreign Studies University.

Chapter 8
Conclusion

8.1 I

There are many scientific methods for understanding human socio-economic actions, but interestingly, 'the main flaw of traditional epistemology is its neglect of human action',[1] which is why Mises criticized traditional epistemologists from isolating thoughts from other forms of human activity.[2] The author is deeply impressed by this criticism, as a review of many studies on intellectual property issues in the legal field reveals that they indeed often detach logical inquiry from the substantive content of thought, and the results eventually lack of logics. The original intent of this book is to avoid falling into the conventional traps that frequently appears in researches on intellectual property system, aiming to return to the level of human action, namely, it attempts to analyse how the intellectual property system guides market participants in creating and managing knowledge assets from a behavioural perspective, thereby truly appreciating that the intellectual property system is fundamentally an economic mechanism, and testing whether the legal framework aligns with the idea that 'intellectual property can only arise in the market and can only be realized in the market'.

In summary, this book aims to answer why both developers and users can benefit from intellectual property simultaneously. It seeks to explore how the intellectual property regime provides systematic supply to facilitate the pursuit of utility maximization for both parties. The question of why intellectual property can generate profits may seem straightforward, as intellectual property enables right holders to sell products at the same price but with lower costs.[3] In fact, this issue is more complex than it looks, as 'competition' and 'the pursuit of profit' will drive the spillover effects

[1] Mises, L. (2015). *The ultimate foundation of economic science: An essay on method* (Zhu, Y. trans.). Beijing: Commercial Press. 6.

[2] Ibid.

[3] Greenhalgh, C. & Rogers, M. (2017). *Innovation, intellectual property, and economic growth.* (Liu, S. & Li, W. trans.). Beijing: Intellectual Property Publishing House. 126.

© Intellectual Property Publishing House Co., Ltd. 2025

M. Yang, *Basic Theories of Intellectual Property Transaction*,
https://doi.org/10.1007/978-981-96-7039-0_8

of intellectual property.[4] Thus, intellectual property is not something over which the right holders can exert complete and unilateral control. Therefore, we must not only consider the issue from the perspective of the property owner but also from the perspective of the user, encompassing not only short-term effects but also long-term considerations.

Briefly speaking, only by starting from a multidimensional and integrated analytical framework of 'institution—market—behaviour' can we clarify the inherent logic between the operation of the system and the market, thereby exploring the effects of the intellectual property system and answering the question of how intellectual property can bring benefits to society as a whole. On this ground, this book focuses on the interactivity between intellectual property transactions and the intellectual property legal system, analysing specific operational behaviours in intellectual property transactions to reveal the how the system impacts the behaviours of the parties involved. Ultimately, this book lands on a series of reflections on the current intellectual property system in China, and offers suggestions for improving the rationality of the institutional design of intellectual property system as well as the efficiency of system operation.

8.2 II

This book first examines the issue of property rights claims in the creation of intellectual property. Through a thought experiment on the behavioural choices of market participants in the process of intellectual property creation, it reveals how the current institutional arrangements of intellectual property law in rights entitlements affect people's business activities which consequently enable them to gain a competitive advantage in the market. In terms of the impact of intellectual property protection on cumulative innovation, the book answers how the entitlement of intellectual property rights achieves a balance between the free use by rights holders and the public's access from the perspectives of the length and breadth of intellectual property protection.

The book then points out that for intellectual property, a system that originates in the market and can only exist within the market, conducting the so-called institutional research isolated from market is significantly flawed. This is because the intellectual property system and intellectual property transactions are mutually responsive. Therefore, it is necessary to approach the study on the 'system-transaction' complex by using a systematic analytical framework of 'system-market-behaviour' from a behavioural perspective, so as to better understand the observed the operational effects of the system and to examine the rationality of its design.

Since contracts represent a fundamental institutional form of intellectual property transactions, contract theory can be used to explain the various issues that may arise in

4 Here, the author refers to Baumol's view that these two factors prompt companies to spread new technologies, see Baumol, W. (2016). *Innovation: The magic of economic growth* (Guo, M., Tang, Y., Peng, J. & Li, Q. trans.). Beijing: CITIC Publishing Group. 74–79.

intellectual property transactions. This book focuses on the various problems that may arise during the contracting process and their impact on the formation of contracts. Based on the principles and system of contract theory, the book further explores the application of contract theory in intellectual property transactions, combining the characteristics of intellectual property transactions and examining its application from both the legislative and judicial perspectives.

The core issue of intellectual property transactions is pricing, which is also a key distinction between intellectual property and tangible property. Price theory is the most direct theoretical study on pricing, as it not only reveals the process of price formation and the laws of price fluctuations, but also systematically summarizes the impacts of price. Through the study of price theory, this book aims to assist the intellectual property academia gain a deeper understanding of the price formation process in intellectual property transactions, thereby facilitating a more confident approach towards pricing issues when making judicial decisions. To this end, the book first outlines the basic system of price theory, based on this framework, it further discusses its specific application in intellectual property transactions.

After the study of contract theory and price theory, this book shifts its focus to different types of intellectual property transactions. In the process of analysing specific transactions, it attempts to highlight the analytical logic of 'system-market-behaviour'. What the book aims to emphasize is that the study of market transaction behaviour is, in fact, the study of the formation process of equilibrium price games in intellectual property transactions. Therefore, based on an analysis of key transaction models such as intellectual property licensing, assignment, and capitalization, the book examines the specific legal issues associated with these transaction models. It also analyses the regulatory methods within the existing framework and offers corresponding suggestions for improving the current system.

The goal and outcome of intellectual property transactions are the allocation and redistribution of intellectual property resources, which are closely related to market competition. Intellectual property holders, possessing strong bargaining power, may be motivated to abuse their market position and use transaction arrangements to exclude or restrict competition in relevant markets. Therefore, the study of intellectual property transactions should not overlook competition law issues. Based on the previous categorization of intellectual property transaction behaviours, this book also conducts a targeted study of monopoly issues. It provides a detailed discussion on the potential monopolistic phenomena, the application of existing legal rules of antitrust, as well as the challenges in determining the nature of behaviours and defining regulatory content within the current analytical framework. The book further offers suggestions on how to overcome these challenges.

8.3 III

Overall, this book adopts a market perspective and starts from the theory of behavioural choices to explore the basic theories and operational mechanisms of intellectual property transactions. Its aim is to gain a deeper understanding of how market competition unfolds through the external forms of institutional operation. Of course, the author is well aware that 'the relationship between market coordination and the realization of social efficiency is never so simple'.[5] Although the book makes considerable efforts, given its designated perspectives and methodologies, flaws and errors are inevitable. The author hopes that this limited interpretation of the economic mechanisms underlying the intellectual property system, from both theoretical and practical perspectives, will offer some trivial insights to fellow scholars in the field of intellectual property.

References

Baumol, W. (2016). *Innovation: The magic of economic growth.* (Guo, M., Tang, Y., Peng, J. & Li, Q., Trans.). CITIC Publishing Group.

Greenhalgh, C. & Rogers, M. (2017). *Innovation, intellectual property, and economic growth* (Liu, S. & Li, W., Trans.). Intellectual Property Publishing House.

Kozan, I. (2012). *The meaning of market process* (Feng, X., Jing, C., Tan, X. & Zhu, H., Trans.). Social Sciences Academic Press.

Mises, L. (2015). *The ultimate foundation of economic science: An essay on method* (Zhu, Y. trans.). Commercial Press

[5] Kozan, I. (2012). *The meaning of market process* (Feng, X., Jing, C., Tan, X. & Zhu, H. trans.). Beijing: Social Sciences Academic Press. 15.

GPSR Compliance

The European Union's (EU) General Product Safety Regulation (GPSR) is a set of rules that requires consumer products to be safe and our obligations to ensure this.

If you have any concerns about our products, you can contact us on ProductSafety@springernature.com

In case Publisher is established outside the EU, the EU authorized representative is:

Springer Nature Customer Service Center GmbH
Europaplatz 3
69115 Heidelberg, Germany

Batch number: 10725802

Printed by Printforce, the Netherlands